NEW WORLD POSTCOLONIAL

ILLUMINATIONS:

Cultural Formations of the Americas Series

JOHN BEVERLEY AND SARA CASTRO-KLARÉN, EDITORS

NEW WORLD POSTCOLONIAL

The Political Thought of Inca Garcilaso de la Vega

JAMES W. FUERST

University of Pittsburgh Press

To a scattered dynasty of solitaries

Published by the University of Pittsburgh Press, Pittsburgh, Pa., 15260

Manufactured in the United States of America
Printed on acid-free paper
10 9 8 7 6 5 4 3 2 1

Cataloging-in-Publication data is available from the Library of Congress

ISBN 13: 978-0-8229-6540-4

Cover art: *Nieuwe en "meest nauwkeurige" wereldkaart door Joan Blaeu* (New and "most accurate" world map, by J. Blaeu) 1664, via Wikimedia Commons.

Cover design by Jordan Wannemacher

CONTENTS

ACKNOWLEDGMENTS

In preparing the earlier version of this text, I am deeply grateful for the help and guidance of Richard Tuck, José Antonio Mazzotti, and Pratap Mehta, Doris Sommer for first introducing me to Inca Garcilaso, the faculty, students, and staff at the Centro Bartolomé de Las Casas in Cuzco where I studied for a summer and the Foreign Languages and Area Studies Grant from Harvard that enabled me to do so, Anthony Pagden and Jennifer Pitts for their comments on some of my initial research, Sankar Muthu for kindly securing me access to Bobst Library, and a Minority Dissertation Fellowship from the Ford Foundation that generously funded my writing. As for this version of the text, I owe a debt of gratitude to John Beverley and Sara Castro-Klarén for selecting it for the Illuminations series, to Alcira Dueñas, whose work on Andean intellectuals introduced me to Juan de Cuevas Herrera and who then helped me obtain a copy of his manuscript from the Biblioteca Real del Palacio de Madrid, and to the many Latin Americanists, Peruvianists, colonialists, postcolonialists, and garcilacistas who have offered invaluable suggestions, encouragement, and support at various times over the years, including Sharonah Fredrick, Christian Fernández, Walter Mignolo, John Beverley, Margarita Zamora, José Antonio Mazzotti, Sara Castro-Klarén, and

Rolena Adorno, among others. Finally, I would like to thank Josh Shanholtzer and Alex Wolfe at University of Pittsburgh Press, the anonymous reviewer whose insightful comments helped me to sharpen chapters 5 and 6, family and friends for putting up with me, and Ellen V. Holloman for her undying confidence that this work would one day make it into print.

FOREWORD

Thus far the work of Inca Garcilaso de la Vega has not been chiefly interpreted as an intervention in political thought. Drawing from the extensive bibliography on Inca Garcilaso in Spanish and the new and expanding bibliography in English, James Fuerst navigates a series of hidden and coded passages in the *Royal Commentaries* and its second part *General History of Peru* in order to bring together a significant number of texts and questions that enable him to sketch a map of Garcilaso's political preoccupations as he narrates the history of the Inca dynasty and the government that is to come after the Spanish conquest of the Andean empire. Fuerst is not only attentive to Garcilaso's overt and implicit discussions of Renaissance political theory, but he is particularly keen in locating and excavating any subterranean presence, allusion, or vibration of Andean political concepts and practices that might illuminate Inca Garcilaso's narration of political events and actions by the various personages that populate the thousands of pages of his narrative.

Fuerst's examination of the political thought of Inca Garcilaso is placed in the grid of current imperial studies, and to some extent it is written in the hope that imperial studies in English about the English invasion and settlement of North America find in this study a call to consider the questions raised by imperial studies with respect to deeds of Spain and Portugal and their colonial subjects. Perhaps more to the point, Fuerst's study pushes to the front of imperial studies the person and character of Inca Garcilaso, who writes not from the position of an official or central imperial subject, but rather from that of a newly inaugurated subaltern intellectual acting in the context of the coloniality of power. Fuerst has engaged elsewhere Locke's reading of Garcilaso in theorizing his concept of "state of nature." (See "Locke and Inca Garcilaso: Subtexts, Politics, and European Expansion" in *Inca Garcilaso and Contemporary World-Making*.) Locke's commentators have always been puzzled by Locke's references to Inca Garcilaso's work. Fuerst has highlighted the point that Locke had been involved in matters related to imperial expansion and conquest at the practical level when he served as secretary to the Lords Proprietors for Carolina (1668–1675). In order to begin rethinking Locke's interest in reading not just *The Royal Commentaries* and Inca civilization, but *La Florida del Inca*, we need to keep in mind that one of his tasks relating to the English colonies in America was to draft the *Fundamental Constitutions for Carolina* in 1669.

By bringing to the fore Andean historical and political concepts such as *pachakuti* (upheaval, cataclysm, the turning of the world, renewal), Viracocha Inca, Viracocha Apparition, Viracocha-Divine Creator as well as López-Baralt's understanding of *tinku* (complementarity) and *ayni* (reciprocity), Fuerst moves beyond the parameters previously established by exclusively focusing on "influences" believed to be part of a misunderstood univocal renaissance. Fuerst moves our understating of Inca Garcilaso's sense of writing the past beyond what has been attributed to be Cicero's rhetorical sense of history writing. Indeed, in relation to the dynastic organization of time, common in European historiography, Garcilaso introduces a conundrum when he envisions the possibility of a shared and dual rule of postconquest Peru. What for some readers appears simply as infantile utopia, given the unilineal conception of history and dynasty in Europe, from the Andean perspective, imbued with a positive sense of duality as expressed in the practice of "Inca by privilege," shared rule appears to be a more practical approach to the aftermath of conquest, a political situation in which conquered and conqueror must find accommodation (not unending destruction) in order to go forward.

This volume on Garcilaso's political thought is thus a welcome addition to colonial and imperial studies. Intellectual history also benefits, for it receives some input from Andean political thought and its approach to conflict resolution. One of the many strengths of this study is its demonstration of Garcilaso's ability to nourish his thought and his arsenal of political questions from more than one archive at a time. Fuerst's keen exploration of the concept of pachakuti (cataclysm, the turning of the world) and the consequent notion of cyclical history has much to say to current discussions of European concepts of an infinite time in which the new will always avert the coming of the Anthropocene, ironically a stage in human history that began with the destruction of Amerindian civilizations. Another is Fuerst's showing how Garcilaso grapples with a profound sense of irrecoverable loss and yet finds the personal and intellectual wherewithal to continue to explore avenues for reconciliation based in López-Baralt's concept of ayni and tinku.

However, studying the search for shared governing political structures is not to say that this study diminishes in any way the power of Garcilaso's critique of Spanish historiography and ways of knowing in general. In this sense Inca Garcilaso's critique of history writing remains to be rediscovered after the studies by Margarita Zamora, Walter Mignolo, and this writer by current English-speaking scholars and commentators who dwell on the provincialism of the European sense of world temporalities but do not engage colonial critiques such as Inca Garcilaso's work. While an elucidation of tinku and ayni may emphasize Andean concepts of government put to the fore by Inca Garcilaso in the second part of his *Royal Commentaries*, readers should not forget that the work has also been linked to the cradle of uprising and revolutionary action in Latin America's history, as was the case with the Túpac Amaru II rebellion at the end of the eighteenth century, the thinking of nineteenth-century liberators such as Simón Bolívar and José de San Martín. Nothing offers a more telling testimony on the capacity of Inca Garcilaso's political thought and his evidentiary presentation to affect both thought and action than the Spanish authorities' decision to forbid the circulation of *Royal Commentaries* in its two parts, to gather all copies available after 1781, for the king himself feared that its continued reading would lead to further disauthorization of Spanish colonial rule. Thirteen days before the order for the execution of Túpac Amaru II was made public, the Royal Inspector José Antonio de Areche wrote to the court asking that Indians be forbidden to read the book. In April 1782 the Spanish king wrote the viceroy in Lima lamenting the Indians' desire to "preserve the memory of their ancient pagan costumes." The king then ordered his bureaucrats to collect with "caution and sagaciously" all copies of the *Historia* of Inca Garcilaso, where the Indians have "learned many prejudicial things" (cited in John Grier Varner, *El Inca. The Life and Times of Garcilaso de la Vega*, 1968, 381–82). Regardless of the royal prohibition, the book continues to circulate and garner new readers for its stand against epistemological and political tyranny remains vibrant.

Sara Castro-Klarén
Johns Hopkins University
Baltimore, June 2017

NEW WORLD POSTCOLONIAL

INTRODUCTION

The son of a Spanish conquistador and an Inca princess, El Inca Garcilaso de la Vega (1539–1616) was a child of conquest and a member of the first generation of mestizos born in Peru. As the translator of Leon Hebreo's *Dialoghi di Amore* from Italian into Spanish (published in 1590), the historian of Hernando de Soto's failed conquest of the Mississippi region of North America titled *La Florida del Inca* (The Inca's Florida, 1605) and a two-part history of Inca civilization, Spanish conquest, civil wars, and colonial consolidation in Peru called the *Comentarios reales* (*Royal Commentaries*, 1609–1617), Inca Garcilaso is the founding figure of American letters and the first self-identified person of indigenous descent to publish books about the New World in the Old. Over the centuries he has been hailed as a translator, a humanist, a historian, a linguist, an ethnographer, a commentarist, an expert prose stylist, a cultural go-between, a proto-novelist, even America's first Neoplatonic philosopher (Flores Quelopano: 2008), and to greater or lesser extents he is all of those things. Nevertheless, Inca Garcilaso is best understood as a political thinker, one of the most well known of the seventeenth and eighteenth centuries in Europe as well as Peru (see chapter 2 for details), and his masterpiece, the *Royal Commentaries*, is an indispensable work of political thought in the early modern period.

There are complete, highly readable translations of Inca Garcilaso's histories—John Grier Varner's *The Florida of the Inca* (1951) and Harold V. Livermore's *The Royal Commentaries of the Incas and the General History of Peru* (1966)—two informative and reputable biographies (Varner 1968; Castanien 1969), and a handful of seminal, full-length studies and anthologies examining his oeuvre, all in English.[1] Despite the ready availability of his texts as well as enlightening commentaries on them, however, Inca Garcilaso remains almost unknown to students and scholars of political thought in English-speaking college and university departments across North America. This is in part because, as products of and responses to Spanish imperialism and colonialism of the late sixteenth and early seventeenth centuries, Inca Garcilaso's texts have historically fallen into gaps within the study and teaching of political thought in the United States. In "Political Theory of Empire and Imperialism," Jennifer Pitts states, "political theory has come slowly and late to the study of empire relative to other disciplines" and "for much of the 1980s and 1990s was remarkably untouched by . . . powerful theoretical and thematic developments" in world history, anthropology, colonial, postcolonial, literary, and cultural studies, among others (Pitts 2012: 352, 353 respectively). But as Pitts's own work admirably demonstrates (Tocqueville and Pitts 2001; Pitts 2005, 2012b), students and scholars of political thought have indeed made a more concerted "turn to empire" (her phrase) in the first decades of the twenty-first century, a turn that may finally be creating space for new critical perspectives on the history of political thought as well as the inclusion of traditionally excluded or marginalized figures in a field that has predominantly focused on European writers and thinkers.[2] As advances in colonial and postcolonial studies have shown us, however, the various forms of European imperialism and colonialism were not simply about what Europeans thought, wrote, or did; they were also, and continue to be, about the complex, constrained, and creative ways those whom Europeans sought to dominate or even vanquish struggled to survive, adapt, resist, and respond, which on its own is a compelling argument in favor of encountering a figure like Inca Garcilaso.

However that stands, the general lack of familiarity with Inca Garcilaso's works in North American political thought (or Guaman Poma de Ayala's or Sor Juana Inés de la Cruz's, for that matter) is also in part due to the enduring divide between the studies of English colonialism and Spanish colonialism in the Americas. For instance, while researching his sweeping comparative history of the two colonial systems for *Empires of the Atlantic World: Britain and Spain in America, 1492–1830* (2006), J. H. Elliott concluded:

> There was high-quality literature on both British and Spanish colonial America, but I could not fail to be struck by the degree to which the two literatures were unrelated to each other. Each world seemed to exist in a self-contained compartment, with little or no reference to what was happening simultaneously in the other, although the fact that the two touched hands at certain points had led to the development in the United States of a subfield of history of the Spanish borderlands, which, however, remained relatively isolated from the mainstream of North American history. (Elliott 2012: 85)

In this bifurcated historiography Elliott discerned "a profound belief in the United States and its manifest destiny" as well as "what was assumed to be the innate superiority of Anglo-American to Iberian civilization" that became more "strident" and "acute" in the nineteenth and twentieth centuries (Elliott 2012: 85–86). While it is beyond the scope of this introduction to interrogate nationalistic and chauvinistic biases within various fields of historical scholarship, it is enough to note that such biases create institutional disincentives and barriers to the study of Central and South American colonial writers in North America, and this has undeniably been the case for Inca Garcilaso and others.

I have only briefly touched on these initial obstacles here because they pertain to the context in which this investigation was produced and to which it in part responds. But it must also be said that such obstacles are by no means insurmountable. Rather, if we attend to the moments at which English and Spanish (or French, Dutch, or Portuguese) colonial histories "touch hands," in Elliott's words, no matter how unlikely a particular conjunction or intersection may seem, we may nonetheless find fertile ground for research and publication. Such has been my experience with Inca Garcilaso, whom I encountered while reading John Locke's *Second Treatise of Government* (1691), during preparation for my general exams as a graduate student in the mid-1990s. At the time I knew next to nothing about Inca Garcilaso save a couple of intriguing notions I'd heard at a lecture the previous fall, and yet there he was in §14 of the *Second Treatise*, there he had *always* been, in fact, in one of the foundational texts of early modern liberalism, a book I must have read ten or twelve times at that point without ever having noticed or registered "Garcilasso De la vega, in his *History of Peru*."

Despite Locke referring to Inca Garcilaso with regard to the state of nature (a central but notoriously slippery concept in Lockean political thought) the secondary literature on Locke was just as baffled about his use of Inca Garcilaso as I was. No one had analyzed the passage in the *Royal Commentaries* to which Locke had alluded, on the one hand, and it likewise seemed (as if exemplifying the obstacles mentioned above) that many commentators did not know who Inca Garcilaso was, on the other. The omissions nevertheless gave me encouragement to explore the matter further, in the hopes of perhaps writing an article on Locke's engagement with the mestizo historian through the lens of a shared context and area of concern. For as I had already begun to learn, Locke had been actively involved in a number of English overseas ventures, not least of which was serving as secretary to the Lords Proprietors for Carolina (1668–1675). In this position he oversaw correspondence for the Carolina colony and drafted its charter, the *Fundamental Constitutions of Carolina* (1669), activities that comprised a sphere of practical and intellectual interest for Locke located in the very region about which Inca Garcilaso had already written a history, *La Florida del Inca*, more than a half-century earlier. Although the precise connections between the two thinkers were still unclear, it was increasingly apparent that their shared area of concern could broadly be construed as "American."

While reorienting both figures toward an American context helped to elucidate stark differences in their conceptions of the New World (see Fuerst 2016), it also made me aware of the need for a full-length work dedicated solely to Inca Garcilaso. There were precious few monographs devoted to him in English, and beyond that there were none in any language that treated the *Royal Commentaries* first and foremost as a work of political thought, the kind of treatment that would enable students and scholars to situate Inca Garcilaso's work more readily in relation to other thinkers in the canon. English-speaking readers would especially benefit, I thought, from a historically sensitive treatment of the *Royal Commentaries* that interpreted it against multiple contexts while attempting to keep track of the social and political interests that grounded and informed Inca Garcilaso's mestizo perspective.

Having already read José Antonio Mazzotti's *Coros mestizos del Inca Garcilaso: Resonancias andinas* (1996a), which opened new possibilities for unearthing potential Andean subtexts in the *Royal Commentaries*, I realized that attempting to historicize Inca Garcilaso's *mestizaje* would bring with it additional challenges and risks. As for the challenges, exploring possible Andean meanings in Inca Garcilaso's work necessarily meant engaging indigenous Andean culture and civilization, quite literally an "other" conceptual universe with which I had no previous experience and upon which I would be starting from scratch. As for the risks, if political thought at the time tended to neglect examinations of empire and there was also something of a dialogical chasm between the study of English and Spanish colonialism, then delving into the subaltern realms of Andean contexts in the sixteenth-century viceroyalty of Peru threatened to push my research off the map of political thought altogether.

And yet, it seemed to me that these were analogous to the kinds of challenges and risks that Inca Garcilaso wanted his readers to take. Time and again he faulted Spanish imperial historians and religious and colonial administrators for their lack of facility with indigenous languages, and then for using their faulty understandings to misconstrue indigenous religions, cultures, and peoples as inferior to Spaniards and Europeans, thereby providing justifications for their own political and economic designs. By comparison, he was also at pains to note that Andean oral traditions had proven insufficient repositories of the indigenous past in light of the cultural devastation wrought by foreign conquest and rule. Whereas Inca Garcilaso's criticisms encourage Spaniards and Europeans to meet indigenous Andeans (and Amerindians writ large) on the level of the latter's own self-understandings in the service of mutual comprehension, they also simultaneously exhort indigenous Andeans to preserve their languages and traditions and to restore their former status in the face of a dominant and hostile culture by appropriating that culture's most advantageous tools, such as Christianity, literacy, and writing. As such, political reconciliation and social justice in Peru and across the New World depended for Inca Garcilaso on both natives and newcomers crossing camps, as it were, and becoming *cultural mestizos*. This kind of mutual engagement and interchange, which lies at the very heart of Inca Garcilaso's moral and political project, necessarily entails wagering some amount of faith in the "other" and taking risks.

Just as importantly, if there were in fact Andean meanings embedded within the *Royal Commentaries*, then they could potentially hold profound implications for how the text was understood. For example, the scholarly consensus on Inca Garcilaso then was that he had been steeped in Renaissance humanism and Neoplatonic philology and philosophy, as evidenced by his translation of Hebreo's Neoplatonic *Dialoghi di Amore*, and his histories, falling squarely within the rhetorical tradition of historiography as theorized by Cicero, were intended solely for European audiences, in order to challenge and correct their distorted and disparaging views of Incas, Peruvians, Floridians, and multitudinous other Amerindians throughout the New World. In this light, the *Royal Commentaries* spoke about the origins, growth, and flourishing of the Inca empire, its former rulers, political structures, religion, language, and culture without speaking *to* its indigenous or mestizo descendants at the turn of the seventeenth century. But the discovery or reconstruction of Andean meanings within the *Royal Commentaries* at the very least implied an audience (whether actual or projected) capable of understanding those meanings, which in turn suggested that the *Royal Commentaries* might not simply contain one book, but rather two: a primary Spanish text intended for and open to Hispano-European audiences, and a purloined Andean text, which, for those without access to indigenous language and culture, would be hidden in plain view.

Sara Castro-Klarén has recently characterized the textual structure of the *Royal Commentaries* as "double-stranded" for its interweaving of Hispano-European and Inca-Andean cultural codes and she is careful to remind us that "when reading Garcilaso, it is always important not to neglect the possible Andean source of his concepts or solutions (Castro-Klarén 2016b: 4, 15 respectively). These statements demonstrate the extent to which reading the *Royal Commentaries* through dual cultural lenses has gained both acceptance and currency not only in the secondary literature on Inca Garcilaso but also in broader theoretical debates on Latin American coloniality and postcoloniality (see Castro-Klarén 1994 and Moraña 2010 as two important examples), although such was far from the case when the first version of this work was completed in 2000. In the intervening years, however, several scholars have investigated Andean sources, motifs, and concepts at work in the *Royal Commentaries*, some of the most notable being Christian Fernández's examination of the *Royal Commentaries*' paratexts (2004), Mazzotti's enumeration of the resonances between elements within Andean cosmology and the Neoplatonic theories of nature espoused by Hebreo in the *Dialoghi di Amore* (2006), Elena Romiti's analysis of the *Royal Commentaries*' *quipu* (cords of knotted beads used for record keeping) structure (2009), and the text's interplay of *tinku* (complementarity) and *ayni* (reciprocity) explicated by Mercedes López-Baralt (2011: 195–221), among others. I mention these at the outset because, from different fields, specializations, and perspectives, a number of commentators have come independently to conclusions similar to ones drawn here, a circumstance in part due to the many years it has taken to find this work a publisher. Nevertheless, I consider those and other studies to be rich and congenial perspectives, ones from whose various insights I have benefitted and learned much and have integrated in what follows. I am delighted to have my own research be in conversation with them.

Regarding what lies ahead, first, as mentioned above, I argue that Inca Garcilaso is best characterized as a political thinker. Second, an inextricable corollary of the first, in order to fully appreciate Inca Garcilaso's contributions to Spanish, European, and American political thought, his work must be read in light of Andean as well as European contexts. Before jumping in to the argument proper, however, chapter 1, "Becoming an Inca," offers a sketch of Inca Garcilaso's life, written with a view toward highlighting the political events that contributed to his adoption and acceptance of his mestizo persona and perspective. For "the Inca Garcilaso de la Vega" was not born so, but became so by making a conscious choice to change his given name; both the privileges and burdens of his self-naming echo throughout his work.

Chapters 2 and 3 both deal with Inca Garcilaso's conception of history, but from different angles, and both are guided by formal textual characteristics more usually associated with literary criticism than political science. In "Mestizo Rhetoric," I focus on the style of the *Royal Commentaries*, for it was through style that rhetorical historiographers of the Renaissance directed their narratives and arguments toward the conventional understandings of those they intended to reach with their works. This chapter also represents the crux of all that follows in that it attempts to demonstrate Inca Garcilaso indeed intended the *Royal Commentaries* to be read by a diverse Peruvian audience, and that the very *European* concepts available at the time encouraged him to include Andean meanings within his texts in order to fulfill his moral duty as a mestizo historian. This chapter also polemically challenges the predilection for reading Inca Garcilaso solely in light of European contexts by not simply beginning with those contexts, but also by showing how they insufficiently account for the way he presents his authorial personae in the *Royal Commentaries*. Instead, I argue that Inca Garcilaso's mestizo rhetoric inaugurates a dual and heterogeneous form of colonial discourse while easing readers into Andean subtexts by showing this mestizo rhetoric in action through a close reading of select passages. Where chapter 2 focuses on style, chapter 3, "The Many Faces of Viracocha and the Turning of the World," analyzes the structure and, more specifically, the allegorical meaning of the dual historical framework winding through the first and second parts of the *Royal Commentaries*. This is a second and different approach to Inca Garcilaso's conception of history that concentrates on his labyrinthine deployment of symbols, historical alterations, and his expansive notion of "Inca" in order to create an implicit dynastic link between Incas and Spaniards, and to transform a tale of tragic devastation into a parable of possible rebirth and renewal. The analysis relies heavily on Andean contexts and meanings, but in both chapters 2 and 3 pains are taken to demonstrate the precise social and political interests informing both the style and structure and, therefore, the entirety of the *Royal Commentaries*.

Having laid out the cyclical indigenous structure of the *Royal Commentaries*, which is punctuated by recurring moments of upheaval and cataclysm, or *pachacuti*, I turn to detailed examinations of three such moments in chapters 4 through 6. In chapter 4, "*Auca*," I explore Inca Garcilaso's account of the initial moments of the Spanish conquest and Francisco Pizarro's execution of Atahualpa. Shuttling between Inca and Hispano-European perspectives and politics, Inca Garcilaso both justifies and criticizes the Spanish invasion by portraying Atahualpa as a tyrant and by appealing to the doctrine of tyrannicide to prepare the ground for a potential political alliance between Francisco Pizarro and the "legitimate" heirs to the Inca throne, represented by Inca Garcilaso's own *panaca* (royal kinship unit). Surprisingly, at stake in his version of the conquest are not the rights of the Spanish monarchy to control over Peru, but rather explaining how what should have been a legitimate and peaceful transfer of power between implicit brothers resulted in ruin. Chapter 5, "'Die a King,'" looks at how Inca Garcilaso initiates an insurrectionary and potentially revolutionary ideology in the service of an independent, Peruvian mestizo polity against the abuses of the Spanish monarchy and viceregal government. Of particular note in this chapter are Inca Garcilaso's family connections to and use of arguments from the *comunero* movement (1520–1521) both to justify and defend the neo-Inca's, i.e., Gonzalo Pizarro's, armed rebellion against the New Laws in Peru. The last moment in this cycle, the present of Peru at the turn of the seventeenth century when the *Royal Commentaries* was written, is also a return of the first, the chaotic First Age of Andean prehistory before the advent of the Incas. And in chapter 6, "Jesuit Amautas," the question of Inca Garcilaso's views on and suggestions for political reform in the colonial Peruvian society of his day is posed. Insofar as I argue throughout that Inca Garcilaso is in fact a political thinker, this hypothesis is put to the test of practical politics and specific policy recommendations to be found in the *Royal Commentaries*; a test, moreover, almost never put to Inca Garcilaso's work in any systematic way. It was a productive experiment, however, for Inca Garcilaso has much to say both to and about Jesuit evangelical and educational practices in Peru, and even a way of expressing this to potential Indian, mestizo, and Creole readers.

In preparing this work for publication, I have updated the research to reflect relevant developments across a number of fields, especially the raft of essays and articles on Inca Garcilaso occasioned by the series of quadricentennials celebrated in the early part of this century: the four-hundredth anniversary of the publication of *La Florida del Inca* (1605/2005), of the publication of the First Part of the *Royal Commentaries* (1609/2009), of Inca Garcilaso's death (April 23, 1616/April 23, 2016), and of the publication of the Second Part of the *Royal Commentaries, the General History of Peru* (1617/2017). In anticipation of this last, I have added a translation of the Prologue to the Second Part of the *Royal Commentaries* in the Appendix, which Inca Garcilaso dedicated to the *Indios, mestizos y criollos* of Peru. The Prologue represents a key moment in Inca Garcilaso's overall opus as well as his political thought; this is the first translation of it to appear in English.

As a final note, Inca Garcilaso has been involved in the discourses of early modern Europe and the Americas right from the beginning in ways that are both tied to and transcend particular Andean, Spanish, Peruvian, and Latin American contexts, and he continues to be read, relevant, and influential today. For instance, Peruvian author and essayist Miguel Gutiérrez's 1995 novel *Poderes secretos* (Secret Powers), which imaginatively explores Inca Garcilaso's relationship to the Jesuits and especially the mestizo Jesuit Blas Valera, one of his favorite sources on Peru, was so popular that it went through a reedition in 2010, and the future Nobel prize–winning author Mario Vargas Llosa penned an encomium to the patriarch of Peruvian and American letters in 2006 titled "El Inca Garcilaso y la lengua de todos" (El Inca Garcilaso and the Language of All) for a conference commemorating the four-hundredth anniversary of the publication of *La Florida del Inca*. A bit closer to the United States, Junot Díaz's 2007 Pulitzer Prize–winning novel *The Brief Wondrous Life of Oscar Wao* features a character named La Inca, the "mother aunt" of the formerly orphaned Beli, who is in turn the mother of eponymous Oscar. La Inca, proprietress of a bakery in middle-class Baní in the 1950s, is the very incarnation of propriety and respectability, of "suffocating solicitude" and endless reminders of the "inescapable fact of her Family's Glorious Golden Past," yet who is unfazed by the blackness of daughter-niece's skin and is above all concerned to provide her with a proper education (88, 81). "Your father was a doctor, La Inca repeated, unperturbed. Your mother was a nurse. They owned the biggest house in La Vega" (82). La Inca from La Vega with the Glorious Golden Past is assuredly a modern-day parody and caricature of El Inca Garcilaso de la

Vega of the *Royal Commentaries*. The portrait of El Inca himself may be a bit thin, but in fiction that matters little, and the allusion is still properly viewed as an homage, an acknowledgment and implicit thanks by a writer who was born in the Dominican Republic, raised in New Jersey, and plies his craft in English to the native Cuzcan whose first language was Quechua, who lived his adult life in Spain, and plied his craft in Spanish. Perhaps there is something peculiarly "American" about the specificities and multiplicities that Inca Garcilaso's mestizo rhetoric forces or even inspires us to consider, but there can be no doubt that it continues to speak to our world in the present.

1
BECOMING AN INCA

Life, Works, and Context

In the weeks and months leading up to April 23, 2016, there were innumerable conferences and celebrations in England, Spain, Peru, and the world over to commemorate the quadricentennial of the deaths of three towering literary figures: William Shakespeare (1564–1616), Miguel de Cervantes Saavedra (1547–1616), and El Inca Garcilaso de la Vega (1539–1616).[1] Shakespeare and Cervantes are in no need of introduction to readers across the globe, yet the last member of this legendary triumvirate is far less known to North American and English-language readers despite his unprecedented literary achievements. This is a rather odd circumstance when one considers that the Peruvian mestizo historian is the first American-born author to self-consciously identify himself as a member of a conquered indigenous race and to publish highly acclaimed texts about the New World in the Old.[2] For this reason, among others, it is necessary to give a brief account of his life before moving on to an estimation of his work.[3]

When Gómez Suárez de Figueroa (only later did he take the name Inca Garcilaso de la Vega) was born on April 12, 1539 in the imperial city of Cuzco, he came into the world amid constellations of civil strife, miscegenation, illegitimacy, and nobility that were to influence the rest of his life.[4] Within the decade prior to his birth Peru had seen the civil war between Inca rivals Atahualpa and Huáscar, which resulted in the ascendancy of the former and the slaughter of the latter and his supporters, and the conquests of Francisco Pizarro and Diego de Almagro, which resulted in the capture, ransom, and execution of Atahualpa (1532–1533) and ceded control of Tahuantinsuyu to the Spanish invaders.[5] Moreover, it witnessed the failed indigenous rebellion of Huáscar's brother, Manco Inca, against the Spaniards in Cuzco (1536) as well as the incipient stages of infighting among the Spaniards that led to the executions of both Almagro (1538) and Francisco Pizarro (1541) and launched a series of civil wars in Peru that would endure until the mid-1550s.[6] The disputes between the Spanish invaders primarily revolved around distribution of the spoils gained in conquest: the enormous riches in gold and silver gained in the ransom of Atahualpa and the *repartimientos* or allotments of Indian laborers and servants, called *encomiendas*. Cuzco was itself unique in that most of the territories in and around the city belonged to the *panacas* (royal families) of the Incas or their ancestral *mallquis* (mummy bundles), which accounted for the large number of Inca nobility residing there. The imperial city, founded as a Spanish municipality by Pizarro on March 23, 1534, then became a major locus of operations for the conquistadors and *encomenderos* (those Spaniards who were rewarded for their services with encomiendas, which were grants of Indian labor) in their early attempts to control the territories increasingly within their possession.

Maternally, Gómez Suárez was a descendant of the Inca ruling classes. His mother, Ñusta Isabela Suárez Chimpu Ocllo (d. 1572?), was the daughter of Huallpa Túpac Inca Yupanqui and Palla Cusi Chimpu; she was also the niece of Huayna Cápac, the twelfth Inca, and cousin to both Huáscar and Atahualpa. Her grandfather had been Inca Túpac Yupanqui, the eleventh Inca, and the panaca of his descendants (of which Chimpu Ocllo and her relatives were members) was based in Cuzco where they enjoyed their major sphere of influence. Gómez Suárez's father was Captain Sebastián Garcilaso de la Vega y Vargas (1500?–1559) from Badajoz, Extremadura, who came to Peru with the second wave of conquistadors under Pedro de Alvarado, governor of Guatemala, in 1534. Captain Garcilaso de la Vega, similarly, was the progeny of high birth. His mother, Blanca de Sotomayor Suárez de Figueroa, was the great-niece of the first Count of Feria, and her lineage stretched back to the legendary Garcí Lasso de la Vega, the namesake of the great Castilian poet Garcilaso de la Vega (1501?–1536) who was her first cousin. Captain Garcilaso's father was Alonso de Hinestrosa de Vargas, Lord of Valdesevilla on the frontiers of Extremadura, who received the Vargas patronymic from Garcí Pérez de Vargas, Knight Commander of Holy King Ferdinand III of Castile (1217–1252) during the thirteenth-century *reconquista* of the Iberian Peninsula from the Muslims (Elliott 1963: 26). The patriarchs at the root of both branches of Captain Garcilaso de la Vega's family tree, Garcí Pérez de Vargas and Garcí Lasso de la Vega, were deeply ensconced in the early national mythologies of Spain: both were exemplary knights and nobleman who had taken the field against the "infidel" Muslims for the greater glory of Christianity and Castile, and their fame in the chivalric lore of sixteenth-century Spanish culture approached that of Amadís of Gaul and El Cid (Varner 1968: 20–24; Garcilaso de la Vega 1951). Both the Inca and Spanish relatives of Gómez Suárez de Figueroa occupied positions of power, privilege, and prestige in the political and military hierarchies of their respective lands, and this young mestizo, part of the first generation of mestizos born in Peru, was to bear the full brunt of these vaunted legacies.

Although it appears that Gómez Suárez enjoyed and maintained close relations with both his parents—he was raised primarily by his mother and her relatives (from whom he took his first language, the *runasimi* [people's language] or Quechua) and was recognized by Captain Garcilaso as his "natural son" in his will—Captain Garcilaso de la Vega and Chimpu Ocllo never married. How Captain Garcilaso regarded the Inca princess is undocumented and unknown, but she was one of at least two concubines he had in Peru.[7] Whatever the truth, Chimpu Ocllo was married off to an undistinguished Spaniard, Juan del Pedroche, around the same time that Captain Garcilaso was exchanging vows with the fourteen-year-old Louisa Martel de los Ríos in 1549.[8] Whether or not it disturbed Gómez Suárez to see his mother rejected in favor of a stepmother who was only four years his senior, his mother's marriage seems to have caused him discomfort, as he never mentions it in any of his works.

Little is known about the early education of Gómez Suárez, save for what he himself tells us in his writings. In the formal European sense, his schooling was first entrusted to Juan de Alcobaza sometime in the early 1540s. Alcobaza was guardian and tutor to Gómez Suárez and overseer of Captain Garcilaso's property in Cuzco. Alcobaza's son, Diego de Alcobaza, also a mestizo, was born in the de la Vega home, raised along with Gómez Suárez as his friend and classmate, and later became a priest. From Juan de Alcobaza Gómez Suárez would learn the "be-a-ba" (abc's), but just how long this situation lasted is unclear. Peru of the 1540s was wracked with violent convulsions, most notably the rebellion of Gonzalo Pizarro (1544–1548), the younger half-brother of Francisco, to which the young mestizo was witness and in which Captain Garcilaso's involvement during the battle of Huarina was to cause many difficulties for Gómez Suárez later in life. As a result, Gómez Suárez's early training was interrupted and intermittent; he claims to have been through several different instructors and indoctrinated primarily in "arms and horses" until the arrival of Licentiate Juan de Cuéllar, created as the Canon of the Cathedral of Cuzco in 1552 (Part 1, Book II, Chapter XXVIII, vol. 1, 139).[9] With Cuéllar, Gómez Suárez and his classmates were no doubt trained in the rudiments of Spanish and Latin grammar and rhetoric, but the precise character of their education remains open to speculation (Part 2, "Prologue").[10] It is worth noting that the class was overwhelmingly composed of mestizos, save for two Indians of pure blood, Felipe and Carlos Inca (sons of Paullu Inca and Catalina Ussica), and one Creole, Gonzalo Mexía de Figueroa (son of Nuño Tovar), so that Gómez Suárez was daily surrounded by a group of peers who were much like himself.

Just as important as the initiation into Spanish and Latin culture that Gómez Suárez was receiving at this time was his continual exposure to and increasing curiosity about the culture and history of the Andes region and his Inca forebears. As noted above, his first language was Quechua, and this provided Gómez Suárez with the advantage of having direct access to the oral histories of the Incas.[11] He claims to have been regaled with the myths and legends of the Incas first by his mother, from whom he poetically describes having imbibed such stories along with her milk, and then from his uncle Don Fernando Huallpa Túpac Inca Yupanqui, his great-uncle Cusi Huallpa, and two captains of Huayna Cápac's guard, Don Juan Pachuta and Chauca Rimachi, among other Incas and Pallas (Part 1, Book IX, Chapter XIV). Later in life he would reflect fondly upon their weekly visits and numerous conversations, declaring that his Inca relatives had treated him as if he were a "natural son" and basing large portions of the *Comentarios reales* (*Royal Commentaries*) upon the information he had received from them (Part 1, Book I, Chapters XV and XIX). Additionally, the future historian claims to have learned much from traveling through various parts of the recently despoiled Inca empire and observing first-hand the religious practices and festivals of both Inca and non-Inca Indians. The reign of the Incas had certainly reached its nadir, but the diverse inhabitants of the Andes did not relinquish their cultural practices overnight. It was in this atmosphere of indigenous resistance and accommodation to the demands of their Spanish conquerors that Gómez Suárez was to learn some of his most enduring lessons.

Shortly after Francisco Hernández Girón's rebellion had been quelled and its leader beheaded (1553–1554), during which Captain Garcilaso was forced to flee Cuzco for fear of his life, a period of relative calm ensued in Peru. Captain Garcilaso was named corregidor (magistrate) of Cuzco by power of the Audiencia (court) at Lima on November 16, 1554 and served in that capacity until he was removed by Andrés Hurtado de Mendoza, Marquis of Cañete and third Viceroy of Peru, on July 23, 1556. It was during this time (1554–1555) that the Peruvian encomenderos submitted a petition to King Charles V requesting that their repartimientos of Indians be granted in perpetuity, rather than for the "two lives" stipulated in the redaction of the New Laws in 1545. This request was countered by a petition brought before the *Concilia de Indias* (Council of the Indies) by the Dominican Friar Domingo de Santo Tomás, Lascasian sympathizer and author of the first Spanish–Quechua dictionary, on behalf of the *curacas* (local ethnic chiefs) to abolish the encomienda system altogether (1559–1560).[12] Although the decision of the Council on these petitions was delayed and the report on the status of the encomiendas filed by Diego López de Zuñiga y Velasco, Count of Nieva and fourth Viceroy of Peru, recommending that encomiendas should not be granted in perpetuity did not appear until 1562, the young Gómez Suárez, now in his teens, would have had notice of the beginning of these developments because he was acting as his father's scribe while the latter was corregidor. Gómez Suárez saw his father begin construction on the Hospital de Naturales (Hospital of the Natives) and its annex, Iglesia de Nuestra Señora del Remedio (Church of Our Lady of Remedy), in July 1556, and apparently the "dual" education of Gómez Suárez had progressed to the point that his father trusted him to handle political correspondences in Spanish and enlisted his assistance in reading the *quipus* (knotted cords used by Andeans for record keeping) in order to collect tribute from Indians (Part 1, Book VI, Chapter IX, vol. 1, 348).[13]

Besides gaining some familiarity with affairs of state, Gómez Suárez was introduced to a role that he would take on much more explicitly in his literary endeavors: a mediator between two different cultural worlds. At this time, he also very likely witnessed one of the many ways that political power affects knowledge. On December 8, 1557, there was a celebration in Cuzco to announce the abdication of King Charles V and the accession to the throne of his son, newly crowned King Philip II. According to Sabine MacCormack, during the lengthy ritual to commemorate the removal and installation of sovereign monarchs, "the Inca past of Cuzco was not acknowledged with even a single gesture" (MacCormack 2001: 361 n11). Although Inca Garcilaso makes no mention of this event in his works, it is difficult to imagine that such a blatant, official erasure of the Inca past and present would be lost on the young mestizo scribe and handler of quipus.

Just over two years later, in May 1559, shortly after Gómez Suárez's twentieth birthday, Captain Sebastián Garcilaso de la Vega died following a prolonged illness. In Captain Garcilaso's will provisions were made for 4,000 pesos in gold and silver to be left in the trust and discretion of Antonio de Quiñones so that the "natural son" of the deceased could travel to Spain and finish his education (Valcárcel 1939: 52–54).[14] Captain Garcilaso's decision in these matters was most likely provoked by a series of royal decrees issued by Charles V in 1549–1555 that prohibited mestizos from holding public office, having charge of Indians without a special royal license, and being ordained as priests. These decrees were followed in the late 1560s by further constraints that prohibited mestizos from becoming *caciques* (chiefs) of Indian villages and from carrying arms. All these restrictions were intended to stymie the influence and excesses of the steadily growing mestizo populations of the New World, populations that were considered potentially seditious by the crown and its overseas administrators (Konetzke 1946b; López Martínez 1971: 14–17; Hemming 1970: 342).[15]

In early 1560, with many of the opportunities for social advancement in Peru closed to him due to his racial background, Gómez Suárez set sail for Spain, but not before one final and remarkable experience. In 1559 Licentiate Polo de Ondegardo, then Corregidor of Cuzco, discovered a group of Inca mallquis, which he offered to show to Gómez Suárez so the young man might have something to talk about when he arrived in the Old World. In Ondegardo's home the wonderfully preserved remains of Inca Viracocha and his wife Mama Runtu, Túpac Inca Yupanqui (Gómez Suárez's great-great maternal grandfather), Huayna Cápac and his mother Coya Mama Ocllo lay before the mestizo.[16] Gómez Suárez later regretted not having studied them more carefully, but he had not yet considered writing about them. He did, however, touch the finger of Huayna Cápac, Inca ruler and father of the warring half-brothers Huáscar and Atahualpa. In January 1560, Gómez Suárez left Cuzco for Lima, whence he departed Peru, never to return (Part 1, Book V, Chapter XXIX, vol. 1, 320–21).

Gómez Suárez disembarked from his Atlantic passage at the port of Lisbon, made his way down to Seville, and then set off for Badajoz in Extremadura, the site of Captain Garcilaso's birth and the region in which the conquistador's eldest brother, Gómez Suárez de Figueroa y Vargas, held sway as the Lord of Torre del Águila y Tesorero. Captain Garcilaso had been the third of four brothers (and five sisters) born to Blanca de Sotomayor Suárez de Figueroa and Alonso de Hinestrosa de Vargas, two of whom were still living when Gómez Suárez entered Spain. As mentioned above, Captain Garcilaso died in Cuzco in 1559, which precipitated his son's departure, and the youngest of the brothers, Juan de Vargas, had also died in Peru as a result of the harquebus wounds he had suffered in the battle of Huarina (1547) (Part 2, "Prologue"). The two remaining sons were the aforementioned Lord of Torre del Águila y Tesorero and Alonso de Vargas, the second in line, who had been a military captain under Charles V from 1517 to 1555 and resided in Montilla. It appears that Gómez Suárez first presented himself to the Lord of Torre del Águila y Tesorero, where he encountered a lukewarm reception if not outright rebuke due to the fact that he was illegitimately conceived and of mixed blood (Varner 1968: 199–206). It should be remembered that in Spain at this time the fifteenth-century rationale of *limpieza de sangre* (purity of blood), which originally debarred recently converted Jews (then Muslims, or *Moriscos*) from occupying positions in Spanish political and religious institutions by requiring proof of four generations of Christian descent on *both* sides of an applicant's family tree, was modified and applied to the Indians and mixed-race progeny of the Spanish conquests, to which the prohibitions against mestizos forcefully attest.[17] Of course, whether Gómez Suárez was subjected to racial prejudice at the estate of the Lord of Torre is open to question. Nevertheless, the facts that he took up residence with his other, much less wealthy uncle Alonso de Vargas and that his relations with the Figueroas, who represented the ruling houses of Feria and Priego, would remain strained for the rest of his life suggest this may have been the case.

Gómez Suárez's relationship with Don Alonso de Vargas turned out to be a very close one, and the elder captain not only treated his nephew with kindness, but also formally adopted him and made him coexecutor of his estate when he died in 1571. Gómez Suárez moved to Montilla no later than September 1561, where sometime before or shortly thereafter he received news from Peru that his two half-sisters, Blanca de Sotomayor and Francisca de Mendoza, the daughters from Captain Garcilaso's marriage with Luisa Martel, had both died within a seventeen-day period in May 1560. This meant the repartimiento of Indians that Captain Garcilaso had left to his legitimate daughter Blanca de Sotomayor would revert to the crown, having surpassed the two-life limit of the New Laws. The only remedy was to bring a suit seeking exception before the Council of the Indies requesting title to the encomienda, which Gómez Suárez's stepmother and her new husband Gerónimo Luis de Cabrera were doing in Peru. This was probably what Gómez Suárez had in mind when he arrived in Madrid in early 1562 to petition King Philip II for pecuniary recognition of his father's services and the restitution of his mother's patrimony (Varner 1968: 201–07). Since his uncle had helped him with a similar petition for a share in his father's legacy when Captain Garcilaso's other illegitimate daughter, Leonor de la Vega, who lived in Spain, passed away in 1561, Gómez Suárez may have held out some hope of success.

The petition was rejected, and there are many reasons why the requests made by Gómez Suárez were probably doomed to fail from the start. However, since many garcilacistas agree that this was an important turning point in the life of the historian, it would be well to consider some of them here. First, it is not clear what Gómez Suárez might have been requesting of the crown other than an exception of some sort. He possessed no rights to the succession of his father's encomienda, because he was born out of wedlock and his parents never married, leaving him illegitimate. The succession of encomiendas was permitted only to the legitimate children of encomenderos and, again, only for the generation immediately following the original holder. This may be why Captain Garcilaso left his repartimiento to his daughter instead of his son in the first place, but the question of legitimacy was certainly one that differentiated Gómez Suárez's petition from that of his mestizo classmate from Cuzco, Pedro del Barco (whose Spanish father and Indian mother had married), which was made about the same time and succeeded, despite the fact that del Barco was imprisoned in Cordoba for having attempted to murder his wife (Varner 1968: 205). So, if Gómez Suárez was making a claim on the remains of his father's encomienda, it seems he had very little legal ground upon which to base it.

Second, it is just as unclear what he may have sought in requesting the recovery of his mother's patrimony (Castanien 1969: 34). Though she had married Juan del Pedroche, until her death Isabela Chimpu Ocllo continued to receive rents from Captain Garcilaso's coca plantation in Havisca, located in the region of Antisuyu near Paucartambo. She was able to collect this income because she shared the plantation with her son, Gómez Suárez. According to Varner, Captain Garcilaso had found a way of permanently conferring the property on his son and a cousin, García Suárez de Figueroa, despite the apparent legal snags, and in 1559 Gómez Suárez was able to buy the portion of the plantation that had belonged to García Suárez with a promissory note. He then assigned half of it to his mother for a small payment in gold (Varner 1968: 189). Unless Gómez Suárez was either trying to increase this holding or have the expense of the promissory note covered by the crown, it is difficult to see what kind of restitution there could have been on lands that he and his mother already controlled.

It thus seems most likely that Gómez Suárez was petitioning for the recognition and reward of Captain Garcilaso's services to the Spanish monarchy. Like many other conquistadors, Captain Garcilaso had participated in the endeavors in the New World, at least initially, at his own expense, with the promise of sharing in the spoils as his only financial guarantee (Varón Gabai 1997: 9–12). The gains won in conquest were divided in proportion to rank and economic investment, with one-fifth of the total take set aside for the King ("the Royal fifth"). Since Sebastián Garcilaso de la Vega was both the legitimate son of nobles and a military captain, it was understood that his portion should be greater than that of a person of lesser birth or rank. Though Captain Garcilaso was ultimately able to provide not only a comfortable existence for himself, but also (as it turns out) economic assistance to his wife, concubines, and children, it was not unusual for additional considerations (such as pensions, annuities, tax exemptions, and honorary titles) to be given to those who performed exemplary service. Such was the case with Don Alonso de Vargas, Gómez Suárez's uncle, who had served Charles V faithfully for nearly four decades and been rewarded.[18] Such requests for royal compensation would involve consideration of the quality and character of the services done for the crown and the loyalty of the one who performed them.

Beyond any feelings he had for his father, Gómez Suárez probably had reason to think there was some chance that either he or his mother might profit by a petition of this sort. After all, his father had helped to conquer one of the richest and most splendid empires of the New World at peril of life and limb, he had survived various assassinations and civil wars, he had served in a governmental post, and he was related to the houses of Feria and Priego, two of the most powerful in all of Spain.[19] And although the supplicant was an illegitimate mestizo, he still had the advantage of having the blood of both Spanish and Inca aristocrats in his veins. The outcome of Gómez Suárez's request would involve a consideration of all these factors, yet the *honra* (reputation) of his father, concerning which he seems to have had little doubt, would be crucial.

It was here that the shadow of Captain Garcilaso's questionable involvement in the battle of Huarina (October 21, 1547), one of the high moments of Gonzalo Pizarro's rebellion against the Spanish monarchy, caught up with Gómez Suárez. In brief, when the New Laws were promulgated on November 20, 1542 by Charles V from Barcelona, their ostensible purpose was to protect the lives and souls of Indians from the harsh abuses and often obscene forms of exploitation they were suffering at the hands of conquistadors and encomenderos throughout the Indies. The practical consequences of these measures were drastic reductions in both the amount and kind of tribute that encomenderos could extract from their Indians as well as a limitation on the succession of encomiendas from perpetuity to a single generation (the life of the encomendero and no other), after which the Indians would revert to the crown. Needless to say, encomenderos all over the New World were scandalized and outraged, for with one swift blow Charles V had not only effectively taken back what they felt they had risked their lives and fortunes to attain, but he had also thoroughly undermined the foundation upon which the encomenderos' political and economic power was based—indigenous labor.[20] The news was taken especially hard in Peru, where the largest number of encomenderos resided and where the newly arrived first Viceroy of Peru, Blasco Núñez Vela (May 1544), was ensuring that the reforms were implemented with draconian precision. In October 1544 Núñez Vela was expelled from Peru by Gonzalo Pizarro, who had roused troops, taken Lima, and been elected governor by the Audiencia. Peru was in revolt, and the next decisive moment would come on January 18, 1546, when the forces of Pizarro routed those of Núñez Vela at Iñaquito, and the viceroy, technically an extension of the very body of the King, was executed.

Pizarro had succeeded in removing Peru from monarchical control, but Charles V emended some of the more caustic clauses in the laws and endowed Licentiate Pedro de la Gasca with broad powers to quell the rebellion. Pizarro's reign and life would eventually come to an end thanks to Gasca's troops and the desertion of his own forces at the battle of Sacsahuana, just outside Cuzco on April 9, 1548, but not before another stunning victory against royalist forces at Huarina on the shores of Lake Titicaca on October 21, 1547. The royalists were led by Diego Centeno and counted Captain Garcilaso among their ostensible supporters, if not their numbers. At the time of battle, Captain Garcilaso was Pizarro's "captive" and had been since 1544, and although one man was prisoner of the other they were far from enemies; both were Extremadurans (Pizarro from Trujillo) and *vecinos* (citizens) of Cuzco, and they had been on a successful conquest together to Collao in 1538.[21] During the fighting, Gonzalo Pizarro was knocked from his horse, and it began to appear as if the day would belong to the royalists. Yet, in a move that was to become infamous regardless of how or when it occurred, Captain Garcilaso is said to have responded by offering Pizarro his horse. Pizarro mounted, rallied his troops, and sent an embarrassing defeat to the king as a symbol of his defiance.[22] The sincerity of Captain Garcilaso's commitment to the crown has been in question ever since.

However flimsy or firm his other claims may have been, the interpretation given to this event by Licentiate Lope García de Castro, head of the committee of the Council of Indies reviewing Gómez Suárez's petition and soon to become president of the Audiencia in Lima (he arrived September 1564), punctured the mestizo's pretensions (Part 2, Book V, Chapter XXIII). García de Castro had at his disposal not only the unfavorable testimony regarding Captain Garcilaso's character from the correspondences of the Marquis of Cañete, third Viceroy of Peru (the man who had removed Captain Garcilaso from his post of Corregidor in 1556), but also the chronicles of the Peruvian civil wars that had been published in the mid-1550s. Both Francisco López de Gómara's *Historia general de las Indias y conquista de México* (General History of the Indies and the Conquest of Mexico, 1552), who had been the chaplain of Herán Cortés after the latter's return to Spain, and Agustín de Zárate's *Historia del descubrimiento y conquista del Perú* (History of the Discovery and Conquest of Peru, 1555), who had served as the General Accountant of Peru under first Viceroy Núñez Vela, had either explicitly or implicitly implicated Captain Garcilaso in the affair.[23] Yet it was the unpublished manuscript of Diego Fernández de Palencia the Palentine, who had been recruited by the Marquis of Cañete to write a history of Peru's civil wars, that proved to be the most damning. In his *Historia del Perú* (History of Peru, 1565), Fernández repeated a rumor circulating in Peru that the rebellion of Francisco Hernández Girón (1553–1554) had simply preempted one concurrently planned by Captain Garcilaso and his brother-in-law Antonio de Quiñones. Further, about the battle of Huarina, Fernández wrote, "Gonzalo was thrown to the ground in this encounter [during the attack by royalists Pedro de los Ríos and Antonio de Ulloa], and Garcilaso (who had remained in the saddle) dismounted and gave him his horse and helped him to mount" (Fernández de Palencia 1913–1914: Part I, Book II, Chapter 79, Part II, Book II, Chapter 25).

Armed with this unflattering portrait of Captain Garcilaso, García de Castro is said to have confronted Gómez Suárez with these words: "What reward do you expect His Majesty to grant you when your father did as he did at the battle of Huarina and gave Gonzalo Pizarro that great victory?" When Gómez Suárez challenged the veracity of those reports, García de Castro continued, "The historians have written it: are you going to deny it?" (Part 2, Book V, Chapter XXIII, vol. 2, 216). This, at any rate, is how Inca Garcilaso was to record his experiences in Madrid many years later in his *Royal Commentaries*. Regardless of whether the central lesson of this encounter, the connection between political interests and colonial historiography, was already known to Gómez Suárez thanks to the oral traditions of his Inca relatives, was only then realized by the then twenty-four-year-old mestizo (the committee finally handed down its decision in the spring of 1563), or would arise through his later engagement with the rhetorical historiography of the late Renaissance, one point stands out. Gómez Suárez had experienced a jarring collision between the machinery of the Spanish state, the historical records of Spanish expansionism, and at least one prominent facet of his own identity.

The personal disappointment and political defeat that Gómez Suárez suffered in Madrid were due in large part to the words of historians, and this incident, upon which he would dwell in his works, certainly provided one of the primary motivations for his intellectual endeavors. Yet although he would go on to write corrective histories of Inca civilization, Spanish conquest, and the Peruvian civil wars of the early colonial period, he was by no means transformed overnight. In fact, after the decision was rendered, Gómez Suárez submitted another petition to the Council, this time requesting permission to return to Peru. His request was granted on June 27, 1563, but he never boarded the ship that would have transported him back to his native country. This can most probably be explained by the fact that on August 8, 1563 King Philip II named Lope García de Castro, the same man who had just scolded Gómez Suárez in the Council's chambers, president of the Audiencia in Lima to replace the fourth Viceroy of Peru, Diego Lopez de Zuñiga y Velasco, Count of Nieva (Part 2, Book VIII, Chapter XV; Varner 1968: 224; Miró Quesada 1971: Chapter V). Over and above the restrictions placed upon mestizos in the New World, Gómez Suárez would have been forced to negotiate an administrative regime that was not only familiar to him, but regarded him with suspicion, if not open animosity. Like the hope of gaining both the recognition of and commensurate pecuniary reward for his aristocratic status in Spain, the slim prospects of living as a mestizo settler in Peru were now closed to him as well.

Before leaving Madrid to return to his uncle's home in Montilla, Gómez Suárez encountered two veterans (among several others) of Spanish endeavors in the New World whose diametrical views on the conquest and differing receptions of the mestizo are worth recording. The first was the legendary Dominican Friar Bartolomé de Las Casas, first Bishop of Chiapas, whose crusade against the cruelties and injustices perpetrated by conquistadors and encomenderos in the New World earned him the title "Apostle of the Indians," the ears of Charles V and Philip II, and the enmity of conquerors and settlers throughout the Spanish overseas possessions (Hanke 1974: 73–112; Pagden 1982: 119–45; Brading 1991: 59–102). At the time, both Las Casas and Domingo de Santo Tomás had been appointed by Peruvian curacas to represent their petition/offer to abolish the encomienda system to the court. While Las Casas's call for restitution to the legitimate "natural lords" of indigenous civilizations is well known, the curacas' petition represented a complex interplay of Peruvian political interests. The first goal was to wrest control of labor and local government from the encomenderos. The second implicit goal, however, stemmed from the curacas' ongoing attempts to regain the autonomy they had lost to their Inca masters, whom indigenous Andeans were beginning to portray as usurpers.[24] When Gómez Suárez met Las Casas in Madrid, it is said that once the bishop recognized the young man as being from the Indies he gave the mestizo his hand to kiss. Although the historian tells us that Las Casas had very little to say when he realized Gómez Suárez was from Peru instead of Mexico, it is more likely that the Defender of the Indians was disturbed to see the mestizo son of an encomendero and an Inca princess pressing claims for "reward" to the Spanish Crown.[25] The experience was not a pleasant one for Gómez Suárez, but it marks yet another instance of his encounters with the political battles swirling around his own mixed heritage.

The other person encountered by Gómez Suárez in Madrid was an old acquaintance from Cuzco, Gonzalo Silvestre, a native of Herrera de Alcántara in the province of Cáceres, a captain in Hernando de Soto's ill-fated expedition to Florida (1539–1543) and a Peruvian expatriot banished by Viceroy Marquis de Cañete (Varner 1968: 157). Silvestre had traveled to Peru after being one of the few to survive Soto's disaster (Soto was not so fortunate) and promptly joined Diego Centeno's royalist forces against Gonzalo Pizarro at Huarina. He entertained the children of Cuzco with stories of exploration and conquest when Gómez Suárez was still a youth, and now the two were reacquainted in

Madrid. Whereas Las Casas treated Gómez Suárez coolly, the elder conquistador appears to have embraced the young man, and the two formed a friendship that would last until Silvestre's death in 1592. The meeting is significant for, although it is not known exactly when Gómez Suárez decided to pursue a life of letters, this friendship spurred a literary collaboration in which Silvestre became the principal eyewitness source for Inca Garcilaso's first published history, the novelesque *La Florida del Inca* (The Florida of the Inca, 1605).[26]

Gómez Suárez only spent a year and a half in Madrid, yet in many respects the course of his life had been set in these few trying months. He would receive no recognition from the crown; he had experienced the profound limitations of his mestizo heritage; he would never return to Peru; and somewhere along the way his conversations with Gonzalo Silvestre would produce a manuscript. Although his precise thoughts at this time are unknown, a change had indeed come over Gómez Suárez as he headed back to Montilla. While acting as a godfather in the Church of Santiago in Montilla on November 17, 1563, Gómez Suárez signed the baptismal ledger not as Figueroa (the name he had been given), but as Gómez Suárez de la Vega. Five days later, standing in the same capacity for another child, he renamed himself again. From this moment on, he would be known as Garcilaso de la Vega (Varner 1968: 225).

In Montilla, Garcilaso settled into the life of the rural *hidalgo* with which the generosity of his inheritance and his uncle Don Alonso de Vargas provided him.[27] He spent his days tending to his uncle's vineyards and raising horses, an affinity and skill for which he had already begun to develop in Peru and in pursuance of which Don Alonso de Vargas added stables to his household for Garcilaso's private use (Castanien 1969: 35; Part 2, Book II, Chapter XXV and Book V, Chapter XXII). If Garcilaso had begun to consider writing as a vocation, living in the modest comforts of his uncle's home would have provided him with ample time to pursue his interests, and in 1564 it appears that Garcilaso went to Seville to perfect his Latin under the scholar and theologian Pedro Sánchez de Herrera (Varner 1968: 231). These seem to have been quiet years for Garcilaso (1563–1570), and what little is known about them comes primarily from the archives of Spanish legal documents. Yet there are a few events that either occurred or began at this time that would prove to be important developments in the historian's life.

First, perhaps at the "well-known and excellent library" of his relative the

Marquis de Priego (del Pino-Díaz 2011: 16), Garcilaso chanced upon a copy of *Dialoghi d'Amore* (Dialogues of Love, 1536) written by Judah Abrabanel, more commonly known as León Hebreo, the Neoplatonic philosopher and exiled Portuguese Jew. Hebreo's work, which takes the form of a three-part conversation between the love-stricken Philo and the aloof, desired Sophia, is a complex and sweeping attempt to reconcile the philosophies of Plato and Aristotle, the teachings of Moses and Maimomides, and the theology of St. Thomas Aquinas with the commentaries of Averroes in a syncretic and unified whole that demonstrates God is love. It treats the different forms of desire as well as the origin and universality of love with extensive discussions of the kernels of truth contained in Greek and Roman myths, astrology, cosmology, and the Cabbala. All of this is contained within an underlying Empedoclean framework in which different historical epochs are determined by the eternal struggle between Love and Hate. Garcilaso was obviously taken with this text, most likely for its explicit attempt both to valorize and reconcile the myths and wisdom of pagan civilizations with the religious truths of Judaism and Catholic theology (Sommer 1996a, 1996b; Mazzotti 2006: Castro-Klarén 2016c). More important, perhaps, is the clear message of ecumenical tolerance in the *Dialoghi*, based on the idea that we are all the rational creatures of God; for if God is love and we naturally desire his likeness, then we, too, should love one another. As such, the *Dialoghi* tends to defend and celebrate plurality and cultural difference as well as the fundamental dignity and interconnectedness of all God's children. A powerful argument indeed for a young man whose Inca relatives were seen as "barbarians" and "savages," and Garcilaso would later translate it into Spanish from the Italian as his first published work (1590). Although this task would not be completed until 1586, it appears that Garcilaso's initiation into the soothing and heady logic of Renaissance Neoplatonism occurred in the mid-1560s.[28]

Second, Vargas introduced Garcilaso to the clergy at the Church of Santiago in Montilla, which the former attended regularly, and this is most likely where Garcilaso became more formally acquainted with the religious intelligentsia in southern Spain. Beyond the rectory of the church, the Jesuits were operating a college in the area (Castanien 1969: 36), and since Garcilaso's residence in Montilla coincided with the arrival of the first Jesuit missionaries in Peru, it is difficult to believe that the ever curious brethren of the Society of Jesus would fail to take notice of a Peruvian mestizo in their midst.[29] Precisely whom he met and the depth of his early interactions are impossible to gauge.[30] However, considering the friendship of the many Jesuits he would later enjoy (such as Juan de Pineda, Francisco de Castro, Miguel Vásquez de Padilla, Jerónimo de Prado, Pedro Maldonado de Saavedra, and Jerónimo Ferraz), the outward praise he gives the Jesuits in his texts, his admiration for and liberal use of the works of the Peruvian mestizo Jesuit Blas Valera and José de Acosta, and the fact that his relatives the Marquises of Priego were generous supporters of the Society all suggest a longer association with the Jesuits than the one that seems to materialize rapidly after the publication of Garcilaso's translation of the *Dialoghi d'Amore* and his move to Cordoba (1590–1591). At any rate, it appears that through the assistance of his uncle and his proximity to a broader intellectual community Garcilaso began to dedicate time to his studies.[31]

Finally, there is evidence to suggest that Garcilaso remained in contact with his Peruvian compatriots as he claims to have done in his texts (Part 1, Book I, Chapter XV). Gonzalo Silvestre had moved to nearby Las Posadas, and that the two had occasion to continue the conversations they had begun in Madrid is attested to by the fact that Garcilaso purchased a white female slave, Juana, from Silvestre in 1567 and by annotations and margin comments the two made in a copy of López de Gómara's *Historia general de las Indias* (Varner 1968: 237; Rivarola 2011). As Garcilaso and Silvestre were hashing out the "true account" of Soto's Florida expedition as well as the rebellions of Gonzalo Pizarro and Francisco Hernández Girón, in both of which Silvestre had taken part, news from Peru was shortly to arrive with the visit paid to Garcilaso by his Cuzqueño classmate and fellow mestizo, Juan Arias Maldonado.

During Garcilaso's absence the conditions for mestizos in Peru had worsened as a result of the continued wrangling over the perpetuity of encomiendas and the increased restrictions placed upon mestizos by the crown. A group of embittered young men decided to take action. A rebellion had been slated for January 1567, the leaders of which were Juan and Cristóbal Maldonado, sons of Diego Maldonado the Rich, owner of the wealthiest encomienda in Peru; Pedro del Barco, son of a conquistador with the same name; and Carlos Inca, son of Paullu Inca. Their plot was far-reaching in its aims: one retinue would assassinate President of the Audiencia Lope García de Castro in Lima; then, having taken Lima, they would send word to overthrow Jerónimo Costilla, Corregidor of Cuzco, where arms had been stockpiled in the home of Carlos Inca. After this, the rebels planned to enlist the aid of Titu Cusi Yupanqui, who was orchestrating Inca resistance from the mountain stronghold of Vilcabamba, and, if possible, send all of Peru hurtling into revolt. The plot was betrayed by Juan de Nieto, who revealed the conspiracy to Augustinian Prior Juan de Vivero during confession. Within days the conspirators were rounded up by García de Castro, and many of those implicated had their estates confiscated and were banished from Peru (López Martínez 1971: 13–47; Hemming 1970: 42–44).

This turn of events forced Juan Arias Maldonado to Spain, where he renewed his association with Garcilaso in Montilla in the early 1570s (Varner 1968: 265). There is no record of their exchange, yet here was a young man much like Garcilaso himself who had been pushed by the policies of the crown and the iniquities of the Peruvian colonial regime to the very brink of armed conflict. It is certain that Maldonado recounted the removal of himself and his brother Cristóbal to Spain, Pedro del Barco's exile in Chile, and the active persecution of the sons of encomenderos and Indian princesses by Peruvian administrators. If Garcilaso were still smarting from his rejection in Madrid a few years before, perhaps Maldonado's visit provided him with more fuel for an already smoldering fire. At the very least, news of colonial politics and the thwarted rebellion probably reinforced Garcilaso's lingering solidarity for his mestizo comrades, a solidarity he also held for his Inca relatives and the first Peruvian encomenderos. In the *Royal Commentaries* he would defend all three groups, sometimes altering the historical record in order to do so, and it is interesting to wonder where Garcilaso would have stood in January 1567 had he returned to Peru in 1563.

Garcilaso was not living in Peru during the mestizo conspiracy so he was never faced with the choice between loyalties that his classmates (or his father, for that matter) had experienced. However, when the call for battle came in Spain during the Morisco revolt at Alpujarras in Granada (1568–1570), Garcilaso embarked upon his own, short-lived military career.[32] Perhaps he was motivated by the martial examples of his father and uncle, or by the desire to solidify his uncertain social status with a military commission, both of which concerns may have been more urgent at the moment, regarding his circumstances. On March 17, 1570, Don Alonso de Vargas, the uncle who had adopted Garcilaso as his own son, died. Vargas named Garcilaso, along with the former's wife, Doña Luisa Ponce de León, and local prelate Francisco de Castro, coexecutors of his estate, and although Garcilaso would continue living with his aunt in Montilla until she moved to Cordoba in 1580 (where she died in 1586), he was now effectively on his own. At the end of March or early April 1570, just before his thirty-first birthday, Garcilaso set out with the men he had gathered and trained and the supplies he had provided to serve under Don Juan of Austria, the Habsburg half-brother of Philip II.

Little is known about Garcilaso's military service, save that he attained the rank of captain, granted to him by both Philip II and Don Juan of Austria, and that his tenure was very brief. Having departed Montilla in late March or early April, he had returned no later than July 19, 1570. He was called again on August 8, reported for duty on August 25, and was home again on September 24, 1570, serving (as he frequently did) as a godfather in the Church of Santiago and signing his name "señor Capitán Garcilaso de la Vega." He seems to have neither distinguished nor disgraced himself in battle, and the only spoil that he appears to have claimed was a female slave, a *morisca* whom he named María de Flores and sold the next year. It is known, however (striking the chord that sounded so frequently in Garcilaso's life), that he served at his own expense and was neither rewarded nor reimbursed for his efforts and expenditures (Varner 1968: 244–48).

There would soon be additional sorrow and then outrage added to the loss of his uncle and the continued snubs from the crown. Between the end of 1571 and the beginning of 1572, Ñusta Isabela Suárez Chimpu Ocllo, granddaughter, niece, and cousin to Inca potentates, concubine of Captain Sebastián Garcilaso de la Vega, wife of Spanish commoner Juan del Pedroche, and mother of Garcilaso de la Vega, died.[33] In addition to her son she was survived by two daughters, Ana Ruiz, wife of Martín de Bustinza, and Luisa de Herrera, who married Pedro Márquez Galeote. Garcilaso is likely to have received the news of his mother's death from his sister Luisa de Herrera, with whom he remained in contact and whose son, Alonso Márquez de Figueroa Inca, both visited and had a close association with Garcilaso when he traveled to Spain (1604–1614) (Miró Quesada 1948: 258). Unlike Captain Garcilaso, to whom he dedicated several passages in the Second Part of the *Royal Commentaries*, including a lengthy funeral oration (Part 2, Book VIII, Chapter XII), Garcilaso wrote very little about his mother. Nevertheless, thanks to her will and a sentence in the "Dedication" to the Second Part of the *Royal Commentaries*, we do know that Chimpu Ocllo died a Christian.[34]

With the visitation of Juan Arias Maldonado and the recent death of his mother, Garcilaso's thoughts may have once again been turning to Peru as the Incas were about to suffer their final and perhaps most devastating calamity. On November 30, 1569, Francisco de Toledo, fifth Viceroy of Peru, arrived in Lima with a mission. Toledo had been sent by King Philip II to implement a sweeping plan of reform that would stabilize the often chaotic Peruvian territories, increase the economic output of the area, and bring an end to Inca resistance, which had been conducted alternately from Vitcos and Vilcabamba since the mid-1530s (Hemming 1970: 392–456). In 1567 Titu Cusi Yupanqui, son of Manco Inca and current ruler of the "Neo-Inca state," performed a written act of submission to Spain, and in January 1569 Philip II ratified the Treaty of Acobamba between the indigenous leader and Lope García de Castro (Kubler 1947: 189–203). Toledo was instructed to conclude the negotiations begun by his predecessor, but during the first year of his term the viceroy only managed to exchange letters with Titu Cusi Yupanqui, to no avail. As Toledo's impatience grew, Titu Cusi Yupanqui died under mysterious circumstances, and the viceroy, who had already begun to consider an armed resolution to the negotiations and was unaware of Titu Cusi's death, interpreted the break in talks as recalcitrance.[35] Túpac Amaru, legitimate son of Manco Inca, had secretly acceded to the throne by the time Toldeo's emissaries, led by Atilano de Anaya, arrived outside Vilcabamba in March 1572 to remind the Inca, who was still thought to be Titu Cusi, of his promises to the King. When Atilano de Anaya, a respected citizen of Cuzco and intermediary between Spaniards and Incas, was murdered by the indigenous guards surrounding the Inca encampment, Viceroy Toledo responded with a declaration of war on April 14, 1572. By September 21, 1572, Túpac Amaru, the last legitimate heir to the Inca throne, was led to Cuzco in chains by his captor Don Martín García de Loyola, the grandnephew of Saint Ignatius of Loyola, founder of the Jesuits. For three days Túpac Amaru was instructed in the Christian faith and baptized while he underwent a sham trial for murder and insurrection, and Jesuits priests such as Alonzo de Barzana begged Toledo to spare the Inca's life. Toledo would not be swayed (Hyland 2003: 53). On September 24, 1572, in the main square of Cuzco, former capital of the Inca empire, amid the protests of Spanish clergymen and the wailing of his indigenous subjects, Túpac Amaru was beheaded (Hemming 1970: 444–49).

This event was the shocking coup de grâce to four decades of insult and injustice meted out to the shattered Inca dynasty, beginning with Francisco Pizarro's execution of Atahualpa in 1533. The years of resistance and the continual negotiations between the Incas and Spaniards for coexistence, restitution, and restoration had culminated in the arrogant and gory spectacle of Túpac Amaru's public decapitation. As if this were not enough, the official reports sent by Viceroy Toledo to Philip II, *Informaciones acerca del señorio de los Incas* (Information regarding the reign of the Incas, 1572), and the histories written by Toledo's agents, Juan de Matienzo and Pedro Sarmiento de Gamboa, both of which were buttressed by the testimonies of indigenous eyewitnesses, put forward the view that the Incas had been nothing more than recent conquerors and cruel tyrants (Brading 1991: 128–46). Whereas Dominican theologian Francisco de Vitoria and Bartolomé de Las Casas had earlier argued, respectively, that the Incas were *señores naturales* (natural lords) and virtuous, noble gentiles, the works of the Toledan school revived the neo-Aristotelian arguments of Juan Gínes de Sepúlveda, and claimed that the native inhabitants of Peru were "natural slaves" who had succumbed to Inca dominion through warfare and terror.[36] Even as the remnants of the Inca panacas were being eradicated, the Toledan school was initiating a new justification of the Spanish conquest that represented the latter as a form of Christian emancipation from savage, pagan despots.

Garcilaso's familiarity with the actual works produced by the Toledan school is doubtful at best since Philip II ordered all documents pertaining to the conquest of the New World to be collected and sealed in an archive at Seville in 1577 (Brading 1991: 143). Nevertheless, it is relatively safe to assume that Garcilaso caught wind of their gist when his contacts in Peru informed him of Túpac Amaru's execution and the concomitant policies of Toledo's viceregal regime. It is possible that both the dispatch of the last Inca and Toledo's reign (1569–1581) provided the final impetus for Garcilaso's decision to undertake the difficult task of writing his own version of Inca civilization and the Spanish conquest.[37] However that may be, the complicated political sensibility that was to inform Garcilaso's works was beginning to fall into place. He had already seen the ill-treatment reserved for both Peruvian encomenderos and mestizos, and now this final and flagrant disregard for the rights and lives of the Inca elite could be added to the stories he had heard from his Inca relatives while in Cuzco. On top of everything was Toledo's claim that the Incas had never been "kings" in the true sense of the term; they had been little more than murderous thugs lording it over timid simpletons. Perhaps what made the words and deeds of Toledo all the more galling to Garcilaso was that they were coming from a member of his own family: the viceroy was a distant cousin through the Figueroas (Varner 1968: 266; Markham 1999: xix n1).

Although there can be little doubt as to the importance of the events of 1572, it would be another four and a half decades before Garcilaso's thoughts on these matters were published.[38] In fact, almost twenty years would elapse before his translation of Leo Hebreo's *Dialoghi d'Amore* was printed by Pedro Madrigal in Madrid in 1590.[39] Garcilaso frequently blames his somewhat belated entrance into the republic of letters (he was in his early fifties when the translation appeared) on the poor schooling he received as a child, the interruptions of his military service, and financial distress.[40] On at least one of these counts, his pecuniary predicament, Garcilaso is known to have exaggerated (Varner 1968: 309; Fernández 2016: 24). Yet in the dedicatory letters to Don Maximiliano of Austria, Chief Abbot of Alcalá la Real and grandson of Charles V, and to King Philip II in *La traduzión del Indio*, Garcilaso informs us that he had completed roughly one-fourth of *La Florida* and, at the very least, had determined to write, if not already begun, a history of Peru.[41] In addition to what these letters tell us about his personal aspirations at the time, they demonstrate the intellectual endeavors that would occupy the rest of his life were well under way as of the mid-1580s. More importantly, as Garcilaso was presenting himself to posterity and offering this literary "first fruit" from a native Peruvian to Philip II, he explicitly accepted the challenges of his precarious, dual heritage. In both the title of the translation and the prefatory letters, Garcilaso describes himself alternately as *Indio* (Indian), *Ynga* (Inca), son of Peruvian kings and noble Spanish conquistadors—in short, as a mestizo. Now acting as the first literary representative of three despised and disparaged groups, he would be known forevermore as Garcilaso Inca de la Vega.

It was around this time that things started to change for the better for Inca Garcilaso. In 1580 his aunt Doña Luisa Ponce de León, with whom his relationship had always been more expedient than affectionate, moved to Cordoba while he remained in Montilla. Upon her death in 1586, Inca Garcilaso became the sole proprietor of his uncle's estate, as dictated in the latter's will. Although he would experience continued difficulties collecting debts that had been owed to Alonso de Vargas, Inca Garcilaso was now both a captain of the military and a man of considerable property.[42] He would eventually sell his home of thirty years in Montilla on October 11, 1591 and resettle in Cordoba, where his writing and reputation would flourish (Varner 1968: 301).

Between the time of his aunt's death and his own relocation, Inca Garcilaso not only prepared the final copies of the translation, but he also made numerous trips to the residence of Gonzalo Silvestre in Las Posadas to work on *La Florida*.[43] As Inca Garcilaso states in the preface, the work had been at least twenty years in the planning, but now that Silvestre's health had begun to deteriorate, the completion of the task became more urgent (*La Florida*, "Preface").[44] Considering the apparent paucity of written accounts at their disposal, Silvestre's contribution to *La Florida* must be regarded as considerable, and in a characteristic display of false modesty Inca Garcilaso claims to have acted solely as the former's amanuensis and scribe.[45] The collection, organization, and substantial revision of Silvestre's first-hand recollections would not be submitted to the Office of the Inquisition for approval by Inca Garcilaso until 1604.[46] It was finally published under the title *La Florida del Ynca. Historia del Adelantado Hernando de Soto, Gouernador y capitán general del Reyno de la Florida, y otros heroicos caualleros Españoles e Yndios, escrita por el Ynca Garcilasso de la Vega, capitán de su Magestad, natural de la gran ciudad del Cozco, cabeça de los Reynos y prouinçias del Peru* (The Florida of the Inca, a history of Adelantado Hernando de Soto, Governor and captain general of the Kingdom of Florida, and of other heroic Spanish and Indian cavaliers, written by the Inca Garcilaso de la Vega, captain of His Majesty, native of the great city of Cuzco, head of the Kingdoms and provinces of Peru) by the printing house of Pedro Crasbeeck in Lisbon in 1605.[47] Yet only one of the two collaborators would live to see the realization of their efforts: Silvestre had died in 1592, bringing to an end a friendship between the two men that had lasted nearly forty years.

Although it is easy to see how Inca Garcilaso would have been affected by Silvestre's death, one should nevertheless take his statement that he had been reduced to the "rincones de la soledad y pobreza" (corners of solitude and poverty; *La Florida*, "Preface") with a little salt.[48] In the first place, it had become a commonplace for authors in late-sixteenth- and early-seventeenth-century Spain, a Spain whose greatness was clearly in decline, to present themselves as *desengañados*, persons who had been "undeceived" and therefore stoically removed from the vanities and false hopes of the material world. Second, Inca Garcilaso was neither impoverished, as we have seen, nor completely isolated. In fact, he appears to have had a "family" of his own. Somewhere between the late 1570s and early 1580s, one of his female servants, Beatríz de Vega or de la Vega, gave birth to a son, Diego de Vargas (Miró Quesada 1948: 260–268). Due to the lack of accompanying baptismal records, the date of the child's birth is unknown, and there are no official documents in which Inca Garcilaso either recognizes the boy as his own offspring or declares his intimate relations with Beatríz, whom he never married. Nevertheless, both Beatríz and Diego would accompany Inca Garcilaso to Cordoba and remain with him until his death. Both are explicitly named as beneficiaries in Inca Garcilaso's will, and Beatríz is singled out among his servants as the "favorite." Diego de Vargas acted as Inca Garcilaso's scribe and copyist for portions of the *Royal Commentaries* and he was eventually elected sacristan of the Chapel of the Blessed Souls of Purgatory in Cordoba, where Inca Garcilaso was entombed (Vargas Ugarte 1930:

47–50; Aguilar Priego 1945: 281–300). Despite Inca Garcilaso's silence on these matters, it appears that he cared enough for Beatríz de Vega and Diego de Vargas to make certain they would be provided for after his death (Fernández 2016a: 24). What remains a question, however, is what caused Inca Garcilaso to pass the illegitimacy that had proved so troublesome for him in his earlier years on to his son.

Whatever the state of his private affairs, in public Inca Garcilaso enjoyed the friendship and esteem of some of the most prominent scholars in southern Spain. In the letter to Don Maximiliano dated September 18, 1586, Inca Garcilaso mentions Agustín de Herrera, theologian and tutor of Inca Garcilaso's cousin Pedro Fernández de Cordoba (Marquis of Priego); Jesuit Jerónimo de Prado, lector of scripture in Cordoba; Licentiate Pedro Sánchez de Herrera, Inca Garcilaso's former instructor; and Augustinian Friar Fernando de Zárate, former master of theology at Osuna, as some of those who had read his translation of the *Dialoghi d'Amore* and encouraged him to publish it.[49] These four men were among many associations Inca Garcilaso acquired in Montilla, as he claims "otros religiosos y graves personas" (other religious and serious persons) aided in solidifying his determination to complete the task.

By this time Inca Garcilaso must have been in full possession, if not at the very summit, of his intellectual powers. He was fluent in Quechua and Spanish, had mastered Latin and Italian, and seems to have had at least working knowledge of Greek, Portuguese, and perhaps French.[50] His facility with language most certainly would have caught the attention of his humanist contemporaries, many of whom were nearly obsessed with it, and Inca Garcilaso's achievements in this area would have impressed them all the more considering the scant formal education he had received. Nor would the sheer novelty of encountering an erudite Indian, Inca, and mestizo, one who had tilled the soil of Renaissance Neoplatonism more on less on his own and who possessed extensive knowledge of Inca civilization and Peruvian history, be lost on them. In one telling and humorous anecdote, Inca Garcilaso relates how his translation was received by Francisco Murillo, schoolmaster of the Cathedral of Cordoba. Upon meeting Inca Garcilaso, Murillo is said to have offered this greeting: "An Antarctic, born in the New World, down there below our hemisphere, and who drank the general language of the Indians of Peru with his mother's milk, what does he have to do with being an interpreter between Italians and Spaniards? And that since he has already presumed to be one, why did he not take whichever book and not the one Italians esteemed most and Spaniards knew least?" Seemingly unperturbed by the none too subtle insinuation of prejudice, Inca Garcilaso responded that the endeavor could be chalked up to a soldier's temerity, whereby great deeds are achieved and the victorious are hailed as brave, while those who perish are called crazy (Part 2, "Prologue").[51]

Regardless of whether Murillo's reaction to Inca Garcilaso was indicative of an attitude he daily encountered, the combination of his scholarly aptitude, demonstrated by his translation, and the peculiarities of his background continued to attract the attention and curiosity of learned men in Cordoba. Chief among these was the great patriarch of Andalusian letters, antiquarian, and Royal Historian for the crown of Castile under the patronage of Philip II, Ambrosio de Morales (1513–1591). Morales had studied at Salamanca with his uncle, historian Fernán Pérez de Oliva, then proceeded to Alcalá, where he enjoyed the friendship and guidance of Dominican Melchor Cano and acted as Don Juan of Austria's tutor.[52] He retired to Cordoba in 1581, and somewhere between his arrival there and his death he seems to have taken Inca Garcilaso under his wing. In a letter to Licentiate Juan Fernández Franco, overseer of the estate of the Marquis of Carpio in the village of Bujalance as well as a close friend of Morales, Inca Garcilaso claims that Morales had read his translation of the *Dialoghi d'Amore* as well as the fourth part of *La Florida del Inca*, and had adopted him as a son. Although the duration of their acquaintance is unknown, Morales seems to have had a profound impact on Inca Garcilaso, for the same letter laments that Morales had died just when Inca Garcilaso needed him most (Asensio 1953: 585–86).

In addition to the exchanges with Morales and Fernández Franco, who was a highly respected though unpublished antiquarian in his own right, Inca Garcilaso maintained extensive ties with the Society of Jesus through their college at the Cathedral of Cordoba (Miró Quesada 1971: 165–90; Araníbar 1991: 693, 701–02, 785–86). Miguel Vásquez de Padilla and Jerónimo de Prado, the latter of whom had corrected Hebrew phrases in *La traduzión del Indio*, convinced Inca Garcilaso to remove certain passages on the immortality of the soul from *La Florida del Inca* (Part 1, Book II, Chapter VII, vol. 1, 87). Inca Garcilaso considered revising the poetry of Garcí Sánchez de Badajoz with the help of Juan de Pineda, author of *Commentarorium in Job* (Commentaries on Job, 1597–1601). The project never materialized, but Father Pineda openly lauded Inca Garcilaso in his work (Garcilaso de la Vega 1951b; Miró Quesada 1971: 169). From Pedro Maldonado de Saavedra Inca Garcilaso received the manuscripts of Peruvian mestizo Jesuit Blas Valera that had been damaged during the sack of Cadiz led by Lord Howard of Effingham in 1596 (Part 1,

Book I, Chapter VI).[53] Francisco de Castro, Professor of Rhetoric at Cordoba, gave Inca Garcilaso the *Cartas Anuas* (Annual Letters) of the Jesuits in Peru relative to the indigenous rebellion in Chile and with fulsome praise dedicated his *De Arte Rhetorica, Dialogi Quatuor* (The Art of Rhetoric in Four Dialogues, 1611) to the mestizo historian (Part 1, Book VII, Chapter XXV).[54] Finally, in his attempts to bring the First Part of the *Royal Commentaries* to press, Inca Garcilaso endowed Father Jerónimo Ferraz in Lisbon with all powers necessary to achieve this end in 1609 (Miró Quesada 1971: 373). Inca Garcilaso's constant and manifold associations with the brethren of the Society of Jesus, which began no later than the early 1580s and perhaps much earlier, not only signal the extent of his intellectual activity and proclivities, but also his devotion to the Catholic faith. When Inca Garcilaso joined the ranks of the secular clergy while living in Cordoba in 1597, it is safe to conclude he did so through the Jesuits.[55]

By the turn of the seventeenth century, Inca Garcilaso's career as a historian was in full swing. While publication of *La traduzión del Indio* had brought him viability and renown in elite intellectual circles, it was *La Florida del Inca* and the advanced progress of his masterpiece *Royal Commentaries* (published in two parts, 1609 and 1617), a monumental historical revision of Inca civilization, the Spanish conquest of Peru, and the Peruvian civil wars, that demonstrated to his contemporaries the depth of his knowledge, the originality of his perspective, and his extraordinary capacity for narration. On the one hand, Inca Garcilaso's account of Hernando de Soto's failed attempt to conquer Florida (1539–1543) is a testament to the author's engagement with humanist culture and learning. Echoing Cicero, Inca Garcilaso claims that the aim of his history is to tell the truth, he cites the *Commentaries* of Julius Caesar with approbation, and his depiction of the noble and warlike Indians of Florida owes much to Tacitus's *Agricola* (Book II, Part I, Chapter XXVII and Book V, Chapter I).[56] Further, in the course of the work explicit mention is made of Alvar Núñez Cabeza de Vaca's *Naufragios* (Voyages), Pedro de Mejía's *Historia Imperial y Cesarea* (Imperial and Caesarian History), Pandulfo Collenucio's *Compendio de la Istorie del Regno di Napoli* (Compendium of the History of the Kingdom of Naples), José de Acosta's *Historia natural y moral de las Indias* (Natural and Moral History of the Indies), the poetry of Ariosto and Boiardo, Luis Vives, and Jesuit Pedro de Ribadeneira (Book I, Chapters III–IV; Book

II, Part I, Chapters XX, XXV, and XXVII; Book V, Part I, Chapter VIII; Book VI, Chapter XXII, respectively).

Yet the originality of *La Florida del Inca* resides not in its mastery of humanist historiography, but rather Inca Garcilaso's explicit statement of his multiple political intentions. His primary concern is to persuade Spaniards to undertake the conquest and settlement of the kingdoms of Florida so that the indigenous inhabitants could receive the spiritual benefits of the Catholic faith. Just as important, however, is Inca Garcilaso's desire to rescue the heroic deeds of both Spanish and Indian *caballeros* (cavaliers) from oblivion ("Preface," Book IV, Chapter XIV and Book VI, Chapter IX). So that no injury is done to "either race by recounting the valiant achievements of one while omitting those of the other," Inca Garcilaso attempts to rectify the negative images of conquistadors and Indians prevalent in his day (Book IV, Chapter XIV). Thanks to the often horrific propensity for cruelty they displayed toward Indians, the fact that they represented a significant political obstacle to monarchical control in the New World, and the publication of Bartolomé de Las Casas's *Brevísima relación de la destrucción de las Indias* (A Short Account of the Destruction of the Indies, 1552), by the late sixteenth century the Spanish conquerors were generally viewed as gold-starved thieves and bloodthirsty murderers.[57] In contrast to this view, Inca Garcilaso is careful to demonstrate the numerous difficulties and hardships suffered by those who embarked on missions of conquest in foreign lands as well as their military virtues in confronting them. Although Inca Garcilaso does not hesitate to point out the greed and violence displayed by many conquistadors (Book II, Part I, Chapter XII), Hernando de Soto emerges from the text as a tragic hero (tragic because unsuccessful) and Gonzalo Silvestre as a robust and dashing example of Spanish valor and chivalry.[58]

As for the natives of Florida, Inca Garcilaso openly challenges the view, associated with Juan Gínes de Sepúlveda, that the Indians were "simple folk without reason or understanding who in both peace and war differ very little from beasts and accordingly could not do and say things so worthy of memory and praise" (Book II, Part I, Chapter XXVII, 82). Reminiscent of Tacitus, he puts speeches unequivocally condemning the Spanish conquest into the mouths of Indian chiefs, and he details the religious beliefs, towns, temples, and laws of the natives while stressing the eloquence and undeniably Christian virtues of many indigenous rulers, with special praise for one in particular, Mucozo (Book I, Chapter IV; Book II, Part I, Chapters VII, XVI and XXI; Book III, Chapter XXXIV; and Book IV, Chapter XIV).[59] The overall effect achieved by the narrative is a vivid description of the rational capacities, military prowess, and civility of the so-called barbarians. Inca Garcilaso calls Spaniards and Indians alike "caballeros," despite the fact that the latter lacked horses (*caballos*), yet he manages to do more than simply place the two on equal footing. In describing the magnanimity of Mucozo, Inca Garcilaso declares he has represented the admirable conduct of the "infidel" so that "princes of the faith may make efforts to imitate and if possible surpass him—not in infidelity, as some do who are undeserving of the title of faithful, but in virtue and similar excellences" (Book II, Part I, Chapter IV, 36). Far from exhibiting the characteristics of inferior or servile beings, Inca Garcilaso's Indians are often the very embodiment of the cardinal virtues from whom Christians have much to learn.

Many of these themes would be carried over and extended by Inca Garcilaso in his most ambitious and important work, the *Royal Commentaries*.[60] Even before the *Primera parte de los comentarios reales* (First Part of the Royal Commentaries) had appeared in print in 1609, Inca Garcilaso was already considered an expert on the history of the New World by Andalusian scholars. Evidence of this is to be seen in the fact that three separate authors refer with approbation to Inca Garcilaso's work prior to its publication. Like Juan de Pineda with *La Florida*, Dominican Friar Gregorio García similarly assures his readers that the "history of the kings of Peru" by "Garcilaso de la Vega Inga" will give "great satisfaction and delight to those who read it" in *Origen de los indios del Nuevo Mundo e Indias Occidentales* (Origin of the Indians of the New World and West Indies, 1607). Finally, Jesuit Father Bernardo de Aldrete, Canon of the Cathedral of Cordoba and one of the preeminent Spanish philologists of the early seventeenth century, refers to the authority of the *Royal Commentaries* of "Garcilaso Inca" that are "as yet unpublished" in his *Origen y principio de la lengua castellana* (Origin and Beginning of the Castilian Language, 1606). Appropriately enough, each of the three citations enlists Inca Garcilaso's testimony and support in a philological dispute about the etymology of the word "Peru" and its relation to the mythical Ophir of Solomon (Durand 1976: 138–60).[61]

In addition to his growing reputation as a scholar, it appears that Inca Garcilaso was also an active member of the citizenry of Cordoba. He continued to act as a godfather, principally for members of the artisan classes, and in August 1605 he was appointed majordomo (superintendent) of the Hospital of the Immaculate Conception of Our Lady of Cordoba (Varner 1968: 340–41). He was now spending his time attending to the maintenance and revenues of the hospital (for which he received a salary), the publication of the First Part of the *Royal Commentaries*, and the composition of the *Segunda parte de los comentarios reales* (Second Part of the Royal Commentaries), which would be finished by 1614 and published in 1617. Yet despite the respect and prestige he seems to have achieved later in life, Inca Garcilaso's last few years were spent exorcising old demons. To the eloquent defense of the accomplishments of his Inca ancestors in the First Part of the *Royal Commentaries*, he would add the tale of their conquest, the executions of Atahualpa and Túpac Amaru, the civil wars and Toledo's viceroyalty, as well as a final attempt to clear his father's name, in the Second. As he approached the completion of this work, having revisited a number of painful memories, he may have decided that an accounting and settlement of debts were due. This, at least, may help to explain his renewed efforts to receive recognition from the Crown in 1614–1615 (Varner 1968: 363–65).

If his final plea, taken before King Philip III by Cristóbal de Burgos y Arellano, somehow succeeded where his other attempts had failed, news of it would have come too late, as Inca Garcilaso died on April 23, 1616. Although the outcome of this petition is unknown, the royal recognition he repeatedly tried to attain was not the only thing he did not live long enough to enjoy. The Second Part of the *Royal Commentaries*, the culmination of his life's work, was delayed at the presses and was finally published by the printing house of Doña Lucía de Leries in Cordoba in 1617. Unless they were due to financial concerns, the reasons for the delays are unclear since the approval of the king and the Inquisition are dated no later than January 21, 1614. But there is another oddity. For some reason that has never been adequately explained, the text that Inca Garcilaso always referred to as *Segunda parte de los comentarios reales* and intended as a continuation of the First Part was published under the title *Historia general del Perú* (General History of Peru). If he had lived, the title most certainly would not have been changed, but it is as the "General History of Peru" that the "Second Part of the Royal Commentaries" has mistakenly come to be known.

In 1612, Inca Garcilaso made provisions for his final resting place, purchasing the Chapel of the Blessed Souls of Purgatory in Cordoba. It is rather fitting that Inca Garcilaso, whose life and work had insisted upon the value and integrity of non-Christian cultures from within his own Catholic faith, would chose a former mosque as his burial site. One of the memorial tablets informs us that Inca Garcilaso had perpetually endowed the chapel and dedicated his wealth to masses on behalf of the souls in Purgatory. The other memorial tells us how the deceased wanted to be remembered: "The Inca Garcilaso de la Vega, a renowned man, worthy of perpetual memory, illustrious in blood, accomplished in letters, valiant in arms, son of Garcilaso de la Vega of the houses of the Dukes of Feria and Infantado and of Isabela Palla sister of Huayna Cápac last Emperor of the Indies. He commented upon Florida, translated Leon Hebreo and composed the *Comentarios reales*" (Castanien 1969: 50).

2
MESTIZO RHETORIC

Even before the First Part of Inca Garcilaso de la Vega's *Royal Commentaries* was published in Lisbon in 1609, it had already been praised and cited by prominent scholars in southern Spain, such as Jesuit Bernardo de Aldrete, in his *Origen y principio de la lengua castellana* (Origin and Beginning of the Castilian Language, 1606), and Dominican Gregorio García, in his *Origen de los Indios del Nuevo Mundo* (Origin of the New World Indians, 1607).[1] Immediately after publication, the *Royal Commentaries* was both read and relied upon by such preeminent Spanish intellectuals and literary artists as Francisco de Castro, who dedicated his *De Arte Rhetorica* (On the Art of Rhetoric) to Inca Garcilaso in 1611, Lope de Vega in *El Nuevo Mundo descubierto por Cristóbal Colón* (The New World Discovered by Christopher Columbus, 1611), Miguel de Cervantes in *Persiles y Sigismunda* (1617), Tirso de Molina in *Amazonas en las Indias* (Amazons in the Indies, 1635), and Pedro Calderón de la Barca in *La Aurora en Copacabana* (Dawn in Copacabana, 1653) (Saravia 2011a: 17–18; Amat Olazábal 2012: 73).[2]

Beyond the Iberian peninsula, the first translations of the *Royal Commentaries* appeared in English in London in 1625, in Samuel Purchas's *Hakluytus Posthumous or Purhcas his Pilgrimes*, an edition of Richard Hakluyt's unpublished papers that included excerpts from both the First and Second Parts of Inca Garcilaso's histories, and was followed in 1688 by Sir Paul Rycaut's abridged translation of both parts (Garcés 2006: 206, 214–220).[3] Sir Francis Bacon alludes to the *Royal Commentaries* in *The New Atlantis* (1627) (Saravia 2011a: 18), and in *An Advertisement Touching a Holy War* (1629), he writes to Martius, his fictional interlocutor, "I perceive that you have read Garcilazo de Viega, who himself was descended of the race of the Incas, a Mestizo, and has made the best of the virtues and manners of his country" (Bacon 2005: 37; Martí-Abelló 1950). Thereafter the *Royal Commentaries* would go on either to appear in or inform Thomas Hobbes's *Leviathan* (1651), John Locke's *Essay Concerning Human Understanding* (1689) and both the *First Treatise* and *Second Treatise of Government* (1691), Daniel Defoe's *The Life and Adventures of Robinson Crusoe* (1719), Jonathan Swift's *A Modest Proposal* (1729), and David Hume's *Essays Moral, Political and Literary* (1758), to name but a few luminaries of the Anglophone world, including Thomas Jefferson, who had copies of *La Florida del Inca* and the *Royal Commentaries* in his personal library at Monticello, and the African-born abolitionist John Stuart, originally named Quogna Ottobah Cugoano, who cited Inca Garcilaso in his antislavery work *Thoughts and Sentiments* (1787).[4]

Back on the continent, Jean Baudoin published a full French translation of the First Part of the *Royal Commentaries* in Paris in 1633, followed by a complete version of the Second Part in 1650, during which time Inca Garcilaso's history of Inca civilization had already begun taking France and the Netherlands by storm, its "extraordinary success" resulting in "continual translations" and multiple editions between 1633 and 1745 (Garcés 2006: 204, 211, respectively; also Valcárcel 1939: 55–59; Rose 2010). The Baron de Montesquieu cites the Second Part of the *Royal Commentaries* in *Esprit des Lois* (Spirit of the Laws, 1748), Voltaire's portrayal of the utopian El Dorado in *Candide* (1759), in which "Peruvian" is spoken and the king claims to be a descendant of the Incas, owes an obvious debt to Inca Garcilaso, and Denis Diderot and the abbé de Raynal both read and used the *Royal Commentaries* to compose the third edition of *Histoire philosophique et politique des établissemens et du commerce des Européens dans les deux Indes* (Philosophical and Political History of the Settlements and Trade of the Europeans in the East and West Indies, 1781), among many other French *philosophes* and intellectuals (Montiel 2010: 120–23).

In the New World, copies of the First Part of the *Royal Commentaries* arrived in Peru no later than 1612 (González Sánchez 2010: 33), the bibliophilic extirpator of Andean idolatry Francisco de Ávila made a summary of the work in 1613 (Duviols 1993: 15; Spalding 2006: xxiv; González Sánchez 2010: 33), and according to Ana María Lorandi, the text was used by Jesuits in their *colegios* (colleges) in Cuzco and Lima to educate indigenous *curacas* (local ethnic chiefs) (Lorandi 2005: 67; Dueñas 2010: 17).[5] As to be expected, the first documented readers of the *Royal Commentaries* in Peru were European or criollo members of the religious intelligentsia who mined the work for historical data and critically gauged its accuracy regarding past events, especially indigenous religious practices and beliefs. Most notable among these early efforts were *Historia del reino y provincias del Perú y vidas de las varones insignes de la Compañía de Jesús* (History of the Kingdom and Provinces of Peru and Lives of the Distinguished Men of the Company of Jesus, 1631) by the Italian-born Jesuit Giovanni Anello Oliva and *Memorial de las historias del nuevo mundo, Pirú* (Memorial of the Histories of the New World, Peru, 1630) by Peruvian-born Franciscan Buenaventura de Salinas y Córdoba, which David Brading has called "by far the most powerful, public and eloquent statement of early creole patriotism" (Brading 1991: 315).[6]

As important, although hardly known for centuries, if at all, were the indigenous and *mestizo* readers and receptors of Inca Garcilaso's work, such as Juan de Cuevas Herrera.[7] A mestizo from Chuquisaca, La Plata, Cuevas Herrera was born circa 1590, claimed descent from Inca Cristóbal Paullu (the son of Huayna Cápac and brother of Huáscar), entered the Jesuit college in Lima in 1610, studied liberal arts and law, and took orders as a *cura doctrinero* (a priest of Indian *doctrinas* or parishes), a position in which he served in various provinces throughout Peru for over twenty years (Dueñas 2010: 38). Later in life, around 1650, he penned "Cinco memoriales" (Five Petitions) to King Philip IV, detailing the grave impediments to the indoctrination of indigenous Andeans that he had witnessed firsthand in his career. After opening with a brief account of divine will in Inca and Peruvian history, an account that is little more than a condensed summary of Inca Garcilaso's unique version of the same (see chapter 3), Cuevas Herrera cites as his source "the Commentaries of an author free from all suspicion, an exceptional elder of the pure royal blood from the Inca kings, Garcilaso de la Vega," establishing Inca Garcilaso as an authority on Inca history within Cuevas Herrera's attempts to lobby on behalf of indigenous Peruvians and to secure urgently needed reforms (Dueñas 2010: 212).[8]

From these beginnings, the reception of Inca Garcilaso's work in Peru branched off into two types of overtly political interpretations undertaken by different constituencies of readers (Guibovich 1990–1992: 103–20; 2016: 129–53). Spanish criollos, on the one hand, used the *Royal Commentaries* to construct a Peruvian national identity against the developing chauvinism of European intellectuals that simultaneously established criollo superiority over indigenous subjects in the colonial hierarchy. These readings tended to stress Inca Garcilaso's exaltation of the Pizarro brothers and *encomenderos* (Spaniards rewarded for their services with *encomiendas*, grants of Indian labor) as the foundation of an epic national tradition in contrast to the then current European view that the New World, its flora, fauna, and people alike, were inferior and degenerate.[9] *Mercurio Peruano de historia, literatura y noticias públicas* (Peruvian Mercury of History, Literature, and Public Notices), founded in Lima between 1791 and 1795, later became one of the principal literary vehicles for the articulation of criollo views (Guibovich 1990–1992: 113; 2016: 142–43). Members of the indigenous elite, including both curacas and descendants of the Inca aristocracy in Cuzco, on the other hand, embraced Inca Garcilaso's valorization of the Incas to assert their rights, criticize the policies of the Spanish colonial regime, and demand restoration for the loss of their empire (Guibovich 1990–1992: 110–12; 2016: 139–41). Most notable in this regard was the interpretation of José Gabriel Condorcanqui, Túpac Amaru II, whose reading of the *Royal Commentaries* partially inspired his armed rebellion in 1780–1781 (Rowe 1976). Heir-at-law to the first Túpac Amaru (beheaded by Viceroy Francisco de Toledo in 1572), José Gabriel Condorcanqui was executed for his failed uprising, and for his actions the *Royal Commentaries* was subsequently banned.[10]

Both the criollo and indigenous nationalist interpretations, while perhaps equally partial and incomplete, find ample support in the texts. Inca Garcilaso does exalt the first conquistadors and encomenderos in the Second Part of the *Royal Commentaries*, just as he valorizes the Incas to the brink of idealization and defends the justice and legitimacy of their rule in the First. What is somewhat more remarkable, considering the antagonistic processes of collective identification and the diametric opposition of their political projects, is that very early on both criollos and indigenous elites nonetheless found in the *Royal Commentaries* an authoritative voice and indispensable resource. It is perhaps tempting to chalk this up to the selective reading practices of rival social groups struggling for economic resources, political power, collective identification, and cultural survival in a frontier colonial setting, the totality of which was experiencing (as it had since Francisco Pizarro first landed in 1532) tremendous and frequently cataclysmic change. But it may also be the case that there was something peculiar about the texts, written as they were by someone who claimed to be equally Spanish and Indian, that enabled them to appeal to the interests and collective self-understandings of emerging Creole patriots and descendants of indigenous elites in Peru alike, as well as to diverse European publics.

Given the near universal popularity and authority of the *Royal Commentaries* throughout the seventeenth and eighteenth centuries in Peru, Spain, and the rest of Europe, across cultures and continents, languages, religions, and time, it is tempting to say along with Mario Vargas Llosa that Inca Garcilaso found a way to speak "the language of all" (*la lengua de todos*) (Vargas Llosa 2010: 19–28). Yet it is precisely the substance of Inca Garcilaso's extraordinary literary achievement that poses the starkest challenge to modern readers. Regardless of how his texts were appropriated by the heterogeneous publics of his own time, it cannot be denied that this son of a Spanish conquistador and Inca princess, born and raised amid the ruins of the Inca empire and the storms of civil wars, became one of the chief authorities on Inca civilization and early Peruvian history. He was able to do this despite being educated, as he frequently tells us, "between arms and horses," and having to bear the social stigma of his own mixed heritage in a Spanish culture verily obsessed with caste status and "purity of blood."[11] Mestizo, as he likewise informs us, was a word many of his contemporaries used simply as an insult (Part 1, Book IX, Chapter XXXI, vol. 2, 627). Both an appreciation as well as a critical evaluation of Inca Garcilaso's contribution to Peruvian, European, and American colonial historiography and political thought begin, then, with a recognition of the manifold tensions surrounding Inca Garcilaso as the culturally hybrid and thorn-bearing blossom of the violent collision between two radically different worlds. This facet alone distinguished him from all previous European colonial historiographers, and it is a characteristic upon which his chosen name, "Inca Garcilaso de la Vega," insists.

It is Inca Garcilaso's insistence on his mestizo status, however, that arguably stands as the largest obstacle to modern readers. If being an indio or a mestizo in the sixteenth century carried with it a set of pejorative social meanings that would have predisposed Spanish and European readers to be suspicious, if not outright dismissive, of Inca Garcilaso's texts, then the question of how he was able to overcome this widespread prejudice and, in fact, turn it to his favor is raised. The answer to this question is well known and it has been the most thoroughly discussed aspect of his work: Inca Garcilaso was able to authorize his texts in the eyes of Spanish and European readers because he had thoroughly mastered their language—humanist discourse of the late Renaissance. This is undoubtedly true and any evaluation of Inca Garcilaso's work that disregards his prolonged engagement with and constant use of a vast and varied array of humanist conventions and techniques does so at its own risk. Nevertheless, it does not necessarily follow that Inca Garcilaso's mastery of humanism can account for the authority his texts were granted by indigenous Peruvians, such as Cuevas Herrera or, later, Fray Calixto de San José Túpac Inca, among others.[12] The ethnically and linguistically diverse indigenous peoples of the Andes region had survived, resisted, and adapted themselves not only to the total upheaval of their social universe, but also to the invasion and imposition of Spanish institutions, practices, and beliefs in their everyday lives. In 1552 Dominican Bartolomé de Las Casas, writing for colonial reform on behalf of indigenous peoples throughout the New World, summed up the consequences wrought by the conquest with the phrase "destruction of the Indies" (Las Casas 1992). At the turn of the seventeenth century, the iconoclastic Andean writer, painter, and Inca Garcilaso's contemporary, Don Felipe Guaman Poma de Ayala, wrote that viceregal Peru was a "world turned upside down" (*mundo al rrevés*), and the plethora of injustices indigenous Andeans had endured on every level of society were so severe that there could be "no remedy" (*no ay rremedio*) (Guaman Poma de Ayala 1980: vol. 3, 1025, f. 1126[1136], vol. 2, 848, f. 905[919], respectively). Peruvians of indigenous descent had every reason to be suspicious of the clearly foreign, and for many of them incomprehensible, forms of thought represented by Inca Garcilaso's humanist strategies. How then did the *Royal Commentaries* capture the interest and imagination of such diverse groups?

That the *Royal Commentaries* was immediately susceptible to multiple interpretations by indigenous and Spanish Peruvians is hardly surprising, yet this circumstance allows us to raise a fundamental question about Inca Garcilaso's work. The question concerns the intentions of the texts; in other words, to what ends and for whom was the *Royal Commentaries* written? At the most general level, it is widely known that the purpose of the work is not only to challenge the accounts of Inca civilization provided by previous Spanish imperial historiographers, but also to reconcile the social antagonisms and conflicts in colonial Peruvian society in accordance with the Renaissance ideal of *concordia*. In both the very title as well as the "Preface" to the First Part, Inca Garcilaso renders these intentions explicit; the "commentary" as a sixteenth-century literary genre was a hermeneutical enterprise based upon the explication and interpretation of authoritative texts, and Inca Garcilaso claims that his intention was not to contradict Spanish historiographers, but rather to serve as a "comment and gloss" (Part 1, "Preface to the Reader," vol. 1, 4).[13] Influenced as he was by Neoplatonism, to which his translation of Leo Hebreo's *Dialoghi d'Amore* clearly attests, Inca Garcilaso's avowal of noncontradiction illustrates his adherence to the idea that truth is singular and uniform and that discrepancies in opinion or perspective not only can be reconciled at a higher or more universal level of abstraction, but that it is also a moral duty to do so.[14] As stated in his translation of Hebreo, "one truth cannot be contrary to another, it is necessary to give place to the one and the other and concord them" (Garcilaso de la Vega 1996: 70).[15] There were at least two "truths," according to Inca Garcilaso, that had not been given their proper place: first, the nature or essence of Inca culture, which Spanish historians had distorted and devalued due to their political agendas and ignorance of indigenous languages; and, second, an appropriate estimation of the deeds of the first conquerors and encomenderos of Peru, who had been vilified by the pen of Bartolomé de Las Casas and misused by the Spanish crown. In the first instance, then, the *Royal Commentaries* attempts to reinterpret and correct the imperial historiographical record of Inca civilization and early Peruvian history while simultaneously providing an account of the past that constructs the conditions of possibility for social amelioration, political solidarity, and collective identification between the descendants of conquerors and conquered alike.

When the intentions of the *Royal Commentaries* are viewed in this way, the question of Inca Garcilaso's prospective audience (or audiences) gains an added clarity and relevance. If he can be taken at his word when he declares that the *Royal Commentaries* was motivated by a filial piety for both his Inca relatives as well as his conquering Spanish forefathers (Part 2, Book VIII, Chapter XXI), it seems to follow that he was writing not only *on behalf of* Peruvians of various races, but also *to* them. This is explicitly stated in the "Prologue" to the Second Part addressed to the "Indians, Mestizos, and Creoles" of Peru, in which Inca Garcilaso assures his compatriots that his "desires are only to serve" them by illustrating their "*patria* and parents." Furthermore, he begins the "Prologue" by extending identical motivations to *both* parts of his work: "For these three reasons among others, my gentlemen and brothers, have I written the First, and do write the Second Part of the *Royal Commentaries* of the Kingdoms of Peru" (Part 2, "Prologue").[16] From these declarations alone it is hardly unreasonable to conclude that Inca Garcilaso had a number of audiences in mind, some of which were quite specific, when he was writing the *Royal Commentaries*.

Despite Inca Garcilaso's statements about the purpose of his histories, his explicit address of Peruvian Indians, mestizos, and criollos, and the fact that he intended both parts of the *Royal Commentaries* to be read as a single work to which he ascribed identical motives, it has often been assumed by scholars that the *Royal Commentaries* was intended solely for the correction and instruction of prejudiced or misinformed European readers.[17] At least one version of this argument maintains that neither the restoration and interpretation of Quechua terms that fill the pages of the First Part of the *Royal Commentaries* nor Inca Garcilaso's narrative of Inca history and civilization was intended for indigenous readers, because both constituted the cultural inheritance native Peruvians already possessed (Zamora 1988: 9–10). This view is proposed despite Inca Garcilaso's frequent laments over the corruption, neglect, and misuse into which Quechua had fallen after the conquest and Viceroy Francisco de Toledo's *reducciones* (reductions) as well as his claim that the once rich tradition of Inca oral history recorded in the *quipus* (knotted cords) had become "feeble and miserable" following the change of regime (Part 1, Book VII, Chapter VIII, vol. 2, 433). Once again, such statements illustrate that Inca Garcilaso was not only concerned with the damage that had been done by Spanish conquerors, administrators, and historians alike to the fabric of Inca civilization, but also the consequences such damage held for Peruvian Indians, mestizos, and criollos in their attempts to comprehend and uphold their own history and heritage.[18]

My purpose in focusing on the different receptions, intentions, and potential audiences of the *Royal Commentaries* is to suggest that once Inca Garcilaso's work is situated in relation to the specific groups to which it was directed, a remarkably different interpretation of his contribution to American colonial historiography and political thought begins to emerge. If we take Inca Garcilaso's insistence on his mestizo status seriously, we are strongly encouraged to read his texts in relation to both the European and Andean contexts from which they arose, upon which they comment, and toward which they gesture.[19] Approaching the texts in this way both enriches and necessarily complicates our understanding of Inca Garcilaso's intellectual achievement for the reason that the very possibility of an ideological subtext composed of indigenous meanings opens an "other" avenue of experiencing and interpreting his work, which, by virtue of its "foreign" character, exceeds European concepts and control. This, I would like to suggest, is a central aspect of the task Inca Garcilaso set for himself in reconstructing the Peruvian past. In the *Royal Commentaries* he attempted to weave together dual and heterogeneous forms of colonial discourse that took equally seriously the humanity and cultural traditions of both his Spanish and Inca ancestors as well as their descendants' need to adapt the remnants of their beliefs and practices in light of changing and hostile conditions. As he reveals the biases and shortcomings of previous histories of Peru, Inca Garcilaso offers his readers new accounts: one that challenges the prejudices of Spanish and European observers; and another that attempts to selectively restore, integrate, and construct a hybrid Peruvian perspective. The result of his efforts is a *mestizo rhetoric* constructed from both humanist and indigenous resources that founds and forwards a specific, intercultural subject position as a more authentic and authoritative vantage point from which to relate the Peruvian past, and as the key to cultural regeneration and political action. The continual interplay of Andean and European meanings does not simply record and transmit information about Inca civilization and early Peruvian history to European readers. Rather, the superposition and interspersing of cultural codes represent dual forms of address that almost invariably lead to separate and sometimes conflicting interpretations in the service of specific political interests.

This, of course, is the central thesis not only of this chapter, but also this entire investigation, and as Sara Castro-Klarén reminds us, "The cultural dialectics that constitute the *Royal Commentaries* call for thick description on both sides," European *and* Andean (Castro-Klarén 2016b: 14). Due to the obvious difficulties of rushing headlong into the intercultural vertigo of exploring Andean as well as European meanings in the *Royal Commentaries*, however, it is best to proceed slowly and begin with some basics. Therefore, in order to appreciate the originality and significance of Inca Garcilaso's mestizo rhetoric, it stands to reason that we should first turn our attention to clarifying the notions of rhetoric, and in particular the relationship between rhetoric and humanist historiography, in which the *Royal Commentaries* takes root. Thus, the remainder of this chapter will focus on that all-important question of the Renaissance, the question of style.

As inheritors of ancient traditions of rhetorical theory and criticism, humanists throughout the Renaissance were keen observers and practitioners of the ways in which language could be consciously manipulated to achieve specific effects. Such effects were to be realized through techniques of reasoning, persuasion, and speaking suited to particular occasions and audiences. Uniting the totality of rhetorical techniques and linguistic use in the pursuit of specific ends was an author's style, and it was style that enabled an author's voice to address and stimulate a prospective audience. As William Kennedy put it, the "emphasis on voice and address crystallizes Renaissance views on the moral purpose of rhetoric" (Kennedy 1978: 7). Accordingly, my argument is that Inca Garcilaso, undeniably an erudite and committed humanist, made a self-conscious effort to fashion his own style of historical writing to be amenable to the understandings of both Europeans and Andeans. In attempting to create an authoritative, intercultural account of early Peruvian history with the goal of a possible reconciliation between irreconcilable worlds, Inca Garcilaso had to "invent" discursive strategies, arguments, and registers that were appropriate or fitting not only to the subject matter of his history, but also to the conventions and norms of the diverse groups his work was intended to persuade, console, admonish, inspire, and instruct. Such is the Gordian knot of ethical, political, and rhetorical problems with which Inca Garcilaso was faced as a writer and for which the *Royal Commentaries* offers the unique solution of a mestizo rhetoric. In order to illuminate the relationship between style and historiography in the *Royal Commentaries*, however, we must first situate Inca Garcilaso's work in its proper European context. We will then be able to grasp not only how European traditions of rhetoric and humanism influenced Inca Garcilaso's conception of history, but also how, in being faithful to humanist principles, he went beyond them and created something new.

When Jesuit Francisco de Castro (1567–1631), Professor of Rhetoric at Cordoba, dedicated his *De Arte Rhetorica* to Inca Garcilaso de la Vega in 1611, he claimed to be fleeing the tedium of the ignorant for the cloisters of rhetoric's eloquent multitude, just as the weary prophet Elijah, pursued by Jezebel's wrath, had refreshed himself in the desert under the shade of a juniper tree (1 Kings 19: 1–8).[20] Castro tells his readers that Inca Garcilaso's unique shadow provided him with refuge, protection, and grace from the dual enchantments of vanity and false hopes, and stimulated him with the sweet fragrance of virtue to sustain the latter with the fruit of his work and to defend it with his strength. Castro then describes Inca Garcilaso's royal Inca ancestry, his noble Spanish lineage, and briefly summarizes his works, including the as yet unpublished Second Part of the *Royal Commentaries* (1617). Throughout the dedication Castro praises Inca Garcilaso for his prudence, justice, fortitude, temperance, piety, and modesty, for his elegant style, for his ability to represent historical events with the vivid colors of truth, and for the pleasure and satisfaction his works would bring to the souls of his readers. For Castro, Inca

Garcilaso, with roots spanning two worlds, possessed all the qualities of a true Christian and a prince and was worthy to be emulated by all.

While Castro's encomium to Inca Garcilaso is certainly a testament to their friendship, it is an excellent point of departure for at least three reasons. In the first place, as Aurelio Miró Quesada noticed several decades ago, after moving to Spain in 1560, Inca Garcilaso maintained numerous ties to the Society of Jesus until his death in 1616 (Miró Quesada 1948: 155–64).[21] José Durand suggests that as early as the mid-1560s, while living with his uncle Don Alonso de Vargas in Montilla, Inca Garcilaso was introduced to the Society of Jesus through Juan de Ávila the Apostle of Andalusia, who had been a personal friend of St. Ignatius of Loyola and preached at the dedication of the Jesuit house in the area (Durand 1964: 25–26). Further, the Jesuit college in Montilla, established in 1558, owed its existence to the patronage of Catalina Fernández de Córdoba y Figueroa, the Marquess of Priego, who was Inca Garcilaso's aunt through marriage.[22] Through proximity and a family tie, it is quite possible that well before he turned his attention to writing Inca Garcilaso had been exposed to and learned from Jesuit humanists. Regardless of when or through whom he became acquainted with the Society of Jesus, however, it is certain that he had both established contacts and enlisted the help of Jesuit scholars while he was translating Leo Hebreo's *Dialoghi d'Amore* in the 1580s. In fact, Jesuit scholars were involved at some level in the writing, editing, and publication of each one of Inca Garcilaso's works. Jesuit Jerónimo de Prado, Reader of Scripture at Cordoba, edited Hebrew phrases in Inca Garcilaso's translation of the *Dialoghi d'Amore*,[23] and he, along with Jesuit Miguel Vásquez de Padilla, later encouraged Inca Garcilaso to remove passages on the immortality of the soul from *La Florida del Inca* (Part 1, Book II, Chapter VII, vol. 1, 87). Inca Garcilaso discussed collaborating on an edition of Garcí Sánchez de Badajoz's poetry with Jesuit Juan de Pineda that was never completed, but he nevertheless went on to praise Inca Garcilaso in his *Commentarorium in Job* (Commentaries on Job, 1597–1601) (Garcilaso de la Vega 1951; Miró Quesada 1971: 169; and Durand 1979). Jesuit Pedro Maldonado de Saavedra, Reader of Scripture at Seville, gave Inca Garcilaso the mangled Latin manuscript of mestizo Jesuit Blas Valera's history of Peru, which Inca Garcilaso subsequently used as a principal source for his discussion on Inca civilization in the First Part (Part 1, Book I, Chapter VI, vol. 1, 19), and in his attempts to bring the First Part of the *Royal Commentaries* to press, Inca Garcilaso endowed Jesuit Father Jerónimo Ferraz in Lisbon with all powers necessary to achieve this end in 1608 (Miró Quesada, 1971: 373).

Francisco de Castro (mentioned above) provided Inca Garcilaso with the annual reports from the Jesuits stationed in Peru regarding an indigenous rebellion in Chile (Part 1, Book VII, Chapter XXV, vol. 2, 477), and later was the censor who personally approved the Second Part of the *Royal Commentaries* for publication on January 26, 1613.[24] So for at least thirty years, and perhaps closer to fifty, Inca Garcilaso was in continual personal communication and intellectual exchange with members of the Society of Jesus, some of whom made invaluable contributions to his work.

The second reason, related to the first, is that both Castro's dedication and Inca Garcilaso's affiliations with the Society of Jesus allow us to more properly situate the *Royal Commentaries* in the context of standards and expectations with which his texts were received and evaluated by his Spanish contemporaries. Ever since the comments of Spanish literary critic Marcelino Menéndez y Pelayo, it has often been customary to link Inca Garcilaso to influential writers of the early sixteenth century, such as Desiderius Erasmus and Thomas More, rather than humanists who were alive and active when Inca Garcilaso was writing at the turn of the seventeenth.[25] The influence of Erasmus on Spanish humanism, amply demonstrated by Marcel Bataillon's classic study, was as profound and enduring as it was hotly contested, with the appearance of Erasmus's works in the Index of Prohibited Books in 1560 perhaps being symbolic of all three (Bataillon 1991: 699–737). I do not mean to suggest that Erasmus or Erasmian humanists, such as Juan Luis Vives or Alfonso de Valdés, had no impact on Inca Garcilaso's intellectual formation, for similarities running through Inca Garcilaso's texts have rendered this influence apparent to numerous scholars. What I am suggesting, rather, is that in post-Tridentine Spain the Society of Jesus not only provided the shock troops for the defense and increase of orthodox Catholicism against its enemies, but many of the humanists trained in that order closely approximated the kind of intellectual commitments and praxis previously associated with the embattled Erasmians.[26] Despite differences on questions of Catholic dogma and the role clergy were to play in shaping it, the Jesuits had taken membership, like Erasmus, in what Richard Tuck has described more generally as the "cult of Cicero" (Tuck 1993: 6, 16–18 and 131–36). In fact, the Society was so committed to Ciceronian principles that, well before their unique and autonomous educational program was codified in the monumental *Ratio studiorum* of 1599, their pedagogical objective in humanities had been the development of *eloquentia perfecta et Ciceroniana*, or perfect Ciceronian eloquence (Farrell 1938: 177–80).[27] This penchant for combining the works and values of the Roman orator and statesman with the imitation of Christ is what connects Jesuit humanists with Erasmian humanists, and it links Inca Garcilaso with both.[28]

Finally, Castro's comments to Inca Garcilaso (all the more revealing coming as they do from a professor of rhetoric) are representative of a dominant mode of historical criticism practiced in sixteenth-century Spain. Historiography was seen as a moral, political, and rhetorical endeavor par excellence (Nadel 1964: 291–315), and Spanish humanists as diverse as Juan Luis Vives, Paez de Castro, Sebastián Fox Morcillo, Pedro Mejía, Jesuit Juan de Mariana, and Luis Cabrera de Córdoba were in general agreement that the value of historical works was found in their stylistic and literary merits, their pragmatic and exemplary functions, their social utility, and the moral authority of their authors (Montero Diaz 1948: xi–lvi; Costas Rodríguez 1996: 543–54). For Jesuit humanists history was aesthetic creation, the primary resource in political education, and a form of prudential praxis. Moreover, the conventions or "rules" of historiography were principally derived from Cicero's views on the theory and practice of rhetoric.[29] It is hardly surprising, then, that Castro praises both Inca Garcilaso's personal character and his historical works for their conformance to the Jesuit version of *philosophia christi*—an unwavering fidelity to orthodox Catholicism couched in an elegant and compelling Ciceronian style that would shape the moral character of readers by reinforcing classical and Christian virtues. To Cicero, therefore, we now turn.

The influence of Marcus Tullius Cicero (106–43 BCE) throughout the Renaissance was manifold indeed, yet it primarily arose from his contributions to the study and practice of rhetoric, in which humanists, beginning with Petrarch, found not only a powerful theoretical justification for eloquence, but also a model of its practical application in Cicero's prose (Siegel 1968: 3–62).[30] Cicero's theory of oratory expounded upon the need to combine philosophy (the pursuit of wisdom) and rhetoric (the pursuit of eloquence) in a harmonious and efficacious union. The ultimate aim of this union was to harness, control, and direct the effects of discourse toward the perfection of individual moral character and the promotion of socially beneficial ends. Having set as his purpose the resolution of the "quarrel" between philosophy and rhetoric stemming from ancient Greek thought (Struever 1970: 5–39), Cicero argued that the goal of the orator was to conjoin wisdom and eloquence in a "style that is dignified and graceful and in conformity with the general modes of thought and judgment" (Cicero 1997b: I.xii.54). Reason and speech elevated mankind above the rest of nature's creations, yet the improvement or perfection of each often tended in antithetical directions. Following Socrates, Plato, and the Stoics, various philosophical schools had divorced themselves from the public domain, whether in the interests of a private pursuit of truth or through their use of terse reasoning and syllogistic language. Rhetoricians, following Gorgias, had committed themselves to linguistic dexterity and public activity, but insofar as they lacked training in philosophy, they were often prone to use their skills to plead morally suspect cases or, worse, to instigate vicious behavior (Cicero 1997b: III.xv.56–xix.73). Thus, neither reason nor speech was sufficient on its own terms to secure the public good: "wisdom without eloquence does too little for the good of states," and, "eloquence without wisdom is generally highly disadvantageous and is never helpful" (Cicero 1976: I.i.1). When the two were united, however, they had the power to civilize the barbarous, found republics, cement the social bonds between citizens, and inspire the latter to a life of civic virtue in the service of the state. It was after all an orator, as we are told in the famous passages opening *De Inventione*, who had created the very possibility of civil life and ethical behavior by assembling the wild and brutal humans who roamed like beasts of the field into communities and by instructing them in every honorable and useful occupation. Since speech was the very mortar of communal life as well as the medium in which rational precepts were rendered concrete and effective, systematic instruction in rhetoric was absolutely necessary for individuals to realize their highest potentials as social beings and, therefore, it was an essential component of political or civil science (*civilis scientiae*) (Cicero 1976: I.i.1–v.6).

Given the orator's overriding concern for the public good, Cicero saw eloquence as one of the "supreme virtues," partly due to the orator's ability to shape public opinion, inculcate morality, and inspire virtuous conduct in his audience through persuasive speech (Cicero 1976: I.v.6), and partly due to the numerous difficulties involved in the very cultivation of this ability. By stressing both the union of wisdom and eloquence as well as the social functions of oratory, Cicero extended the domain of rhetoric to include practically all branches of learning and all occasions of public speaking. The vast cultural attainment required of the ideal orator was expressed in this way: "eloquence is so potent a force that it embraces the origin and operation and developments of all things, all the virtues and duties, all the natural principles governing the morals and minds and life of mankind, and also determines their customs and laws and rights, and controls the government of the state, and expresses everything that concerns whatever topic in a graceful and flowing style" (Cicero 1997b: III.xx.76). Due, moreover, to the lack of a general theory of prose in antiquity, rhetoric was extended to encompass every form of written discourse as well (North 1956: 234–242). Tragedy, comedy, and history were different species of the same rhetorical genus: they were forms of *narratio*, a subheading of the technique of "invention" (*inventio*).[31] What distinguished the three genres was the correspondence of their respective contents or subject matter (*res*) with the criteria established for narratio properly so called. Narration had to be brief, clear, and above all plausible, as narratio was itself defined as an "exposition of events that have occurred or are supposed to have occurred." Tragedies (*fabula*) were narrative forms that were neither true, i.e., never happened, nor displayed verisimilitude (*verisimilis*). Comedies (*argumenta*) were untrue but could have happened and therefore had a higher degree of realism. Histories (*historia*), however, were accounts of public actions that had actually occurred in the past and for this reason they displayed the highest degrees of realism and plausibility (Cicero 1976: I.xix.27).[32] Although the different forms of narrative represented a broad spectrum of discursive possibilities, Cicero elsewhere remarked that of the three history was especially oratorical (*oratorium maxime*) (Cicero 1994: I.ii.5).[33] History, then, not only shared the explicitly moral, political, and didactic aims of oratory, but the full complement of rhetorical techniques that rendered a discourse effective and useful fell within the historiographer's provenance as well.[34]

If Cicero could claim in his day that the "rules" for historiography "lie open to view," i.e., that the historian should say nothing but the truth, make bold to tell the whole truth, and show no hint of partiality or malice in his works, they were just as evident, if not more so, during the Renaissance. As Donald Kelley put it, "history was the centerpiece of the humanist world view" (Kelley 1970: 19ff.), and the rules expounded by Cicero on the content and form of history in *De Oratore* (II.xv.62–64) were both the foundation and an argumentative commonplace for historical writers and thinkers throughout the sixteenth century.[35] The intimate connection Cicero drew between rhetoric and history in such famous statements as "do you see how great a task history is for an orator?" or again, "by what other voice than that of the orator, is history, the evidence of time, the light of truth, the life of memory, the mentor of life, the herald of antiquity, committed to immortality?" were among the most quoted in the historical discussions in various humanist circles across Europe (Cicero 1997b: II.ix.36). For instance, in his discussion of history in *De ratione dicendi* (The Art of Speaking, 1532), the eclectic Spanish humanist Juan Luis

Vives cited verbatim the entirety of Cicero's passages on the subject in *De Oratore* (Vives 1948: vol. 2, 780–88, especially 784). Even those authors who are known to have transformed or consciously parted with the usual conventions of rhetorical historiography, many either aligned themselves with this tradition of thinking or took it as their point of departure. In a free-leaf opening the manuscript of *Storia d'Italia* (History of Italy, 1561), Francesco Guicciardini included a translation of the passages on history in *De Oratore* (Gilbert 1965: 272–73); and the French historian and political thinker Jean Bodin, who established a new approach to historical criticism that intentionally verged from the rhetorical tradition, prefaced his *Methodus ad facilem historiarum cognitionem* (Method for the Easy Comprehension of History, 1566) with the Ciceronian view (Brown 1939: 60). As for those who wrote of their experiences in the Americas, "Cicero's definition of history," Mignolo notes, "was often repeated by historians of the New World" (Mignolo 1995: 135).[36] Finally, and rather unsurprisingly, Eric Cochrane has argued that Jesuit historians of the latter sixteenth century, despite the availability of new approaches to research and methods of criticism, steadfastly clung to the rhetorical roots of historiography (Cochrane 1980: 21–38, especially 34–36).[37] Inca Garcilaso, who had read Vives, Guicciardini, and Bodin (among many other notable figures), had meticulously perused the histories of the New World, and was closely associated with the Jesuits, undoubtedly began with the Ciceronian tradition as well.[38]

In Cicero's *De Oratore*, historiography, like any other discourse, depended upon the mutual and reciprocal adequacy of its two constituent parts: subject (res) and language (*verba*).[39] And since the primary function of the historiographer *qua* orator in prose was to undertake a discourse on the past that would stimulate readers to embrace virtue and shun vice, both the content (res) of historical narrative and its style (verba) had to be accommodated to the commonly held beliefs and normative conventions of a prospective audience. As a form of narratio, the "truth" of historiographical content was not governed by strict fidelity to facts or *veritas*, but rather the plausibility or verisimilis of the exposition.[40] For historical narratio to be expressed clearly and convincingly the historian had to include specific contents, such as topographical descriptions, accounts of memorable actions or battles, speeches of notable persons, and digressions, while maintaining the proper temporal order of events. The historiographer was to take especial care in detailing the intentions and consequences of actions in order to expose the reasons, causes, motivations, and moral characters of those who contributed to what was said and done. It was expected that the historian, following the example of Thucydides, would use invented speeches to demonstrate not only what was said and by whom, but the manner in which it was stated as well as its effects. While the subject matter of historical narrative was arranged in these ways to render it more lifelike and plausible, the historiographer had the additional and simultaneous obligation of drawing out the practical moral and political lessons for readers. The historian was to accomplish this by exercising his power of judgment (*judicium*) throughout the narration in order to relate which actors merited his, and hence the reader's, approval or censure (Cicero 1997b II.xv.62–64). In the exposition of content alone, therefore, the rhetorical historiographer did not simply report "facts," but rather took an active role in structuring the verisimilitude of the past into a meaningful linguistic edifice that created the moral *exempla* readers were to emulate by engaging their commonly held beliefs.

In the historian's use of language (verba), the relationship with the audience was even more pronounced. It was style that imbued speech or writing with its affective power to "impel the audience wherever it inclines its force" (Cicero 1997b: III.xiv.55), and without a proper or elegant style the practical value and social utility of historiography would be lost. A truly eloquent style, according to Cicero, was both ornate and appropriate (Cicero 1997b: III.xxiv.91). Ornamentation included the use of pure language (in his case Latin), copiousness and variety of diction, amplification, and adornment with figures of speech and thought to provoke the delight of an audience or readership without tiring or sating them. The richness of a speech or narrative, in this sense, was tied to a set of publicly held aesthetic criteria and argumentative common places that would elicit pleasure in listeners or readers as they were being instructed and informed. While a writer of true elegance could not refrain from embellishing, amplifying, or adorning a work with the "flowers" of thought and speech, these creative flourishes were to be distributed (*dispositio*) selectively, moderately, and fluidly so that the intended audience remained attentive and entertained but not overwhelmed (Cicero 1997b: III.xxv.96–97).

Whereas an ornate discourse provided the power to charm, enthrall, or incite an audience, even the strongest of arguments uttered in the sweetest of words would fall upon deaf ears if the speech was inappropriate for its specific occasion. The burden placed upon the speaker or writer in this sense was heavy indeed. If the historian was to succeed in rendering his narrative effective, like the orator, he must "accurately divine what his fellow citizens, and all those whom he wishes to convince on any subject by his eloquence, think, feel, imagine or hope. He must penetrate the inmost recesses of the mind of every class, age, rank and must ascertain the sentiments and notions of those before whom he is pleading or intends to plead" (Cicero 1997b: I.li.223–lii.224). Cicero realized, given the multitude of arguments, subjects, forms of discourse, occasions of speaking or writing, and potential audiences, that no single form of oratory would be suitable in all circumstances. Rather, it was the speaker's sense of propriety (*decorum*), which for Cicero was closely related to prudence and the moral rectitude of behavior, that allowed the orator to know what was appropriate to each particular occasion (Cicero 1997b: III.lv.211).[41]

As Nancy Struever has argued, of all the rhetorical canons adopted by Renaissance historiographers, the principle of decorum was perhaps the most crucial (Struever 1970: 67).[42] Expressing the same idea, "nor can it be too oft repeated," warned Erasmus in *Ciceronianus*, a dialogue on the proper imitation of Cicero published in 1528, "that fitness is absolutely essential to good style" (Erasmus 1908: 86). The revival of rhetorical consciousness in the quattrocento brought with it a heightened sensitivity to the affective powers of language and the ability of discourse to transform behavior by engaging the common understandings of one's contemporaries. This attentiveness to the social context of linguistic performance inaugurated an awareness of the distance, both temporal and sociocultural, separating the "ancients" from the "moderns." The recognition of these differences (the chief one being that the ancients were pagans and the moderns were Christians) exposed the necessity for new ways of speaking amenable to the circumstances and priorities of the present. If "true propriety," according to Erasmus, stemmed "partly from the subject, partly from the character of the speaker and listener, partly from place, time, and other circumstances" (Erasmus 1908: 58), then following the Ciceronian tradition in the modern world would necessarily produce new modes of speaking and forms of address: "Thus it can happen that he is most Ciceronian who is most unlike Cicero, that is, who speaks best and most pointedly, though in a different way; and this is not surprising because the environment is now entirely different" (Erasmus 1908: 78). Against the Italian "ultra-Ciceronians" who favored a literal, exact, and ultimately anachronistic imitation of Cicero's prose (among whom numbered some of the first Jesuits) (Tuck 1993: 17–18), Erasmus emphasized the priority and versatility of individual expression through the internalization of Ciceronian principles. Although "the whole scope of learning and eloquence" was to be directed to knowing and celebrating the glory of Christ (Erasmus 1908: 129), this by no means precluded a multiplicity of approaches or a plurality of styles. In fact, the Christian Ciceronian should rather cultivate versatility and variety as the very foundations of his eloquence. Whereas style was the "dress of ideas" (Erasmus 1908: 59), nature intended speech to be "a mirror of mind" that reflected the natural ability, character, and judgment of an author to his readers. In continuing the metaphor of speech as the mirror of mind, Erasmus writes, "there are as many kinds of minds as there are forms of voices and the mirror will be straightway deceptive unless it give back the real image of the mind, which is the very thing that delights the reader especially—to discover from the language the feelings, the characteristics, the judgment, and the ability of the writer as well as if one had known him for years" (Erasmus 1908: 121). True propriety in this tradition of thinking both allowed and required the writer to be a man of many costumes who dressed his words in garments that accentuated his personality for his readers.

Returning to historiography, and, more specifically, the European conception of rhetorical historiography informing Inca Garcilaso's work, the cultivation of a decorous style enabled the historian to impart to readers, through the subjects he selected for narration, the judgments he rendered, the presentation of his authorial character, his modes of address, and his language, a unique, personal attitude concerning the significance of past events and social life which could then be transmitted to others.[43] The rhetorical impulse affirmed the historian's office as prudential expositor of the past and judicious sculptor of contemporary public opinion, thereby signaling the vitality of historical discourse as the guide of life (*magistra vitae*) for the present and future. The openly didactic aim of historiography accentuated the dynamic relationship between the historical narrative and its receptors, and this relationship was focalized in the historian's ability to engage the values and expectations of his intended audience through his self-conscious manipulation of language and ideas. These social ties and contextual constraints by no means determined each facet of historical discourse (Struever 1970: 198); rather, they compelled the historiographer to make creative and carefully considered decisions regarding the full complement of rhetorical strategies, arguments, and styles to be used relative to the goal of instructing a readership. Historiography's rhetorical edifice, then, would imbue the past with a structure of meaning both relevant and accessible to the present and culminate in a type of moral and political pedagogy that expressed the historian's outlook on the world. This outlook would both reveal the unfolding of historical processes and stimulate the hearts and minds of readers. It also, however, was a product of the historian's participation in and projection of the interests, understandings, and judgments of specific publics, to which the credibility of the work was ultimately tied.

If Erasmus could justify a plurality of styles, voices, and modes of address by writing, "Wherever I turn I see things changed, I stand on another stage, I see another theater, yes, another world" (Erasmus 1908: 62), what different chords these words would have struck with Inca Garcilaso had he chanced upon them in his reading. Inca Garcilaso was a breed of "new man" from the very first generation of Peruvian mestizos, and he was born and raised in a New World, or as he cleverly put it a world called "new" by Europeans (Part 1, Book I, Chapter I, vol. 1, 9). Quechua, which he drank with his mother's milk, was Inca Garcilaso's first language, a tongue completely unknown to Europeans before the conquest. As for the webs of social practices and meanings that comprised the richness of pre-Hispanic Inca culture, they had been rent and torn with the arrival of Pizarro, and as Inca Garcilaso put it, the world of his Inca ancestors "had been destroyed before it was known" (*antes destruida que conocida*) (Part 1, Book I, Chapter XIX, vol. 1, 50).

To the devastating consequences of military conquest, the demographic collapse of indigenous populations through disease, and brutal forms of economic exploitation were added the enduring difficulties of negotiating the linguistic and cultural differences between Spaniards and Indians. In the first instance, European travel writers struggled, in Anthony Pagden's words, "with the problem of how to create a text where none had existed before," that could accurately and authoritatively express the often astounding novelty and diversity of American geography and civilizations to other Europeans (Pagden 1993: 54).[44] For Spanish missionaries in the New World, their primary challenge was somewhat different; they had to develop methods of communication to convince indigenous peoples of the validity of the Catholic faith.[45] As Don Paul Abbott has argued in his study of New World preaching manuals, because Indians were generally seen as lacking intelligence (the work of Las Casas excepted), the style of preaching that developed in the Americas was one that departed from the tradition of Ciceronian rhetoric in favor of incredibly simplistic forms of address and indoctrination (Abbott 1996: 112). The major stumbling block for European historians as well as missionaries (despite the latter's invaluable contributions to the study of indigenous languages), therefore, was none other than language itself (Pagden 1993:

118–19). For someone like Inca Garcilaso, who was concerned not only with the European representations of the Inca past but also with the quality of social and political interactions between Spaniards and native Peruvians, both of these circumstances, the textual and the rhetorical, required a corrective intervention. To make a fitting monument of Inca civilization and to present this legacy in a way that avoided perpetuating the exclusion and dismissal of indigenous voices and values, Inca Garcilaso would have to *speak* differently.

To see that Inca Garcilaso was concerned with the propriety of his language and the characterization of his authorial identity in the *Royal Commentaries*, one does not have to read very far into his opus. When he first publicly announced his intention to write a history of Peru, these were the very notions he chose to emphasize. In a letter written from Montilla to King Philip II bearing the date January 19, 1586, which was published in his translation of the *Dialoghi d'Amore*, Inca Garcilaso (after providing the monarch with a brief resume of his military service and mestizo pedigree) expressed his plan to "summarily treat the conquest of my land, enlarging on her customs, rites, and ceremonies, and in her antiquities: of which, *as her own son I will better able to speak, than another who is not*" (Garcilaso de la Vega 1995: 16; my emphasis).[46] In a second prefatory letter to Philip II written from Cordoba and dated November 7, 1589, Inca Garcilaso picks up the same theme. After summarizing the history of Florida upon which he was working, Inca Garcilaso reminded Philip, "At the conclusion of this account [*La Florida*], I intend to give another of the customs, rites, and ceremonies, that in the gentilism of the Incas former lords of Peru, were kept in their Kingdoms: so that Your Majesty may see them from their origin and principle, written with somewhat more *certainty and propriety* than they have been written until now" (my emphasis).[47] As in the first letter, Inca Garcilaso offers his translation in the "name of Peru . . . as much Indians, as Spaniards," because "from both nations I have ties which oblige them to participate in my successes and failures: which are my father having been a conqueror, and settler of that land, and my mother her native, and myself having been born, and raised between them" (Garcilaso de la Vega 1995: 23–24).[48] Although these statements are brief and undeveloped, Inca Garcilaso had already begun to establish a connection between the uniqueness of his intercultural perspective and a manner of speaking afforded to him that would allow his history of Inca civilization to be more certain and more appropriate to the concerns of diverse Peruvians.

A more pronounced example of the attention Inca Garcilaso paid to adapting his work to the expectations of an intended audience can be seen in his first published history, *La Florida del Inca* (1605). Although Inca Garcilaso's account of Hernando de Soto's failed mission to Florida shares with the *Royal Commentaries* his intention to recount "the many and very illustrious deeds that both Spaniards and Indians performed" (*La Florida*, "Preface," 14), it is unlike his masterpiece in that it was primarily intended for European readers.[49] His "principal purpose" in writing the work, we are told, was "to encourage Spain to make an effort to acquire and populate this kingdom," primarily for the increase of the Catholic faith, but also for the establishment of colonies as the Romans had done (*La Florida*, "Preface," 14v). His ulterior motive in relating the deeds and speeches of Floridian Indians was to challenge the European prejudice that indigenous peoples were "a simple folk without reason or understanding who in both peace and war differ very little from beasts and accordingly could not do and say things so worthy of memory or praise" (*La Florida*, Book 2, Part 1, Chapter XXVII, 82–84). This prejudice, which would undergo a thorough dismantling in the *Royal Commentaries*, was one that Inca Garcilaso had to confront to secure his own authority as an indio mestizo writing before Europeans, and it was one that he was anxious "to destroy by showing just what truth there is in it."[50] Since his history was to be "presented to the entire Spanish republic . . . with the idea of inciting and persuading Spaniards," Inca Garcilaso paid scrupulous attention to the rhetorical strategies through which the veracity and impartiality of his work would be established in their eyes.[51] Following Cicero, he claimed that he would "tell the whole truth," and he made it a point to differentiate his work from "fictions" and especially the popular romance novels of chivalry. Of the latter he declared that he had become their "enemy" after having read the work of Spanish historian Pedro de Mejía, and that he should not be accused of writing fictions simply to praise own his own nation (*La Florida*, Book 2, Part 1, Chapter XXVII, 83). He instead based his account on the eyewitness testimony and written reports of men who had participated in the conquest to furnish his version with immediacy to the events, and he cited their works to offer independent corroboration. As for his fidelity to his primary oral source, the unnamed conquistador Gonzalo Silvestre, Inca Garcilaso asserted that he had acted only as the former's amanuensis and scribe (*La Florida*, "Preface"). As for the literary style suitable for a historical narrative that was "boldly attempting to write the truth," in a characteristic display of false modesty Inca Garcilaso excused himself for composing the work, "not with an excess of hyperbole but rather with a lack of the elegance and rhetoric necessary to give the deeds their proper place of honor" (*La Florida*, Book 2, Part 1, Chapter

XXVII, 84). Yet even here Inca Garcilaso maintained decorum; it was because Soto's disastrous mission had failed to reach the proper place of honor that it could not be written in the highest style.

From Inca Garcilaso's letters to Philip in *La traduzión del Indio*, we know he had been working on *La Florida del Inca* and the *Royal Commentaries* concurrently for a number of years.[52] Despite the differences in the subject matter of the two works, if he were writing both primarily or solely for European readers, one might expect Inca Garcilaso to use the same or similar strategies to authorize the *Royal Commentaries* as he had for *La Florida*, the latter of which had been well received after publication. To be sure, much of Inca Garcilaso's approach remained the same: both texts contain declarations and reassurances of the veracity and impartiality of his work; claims of fidelity to his sources (both oral and written); an emphasis on providing both sides of the story; and mentions of his position as a representative of Peruvian indios, mestizos, and criollos, etc. Upon opening the *Royal Commentaries*, however, one is immediately struck by the differences. For instance, whereas *La Florida* begins with the customary "Dedication" and a "Preface to the Reader," the First Part of the *Royal Commentaries*, rather famously, follows its "Dedication" with two introductory pieces: a "Preface to the Reader" and a "Warning." As Alberto Porqueras Mayo has shown, prefaces or prologues became an independent and ubiquitous genre of writing in sixteenth-century Spanish literature, and it was not uncommon for authors to include multiple prefaces to explain their reasons for breaking new ground or to use them to ease readers into difficult material. In the numerous works he surveyed, moreover, Porqueras Mayo found that declarations of authorial intentions and comments on style were two of the central topics treated in such pieces (Porqueras Mayo 1965: 1–34). Inca Garcilaso takes these oft-trodden paths as his point of departure and he both expresses his intentions and initiates a preliminary version of his critique of Spanish historians in these prefaces. What have been somewhat overlooked by garcilacistas, however, are his comments on the style and, hence, the intended audiences of his work, which are just as revealing.

Although it would perhaps be unwise to push the point too far, it is of no little interest to note that the prefaces to the First Part of the *Royal Commentaries* are distributed into the two elements, res, or content, and verba, or language, of which every speech, according to Cicero, consists. Inca Garcilaso's "Preface to the Reader" discusses the subject (res) of his history, his reasons for writing it, and the manner in which it will be treated. In the *Advertencias* (Warning), the connection to verba is made explicit in the subtitle, *Acerca de la Lengua General de los Indios* (Concerning the General Language of the Indians). In the latter, one finds nothing short of a condensed grammar lesson, in which Inca Garcilaso explains the differences in pronunciation and orthography between Quechua and Spanish and how, through their failure to attend to these differences, both languages had been corrupted respectively by Spaniards and Indians. Taken together, the two pieces form a tightly worded introduction (*exordium*) intended to prepare Inca Garcilaso's readers to look more favorably upon what is to come, and in which he attempts to warn his readers away from misinterpretations of his meaning.[53]

With this in mind, let us turn to a closer examination of Inca Garcilaso's presentation of his authorial perspective and his manner of addressing his audience in each piece. The "Preface" begins: "Although there have been learned Spaniards who have written the republics of the New World, such as those of Mexico and Peru and the other kingdoms in their gentilism, it has not been with the full account that could have been given of them."[54] The next sentence continues: "This I have noticed particularly in the things I have seen written about Peru, of which, as a native of the city of Cuzco (which was another Rome in that empire) I have fuller and clearer information than what writers have provided until now."[55] This opening parry immediately portrays Spanish histories of Peru as being incomplete in terms of their contents and lacking clarity in their presentation. Although Inca Garcilaso allows that previous historians had touched upon many of the great accomplishments of New World civilizations, he faults them for their *style*: "But they have written them [the great accomplishments] *so briefly* that, even those that are very well known to me, *due to the manner in which they are told*, I understand them poorly."[56] Brevity, as we have seen, was a prerequisite of *narratio*, and in terms of Renaissance historiography it was correlated with the task of selecting and recording only the most important events (Struever 1970: 81). As Cicero noted, however, while brevity was a rhetorical virtue on some occasions, it was "very far from being compatible with the general character of eloquence," because too brief an exposition would fail to attain the affective force necessary to sway an audience (Cicero 1939: XIII).[57] Although Inca Garcilaso himself often appeals to brevity to "avoid prolixity," he is stressing the obscurantist tendencies of brevity here. In a few short phrases (perhaps to illustrate his command of rhetoric), he criticizes previous histories not only for being defective in terms of their content, but also for their stylistic improprieties.[58]

Inca Garcilaso's initial maneuvers immediately signal a critical, revisionist stance and raise questions about the appropriate manner of relating the Peruvian past. Propriety, however, was correlated not only with content, but also with an author's relationship to or characterization of his audience; the concept raises questions concerning not only the *what* of Inca Garcilaso's work but also its *whom*. That he expected to have a Spanish readership requires no argument; of all the languages available to him (including Latin, Italian, and Quechua) he chose to write in Spanish. As the First Part of the *Royal Commentaries* was intended to attack the European prejudice against indigenous Peruvians and, therefore, was in part aimed at the instruction of Europeans, it hardly would have been fitting for Inca Garcilaso to dismiss them as an audience and thereby run the risk of losing them as readers. He does, however, establish a firm distinction between Spaniards and native Peruvians, more specifically between those who spoke only Spanish or other European languages versus those who spoke both Quechua and Spanish, which is carried throughout the entire work. By challenging the completeness, accuracy, and "manner" of Spanish imperial histories, Inca Garcilaso has already questioned their adequacy as historical *narratio*, thereby destabilizing the textual bulwark upon which knowledge about Peru rested for Europeans. As if this were not enough, Inca Garcilaso goes a step further and questions their epistemological foundations. European writers describing the Americas had to confront an intellectual double-bind: on the one hand, the often overwhelming difference posed by the flora, fauna, places, and peoples of the New World left them without an authoritative intellectual framework from which they could adequately interpret their surroundings; and, on the other, many of those who wrote such accounts, as soldiers and adventurers, were insufficiently schooled to compose reports amenable to the rhetorical standards of veracity expected from historical works.[59] To counteract both their break from traditional authorities and their lack of proper "science and ornamentation," as Pedro de Cieza de León put it in his *Crónica del Perú* (Chronicle of Peru, 1553), they appealed to the immediacy with which they had observed and inscribed their experiences in the New World as "eye-witnesses."[60] Inca Garcilaso denies whatever guarantees to veracity European claims to first-hand experience in the New World were supposed to provide by erecting a barrier of linguistic and cultural difference between the observers and the observed. Although he claims that in the course of the history "we will not speak of any great circumstance that is not authorized by the same Spanish historians who have touched upon them in part or in whole," he quickly shifts ground and expresses the need to reinterpret the works to which he is referring. The next sentence continues: "My intention is not to contradict them, but to serve as a comment and gloss and as an *interpreter* in many Indian words that, *as strangers to that language*, they interpreted *outside its propriety*."[61] As "strangers" or foreigners to indigenous languages, even those Spanish historians who had based their accounts on their personal experiences in Peru or upon the information they gathered from indigenous informants (such as Pedro de Cieza de León and José de Acosta, to name two Inca Garcilaso cites frequently) find their works accused of a profound and troubling uncertainty. Moreover, by emphasizing the impropriety with which Quechua had been treated by Spaniards, Inca Garcilaso returns to questions of style and raises the possibility of a manner of speaking about the Peruvian past accommodated to both the subject and its audience.

From the very first, then, Inca Garcilaso establishes an epistemological and cultural divide between the two worlds that places European observers on the periphery of Inca civilization and reorients his authorial persona and political solidarity *away* from the Spanish national tradition of imperial historiography. Inca Garcilaso's insistence on the foreignness of Inca culture and language to native Spaniards allows him to separate his perspective from an exclusively European location, and his decision to present his work in the genre of "commentary" further reinforces this posture by providing him with the meta-critical distance necessary to reinterpret the dominant discourse from a different point of view. Insofar as the *Royal Commentaries* addresses Hispano-European readers, the address is projected from a location partially divorced from cultural and political ties to Spain. As we have seen, Inca Garcilaso (in addition to the information provided by his name alone) makes it apparent to his readers that his history is written by a "native of the city of Cuzco" and a few lines later he endows his efforts with the moral force of a patriotic duty: "impelled by the natural love for my country [patria] I offered myself the task of writing these *Comentarios*" (*forzado del amor natural de la patria me ofrecí al trabajo de escribir estos* Comentarios). Insofar as he has offered himself the task of writing for his patria, Inca Garcilaso reinforces the independent character of his work vis-à-vis the official and usually commissioned works of his predecessors.[62] Inca Garcilaso's alternate perspective, however, is not posed as an absolute difference, but rather as an original and enduring cultural rift that is to be alleviated through his offer to serve as an "interpreter" between the two poles. The perspective he adopts and forwards as essential to a full and fitting account of the Peruvian past is one that can negotiate *both* languages and cultures; it is the privilege and burden of a mestizo, and more specifically, a mestizo from the Inca capital of Cuzco.

Compared with the explicit declarations of his intentions and the straightforward address of his Spanish audience in *La Florida*, the strategies used by Inca Garcilaso in the "Preface" to the First Part of the *Royal Commentaries* are much more elaborate and sophisticated. Conspicuously absent from the *Royal Commentaries* are any calls whatsoever to the "Spanish republic" so pronounced in the earlier work. Inca Garcilaso instead reveals his loyalty to his Peruvian patria and then, rather than voicing a similar proclivity for Spanish prerogatives, claims that his work was written "without pretension to any other interest than serving the Christian republic" (*no con pretension de otro interés más que servir a la república cristiana*). Although it might be tempting to see the "Christian republic" as coterminous with Spanish dominions on the European continent and the territories overseas (as did many Spaniards of the time), Inca Garcilaso is referring to the "mystical body of Christ" or the congregation of the faithful in its broadest sense, "so that thanks is given to Our Lord Jesus Christ and the Virgin Mary his mother" (*para que se den gracias a nuestro Señor Jesucristo y a la virgín María su madre*).[63] He commends his work not to the patriotism or national sympathies of his European readers, but rather to their piety: "I offer [this history] to the piety of he who reads it" (*ofrezco a la piedad del que la leyere*). These pious assertions, however, expose a double intention: Inca Garcilaso insists upon the specificity and value of his Peruvian mestizo perspective, and simultaneously requests his European readers to relinquish their particularities (and prejudices) in favor of the more universal moral posture entailed by Christian piety.[64] The accumulation and overlap of Inca Garcilaso's commitments, moreover, present his perspective as the protean link between the particular and the universal; as a Peruvian mestizo from Cuzco and a faithful Christian he not only has better information than previous Spanish historians, but the intercultural position he occupies is normatively superior because it provides him with the ability to speak to both Spaniards and native Peruvians.

All of these maneuvers are intended, as Doris Sommer has argued, to frustrate or forestall the self-assured European presumption of the accuracy of their knowledge and the correctness of both their judgments and actions concerning the indigenous peoples of Peru (Sommer 1996a: 396–403). Inca Garcilaso exposes the limitations of European understanding and close-mindedness and offers himself as a reliable and privileged guide through the distorted and contested terrain of Inca history. His rhetorical strategies, as we have seen, reveal both a complex and semi-autonomous relationship to his European readers as well as a number of ulterior and competing motives. His subtlety and finesse in these opening passages are certainly related to the instability of his authority in the task he has undertaken: the *Royal Commentaries* is a critical reinterpretation of the hegemonic versions of Peruvian history, and as one who has announced both his Inca descent and his loyalty to Peru, Inca Garcilaso must avoid the appearance of an undue partiality that would jeopardize his credibility. While these concerns clearly inform the passages we have been examining, Inca Garcilaso's repeated stress on the indecorous style and inappropriate manner of speaking in Spanish imperial historiography allows him to create a discursive space in which to address native Peruvians more directly.

The first real hint of this comes toward the end of the "Preface" when Inca Garcilaso writes of his work, "I hope it will be received with the same intention as I offer it, because this is the correspondence my volition deserves, although the work may not."[65] Statements such as this were commonplace in sixteenth-century Spanish literature, yet despite its generic character and apparent ambiguity, Inca Garcilaso has already announced his intentions, loyalties, and perspective to his readers and has portrayed his "volition" as having been "impelled by the natural love" for his patria in Cuzco. The implication is that the "correspondence" he desires and "deserves" is one in which the reception of his work will reflect and embrace the mestizo perspective from which it is articulated. The meanings, once again, are twofold. First, Inca Garcilaso wants his readers to accept the work of a mestizo, because mestizos were a socially maligned and politically suspect group across the New World when he was writing, and to assuage this prejudice he portrays himself as the trustworthy representative of this broad racial and ethnic class.[66] Second, by focusing on the call for his text to be "received," we can see that Inca Garcilaso has also put a challenge to his readers to both search out and understand the meaning of his work from the intercultural perspective he has projected. This is something, as he has already led us to believe, no mere "foreigner" could do.

It is in the second preface, the "Warning" on the general language of Peru, however, that Inca Garcilaso more fully reveals what he has in mind. The first thing one notices about the "Warning" is the difference in its tone. Whereas in the "Preface" Inca Garcilaso is magnanimous and pious while he is being critical of previous historians and establishing his position (i.e., claiming not to contradict his predecessors and relying upon their authority, offering himself as an interpreter in loyal service to the Christian republic, and so forth), the very title of the second piece alerts us to the stern, cautionary character of what is to come. It begins by returning to the difficulties Spaniards have had with the general language of Peru, and Inca Garcilaso tells us that, "for the better understanding" of what is written in his history, it would be well to have some notice of the indigenous language. The abbreviated Quechua grammar lesson that follows is both outwardly didactic and stated rather matter-of-factly, in stark contrast to the wording of the "Preface." Inca Garcilaso tells us that each syllable of words in what he calls the "general language of Cuzco" can be pronounced in three different ways, with each pronunciation signifying a different meaning. He then informs us that indigenous words are usually accented on the penultimate or antepenultimate syllables and never on the last. He asserts this doubly aware that "barbarian words" were accented on the last syllable and that "barbarian," as a category of linguistic difference and cultural inferiority dating back to ancient Greece (Pagden 1982: 15–26), had been applied by Europeans to describe Amerindians. Inca Garcilaso assures his readers that his view of the general language of Cuzco "does not contradict those who say that barbarian words are accented on the last [syllable], which they say because they do not know the language."[67] Rather than confront centuries of European learning, Inca Garcilaso maintains that the linguistic category "barbarian," and the inferior intellectual and moral status it entailed, simply does not apply to the speech of indigenous Peruvians. He is not as hesitant, however, to imply that Spaniards could be seen as "barbarians" in the eyes of native Quechua speakers. After enumerating the letters lacking in the general language of Cuzco in comparison to Spanish (b, d, f, g, j, l, rr, and x), Inca Garcilaso states, "the Spaniards add these letters to the detriment and corruption of the language" (*Los españoles añaden estas letras en perjuicio y corrupción del lenguaje*). The charge is more serious than it seems. According to Antonio de Nebrija's famous Spanish grammar of 1492 (an author lauded by Inca Garcilaso later in the text), a "barbarism" (*barbarismo*) was any intolerable pronunciation or spelling of a word, which was not only a linguistic corruption but also a "vice" (*vicio*) (Nebrija 1926: 123).[68] Inca Garcilaso's critique of Spanish abilities both to comprehend and communicate with indigenous Peruvians is intensified, and at this point the connection between the Spanish corruption of Quechua and their disfiguration of Inca history is fully brought to light.

Whereas Spaniards added extra letters to their pronunciation and spelling of Quechua, Inca Garcilaso admits almost in passing that Indians usually mispronounced Spanish words due to the phonetic differences between the two languages: "And as the Indians do not have them [the missing letters], they commonly mispronounce the Spanish words that do."[69] The problem signaled here is that when dealing outside the confines of their respective languages, both Spaniards and Indians appear to each other as barbarians, because each corrupts the language of the other. The charge of "barbarism" cuts both ways, yet the indictment is thereby relativized and quarantined within the problem of linguistic (in)competence. To rectify the fundamental breakdown in communication and the social antagonisms that have resulted therefrom, Inca Garcilaso offers a surprising remedy: "In order to halt this corruption, it may be permissible for me, since I am an Indian, *to write like an Indian in this history using the same letters* with which those words should be written."[70] In the philological terms with which he was so adroit, Inca Garcilaso proposes a restoration of the general language of Cuzco from its most basic elements as a central and conspicuous element of his history (Zamora 1988: 12–38, 62–84; Garcés 1991). He goes further in the next sentence and defends this innovative departure: "And let none who read take it as wrong to see the present novelty in opposition to the poor usage [already] introduced, one should rather enjoy reading the nominatives in their *propriety and purity*."[71] As in the "Preface," Inca Garcilaso illustrates his concern for the "propriety and purity" of indigenous speech, or in other words, the appropriateness and authentic significance of linguistic utterance relative to the sociocultural complex to which it is tied.

The most provocative claim, of course, is Inca Garcilaso's avowal to "write like an Indian," and not simply because the Incas lacked alphabetic writing or because most Europeans thought indigenous peoples were incapable of doing so.[72] This claim pushes Inca Garcilaso beyond merely acting as a representative of Inca civilization for the edification of European readers. It renders him accountable to the understandings of those who had inherited Inca language and culture, and Inca Garcilaso immediately recognizes it as such. In winding down his warning on the general language of Cuzco, he writes: "In many other aspects this language is very different from Spanish, Italian, and Latin, *which will be noted by learned mestizos and criollos*, since they [the differences] are in their language."[73] With these words, Inca Garcilaso has not only assumed the existence of an audience composed of "learned mestizos and criollos" as receptors of his work, but he also has appealed to their knowledge and judgment as corroboration for the veracity of his views on the general language of Cuzco.[74] The juxtaposition of the faults of "learned Spaniards" (*españoles curiosos*) that opens the "Preface" with the expertise of "learned mestizos and Creoles" in the "Warning" clearly favors the latter and places them in the preferred position to understand and interpret Inca Garcilaso's work. At this point, after having captured the attention of potential mestizo and Creole readers, Inca Garcilaso takes the opportunity to address them more directly: "It is well that I point out from Spain the principles of their language, so that they may maintain its purity, for it is certainly a shame for so elegant a language to be lost or corrupted."[75] There is an instantaneous change from the curt, pedantic, and critical tone in the previous passages to that of a gentle reminder and sympathetic commiseration. Further, the idiomatic Spanish expression for "point out" (*señalar con el dedo*) literally means "signal with a finger," and Inca Garcilaso's use of it here evokes the poetic image of him reaching out from across oceans and continents to touch upon the issues he shared with his mestizo and Creole compatriots. It is at once a gesture of praise for the elegant language and culture of Cuzco as well as an expression of Inca Garcilaso's commitment to the interests of native Peruvians in the restoration and perpetuation of their heritage.

From a close reading of these introductory pieces it can be concluded that Inca Garcilaso had not only considered the possibility of a native Peruvian audience, but that he had also self-consciously positioned his authorial character to address their specific understandings and interests. This conclusion gains additional confirmation with the "Prologue" to the indios, mestizos, and criollos of the Second Part, in which the subtle and indirect address of native Peruvians found in the opening moments of the First Part is expressed both candidly and copiously. Since a translation of the "Prologue" to the Second Part is included in the Appendix, there is no need to quote it extensively here. It is sufficient to note that Inca Garcilaso once again praises the intelligence of native Peruvians as well as their capacity to excel in all arts and faculties, and he implores them to "press forward in the exercise of virtue, study, and the art of war, turning themselves to their good name, to that which will make them famous on earth and eternal in heaven." Inspiring such conduct, he tells us, falls within his first reason for writing both parts of the *Royal Commentaries*, thereby explicitly linking the entirety of his work with the reception and use of his Indian, mestizo, and criollo compatriots.

Inca Garcilaso's address of native Peruvians (both direct and indirect), his valorization of a mestizo perspective, and his numerous remonstrations over linguistic performance and propriety significantly alter the interpretive possibilities of his work. In simplest terms, if it can be fairly said, and as I hope to have demonstrated, that the *Royal Commentaries* was written not simply on behalf of native Peruvians for the instruction of European readers, but also *to* native Peruvians for their own perusal and benefit, then this gesture serves to usher in non-European meanings and modes of articulation as semi-autonomous codes within the verbal structures of the texts. Given the importance of decorum in Renaissance thinking and the premium humanists placed on developing a style that reflected the author's personality while actively engaging the common understandings of an audience, it is difficult to think that Inca Garcilaso had either failed to comprehend the full implications of these principles or simply neglected to apply them in his work. If such were the case, however, it would be difficult indeed to continue to maintain that Inca Garcilaso was, after all, a great humanist. For there is an obvious contradiction in lauding Inca Garcilaso's status as a humanist in a Ciceronian or Erasmian tradition, on the one hand, while implying that he had such a limited understanding of the central principles within the tradition that he failed to grasp the novel discursive possibilities they both made available and partially authorized for him, on the other. Fortunately, however, the evidence runs to the contrary. In fact, to gloss his comments in the "Preface" and "Warning," Inca Garcilaso portrays his effort to compose a more appropriate history of Inca civilization from a mestizo perspective as a moral duty. This pledge of propriety is fundamental to Inca Garcilaso's approach and, as we have seen, it operates on many levels: in grammar and philology, content, translation, and interpretive commentary. Most importantly, however, insofar as Inca Garcilaso poses language itself as the key to comprehending Inca culture, he has focused attention on his own language as both the mediator between and medium in which the different meaning systems are placed in dialogue and interwoven. The renewal and, hence, audibility of Inca voices within the cacophonous stutter of the dominant Spanish discourse turns on a question of style.

Inca Garcilaso inaugurates a major shift in his style as he begins to relate the origin of the Incas in Book I, Chapter XV of the First Part. In the preceding fourteen chapters he has further established his independence and authority as a historical narrator by offering critical commentary on questions of natural philosophy (including whether there is one world or two, the habitability of different climatic zones, the existence of the antipodes, etc.), historical anecdotes (such as the discovery of the New World by an "unknown" sailor named Antonio Sánchez de Huelva rather than Columbus, and the shipwreck of Pedro Serrano), and the etymology of the word "Peru" mistakenly applied by Spaniards to Tahuantinsuyu.[76] The last cluster of these chapters (Part 1, Book I, Chapters IX–XIV), in which Inca Garcilaso vividly describes the savage practices of indigenous peoples before the Incas (practices such as cannibalism and incest), are the most important. Inca Garcilaso creates a fundamental distinction, at once chronological and cultural, between the primitive First Age of Peruvian history and the Second Age, which is characterized by the civilizing mission of the Incas.[77] These chapters separate the Incas from the darkness and barbarism of the earlier age as well as from their non-Inca Andean contemporaries, and they provide a dramatic segue into the account of Inca origins. In fact, all of the preceding material—the prefaces, the numerous digressions, the repeated illustrations of Spanish ineptitude with indigenous language, and the appalling state of Andean culture prior to the Incas—gradually builds up to this crucial moment.

The chapter opens with the providential rationale behind Inca civilization, with Inca Garcilaso playing the role of primary historical narrator (Part 1, Book 1, Chapter 15). In order to bring primitive Andeans out of the obscure darkness in which they dwelt, God, the "Sun of Justice" (*sol de justicia*), sent them a "morning star" (*lucero del alba*) to instruct them in natural law, urbanity, and the respect men owe to one another. The Incas were selected by divine grace to transform the savages into rational beings capable of receiving all good doctrine. More importantly, God had done this so that indigenous peoples would be rendered "more docile to receive the Catholic faith and the teaching and the doctrine of our Holy Mother the Roman Catholic church" (Part 1, Book I, Chapter XV, vol. 1, 39).[78] Following authors such as Las Casas and Jerónimo Roman, Inca Garcilaso portrays the origin and expansion of the Inca empire as a divinely ordained *praeparatio evangelica* whose ultimate aim was to prepare the indigenous peoples of the Andes to receive the gospel (MacCormack 1991: 234). The notion of praeparatio evangelica was first expounded by Eusebius of Caesarea and, later, St. Augustine to account for the power and prestige of pagan Rome and the advantages that Roman civilization afforded the early church. Inca Garcilaso's use of it places the Inca empire on par with the achievements of the Romans, solidifying Cuzco's position as "another Rome."[79] This providential explanation, furthermore, not only legitimizes Inca dominance over the indigenous peoples of Tahuantinsuyu, but it also places the Incas in a privileged position in the European conception of universal (which is to say Christian) history as the necessary precursor to the establishment of the church in the New World.

By opening with this providential explanation of Inca civilization, Inca Garcilaso alerts us to the extent to which his account of origins includes the moral and political justifications of the empire. What follows is the record of a conversation between Inca Garcilaso as a youth in Cuzco and his aged uncle Cusi Huallpa, which is brought about by the impetuous curiosity of the young mestizo regarding the Inca past.[80] The question that initiates the tale of origins is about "history" itself. The young Inca Garcilaso asks, "Inca, my uncle, though you have no writing, which is what preserves the memory of past events, what information do you have of the origins and beginnings of our kings?" (Part 1, Book I, Chapter XV, vol. 1, 40).[81] This question encapsulates the current European view, hence the problem, that alphabetic writing was a prerequisite for the inscription and transmission of meaningful accounts of a people's past. In the words of Mignolo, "the concern was the Amerindians' qualifications to have history (because of their lack of letters) and their competence to tell coherent narratives" (Mignolo 1995: 127). Inca Garcilaso confronts this assumption and its attenuating difficulties head on, and the ensuing dialogue not only demonstrates that the Incas preserved detailed knowledge of their past despite their lack of letters, but is also intended as an illustration of the *manner* in which this knowledge was related.

In the passages between the invocation of praeparatio evangelica and the beginning of the conversation with Cusi Huallpa, Inca Garcilaso registers a new set of intentions and forecasts the shift in perspective and style he is to make. First, Inca Garcilaso's turn to the Inca oral tradition as represented by Cusi Huallpa is posed as a deliberate choice that he conspicuously marks off from the prior narrative. He writes, "since we are at the portal of this great labyrinth, it will be well if we move forward and give notice of what is inside."[82] The "labyrinth" is the monument of Inca history itself, the multicursal complexity of which reinforces Inca Garcilaso's role as a guide for his readers.[83] He then goes on to say:

> After having performed many designs and taken many paths to begin to give an account of the origin and beginning of the Incas, formerly natural kings of Peru, it seemed to me that the best design and the easiest and simplest path was to recount what I heard many times in my youth from my mother and her brothers and uncles and other elders about this origin and beginning. For everything that is said about it from other routes comes to resolve itself into the same as we shall relate. And it will be better that it is known in the very words that the Incas tell it rather than those of other foreign authors. (Part 1, Book I, Chapter XV, vol. 1, 39)[84]

Just as Cuzco was the "navel" of Tahuantinsuyu (Part 1, Book II, Chapter XI, vol. 1, 95), the oral history of his Inca ancestors becomes the very core and "first stone" of Inca Garcilaso's edifice (*la primera piedra de nuestra edificio*) (Part 1, Book I, Chapter XIX, vol. 1, 48; Garcés 1991: 133). The metaphor of history as an "edifice" was prevalent in Renaissance historiography, and its invocation in this instance illustrates the extent to which Inca Garcilaso is pursuing a rhetorical strategy. The account we are given, however, is not in the "very words" (*propias palabras*) of the Incas, because it is written in Spanish instead of the general language of Cuzco. After relating the divine origin of the first Incas (Manco Cápac and his wife-sister Mama Ocllo Huaco), the foundation of the city of Cuzco, and the first peoples subdued by the Incas, Inca Garcilaso clarifies this discrepancy. Of the relation his uncle gave him, he says, "I have tried to translate it faithfully from my mother tongue, which is that of the Inca, into the foreign one, which is Castilian" (Part 1, Book I, Chapter XVII, vol. 1, 45).[85] Although he admits that he has not written with the same majesty that the Inca's speech exhibited nor with the full significance of each word (because doing so would have made the account too long and he has intentionally omitted the odious), he has conveyed the "true meaning" (*verdadero sentido*), which is suitable for history (Part 1, Book I, Chapter XVII, vol. 1, 45).[86]

Realizing that Inca Garcilaso has made a conscious decision to portray the narrative as a true translation of the oral tradition of his Inca relatives from Cuzco leads to three very important insights concerning his work.[87] First, this stratagem privileges the oral histories of Inca royalty as the central, authoritative warrant of Inca Garcilaso's texts. As we have seen, the Inca's words are forwarded as the point at which all other versions, both European and indigenous, converge, "resolve" themselves, and are reconciled. To illustrate this, as the account of Inca origins proceeds (Part 1, Book I, Chapter XV) both the foregoing chapters on the savagery of the First Age (Part 1, Book I, Chapters IX–XIV) and the notion of praeparatio evangelica that introduces Inca Garcilaso's shift in perspective are repeated in condensed form as the speech of Cusi Huallpa. The separation of Andean history into two epochs does *not* receive its warrant solely from the requirement of European historiography to maintain the proper chronological order nor from the Spanish historians (such as Cieza de León, Las Casas, or Sarmiento de Gamboa) who had come to the same conclusion. The distinction is warranted and, therefore, presented as "true" because it forms part of the Incas' own understanding of their past. Further, the Christian and Neoplatonic symbolism of God as the Sun of Justice undergoes an immediate revision to resemble the high deity of the Inca solar cult from whom the Incas claimed both descent and political authority.

In the words of Cusi Huallpa, God the Father becomes "our father the Sun" (*nuestro padre el sol*) (Part 1, Book I, Chapter 15, vol. 1, 41) who takes pity on the savages and sends them his son and daughter to rescue them from barbarism. The European version of praeparatio evangelica presented by Inca Garcilaso in his role as narrator and the Inca myth related through Cusi Huallpa are so transparently connected as to be effectively the same story. Nevertheless, they are presented as *different versions* that arrive at the same, deeper truth: the truth that the Incas operated under divine mandate and that they were the legitimate and necessary forerunners of Christianity in Peru.

Second, Inca Garcilaso's appeal to the Inca oral tradition as the guiding thread through the labyrinth of the Peruvian past allows us to situate his work in a specific Andean context. Social life throughout the Andes revolved around extended kinship groups called *ayllus*, which were internally and externally structured through complex systems of reciprocity. Inca rulers and elites, such as Inca Garcilaso's mother and uncles, belonged to royal ayllus known as *panacas*, matrilineal kinship groups centered in Cuzco whose coalitions and conflicts were the very substance of Inca political life (Rostworowski 1999: 7, 15–19). More specifically, Inca Garcilaso identifies his lineage as stemming from Cápac Ayllu, the *panaca* of Túpac Inca Yupanqui, the eleventh ruler of the dynasty (Part 1, Book VIII, Chapter VIII and Book IX, Chapter XIV), located in Hanan Cuzco (Upper Cuzco) (Part 1, Book I, Chapter XVI).[88] The notable aspect of this information for the present purposes is that each panaca kept a history of the deeds of its Inca founder as a family history in poems, painted panels, and quipus. The quipus were knotted cords used as mnemonic devices containing vast amounts of compressed, specially coded data that were both recorded and interpreted by officially designated accountants called *quipucamayus*. While most of the information stored in the quipus was numerical in character and related to tribute tallies, labor obligations, and census counts, they were also used for recording important historical events (Ascher and Ascher 1981: Chapter 4). Inca Garcilaso himself notes that the quipus contained, "everything that could be counted by number, even battles and skirmishes, all the embassies that had been brought before the Inca, and all the speeches and arguments made by the king" (Part 1, Book VI, Chapter IX, vol. 1, 346).[89] The quipucamayu, "he who has charge of the accounts" (Part 1, Book VI, Chapter VIII, vol. 1, 345), occupied himself with committing this information to memory and was called upon to reconstruct it during state rituals and religious ceremonies. Further, it was also his office to pass these accounts on to *amautas* (philosophers) and *harauicus* (poets), who would rework them into allegories and poems, respectively (Part 1, Book VI, Chapter IX). Insofar as quipucamayus were officially designated accountants and expositors of the notable accomplishments of a particular Inca and his descendants (panaca), the stories they transmitted were partisan, highly selective, and served to exalt the accomplishments of one royal faction to the exclusion of others. According to Susan Niles, royal Inca histories took the form of "praise narratives" that underwent constant revision and customarily omitted ignominious deeds and failures of an Inca and his panaca to "represent a privileged and idealized version of historical events" (Niles 1999: 1–27, quote on 27). In this sense, Inca Garcilaso's preferment of the accounts of his Inca relatives is indicative of a standard practice in Andean oral traditions, and it firmly aligns him with the interests of the *panaca* of Túpac Inca Yupanqui to which his mother and uncles belonged.

Third, the representation of his work as a faithful translation of the oral histories passed down to him from his Inca relatives allows us to fill in the significance of Inca Garcilaso's claim to "write like an Indian." The claim, of course, appears to be a paradoxical one for the obvious reason that indigenous Andeans lacked alphabetic writing, and Inca Garcilaso, as we have seen, admits as much. It is precisely in his description of the quipus and the function of quipucamayus, however, that this conundrum is resolved. After detailing the information stored in the quipus and the roles played respectively by quipucamayus, amautas, and harauicus in the perpetuation and ritual recitation of Inca history, Inca Garcilaso returns to the question of writing that initiated Cusi Hualipa's tale of Inca origins. As experience has shown, Inca Garcilaso tells us, the expedients used by the Incas to record their past proved to be highly susceptible to decay and ruin. He continues:

> for letters are what perpetuate deeds, but as those Incas did not attain them they availed themselves of what they could invent. And *as if the knots were letters* they selected historians and accountants (which were called quipucamayus, that is, "he who has charge of the knots") so that through them—and by the threads and their colors and with the help of stories and poetry—*they wrote and retained* the tradition of their deeds. *This was the manner of writing the Incas had in their republic.* (Part 1, Book VI, Chapter IX, vol. 1, 347)[90]

Inca Garcilaso goes on to say that the leaders of each province turned to the quipucamayus to learn the accomplishments of their ancestors and other notable events such as were kept in the "*quipu* annals" (*los quipus anales*), which as "scribes and historians" (*como escribanos y como historiadores*) the quipucamayus were duty-bound to study constantly and learn by heart. Fittingly enough, while Inca Garcilaso is equating the quipus to writing, he also likens the Inca oral tradition to the annalistic records of ancient Rome. "History began," according to Cicero, "as a mere compilation of annals," which were "bare records of dates, personalities, places, and events" that occurred in the course of a year (Cicero 1997b: II.xii.52–53). The similarity between the contents and purposes of Roman annals and Inca "quipu annals" carries over into a correspondence between the tasks of historiographer and quipucamayu. The latter committed the notable events in the "quipu annals" to memory because it was his responsibility to organize and elaborate them into historical narratives: "because, as historians, they had to relate such matters when asked" (*porque como historiadores tenían dar cuenta de ellos cuando se la pidiesen*) (Part 1, Book VI, Chapter IX, vol. 1, 347). Akin to European historiographers, the quipucamayus were the Ciceronian "life of memory" (*vitam memoria*) in that they preserved the past from careening into oblivion and transmitted it to future generations who would otherwise be heedless of their own traditions. "The Indian who had not learned by tradition and memory the accounts (or whatever other history had passed among them)," Inca Garcilaso explains, "was as ignorant of the one and the other as a Spaniard or any other foreigner" (Part 1, Book VI, Chapter IX, vol. 1, 347–48).[91] Among those ignorant of the intricate logic of the quipus and the conventions of their interpretation and exposition, Inca Garcilaso was not to be counted. "I handled the quipus and knots with my father's Indians and other curacas," he concludes the chapter, "when they came to the city to pay tribute on St. John's Day and Christmas."[92] The reason for this was simple enough: the Indians were skeptical of Spanish accounting and needed someone they could trust to compare and verify their records. In providing this service Inca Garcilaso came to understand the quipus "as well as the Indians" (*Y de esta manera supe de ellos tanto como los indios*) (Part 1, Book VI, Chapter XI, vol. 1, 348), and he could therefore present himself to his Andean readers as a mestizo quipucamayu who knew how to write.[93]

If Inca Garcilaso's self-characterization is more than an empty "rhetorical" gesture, the proof should be in the writing; that is, in his style. The style of the *Royal Commentaries*, once identified as Ciceronian by Luis Arocena (Arocena 1949: 50), is much more intricate than it first appears, and fortunately for our purposes the formal and structural elements of the texts have been meticulously analyzed, documented, and interpreted by José Antonio Mazzotti.[94]

Mazzotti's study suggests that Inca Garcilaso's deferral to the character and speech of Cusi Huallpa as the legitimate authority on Inca origins inaugurates a manner of speaking/writing that simulates the patterns and cadences of the oral tradition in Cuzco. As Cusi Huallpa's speech unfolds, a polyphonic and contrapuntal "chorus" of voices emerges analogous to the "mestizo discourse" that resulted from the earliest efforts of Spaniards to translate and record indigenous speech in the Andes (Mazzotti 1996a: 60–99, 107–18; 2008: 55–77, 83–93).[95] Moreover, the syntactic structures of the words spoken by Cusi Huallpa, the Sun, and Manco Cápac (in Chapters XV–XVII, Book I of the First Part) evoke a formulaic organization indicative of ritualized speech in oral traditions. This pattern is then constantly repeated when Inca Garcilaso returns as the principal historical narrator (Part 1, Book I, Chapter XX) to recount the deeds and conquests of *each* successive ruler.[96] If it is recalled that we have been alerted to the extent to which the myth of origins contains the moral and political justifications of Inca civilization and that Cusi Huallpa's recitation of this myth is laid as the "first stone" of the historical edifice, it then becomes apparent that Inca Garcilaso adopted a style that strove to epitomize and unite the magnitude of the occasion with the language of its (translated) expression. The simulation of Andean voices Inca Garcilaso attempts to conjure and then appropriates as part of his "own" voice in his role as principal narrator establishes his authority for a prospective indio, mestizo, and criollo audience by replicating a cadence and "manner of speaking" at once familiar and accessible to them as inheritors of indigenous oral traditions of Cuzco. If, as Inca Garcilaso tells us, "all of them [Incas], as much the kings as those who were not, prided themselves in imitating in everything the character, works, and customs of the first prince Manco Cápac," then he has done just that in the linguistic structures of his text (Part 1, Book I, Chapter XIX, vol. 1, 50).[97] In so doing, he demonstrates his worthiness of being considered a quipucamayu as well as an Inca by his native Peruvian readers. And, of course, *none* of these maneuvers are either intended for or would even be comprehensible to European readers lacking in detailed knowledge of Inca civilization.

When Inca Garcilaso claimed to "write like an Indian in this history using the same letters" at the very beginning of the *Royal Commentaries*, he was not simply referring to orthographic precision in the European sense. The knots of the quipus are "letters" or proto-letters in his conception of history, wanting only the artifice of graphic representation to render them permanent. His task, then, is as much transcription as translation, and he offers his Peruvian compatriots a new form of *material* representation to Inca history that endeavors to capture and immortalize the essential or "true meaning" of the empire. The "true meaning," as we have seen, is contained in the providential purpose and civilizing mission of the Incas, which in turn reflects and illuminates the outstanding rational capacities, political organization, and moral character of the rulers and citizens who imitated the Sun and his emissaries. The "true meaning," moreover, both recalls and clings to the spoken words of the Incas, the translation of which conforms to the criteria of what, as Inca Garcilaso says, "is suitable for our history" (*es lo que conviene a nuestra historia*) (Part 1, Book I, Chapter XVII, vol. 1, 45). The proposed transcription, translation, and commentary, therefore, are simultaneously semiotic, insofar as they move from one system of material signs to another; linguistic, in that they proceed back and forth between Quechua and Spanish; and ideological in that they constantly negotiate two distinct ensembles of meaning. Further, in explicitly adopting the roles of translator, historian, and quipucamayu as his primary authorial functions, Inca Garcilaso ties the "truth" of his plural history ("our history," nuestra historia) to *both* the requirements of plausibility and propriety in humanist historiography as well as the rhetorical conventions of the praise narratives of his panaca in the Inca oral tradition. "Indian writing," or mestizo rhetoric, as such, signifies Inca Garcilaso's extraordinarily creative effort to resurrect and inscribe a verisimilitude of the Inca oral tradition, "the memory of the good lost" as he calls it (*la memoria del bien perdido*) (Part 1, Book I, Chapter XV, vol. 1, 40), within the verbal structures and discursive constraints of a predominantly Spanish text.[98]

Having laid the "first stone" of this investigation, I hope to have demonstrated not only that the *Royal Commentaries* was in fact intended to address the common and diverse cultural understandings of both European and Andean readers, but also that in failing to interrogate the Andean contexts and meanings dispersed throughout the texts one misses *at least half* of the arguments within. Of course, it is precisely this fundamental, yet often latent, duality of the *Royal Commentaries* that the remainder of this work will explore, primarily at the level of how Inca Garcilaso's multiple and intercultural political interests both inform and shape his representation of Inca civilization and Peruvian history. It perhaps hardly needs repeating at this point that, inasmuch as Inca Garcilaso's mestizo rhetoric emerges from and maneuvers between Andean and European meanings, we should not expect his political thought to be reducible to European models in every, or for that matter any, instance. The reason being that no matter how imperfect Inca Garcilaso's knowledge, memory, or portrayal of Inca civilization might have been, begun as the *Royal Commentaries* was over two and a half decades after he had been permanently divorced from indigenous Peruvian language and society, he emphasizes that he has at his disposal an "other" conceptual universe. Fully comprehending Inca Garcilaso's political views, then, requires an attempt to grasp the differences between Andean and European concepts while simultaneously assessing Inca Garcilaso's use of them to forward his own agenda and views. And perhaps nowhere is the richness, complexity, and "difference" of Inca Garcilaso's political thought more patent than in the dual historical structure of the *Royal Commentaries*, to which we turn in the next chapter.

3
THE MANY FACES OF VIRACOCHA AND THE TURNING OF THE WORLD

Tragedy, Conversion, Rebirth

It is quite well known among garcilacistas that the First Part and the Second Part of the *Royal Commentaries* constitute two halves of a single history. It has also been a scholarly commonplace not only to highlight the differences between the First Part (which details the lives, deeds, and conquests of the Inca rulers and is intercalated with abundant digressions on the totality of indigenous culture) and the Second Part (which treats of the Spanish conquest and civil wars of the early colonial period), but also to laud the First to the detriment of the Second.[1] Despite the divergences in style and content between the parts and foregoing any debates about the superiority of one over the other, it is nevertheless clear that Inca Garcilaso intended the First and Second parts to be read together as a unified work.[2]

From this observation, I would like to suggest two points worth keeping in mind while reading the *Royal Commentaries*. First, if we attend to the progression of the historical narrative through both parts of the work, it becomes apparent that all of the actions and events in the *Royal Commentaries* are situated *within* the Inca dynastic tradition. After a handful of highly significant, "introductory" chapters, the history of the Incas begins with the myth of their origins in Book I, Chapter XV of the First Part. This history, and the entire work for that matter, comes to a rather abrupt close with Viceroy Francisco de Toledo's execution of Túpac Amaru and his exile of the royal Indians and mestizos in Book VIII, Chapters XVII–XIX of the Second Part. Between these two textual landmarks stand the birth, growth, and demise of the Inca empire, the Spanish conquest, civil wars, and rebellions, and the arrival of Toledo and the extinguishing of the Inca lineage. As Inca Garcilaso writes in his "Declaration" about the history, his work encompasses "the beginning, middle and end" of the Inca monarchy (Part 1, Book I, Chapter XIX, vol. 1, 50). To the account of the thirteen successive Incas in the First Part, in which he includes Huáscar, Inca Garcilaso adds five more (Manco Inca, his two sons, Sairi Túpac and Túpac Amaru, and two grandsons) who "never possessed anything of the kingdom other than a right to it," in the Second, bringing the total to eighteen (Part 2, Book VIII, Chapter XXI, vol. 3, 254). The fact that the actions of Spaniards dominate the Second Part does *not* alter the overarching structure or continuity of this sequence. For as we shall see below, Inca Garcilaso presents some of the Spanish conquerors as Viracochas, potentially legitimate heirs and family members of the Incas, and in so doing his account of their travails in the Second Part becomes an essential element of a larger, indigenous drama.

The second point, a highly conspicuous characteristic of Inca Garcilaso's magnum opus, is that the *Royal Commentaries* weaves a tale of overwhelming loss. Following the conquest, the oral tradition of Inca Garcilaso's indigenous ancestors painfully reflected on "the memory of the good lost" (*la memoria del bien perdido*), and with tears of mourning in their eyes the relatives of the young mestizo would conclude the tales of their once glorious past with the lament, "Our reign has turned to vassalage!" (*¡Trocósenos el reinar en vasallaje!*) (Part 1, Book I, Chapter XV, vol. 1, 40). In this the Incas were not alone; many of their Spanish conquerors likewise suffered military and political defeat as well as impoverishment and violent death as recompense for their services to the Spanish Crown. The words attributed to Francisco Pizarro by Inca Garcilaso are indicative of the conquerors' complaint: "Wretched are we who perish struggling to win foreign empires and kingdoms neither for ourselves nor our children, but for others!" (Part 2, Book I, Chapter XIII, vol. 1, 44).[3] As the offspring of a Spanish conquistador cum *encomendero* and an Inca princess, a select group of conquerors and conquered thus comprised the culturally heterogeneous strata with which Inca Garcilaso's political interests were most closely aligned. It is hardly a secret, moreover, that he viewed the inability of these two parties to establish a lasting social and political union, as well as the subsequent erection of a brutal viceregal regime in Peru, as the signal failure of the early years of the Hispano-Inca encounter in Tahuantinsuyu (the four corners of the world). For Inca Garcilaso, the utopian promise of the Spanish conquest lay in the possibility of creating, in David Brading's words, "a Holy Inca empire, based on the marriage of conquerors and Inca noblewomen, ruled by a mestizo *encomendero* class (Spaniards rewarded with *encomiendas*, allotments of Indian laborers and servants), Christian in religion, ruling a native peasantry in accordance with the principles of Inca legislation" (Brading 1991: 271). This imperial ideal, however, never materialized and its promise remained unfulfilled. For this reason, above all else, Inca Garcilaso famously remarked that the historical legacy of early Peru "in everything is a tragedy" (*en todo sea tragedia*) (Part 2, Book VIII, Chapter XIX, vol. 3, 251).

The tragedy depicted in the *Royal Commentaries* indeed finds its gravitational center in the overturning of Inca rule. Yet insofar as the Spanish arrival and conquest stand at the mid-point rather than the finale of this dark saga, we must understand the nomenclature of "Inca," and therefore to whom it can legitimately refer, in a broader sense.[4] At one point, Inca Garcilaso informs us that when applied to a prince the title "Inca" meant "lord" or "king" or "emperor," but, "to interpret it in its full significance, it is to say 'man of royal blood'" (Part 1, Book I, Chapter XXIV, vol. 1, 59).[5] Just prior to this translation, we learned, following the practice of the first Inca, Manco Cápac, the royal title could be conferred to exemplary vassals who were thus created "Incas by privilege" and "adopted sons" of the dynastic line. Further, Manco Cápac "ordered that they [Incas by privilege] and their descendants should always call themselves Incas without any distinction or difference between one another" (Part 1, Book I, Chapter XXIII, vol. 1, 57).[6] Finally, in clarifying who were the legitimate heirs of the Incas, Inca Garcilaso writes "all are descendants from the masculine line, for the female line (as said earlier) was disregarded by the Incas unless they were sons of the Spanish conquerors and those who won Peru (because these were also called Incas, believing they were descendants of their god the Sun)" (Part 1, Book IX, Chapter XL, vol. 2, 648).[7] Although this point will be fleshed out in greater detail below, for now it is enough to say that Inca Garcilaso's conception of "Inca" is expansive indeed, and his transformation of Spaniards into Viracocha Incas should not be construed as an ironic gesture solely intended to deepen his criticism of the Spanish conquest.[8] Rather, it represents his attempt to create a dynastic link between indigenous and foreign rulers and to illustrate the extent to which Incas and conquistadors were to share a common, and for Inca Garcilaso, tragic fate.

These preliminaries, more than simply reminding us that it is absolutely essential to read both parts of the *Royal Commentaries* in order to grasp Inca Garcilaso's political thought, raise two additional considerations that must be mentioned before we proceed. First, and at the risk of being redundant, if the Spanish conquest (Atahualpa's execution in particular) does not constitute the end of the Inca empire but rather an implicit, yet frustrated, transfer of power within the confines of its own development, then it is necessary to investigate how this transfer is realized textually. As is almost always the case in the *Royal Commentaries*, there are two separate and overlapping arguments that carry the weight of this burden. One argument relies on divine providence, which will be left aside for the moment, and another hinges upon the transformation of Spaniards into Viracochas.

In pursuing the second thread, however, one immediately encounters a thickly tangled knot of perplexing associations as well as two of Inca Garcilaso's most notorious and blatant alterations of Inca religion and history. For instance, there are no fewer than three indigenous personae in the First Part with the name Viracocha: one is the indigenous god Viracocha; the second is a phantasm called Viracocha Inca; and the third is the eighth emperor, who adopts the name Viracocha Inca due to his relationship with the phantasm. To complicate matters further, Inca Garcilaso inserts major changes into his account of indigenous civilization to accommodate the multifaceted Viracocha and to use this figure to tell a decidedly political tale. The beneficiary of one historical revision is Pachacámac, who, according to Inca Garcilaso, was the highest god of Inca religion, in obvious contradiction to the accounts of his Spanish contemporaries who claimed that Viracocha, in fact, held this distinction. Also implicated in these revisions is the ninth ruler, Inca Pachacútec, who for many of Inca Garcilaso's contemporaries was the Inca par excellence. In the First Part of the *Royal Commentaries*, however, Inca Pachacútec is robbed of his most important military feat, his defeat of the rebelling Chancas, and hence most of his prestige, which is instead attributed to his predecessor and father, none other than Viracocha Inca.

Much of this chapter, therefore, is dedicated to unraveling and explicating this admittedly confusing series of associations and alterations. Realizing that one of the ways Inca Garcilaso creates a continuity through the First and Second parts is by relating the polyvalent Viracocha with the Spaniards, however, brings us to a final consideration. It is this: once Inca Garcilaso's specific political purposes in transforming Spaniards into Viracochas are understood, then his accompanying modifications of Inca religion and dynastic history gain a rather astonishing relevance. Taken in isolation, Inca Garcilaso's preference for the deity Pachacámac over his alter-ego Viracocha and his concomitant promotion of the ruler Viracocha Inca over Pachacútec Inca look like intellectual idiosyncrasies or political parochialism. Nevertheless, I argue that Inca Garcilaso's intentional manipulations of a sequence that runs through and relies upon the symbolic functions of Pachacámac, Viracocha, and Pachacútec in an Andean context provide the *Royal Commentaries* with a dual historical structure. More pointedly, within and against the linear scheme of the *Royal Commentaries*, which emphasizes the providential growth and flourishing of the Incas in the First Part and their utter decimation in the Second, there is an alternative, cyclical scheme that construes the history of Inca civilization and Spanish conquest as a return to the primordial chaos of the Andean First Age.[9] In Inca Garcilaso's simulation of an indigenous framework, the arrival of the Spaniards represents a moment of uncertainty and tension that could have led either to the final perfection of Inca civilization or its destruction. Since the latter resulted, Inca Garcilaso manipulated a broad field of indigenous symbols and historical actors not only to relate a tale of loss, but also to underscore for his Andean readers the relationship between their current political status and religion. In so doing, the tragic history related in the *Royal Commentaries* is transformed into an allegory for conversion and rebirth.[10]

Any reader of early Spanish histories of Inca civilization will notice at least two major differences between Inca Garcilaso's description of Inca religion and politics and the accounts of his predecessors. First, Inca Garcilaso declares that Pachacámac, a Quechua compound meaning "he who animates the world universe" (*el que da ánima al mundo universo*), was the supreme god of the Inca pantheon. Pachacámac appears in the *Royal Commentaries* as an invisible and unknown god whose cult began with the first Incas, Manco Cápac and Mama Ocllo Huaco, whose worship consisted solely of inward genuflection, and to whom the Incas dedicated neither temples nor sacrifices. This "unknown god" (*dios no conocido*), according to Inca Garcilaso, was the first cause or Prime Mover of the world universe and the seemingly monotheistic inspiration behind Inca adoration of the Sun, the latter of which, he argued, was outwardly worshipped as the material manifestation of this all-encompassing being for the benefits of light and warmth it provided (Part 1, Book II, Chapter II, vol. 1, 70).

The idea that the Incas had in fact worshipped a single, omnipotent creator-god was by no means the brain-child of the mestizo historian. Although pre-Columbian Andean religions were polytheistic, animistic, and fundamentally incommensurate with the religious convictions of European antiquity and the Renaissance, Spanish observers assimilated indigenous myths, beliefs, and rituals to conform to Judeo-Christian concepts (Urbano 1981: XVI–XVII). As a result, indigenous belief in a creator-god had been previously recorded by Bartolomé de Las Casas, Jerónimo Román, Pedro de Cieza de León, Agustín de Zárate, José de Acosta, and other sources to which Inca Garcilaso had access as well as many he did not. All of these commentators, however, reported Viracocha as the principal name of the Inca deity (with the variants Illa Tecce Viracocha, Con Ticci Viracocha, or Ticci Viracocha Pachayachachi). For his part, Inca Garcilaso realized, like Acosta, that Viracocha and Pachacámac were two names attributed to the *same* deity (Acosta 1921, vol. 2, Book 5, Chapter 3, 301–2). For instance, the two are linked in a Quechua poem that Inca Garcilaso found in Blas Valera's manuscript of which Quechua, Latin, and Spanish versions are included in the *Royal Commentaries* (Part 1, Book II, Chapter XXVII, vol. 1, 133). Further, in responding to Friar Vincente de Valverde's condensed explication of Catholic dogma in the *requerimiento*, Atahualpa remarks upon the Christian deity, "perhaps he is the same that we call Pachacámac and Viracocha" (*por ventura es el mismo que nosotros llamamos Pachacámac y Viracocha*) (Part 2, Book I, Chapter XXIV, vol. 1, 71).[11] Although implicitly recognizing the identification of Pachacámac and Viracocha, the most Inca Garcilaso is willing to admit is that "Viracocha is the name of a modern god" worshipped by the Indians (Part 1, Book II, Chapter XXVII, vol. 1, 133). He repeatedly insists, however, that the proper appellation of the Inca high god was Pachacámac: "But if I, who am a Catholic Christian Indian by God's infinite mercy, were now asked 'What is God called in your language?' I would say 'Pachacámac,' because in the general language of Peru there is no other word to name God but this one" (Part 1, Book II, Chapter II, vol. 1, 72).[12]

The second obvious departure from the Spanish imperial record found in the *Royal Commentaries* likewise concerns a figure with the name Viracocha, yet in this instance it is the eighth ruler, Inca Viracocha. In this case, the discrepancy involves which Inca ruler deserved credit for defending and restoring the imperial capital of Cuzco from an attack by the rebelling Chancas, natives of Andahuaylas.[13] According to the Spanish chroniclers Cieza de León, Juan de Betanzos, and Sarmiento de Gamboa, all of whom collected information on the Inca past from members of the indigenous elite in Cuzco (as did Inca Garcilaso), the Chanca attack occurred near the end of Inca Viracocha's reign, and this Inca, along with his eldest and favored son, Inca Urco, fled the capital, leaving it helpless. In these accounts, Inca Viracocha's youngest son, Cusi Yupanqui, who later took the name Pachacuti Inca Yupanqui upon his installation as ruler, prayed to the almighty Viracocha for assistance and received a vision from the deity in which he was promised victory. Thus inspired, Cusi Yupanqui remained in Cuzco, valiantly defended the city, repelled the encroaching forces, and rebuilt the imperial seat (Cieza de León 1985: 137–42; Betanzos 1998: 19–30; Sarmiento de Gamboa 1999: 87–96).[14] Not so, according to Inca Garcilaso. In his version, the Chanca revolt occurred at the end of Inca Yáhuar Huácac's reign, the seventh ruler, whose name means, "he who weeps blood" (Part 1, Book IV, Chapter XVI, vol. 1, 232). It was Inca Yáhuar Huácac's ill-tempered and rebellious son (whose name before he took the scarlet fringe had been forgotten by tradition) who had been visited by an apparition that called himself Viracocha, warning of the Chanca threat and promising both his support and victory to the Inca prince. The anonymous prince left the pastures in Chita to which he had been banished by his father due to his unruly behavior and warned Inca Yáhuar Huácac of the imminent attack. Inca Yáhuar Huácac failed to heed this warning, and when he finally received news of the Chanca advance on Cuzco, it was too late. The Inca decided to flee, yet his son refused to cede Cuzco to the "barbarians" and returned to withstand the Chanca onslaught and to perish if necessary. With the timely help of ally forces, the young prince carried the day, successfully defended and restored Cuzco, and took the name Viracocha Inca, in honor of the phantasm that had aided him (Part 1, Book IV, Chapters XX–XXIV and Book V, Chapters XVII–XXII).

While there are almost as many different versions of Inca history as there were historians in the sixteenth and early seventeenth centuries, several scholars have shown that these glaring discrepancies in the *Royal Commentaries* reflect either Inca Garcilaso's own intellectual proclivities or his specific political interests. For instance, Margarita Zamora has argued that Inca Garcilaso's insistence that Pachacámac was the only Quechua word used to designate the supreme being was primarily motivated by linguistic considerations he had inherited from European traditions of philology and hermeneutics. Insofar as Inca Garcilaso was working within theories of language and truth that entailed "the perfect complementariness of signifier and signified" (Zamora 1988: 126), he opted for Pachacámac, which translates as "animator" or "sustainer of the world universe," to represent the indigenous notion of the godhead over the somewhat less majestic Viracocha, which translates as "sea of fat" (*mar de sebo*) (Part 1, Book V, Chapter XXI, vol. 1, 301). His preference for one name over the other was thus prodded by a set of intellectual and aesthetic priorities that in effect required him to preserve a proper correspondence between the intrinsic attributes and exalted status of the creator-deity and its indigenous terms of reference (Zamora 1988: 122–28).[15] Also considering the influence of European sources on his portrayal of Inca religion, Sabine MacCormack has suggested that Inca Garcilaso, though his version was no simple artifact of his fertile imagination, "did, nevertheless, select and interpret evidence in the light of his Platonist convictions" (MacCormack 1991: 342). More specifically, MacCormack maintains that the conjunction of external, solar worship and internal worship of Pachacámac that Inca Garcilaso ascribes to his ancestors is both a response to theological controversies in Counter-Reformation Spain and "derived, in the last resort, from Platonist sources, in particular Leone Hebreo" (MacCormack 1991: 332–49). In both cases, and albeit from different perspectives, Zamora and MacCormack are quick to point out the subtle ways in which Inca Garcilaso uses a variety of European sources to transform and reinstate the Lascasian defense of the rational capacities, religious practices, and moral character of Amerindians.[16] Through recourse to philological techniques and Neoplatonic concepts, Inca Garcilaso alters Inca religious practices to embody the very apex of natural reason and divine inspiration in the vein of *praeparatio evangelica*, making of the Incas a providentially selected, pagan civilization whose indispensable and privileged historical function was to till the barren, Andean soil in anticipation of Christian seedlings (Zamora 1988: 85ff.; Brading 1991: 262–64; MacCormack 1991: 240–46).

The extent to which Inca Garcilaso both manipulated and selectively represented Inca civilization in the *Royal Commentaries* has not gone unnoticed by interdisciplinary scholars of the Andes region. María Rostworowski de Diez Canseco was first to suggest that Inca Garcilaso credited Viracocha Inca with the defeat over the Chancas, thereby displacing the actual victor, Pachacútec Inca, due to the partisan character of Andean oral history and Inca Garcilaso's own membership, through his mother, in the *panaca* of Túpac Inca Yupanqui, known as Cápac Ayllu. According to Rostworowski, Inca Garcilaso pushed the Chanca war back to the previous generation in order to detract from the prestige of Inca Pachacútec's panaca (royal kinship unit), known as Hatun Ayllu (Rostworowski 1953: 57–68).[17] Inca Garcilaso's motives for doing so, Rostworowski contends, stemmed purely from indigenous concerns. Atahualpa, the ruler at the time of Spanish conquest, was a member of Inca Pachacútec's panaca and had defeated his half-brother and rival imperial claimant, Huáscar, a member of Túpac Inca Yupanqui's and Inca Garcilaso's own panaca, in a civil war shortly before the Spanish arrival. In the course of this battle, many members of Cápac Ayllu were massacred and Huáscar later lost his life at the hands of Atahualpa's captains. Considering the customary practice in Andean oral traditions of selecting, omitting, and rearranging historical events in order to valorize and, if necessary, vindicate the representatives of a specific *ayllu* (extended kinship group) or panaca, Inca Garcilaso's doctoring of the historical record represents an act of "filial piety and posthumous revenge" taken against Hatun Ayllu for the deeds of Atahualpa.[18]

With regard to Inca Garcilaso's preference for Pachacámac over the deity Viracocha, José Antonio Mazzotti has argued this, too, bears the stamp of the mestizo historian's attachment to the panaca of his Inca ancestors.[19] There is a well-documented strand of indigenous myth and history (seen, for instance, in the myths of Huarochirí and the work of Don Felipe Guaman Poma de Ayala), a strand also found in some of the early Spanish chronicles (such as Cieza de León and Fernando de Santillán), that connects Túpac Inca Yupanqui with the cult of Pachacámac, the main deity of the Yunga Indians on the Peruvian coast just south of Lima.[20] Some of these accounts suggest that the Yungas and their splendid temple to Pachacámac were first subdued and incorporated into the empire by Túpac Inca Yupanqui, and others relate that this Inca either conversed with an oracle or received a vision in which Pachacámac revealed that he in fact worked in conjunction with the Inca solar deity and should be worshipped accordingly.[21] In either case, Túpac Inca Yupanqui is generally credited with having introduced this revered coastal deity into the Inca pantheon and for beginning construction of an Inca Temple of the Sun in this region.[22] Mazzotti therefore concludes, insofar as Inca Garcilaso favors the oral tradition of his own panaca, it is most likely that he selected from among a number of different indigenous accounts of Inca religion to privilege the contributions of his own lineage (hence Pachacámac over Viracocha), and to create a resemblance between elements of this family history and notions within Christian Neoplatonism (Mazzotti 1996a: 208–22 and MacCormack 1991: 351–52).[23]

Far from being mistakes on his part, there can be little doubt that Inca Garcilaso's promotion of Pachacámac and Viracocha Inca over the god Viracocha and Pachacútec Inca respectively stems from his political commitments. Furthermore, these modifications illustrate the minimally dual intentions of the *Royal Commentaries* in that Inca Garcilaso's alterations of the indigenous past simultaneously attend to concerns and conflicts in both European and Andean contexts. To be sure, as an intellectual and a historian, Inca Garcilaso was every bit as much the Christian, Neoplatonist, and humanist as he was the descendant of Túpac Inca Yupanqui's panaca, and although these two perspectives and priorities often reside in an uneasy tension and implicit contest in the *Royal Commentaries*, one does not necessarily invalidate the other. The conflict between the ethnohistorical discrepancies in Inca Garcilaso's work we have been considering thus far derives from the explicitly universalizing and idealizing tendencies of Neoplatonism and the partial and partisan nature of Inca oral histories. The reconciliation Inca Garcilaso attempts to realize in this confrontation between the European universal and the Andean particular is twofold: he reformulates elements of Inca religion with symbols and concepts amenable to Christian, Neoplatonic interpretations; and at the same time, he projects the interests and priorities of his panaca, centered in Cuzco, as the universal norms of the Inca empire, much to the detriment and exclusion of other indigenous perspectives. The manifold political orientation and revisionist trajectory of the *Royal Commentaries* thus reveal a double movement, in which each cultural perspective is informed, counterposed, and intersected by the "other," and these intercultural cross-currents both ground and valorize the irreducibly plural mestizo subjectivity from which Inca Garcilaso narrates the indigenous past.

Inca Garcilaso's Neoplatonist convictions and his fidelity to his Inca ancestors by no means exhaust the intellectual resources or the political sympathies informing his work, and it would be unwise to reduce the *Royal Commentaries* to a mere elaboration of these motifs.[24] For instance, Inca Garcilaso makes no effort to disguise the fact that his loyalties extend to those whom he dubs the first and second conquerors of Peru, the Spaniards who had entered the country with Francisco Pizarro, Diego de Almagro, and Pedro de Alvarado, with the last of which companies his father Captain Sebastián Garcilaso de la Vega arrived (Part 2, Book I, Chapter XL, vol. 1, 107). His most vocal exaltations of the Spanish conquerors are primarily found in the Second Part of the *Royal Commentaries*, beginning with the "Prologue." Inca Garcilaso claims that his second reason for composing the *Royal Commentaries* "was to celebrate (if not honorably, at least appropriately) the greatness of the heroic Spaniards who won with their valor and military science, for God, for their King, and for themselves, this rich empire, whose names, worthy of cedars, live in the book of life and will live forever in the memory of mortals."[25] As the Second Part gets under way, we encounter a panegyric to the "name and genealogy of the Pizarros," in which the four Pizarro brothers (Francisco, Hernando, Juan, and Gonzalo) are represented as nothing less than providential agents: "through their great works and incredible deeds, they removed them [the Indians] from the infernal darkness in which they were dying and gave them the evangelical light in which they now live!" (Part 2, Book I, Chapter II, vol. 1, 22).[26] Finally, in the last chapter of the Second Part, Inca Garcilaso reminds us that the latter half of his history had been written to fulfill an obligation to "my father and his illustrious and generous companions" (*a mi padre y a sus ilustres y generosos compañeros*) (Part 2, Book VIII, Chapter XXI, vol. 3, 254).

Given, then, that Inca Garcilaso represents and defends the interests of his Inca ancestors and Spanish forefathers (the conquistadors and encomenderos), an understated, yet nevertheless conspicuous argument of the *Royal Commentaries* is that there was, or rather should have been, a natural progression from Inca rule, as praeparatio evangelica, to the Spanish conquest and the early encomienda system, the consolidation of which would have completed a historical trajectory from the "infernal darkness" of the Peruvian First Age to the "evangelical light" of Christian revelation.[27] Like the Incas, the first conquerors are represented as ministers of a superordinate power: the former had been ordered by the Sun to educate and civilize the indigenous masses and bring them to a level of natural reason and urbanity that would allow them to easily grasp and accept the doctrines of Christianity (Part 1, Book I, Chapter XV); and the latter had performed the supra-Herculean task of bringing the Gospel across unknown oceans and continents with considerable danger to themselves to fulfill the promise of eternal salvation latent within Inca civilization (Part 2, Book I, Chapter II). The conquests of both the Incas and Spaniards are justified through recourse to divine providence, and for Inca Garcilaso the legitimacy of the *translatio imperii* relies upon the extent to which the Spaniards were able to achieve their mission of spreading the faith in Peru, a mission their Inca predecessors had already begun.

Of course, this providential justification of the Spanish conquest, along with the linear and teleological historical movement it entails, is thoroughly European in both its inspiration and intended audience. It is complemented, however, by an account of the Spanish arrival in Peru amenable to the understandings of potential Andean readers. As mentioned above, Inca Garcilaso turns to Viracocha to aid him in this task. On numerous occasions throughout the First and Second parts of the *Royal Commentaries*, Inca Garcilaso explains why the Spanish conquerors were called Viracochas by the indigenous inhabitants of Tahuantinsuyu. First, the phantasm Viracocha that had appeared to the banished prince was bearded, clothed from head to foot, held a strange animal at the end of a leash (Part 1, Book IV, Chapter XXI, vol. 1, 243), and a statue of him with these characteristics was constructed in his honor at Cacha (Part 1, Book V, Chapter XXII). When the Spaniards arrived, the Indians immediately recognized their resemblance to this statue and for this they applied the name Viracocha to the invaders. Second, when the Spaniards captured Atahualpa, the Incas thought they had been sent from heaven as "sons of their god Viracocha" (*hijos de su dios Viracocha*) to liberate Cuzco from the tyrannies of Atahualpa, just as the phantasm Viracocha had inspired and supported the Inca Viracocha in his defense of Cuzco from the rebelling Chancas (Part 1, Book V, Chapter XXI, vol. 1, 302).[28] Next, through the use of omens and auguries the Inca Viracocha had prophesied the arrival of foreigners in the empire after a certain number of Incas had reigned, and that the newcomers would remove indigenous idolatry and displace the Incas from their rule (Part 1, Book V, Chapter XXVIII, vol. 1, 319). This prophecy was kept a royal secret until the reign of the twelfth Inca, Huayna Cápac, when he publicized it after hearing news of strange men off the coast (Part 1, Book IX, Chapter XV, vol. 2, 595–96). The Spaniards were thus called Viracocha after the Inca who had foreseen their arrival and whose prophecy they had fulfilled. Finally, the Indians used the name Viracocha to refer to the Spaniards because of the harquebuses and artillery they brought with them (Part 1, Book V, Chapter XXI, vol. 1, 301). The Indians thought these Spanish weapons resembled the tripartite atmospheric phenomena of lightning, thunder, and the thunderbolt, all of which are included in the Quechua word *illapa*. Illapa, moreover, were objects of respect but not worship within Inca religion, according to Inca Garcilaso, because they were "servants of the Sun" (*criados del sol*) (Part 1, Book II, Chapter I, vol. 1, 68).[29] As such, the Indians were strengthened in their belief that the conquerors were Viracochas, for, as his true sons, the Sun had given them his very own weapons (Part 2, Book I, Chapter XL, vol. 1, 107).

Once again, Inca Garcilaso did not initiate the discourse that equated Spaniards with Viracochas. Rather, and as Franklin Pease has suggested, the notion that indigenous peoples worshipped their conquerors as gods, i.e., Viracochas, appears to have been either appropriated or invented by Spanish historians as a form of self-characterization and supernatural legitimation in the decades following the conquest (Pease 1995: 145–53).[30] For his part, Inca Garcilaso simply adopted the association between Spaniards and Viracochas already in currency and used it in accordance with his own purposes. Pierre

Duviols has argued that these purposes were at least twofold: to establish a symbolic kinship between the Incas and their conquerors; and to allow Garcilaso to legitimately claim the title "Inca" for himself (Duviols 1998: 46–58). In order to understand how the Spaniards are transformed from foreigners into family members through the figure Viracocha, we must recall that the first Inca, Manco Cápac, based the legitimacy of the civilizing mission and political rule of the Incas upon the fable of their divine genealogy.[31] Due to their solar descent and the good works they performed, the Incas called themselves "sons of the Sun" and each member of their dynasty and lineage was referred to as *Intip Churin*, "son of the Sun," by their Indian subjects (Part 1, Book I, Chapter XXIV, vol. 1, 59). When the phantasm Viracocha appeared to the anonymous prince, he addressed the latter as "nephew" and told him "I am the son of the Sun and the brother of Inca Manco Cápac and Coya Mama Ocllo Huaco," making the apparition the ancestral brother-uncle of all Incas (Part 1, Book IV, Chapter XXI, vol. 1, 243).[32] After defeating the Chancas, the prince took the name Inca Viracocha and, as we have seen, later prophesied the advent of the Spaniards. Both the phantasm and the Inca Viracocha share the same ancestry and solar origin, which, for the reasons mentioned above, are extended to include the first and second conquerors. Insofar as the latter resemble the statue of the phantasm and fulfill the Inca's prophecy, they not only inherit this celebrated name but also share this *family tie*. This latent kinship, according to Inca Garcilaso, was recognized by the Incas. At one point Manco Inca hails the Spaniards as "true sons of the god Viracocha and brothers of the Incas" (*verdaderos hijos del Dios Viracocha y hermanos de los Incas*) and remarks that both the Incas and the newcomers "were all of one lineage, sons and descendants of the Sun" (*eran todos de un linaje, hijos y descendientes del sol*) (Part 2, Book II, Chapter XII, vol. 1, 139). Remembering Inca Garcilaso has previously suggested that all the conquerors were called Incas (Part 1, Book IX, Chapter XL, vol. 2, 648) and that his own father was included among them, Garcilaso could then rightfully lay claim to the title "Inca," in Sylvia-Lyn Hilton's words, "through the 'dynastic' authority of his father" (Hilton 1982: XC; my translation).[33]

This overlap between conquerors and Viracochas is therefore central to Inca Garcilaso's revision of the indigenous past in that it allows him to suggest the historically unrealized possibility of a peaceful and potentially progressive resolution to the initial encounters between Incas and Spaniards. It is just as important to notice, moreover, that the first conquerors were honored with this title not simply due to the prophecy of their arrival or their resemblance to a statue, but also thanks to the indigenous expectation that the foreigners would behave like Incas. It will be recalled that the political authority of the Incas was based on a covenant with the Sun-god. The Incas were divinely selected to civilize and rule, yet they were likewise ordered by the Sun always to imitate his example and were "sent to the earth only for the instruction and benefit of those men who live like beasts" (*enviados a la tierra sólo para la doctrina y beneficio de esos hombres que viven como bestias*) (Part 1, Book I, Chapter XV, vol. 1, 42). Part and parcel of this covenant, therefore, is the performance of specific, socially beneficial duties upon which the ethical and political substance of Inca dominance is based. In this sense, the extent to which the new Viracochas conform to the traditional practices of the Incas confirms their implicit membership in the dynastic lineage. Or, in the words of Manco Inca, "we should put more faith in the rectitude of those we take for gods than in our own diligence, for if they are true sons of the Sun, as we believe, they will act like Incas" (Part 2, Book II, Chapter XI, vol. 1, 136).[34]

As soon as the Spaniards arrive, however, there is both dissonance and confusion between indigenous expectation and the developing reality, for some of the conquerors' actions confirm their status as Viracocha Incas and others flatly contradict it. The mere facts of their arrival and their outward appearance, at first, commend the Spaniards as Viracochas due, respectively, to Inca prophecy and the statue of the phantasm. Moreover, in an act that both recalls Inca Viracocha's defense and restoration of Cuzco from the invading Chancas as well as explicitly links the Spaniards with their indigenous ancestor, Francisco Pizarro's execution of Atahualpa actually contributes to rather than detracts from this association (see chapter 4). Insofar as Inca Garcilaso portrays Huáscar as Huayna Cápac's legitimate heir and his half-brother Atahualpa as a usurping tyrant, he assures us that the Indians saw the Spaniards as Viracochas because they had provided a "remedy to the Incas and punishment to the tyrant" (*remedio de los Incas y castigo del tirano*) (Part 1, Book V, Chapter XXVIII, vol. 1, 320). "For this," Inca Garcilaso writes, "they called all the conquerors of Peru Viracocha Inca" (*así llamaron Viracocha Inca a todos los conquistadores del Perú*). Nevertheless, the unprovoked slaughter, looting, and plunder that accompanied the Spaniards on their march through indigenous territory undermined their resemblance to Incas, for, as Inca Garcilaso repeatedly assures us in the First Part, these were actions in which the Incas never engaged. In particular, the foreigners were adored as Viracocha Incas "until the avarice, lust, cruelty and severity with which many of them [the Indians] were treated [by the Spaniards] undeceived them of their false belief, for which they removed the name Inca."[35] According to Inca Garcilaso, the Spaniards retained the name "Viracocha," but those who had shown themselves so inclined to vice and violence forfeited the most august and honorable element of their title. Instead, "Inca: was replaced with *zupay*, a Quechua word, 'which is demon'" (çúpay, *que es demonio*) (Part 2, Book I, Chapter XL, vol. 1, 107).

The Spanish Viracocha is thus a potentially Janus-faced being and a new distinction is drawn between the conquerors as Viracocha Incas, i.e., the potential founders of a new, culturally hybrid dynasty, and Viracocha *zupaycuna*, the diabolical agents of indigenous devastation.[36] Inca Garcilaso's reasons for engendering two species of Spanish Viracochas are rather easy to ascertain. First, the distinction allows him partially to dismantle the villainous monolith of violence and destruction attributed to all Spanish conquerors as a result of the Dominican Friar, first Bishop of Chiapas, and "Defender of the Indians" Bartolomé de Las Casas's withering attack on the conquistadors in his *Brevísima relación de la destrucción de las Indias* (Brief Account of the Destruction of the Indies, 1552). According to Las Casas, the innumerable evils and injustices of the Spanish conquest found their common cause in the atrocious moral characters and egregious deeds of the conquistadors and encomenderos. For Inca Garcilaso, who was raised in the conquistador milieu, Las Casas's views obviously failed to capture the complexity of the situation. While explaining the reasons why some Spaniards were called Incas, Inca Garcilaso proposes that the conquerors should have capitalized on this association in order to disseminate the Catholic faith, which would have been greatly effective. Although he tells us "everything turned out very differently" (*pero pasó todo tan diferente*), he is anxious to point out "it is true that all [Spaniards] should not be blamed, for most of them acted in the office of good Christians" (*es verdad que no se deben culpar todos, que los más hicieron oficio de buenos cristianos*) (Part 1, Book V, Chapter XXI, vol. 1, 301). Inca Garcilaso therefore offers a pluralized view of the moral characters of the conquerors in which some are absolved for their participation in the more horrific and inexcusable aspects of Spanish expansion.

Characterizing some Spaniards as Incas and others as demons, moreover, helps Inca Garcilaso to account for the failure of the Hispano-Inca encounter to realize both the dynastic integration as well as the fusion of cultures and races that are held out in the *Royal Commentaries* as the providential destiny of Peru. At the level of theological causation, however, Inca Garcilaso does not hesitate to credit the Devil with having maliciously intervened to disrupt God's well-laid plans. In fact, following his account of Atahualpa's execution and shortly after informing us that indigenous peoples began calling Spaniards zupay (demons), he explicitly states that the *entire* sequence of disasters recounted in the Second Part had diabolical intercession as its main catalyst. "But the Devil," he writes, "the enemy of the human race, endeavored the opposite, with all his strength and guile, to impede the conversion of the Indians; and although he could not obstruct it completely, he at least impeded it many years, with the help and sound diligence of his ministers, the seven deadly sins, for, in a time of such liberty and opportunity, each of the vices could do what it desired" (Part 2, Book II, Chapter V, vol. 1, 124–25).[37] It is hardly coincidental, then, that Inca Garcilaso has previously linked the new nomenclature and the demonic character of the Viracocha zupaycuna to the mortal sins at the root of their behavior: avarice, lust, and wrath (i.e., cruelty and severity). The Prince of Darkness and his agents are therefore held responsible for the double failure of the early years of Spanish expansion in Peru. They first frustrate God's plan for a just and peaceful union between the Incas and their symbolic Spanish brethren, and then they thwart the establishment and consolidation of encomendero rule by fomenting the civil wars of the early colonial period.

At this point it is legitimate to inquire whether there are any additional and possibly non-European reasons why Inca Garcilaso opted for such an elaborate strategy to depict the potentially congenial and actually catastrophic encounters of Incas and Spaniards through recourse to separate and opposing Viracochas: one of whom, Viracocha Inca, rescues and restores the indigenous empire; and another, Viracocha zupay, who wreaks havoc upon it. It should first be noted that Inca Garcilaso's differentiation between the Spanish Viracochas and his representation of indigenous uncertainty concerning whether the foreigners were allies or enemies may have come from Inca oral traditions in Cuzco rather than his own creativity. For instance, the Spanish historian Juan de Betanzos, who was not only one of the most accomplished Quechua linguists and translators of the mid-sixteenth century but also the husband of one of Atahualpa's former wives, Doña Angelina Yupanque, reports a very similar view in the history he based upon the oral histories of his wife's panaca.[38] In the Second Part of his *Suma y narración de los Yngas . . .* (Narrative of the Incas, 1557), Betanzos records that upon hearing of the approach of the Spaniards, Atahualpa was anxious to learn whether the foreigners were "gods, or men like them, and did they do evil or good." Atahualpa decided to take no action whatsoever against them until he had ascertained whether the Spaniards were "*runa quiçachac*" which means "destroyers of the people" or "*viracocha cuna runa allichac*" which means "gods who are benefactors of the people" (Betanzos 1996: 237–38). At another moment, Ciquinchara, one of Atahualpa's captains, explains to the leader, "I don't call them *viracocha* but, rather, *supai cuna*, which means 'devils.'" (Betanzos 1996: 249). Although some of the Quechua phrases used by Betanzos diverge from Inca Garcilaso's Viracocha zupay and Viracocha Inca, his supai cuna is a match for Inca Garcilaso's zupay, and the emphasis on indigenous uncertainty as well as the portrayal of the characteristics and potential roles attributed to the foreigners are nearly identical in both works. This is by no means conclusive proof that Inca Garcilaso was in fact elaborating upon the oral history of his panaca at this moment in his texts, yet it nevertheless suggests that we should not cursorily dismiss the possibility of an indigenous source and subtext.

Delving further into the possibility of Andean meanings within Inca Garcilaso's figurations of Viracocha, the sheer multitude of Viracochas in the *Royal Commentaries* provides another way of approaching the problem. As we have seen, there are at least five Viracochas (and possibly six if the statue/*huaca* of Viracocha at Cacha is included) with distinct, yet at times complementary and opposing personalities and functions present in the narrative. There is the deity Viracocha (in some instances explicitly equated with Pachacámac), the ancestral phantasm Viracocha, the Inca Viracocha, and the two Spanish Viracochas, Inca and zupay. In a very general and perhaps crude way, the proliferation and mutations of Viracochas in the *Royal Commentaries* appear to resonate with Andean conceptions of this incredibly complex figure. Although early Spanish observers were frequently confused as to whether Viracocha was an ancestor, mythical culture-hero, or a god, modern scholars of the Andes region have shown that Viracocha was a single, multiple godhead that manifested and unfolded into different personalities in accordance with a penumbra of diverse aspects and functions.[39] For instance, in the Inca pantheon the various faces of the Sun (*Punchao/Churi Inti*, the son Sun; *Apu Inti*, the Lord Sun; and *Inti Huauqui*, the Brother Sun), the Moon (*Quilla*), Venus (*Chasca*), the Stars (*cóillur*), the threefold lightning (*Chuquilla*, *Catuilla*, and *Inti Illapa*), and the rainbow (*cuychu*) *all* represented different attributes and specific personifications of the celestial entities and atmospheric phenomena contained within the singular and manifold Viracocha.[40] As a multiple godhead, Viracocha would "unfold" into separate personae at precise moments with particular functions in the agrarian cycles and ritual calendar of the Incas. In the festival of Inti Raymi during the winter solstice in June, when the sun is weakest in the southern hemisphere, the deity took the form of Punchao or Churi Inti, the minor or young Sun. By contrast, in the festival of Cápac Raymi during the summer solstice in December, when the sun in the southern hemisphere is at full strength, the deity appeared as Apu Inti, the Lord Sun. The celestial godhead could unfold into even more specific aspects and functions as in the case of Inti Illapa. Inti Illapa was the servant of Viracocha and the "second cause" of all meteorological and atmospheric phenomena, and, as such, could appear as the tripartite lightning (lightning, thunder, and thunderbolt), rain, wind, hail, snow, comets, or rainbows, and so on (Demarest 1981: 13–41, particularly 27, diagram 4, 41, diagram 7).

There are both historical as well as conceptual reasons, according to Arthur Demarest, for the astounding multiplicity and fecundity of the manifold Viracocha. Historically, it was a common practice of the Incas (as it had been for their predecessors, the Huari and Tiahuanaco) in the course of their expansion to incorporate the regional gods of their allies and subjects into the hierarchical pantheon of the state cult. The Inca gods, Viracocha and the Sun, were of course given prominence and required tribute, yet the worship of local gods continued. The latter were simply supplanted and reassigned to lesser status in the state religion (Demarest 1981: 43–54). For this reason Viracocha came to incorporate other major deities of the Andes, the worship of which antedated Inca contact with their respective regions, such as Tunupa, Illapa, and Pachacámac (Rostworowski 1983: 21–49). Conceptually, in Demarest's words, "pre-Columbian religions emphasized the *movements and transformations of astronomical phenomena*, not merely the deification of specific heavenly bodies," the latter of which was the practice among pagans of European antiquity (original emphasis). "As a consequence, the partially personified pre-Columbian deifications of celestial phenomena overlapped and even transformed themselves into each other just as natural phenomena do in time and space" (Demarest 1981: 72 and 73). Insofar as the delicate ecological balance of life in the Andes required indigenous peoples to attend meticulously to the rhythms of human life-cycles, the change of climatic seasons, and the movements of the sun, moon, and stars, they developed a correspondingly dynamic, fluid, and multi-aspected notion of the divine.

Considering how drastic and completely untranslatable were the differences between the Andean notion of a multiple god-head and both pagan

European as well as Judeo-Christian conceptions of divinity, it is hardly surprising that Inca Garcilaso steadfastly refused to provide a straightforward description of either Viracocha or his proper place in Inca religion. In defending his assertion that Pachacámac was the name of the Inca high god against the reports of his Spanish predecessors, he puts it rather bluntly, "in their histories they give another name for God, which is Ticci Viracocha, by which I do not know what is meant, and neither do they" (Part 1, Book II, Chapter II, vol. 1, 72).[41] Of course, there was the additional difficulty that the polytheism and incommensurability of indigenous religions with Catholicism helped to justify Europeans in their belief that Amerindians were rationally, culturally, and morally inferior. And in this sense, Zamora, MacCormack, and other commentators who have suggested that Inca Garcilaso preferred Pachacámac over Viracocha for the former's greater conformity to Neoplatonic and Christian concepts are indeed correct.

Nevertheless, and as per Mazzotti's research mentioned above, the connection in indigenous oral traditions between Pachacámac and Túpac Inca Yupanqui, the founder of Inca Garcilaso's panaca, certainly contributed to his choice. Read in light of both European and Andean contexts, it can therefore be seen that Inca Garcilaso could ill afford simply to omit Viracocha from his account of Inca civilization despite the numerous difficulties entailed by the complexity of Viracocha for his virtually monotheistic and fundamentally proto-Christian portrayal of Inca religion. Since Viracocha was "the most conspicuous of the gods in the Andean area" (Rostworowski 1983: 30; my translation), completely excluding this deity from his work would have not only blatantly contradicted all currently published knowledge on Peru, but also jeopardized Inca Garcilaso's authority before an indigenous audience for whom the absence of Viracocha would have been troubling indeed. Instead, Inca Garcilaso establishes his own hierarchy of the Inca pantheon in which Viracocha is not erased, but rather demoted. Though he first claims that the Incas confined their worship to the unknown Pachacámac and the Sun as the former's visible manifestation and that these were the only gods in their religion (Part 1, Book II, Chapter II, vol. 1, 70), he later amends this view. He explains that the Spaniards were called Viracocha for their harquebuses and artillery (*illapa*) and comments on Blas Valera's suggestion that in this sense Viracocha meant "'*numen*,' which is will and power of God." Inca Garcilaso continues, "he [Valera] says this not because this is what Viracocha means, but for the divinity in which the Indians held the phantasm, who, after the Sun, was worshipped as a god and given the second place. And after him they worshipped their Incas and kings. And they had no other gods" (Part 1, Book V, Chapter XXI, vol. 1, 301).[42] The new hierarchy runs as follows: Pachacámac, Sun, Viracocha, Incas. Despite his frequent attempts to rationalize away Viracocha's importance and his claims that he was a "modern" and "imagined" god, Inca Garcilaso includes him as a secondary deity within the Inca cult.

Somewhat like the Andean high god, Inca Garcilaso's Viracocha "unfolds" as well. From the god stems the phantasm who communicates with the anonymous prince who, in turn, takes the name Viracocha. From the god-phantasm-Inca complex comes the prophecy of the Spanish arrival, the latter of whom engender two more Viracochas. In the branch of associations that links the Spaniards and their artillery with Viracocha, moreover, the indigenous personification of Viracocha as Inti Illapa, the god of thunder, lightning, and the thunderbolt, controller of meteorological phenomena, and "servant of the Sun," as Inca Garcilaso calls him is maintained. So, too, is Viracocha's role as Inti Huauqui, the Brother Sun of Inca ancestor worship, which was reserved exclusively for the Inca ruling classes.[43] Insofar as the phantasm Viracocha declares himself to be "son of the Sun and brother of the Inca Manco Cápac and Coya Mama Ocllo Huaco," his relationship as brother-uncle is explicitly established. Finally, through his kinship with the Incas, who were called Intip Churin, "sons of the Sun," Viracocha's manifestation as Churi Inti or Punchao, the Son Sun or minor Sun, is implicitly confirmed. A major difference, however, is that whereas in Andean religions the solar godhead was a multiaspected attribute and separable series of referents *within* the incomprehensible Viracocha (Viracocha Pachayachachi), in Inca Garcilaso's revision Viracocha becomes an agent and "son" of the Sun, which is actually the visible face of the invisible Pachacámac.

The personification of Viracocha's solar unfolding that is either completely absent or so thoroughly diminished as to be rendered insignificant in the *Royal Commentaries* is Apu Inti, the Lord Sun of full maturity, who was worshipped during the initiation of young Inca nobles in the ritual of Cápac Raymi held during the summer solstice in December (Araníbar 1991: vol. 2, 687–688). Inca Garcilaso does relate that "they called the principal festival of the Sun *Cápac Raymi*" (*Cápac Raimi llamaban a la fiesta del sol*) (Part 1, Book VIII, Chapter VII, vol. 2, 508), yet in his lengthy description of this "solemn Easter of the Sun" (*la pascua solemne del sol*), he claims that it was held in June and called "*Inti Raymi*" (Part 1, Book VI, Chapters XX–XXIV). The fact is, however, and as Inca Garcilaso was certainly aware through his reading of José de Acosta, Cápac Raymi and Inti Raymi were two separate rituals marking precise moments in the agrarian seasons and charting different phases of the sun's solstitial movement through the southern hemisphere.[44] Inti Raymi celebrated the moment of rebirth and rejuvenation of the Sun following its progressive diminution and weakening through the Andean autumn. As such, the Sun was represented as Churi Inti or Punchao, a figuratively apt "young Sun," and the idol Churi Inti, which Inca Garcilaso never mentions, was actually a gold statue in the shape of a ten-year-old boy. Cápac Raymi, comparatively, gave thanks to Apu Inti, the Lord Sun in its adulthood and fullest resplendence, anticipating the fruition of the agrarian cycle and celebrating the coming of age and initiation (*huaracu*) of aristocratic youths into the ranks of Inca nobility (Demarest 1981: 22–31). Whereas Churi Inti stood for the hopeful beginning of a new cycle, Apu Inti represented its magnificent culmination and Apu Inti was therefore both congratulated and thanked for the abundant life and greatness he provided the Incas. Insofar as Inca Garcilaso intentionally collapses the two rituals into one, i.e., Inti Raymi in the winter solstice of June, he portrays the Incas solely as Intip Churin/Churi Inti/Punchao. As a consequence, Cápac Raymi, Apu Inti, and the fulfillment they symbolize are either displaced or deferred (Mazzotti 1996a: 201). Instead, the climatic and solar cycles that reflect both the equilibrium of the natural environment as well as the religio-political role of the Incas as the superintendents of that equilibrium are ruptured. In the *Royal Commentaries*, Apu Inti, the most glorious Sun, never arrives.

Knowing that Inca Garcilaso structured his version of indigenous history around a gaping omission in the natural evolution and ritual expression of its solar cycle is instructive indeed, because this, for him, was the lacuna that should have been filled by the arrival of the Spanish Viracocha Incas. It is for this reason that Inca Garcilaso went to such lengths to authorize some Spaniards as symbolic kinsmen, legitimate heirs, and prophetic restorers of the Inca dynasty in his own, often idiosyncratic, indigenous terms. When Huayna Cápac finally publicizes the prophecy of Spanish arrival on his deathbed, he says "these new people will come and fulfill what our Father the Sun has told us and will win our empire and become its lords . . . their law will be better than ours and their arms more powerful and invincible than yours" (Part 1, Book IX, Chapter XV, vol. 2, 596).[45] To the extent that the Spaniards were capable of proving themselves to be Viracocha Incas, Huayna Cápac's words suggest they would be Viracochas of a higher and more powerful magnitude. This point is reiterated when Atahualpa welcomes Hernando Pizarro and Hernando de Soto as "Cápac Viracocha" (Part 2, Book I, Chapter XIX, vol. 1,

57). The Quechua word *Cápac*, according to Inca Garcilaso, meant "'rich,' not in goods of fortune, but in excellence and greatness of spirit" (*Cápac quiere decir 'rico,' no de bienes de fortuna sino de excelencia y grandeza de ánimo*), and was also used to refer to "many other similar things they [Indians] wished to exalt with this name Cápac" (*Y así otras cosas semejantes que querían engrandecer con este apellido Cápac*) (Part 1, Book VIII, Chapter VII, vol. 2, 508).[46] Atahualpa thus ascribes an especially dignified status to the new Viracochas and extends their implicit association with Apu Inti shortly thereafter. He turns to his Indian attendants and says, "You see here the very same face and figure and habit of our God Viracocha, just as our ancestor Inca Viracocha, to whom he appeared in this image, left him portrayed in the statue and form of stone" (Part 2, Book I, Chapter XIX, vol. 1, 57).[47] As we have seen, the ritual of Cápac Raymi was consecrated to Apu Inti, the Lord Sun, moreover, it occurred under the patronage of Viracocha (Demarest 1981: 28). As a final piece of evidence, in his drawing of the festival of Cápac Inti Raymi, the Andean artist and writer Guaman Poma de Ayala portrays the Sun with a beard and mustache, the same facial hair Inca Garcilaso identifies with the phantasm Viracocha, his statue, and the Spaniards (Guaman Poma de Ayala 1980: vol. 1, 232, f. 258[260]).

This symbolic representation of the Spanish Viracocha Incas as "Cápac Viracochas" and, hence, the emissaries of Apu Inti's belated arrival, however, is a short-lived one. As we have seen, indigenous uncertainty as to the true nature of the foreigners as well as the latter's propensity for destruction quickly result in the Spaniards being identified as Viracocha zupay. The indigenous notion for cataclysmic events, such as those wrought in the *Royal Commentaries* by the Viracocha zupay (demons and agents of the Devil) is *pachacuti*. The Andean sense of past, present, and future was constituted by a cyclical movement through and a possible return of distinct epochs, with the transitional moments from epoch to epoch being marked by upheavals or pachacuti.[48] For instance, Sarmiento de Gamboa reports that in the Andean First Age before the advent of the Incas, Viracocha Pachayachachi punished the disobedience of the first created humans with an *uñu pachacuti*, "which means 'water that overturns the land'" (Sarmiento de Gamboa 1999: 29). Guaman Poma de Ayala defines *pachacuti* as "the punishment from God" (Guaman Poma de Ayala 1980: 74, f. 94[94]), and goes on to relate how Inca Pachacútec was so named due to the natural disasters that coincided with his rule. In nigh inimitable prose, he writes: "In the time of this Inca there was a very great deal of Indian mortality and hunger and thirst and pestilence and divine punishment, for it did not rain for seven years; others say ten years. And there were tempests, and most of the time was all crying and burying the dead. And for this said Inca was called Pachacuti Inca, enormous punishments from God in this reign and in the world" (Guaman Poma de Ayala 1980: 89, f. 109[109]).[49]

Guaman Poma de Ayala's description of pachacuti nicely captures its sense as supernatural disaster, and, interestingly enough, coincides with Inca Garcilaso's use of the term. Moreover, pachacuti brings us back to Inca Garcilaso's revision of indigenous history in which Inca Viracocha is given the victory over the Chancas rather than Pachacútec Inca. In translating the name "Pachacútec," Inca Garcilaso notes that it is a present participle that means "'he who turns over' or 'he who overturns or reverses the world'" (*'el que vuelve' o 'el que trastorna o trueca el mundo'*). He then expounds upon a Quechua refrain, *pácham cútin*: "'*pácham cútin*: which is to say 'the world is reversed.' And for the most part they [Indians] say this when matters of importance are turned from good to bad. And on rare occasions they say it when they are turned from bad to good, because they say it is more certain that things are turned from good to bad than from bad to good" (Part 1, Book V, Chapter XXVIII, vol. 1, 318).[50] Inca Viracocha, according to Inca Garcilaso, should have been called "Pachacútec," because the flight of his father, Yáhuar Huácac, from the threat of the Chancas had reversed the empire "from good to bad" (*de bien en mal*), and the young prince's heroic stand thus turned it back "from bad to good" (*de mal en bien*). Yet he could not take the name Pachacútec, because all of his subjects already called him Viracocha in honor of the phantasm that appeared to him. Inca Viracocha, therefore, gave the name Pachacútec to his son (Part 1, Book V, Chapter XXVIII, vol. 1, 318). However, insofar as *pachacuti* only rarely signaled a change for the better, we are left to wonder whether Inca Pachacútec's reign represented a turn for the worse in indigenous history. Perhaps, and Guaman Poma de Ayala definitely thought it did.[51] We do know, however, through Atahualpa's future purges of Túpac Inca Yupanqui's *panaca* in the civil war with Huáscar, that Inca Pachacútec's *panaca* would eventually unleash a cataclysm on Inca Garcilaso's own.

This family disaster, as per Rostworowski cited earlier, is one of the major motives behind Inca Garcilaso's drastic revision of these events. It should also be noted, however, that this revision *prefigures and forecasts* a series of events (Atahualpa's purges) that only occur later in both the course of historical development as well as the diachronic progression of the *Royal Commentaries*. Such instances of foreshadowing in the *Royal Commentaries*, often extremely heavy-handed, are far too numerous to even attempt to count, and his exaggerated use of this device, in part, gives the work its static and repetitious feel (particularly in the First Part).[52] There are times, however, when Inca Garcilaso's use of foreshadowing is very subtle and can be easily overlooked. For instance, if we attend to his definition of pachacuti, and in particular his language of turning from good to bad or bad to good (*de bien en mal* and *de mal en bien*), we find that nearly identical language occurs at especially significant moments in the narrative. First, in the chapter on the myth of Inca origins (the importance of which can hardly be overstated), in order to remove the people from the obscure darkness in which they dwelt, God permitted a "morning star" (*lucero del alba*) to emerge and give some notice of natural law, urbanity, and so forth. God further saw fit "that the descendants of that one, *proceeding from good to better*, were to improve those beasts and convert them into men" (Part 1, Book I, Chapter XV, vol. 1, 39).[53] The second instance, as we have just seen, occurs between Inca Viracocha and Inca Pachacútec. Next, Atahualpa has this to say to Hernando Pizarro and Hernando de Soto during their first meeting: "I say that I take these times to be most felicitous, for the God Viracocha having sent such guests in them, and that these same times promise us that *the state of the republic will be turned to a better lot, the change and turn certifying the tradition of our elders and the words of my father Huayna Cápac's testament*" (Part 2, Book I, Chapter XX, vol. 1, 60).[54] Atahualpa turns out to have been mistaken, yet the ambience of tremendous change and the linguistic consistency mark this moment, and the two before it, as a pachacuti.

There are at least two additional occasions earmarked as similarly pregnant with tumultuous change and, therefore, are to be counted as pachacuti as well. The first of these, the defeat of the rebel and temporary ruler of Peru, Gonzalo Pizarro, at the battle of Sacsahuana in 1548, occurs through a series of parallels (Gonzalo Pizarro's rebellion is treated at greater length in chapter 5). For the present purposes, it is sufficient to note that when Inca Garcilaso records the site of Inca Viracocha's great victory over the Chancas, Sacsahuana, he takes the opportunity to inform us parenthetically "and after it was where the battle between Gonzalo Pizarro and [Licentiate Pedro] de la Gasca [occurred]" (*y donde fue después la batalla de Gonzalo Pizarro y el de la Gasca*) (Part 1, Book V, Chapter XVII, vol. 1, 291). Before Gonzalo's defeat at Sacsahuana, he had been victorious at Huarina, in which battle Inca Garcilaso's father played a notoriously controversial role (Part 2, Book V, Chapter XIII). After the victory over the forces of Charles V at Huarina, Gonzalo entered Cuzco, where the Indians were gathered in the plaza and were "hailing in loud voices, *calling him Inca*, and other majestic titles that they used to say to their natural Kings in their triumphs" (Part 2, Book V, Chapter XXVII, vol. 2, 225).[55] Whereas Inca Viracocha's victory at Sacsahuana was a turning of the world for the better, Gonzalo Pizarro's loss at Sacsahuana was a reversal for the worse. This, too, is mirrored almost perfectly in the reasons for their respective outcomes: Inca Viracocha was successful against the Chancas because he received military reinforcements from allies (Part 1, Book V, Chapter XVII); and Gonzalo Pizarro lost the battle and his life to the royalists because his troops and friends deserted him (Part 2, Book V, Chapter XXXIV). As such, Gonzalo's loss is the inverse, or pachacuti, of Inca Viracocha's restoration of Cuzco and the empire.

Finally, Viceroy Francisco de Toledo's execution of Túpac Amaru, the exile of royal Incas and mestizos attributed to him by Inca Garcilaso (Part 2, Book VIII, Chapters XVIII and XIX), and his reform program of *reducciones*, i.e., "reducing" Indians by forcibly resettling them from their ancestral lands into specially designated Spanish towns, summon the final pachacuti. If the "order and mandate" (*orden y mandato*), in other words, the very *speech* of the Father Sun engendered the civil and political life of the Incas from the "living death" (*viviendo o muriendo*) of the First Age (Part 1, Book I, Chapter XV, vol. 1, 39), then the eerie silence at Túpac Amaru's execution is the ultimate and catastrophic undoing of such a divinely inspired existence. Upon mounting the executioner's scaffold, Túpac Amaru "raised his right arm with his hand open, and put it to the right of his ear, and from there he lowered it little by little, placing it on his right thigh. With which, the Indians understanding that he was ordering them to be quiet, their cries and shouts ceased, and *they left such a silence it seemed that there had never been a living soul in the whole of that city*" (Part 2, Book VIII, Chapter XIX, vol. 3, 250).[56] For an oral society such as the Inca, in which the contours of social life were predicated upon ritualized speech, this silence is portrayed by Inca Garcilaso as a violent eruption of meaninglessness and a total erasure of the very vitality of the past.[57]

Moreover, after Manco Cápac founded Cuzco, he established towns in its vicinity in the four *suyus*, or districts (Part 1, Book I, Chapter XX), and provided each local tribe with tokens of dress in order to avoid confusion among them and to allow them to maintain their ethnic identities (Part 1, Book I, Chapter XXII).[58] "A viceroy," however, reduced these villages into large towns, combining five or six villages into one and seven or eight into another, "from which resulted many difficulties, which, being odious, are left unsaid"

(*De lo cual resultaron muchos inconvenientes, que por ser odiosos se dejan de decir*) (Part 1, Book I, Chapter XX, vol. 1, 52). One of the difficulties that arose from Toledo's reductions (mentioned at considerable length) was the resurgence of indigenous dialects and the emergence of a veritable Peruvian Babel. According to Inca Garcilaso, this was the complete reversal of Inca efforts to establish Quechua as the official, nationally unifying, imperial language (Part 1, Book VII, Chapters I–IV). Toledo, therefore, had not only overturned all of the major achievements of the Incas, but he had also extinguished their line. With the help of a passage taken from Blas Valera, Inca Garcilaso could thus relate: "In our days, the Viceroy Francisco de Toledo overturned, changed, and revoked many of those laws and statues established by this Inca [Pachacútec]. The Indians, astonished at his absolute powers, called him 'second Pachacútec,' which is to say that he was the reformer of the first reformer" (Part 1, Book VI, Chapter XXXVI, vol. 1, 409).[59]

There are thus at least five *pachacuticuna*, or turnings, in the *Royal Commentaries*: two of which are for the better (Manco Cápac and Inca Viracocha); two for the worse (Gonzalo Pizarro and Toledo); and one (Spanish arrival/Atahualpa's execution) that is ambiguous, open-ended, and could only *retrospectively* be characterized as the harbinger of misfortune.[60] The final pachacuti, represented by Viceroy Toledo, overthrows everything that precedes it and therefore returns us to the darkness and sociopolitical destructuration of the Andean First Age prior to the advent of the Incas. The First Age, despite the fact that Inca Garcilaso underscores the proclivities for violence and vice of its inhabitants, is actually representative of a rather specific social and political condition rendered in the Spanish term *behetrías*.[61] Inca Garcilaso writes *behetrías* means "without order or government" (*sin orden ni gobierno*), and continues by remarking that the characteristics of those in such a condition were: "neither did they have towns, nor worship gods, nor did they possess the expedients of men. They lived like beasts, scattered through the fields, mountains and valleys, killing each other without knowing why. They recognized no lord, and therefore their provinces had no names" (Part 1, Book VI, Chapter XI, vol. 1, 351).[62] Even the most cursory reading of the chapters in which Inca Garcilaso describes the First Age (Part 1, Book I, Chapters IX–XIV) demonstrates that behetrías was precisely the predicament in which Andeans found themselves before the Incas. Likewise, Toledo's execution of Túpac Amaru and the social disorganization and linguistic confusion caused by the reducciones signal the return of the First Age after the Incas. Inca Garcilaso's baroque shadings of the carnality and savagery in the First Age, therefore, doubly reflect the pre-Inca past and the post-Inca present as a cyclical development from social chaos to social chaos.[63]

After the whirlwind of the approximately 1,500 pages of the *Royal Commentaries*, we return to the beginning. Although it is essential to traverse both parts in their entirety while attempting to chart a course between possible European and Andean meanings in order to grasp their full significance, the final Toledan overturning is forecast very early within the narrative structure of the First Part. The First Age gives way to Manco Cápac and Mama Ocllo Huaco, yet *before* the account of Manco Cápac's life concludes in Book I, Chapter XXVI, we are informed of the disturbances caused by the reducciones of a certain viceroy (Part 1, Book I, Chapter XX, vol. 1, 52). From both this eleven-chapter encapsulation of the First Age and its Toledan return (Part 1, Book I, Chapters IX–XX) as well as the rhetorical orientation of the *Royal Commentaries* as a revision of the indigenous past amenable to the understandings of prospective contemporary audiences, the cyclical trajectory of the *Royal Commentaries* is present in embryonic form from the very outset. It is not unreasonable to suggest, therefore, that through this condensed forecast, Inca Garcilaso was attempting both to signal and defend his alterations of the Inca past to an indigenous audience by appealing to the conditions of their present lives. In other words, if the movement of Inca history is a cyclical development from darkness and social turmoil back to darkness and social turmoil, and the elaboration of this trajectory is anticipated from the beginning, then it may be the case that the *entire* evolution of the Inca empire presented in the *Royal Commentaries* occurs for Andean readers under the inauspicious constellation of its eventual destruction.

If this hypothesis is correct, then there should be some textual evidence of Inca Garcilaso's early invocation of the darkness and turbulence looming overhead as both the past and present of Peru that could be interpreted as such by potential Andean readers. This, I would like to suggest, brings us back to Inca Garcilaso's preference for the "unknown god" Pachacámac over the deity Viracocha, and it represents the last piece of this protracted puzzle. First, in terms of placement, directly following the account of Manco Cápac's life (which closes Book I of the First Part), the opening chapter of Book II first introduces us to Pachacámac and inaugurates Inca Garcilaso's protestations on the status of Pachacámac as the singular, high god of the Inca pantheon as well his concomitant demotion of the god Viracocha. Of course, we already know that Inca Garcilaso's treatment of Pachacámac represents an extremely conspicuous revision of Inca religion, and this most certainly would not have gone unnoticed by a prospective Andean audience. We have likewise seen that Inca Garcilaso champions Pachacámac due to the overlap between the meaning of the Quechua word and concepts within Christian Neoplatonism as well as for the connection in Inca oral traditions between this deity and the founder of Inca Garcilaso's panaca, Túpac Inca Yupanqui.[64] What has remained unexplored by commentators, however, is the symbolic importance of Pachacámac's attributes in indigenous contexts and how those attributes are both carried over, revised, and reappropriated in the *Royal Commentaries*.

Of foremost importance is the portrayal of Pachacámac in Andean mythology as a god who disappears, absconds, or is absent from view. For instance, in the myths of Huarochirí, when Cuni Raya Viracocha arrives in the valley of Pachacámac, he finds Pachacámac's daughters, but not their father (*Hijos de Pariya Qaqa:* 1983: vol. 1, 13). In a myth related by Augustinian Friar Antonio de Calancha, in which the antagonism between Pachacámac and his brother, the Sun's ally, Vichama, is nearly constant, Pachacámac is similarly missing when the moment of battle with Vichama arrives. In her analysis of these and other sources, Rostworowski has argued that, in at least one of his dual manifestations, that of Hanan, Pachacámac was a celestial deity associated with darkness, night, and obscurity whose conflicts with a solar brother-double represented the eternal struggle between night and day.[65] Moreover, in his complementary Hurin manifestation, in addition to his obscurity Pachacámac possessed chthonic and subterranean qualities that indicated his ability to control seismic phenomena, such as tremors and earthquakes, thus marking his appearances in indigenous myths as moments of potential cataclysm (Rostworowski 1983: 42–49). Or, as Pachacámac himself put it directly to Túpac Inca Yupanqui when the latter requested his assistance during a rebellion: "I am the one who shakes you and the whole world. I have not spoken because I would not only exterminate these enemies, but at the same time I would also destroy all of you [Incas] and the entire world." It was for reasons such as these that Pachacámac was also known as *Pachacuyuchic*, for, "when he became angry the world moved" (*Hijos de Pariya Qaqa* 1983: vol. 2, 181, 177, respectively; my translation).

As R. Tom Zuidema has demonstrated, in the religious cult of the Incas Pachacámac and Viracocha were different names for the same, multiaspected deity. He states, "Pachacámac was the same as Viracocha, and the temple and pyramid of Pachacámac was perhaps the most important sanctuary to Viracocha in their realm" (Zuidema 1962: 163). Franklin Pease has added that the Incas' joint worship of Viracocha and Pachacámac represented the duality and opposition of Hanan and Hurin (mountain and coast; high and low, respectively), and in this juxtaposition Viracocha retained his celestial attributes while Pachacámac's chthonic characteristics were emphasized (Pease 1973: 30–39). For his part, we have already seen that Inca Garcilaso acknowledged, yet downplayed, the identification between Pachacámac and Viracocha, and, despite his many refusals, allowed Viracocha a secondary or tertiary place in his version of the Inca pantheon. If we move beyond the associations between Pachacámac and either Neoplatonic symbols or the Unknown God of the Athenians (Acts 17: 22–33), we find that Inca Garcilaso's Pachacámac, too, is a dark and chthonic deity who is present in times of severe trial.

Pachacámac's propensities for darkness are at first established in the *Royal Commentaries* through his refusal to be seen. Inca Garcilaso tells us that although Pachacámac was held in higher veneration than the Sun, no temples or sacrifices were dedicated to him "because they [Indians] said that they did not know him because *he did not allow himself to be seen*" (*porque decían que no le conocían porque no se había dejado ver*) (Part 1, Book II, Chapter IV, vol. 1, 76). The association of Pachacámac with invisibility and sightlessness is reiterated shortly thereafter in one of Inca Garcilaso's characteristically oblique anecdotes. In a discussion of indigenous medicinal herbs, Inca Garcilaso mentions a root called *matecllu*, which was used to restore sight to "ailing eyes" (*ojos enfermos*). He tells us how he himself had used the root to cure a boy whose eye was "jumping out of his skull" (*saltarle del casco*), and how he recommended it to an unnamed Spaniard whose sight had become "completely blinded by clouds" (*totalmente ciego de nubes*). He concludes the anecdote by remarking on the simplicity of indigenous ideas on natural philosophy, astrology, and theology, and reminding us "all of Inca theology was enclosed in the name Pachacámac" (*toda la teología de los Incas se encerró en el nombre Pachacámac*) (Part 1, Book II, Chapter XXV, vol. 1, 126–27). The additional information about Inca theology and Pachacámac appears quite out of place as a summary of the foregoing anecdote until it is understood that the indigenous association of Pachacámac with darkness and obscurity is thereby invoked.

Inca Garcilaso goes further, however, and completes the sketch of Pachacámac as not only a nocturnal, but also a chthonic and potentially destructive deity. During solar eclipses, Indians said "the Sun was angry for some offense they had committed against him, since *he showed his disturbed face, like an angry man*. And they foretold, similar to astrologers, that some grave punishment was coming to them" (Part 1, Book II, Chapter XXIII, vol. 1, 121).[66] This illustrates Inca Garcilaso was indeed aware that the celestial-solar godhead had a number of changing "faces" corresponding to his natural transformations and that some of these manifestations were ominous indeed. The notion of punishment and destruction, however, is accentuated in his description of a lunar eclipse: "During a lunar eclipse, seeing her darkening, they said that the Moon became ill and that if she became completely obscured, she had died and fallen from the sky, striking all those below, killing them, and that the world had ended" (Part 1, Book II, Chapter XXIII, vol. 1, 121).[67] Although the darkening of the eclipsed Moon only vaguely implies the obscurity of Pachacámac, Inca Garcilaso does not allow the connection to remain uncertain: "When they saw that the Moon was little by little recovering her light, they said that *she was convalescing from her illness because the Pachacámac (who was the sustainer of the universe) had given her health and ordered that she not die, so that the world would not perish*" (Part 1, Book II, Chapter XXIII, vol. 1, 122).[68]

In Andean religions and cosmogony, the Moon (*Quilla* or *Mama Quilla*) was the feminine, celestial symbol of the Inca queens, or *Coyas*, similar to the way in which the Sun, or *Inti*, was the major symbol of the Inca kings. Moreover, in the dual conceptual universe of indigenous Andeans the pairing Hanan/Hurin had analogues in male/female, high/low, dry/wet, hot/cold, and so forth. As the chapter on the founding of Cuzco demonstrates (Part 1, Book I, Chapter XVI), Inca Garcilaso well understood the significance of the Hanan/Hurin, male/female, and high/low doublets, and he was likewise cognizant of the divinity of the Moon, "wife and sister" of the Sun (Part 1, Book II, Chapter IV, vol. 1, 76). While he does mention the dedication of a room to the Moon in *Coricancha*, the House of the Sun (Part 1, Book III, Chapter XXI, vol. 1, 191), he claims that the Moon was honored and venerated, but not worshipped (Part 1, Book II, Chapter IV, vol. 1, 76). This last comment, based upon the distinction between *dulia* and *latria* in Catholicism, is intended to reinforce what Inca Garcilaso represents as the implicit monotheism of Inca religion for the benefit of European readers. The same general strategy, as we have seen, is at work when he Christianizes Pachacámac. Nevertheless, in his description of the lunar eclipse, in which the feminine Moon is linked with darkness, Pachacámac, and the threat of world destruction, Inca Garcilaso is able to retain an image of Pachacámac that resonated with conventional indigenous understandings. This is the face of Pachacámac from below, or Hurin Pachacámac, responsible for seismic convulsions.

Pachacámac's capacity to produce earthquakes and tremors, moreover, recalls the notion of pachacuti, the turning or reversal of the world universe. In the myths of Huarochirí, Pachacámac warns Túpac Inca Yupanqui that his words could not only "shake the world," but also "destroy the entire world." The relationship suggested by the indigenous connections between Pachacámac, pachacuti, and darkness, conflict between night and day, and so on is one in which Pachacámac's arrival carries with it the threat inherent in transition or upheaval. In this sense, and insofar as his anger is to be avoided because it unleashes total disaster, Pachacámac appears to have been invoked or his appeasement required in moments of extreme necessity or calamity either to escape possible suffering or to avoid heaping more woes upon those of the present.[69] This, at any rate, is what Guaman Poma suggests in his relation of a peculiar Inca law. This law ordered that in times of frost or hail, or when maize dried up because no water fell from the heavens, Indians were to don cloaks of mourning, blacken their faces with ashes, climb to the hilltops, and beg Pachacámac for rain with their tears (Guaman Poma de Ayala 1980: vol. 1, 165, f. 190[192]). This notion of imploring Pachacámac out of compulsion and necessity in order to avert disaster is captured in Inca Garcilaso's description of the indigenous reaction to lunar eclipses, because it is Pachacámac who keeps the Moon from colliding with the earth. It is also echoed in his remarks on how the Incas regarded the very name Pachacámac, which he claimed was held "in such great veneration that *they dared not utter it*, and *when they were forced to utter it*, it was done with feeling and signs of great reverence" (Part 1, Book II, Chapter II, vol. 1, 70).[70]

By fixating upon and accentuating very specific Andean undercurrents of Pachacámac's more menacing and destructive characteristics, Inca Garcilaso creates a dark god of vengeance, retribution, and loss. This is most clearly illustrated by the subtle, yet remarkably consistent, distinction drawn between the Spanish conquerors as "sons of the God Viracocha" and "messengers of Pachacámac" in the Second Part. It will be remembered that Inca Garcilaso distinguishes the Spanish Cápac Viracocha Incas (the latent brethren, potential heirs, and implicit emissaries of Apu Inti, the Lord Sun, who were to complete or perfect the Inca dynasty), from the Spanish Viracocha zupay (the diabolical agents of destruction). Yet appended to these separate identifications is the name of either the deity Viracocha or Pachacámac, depending upon whether the Spaniards are respectively viewed as allies or enemies by indigenous persons in the text. For instance, in the first meeting between an Inca and the invaders, Atahualpa's brother, Titu Atauchi, addresses Francisco

Pizarro as "Inca Viracocha, son of the Sun" (Inca Viracocha, hijo del sol) (Part 2, Book I, Chapter XVII, vol. 1, 51). Similarly, when Atahualpa first encounters Hernando Pizarro and Hernando de Soto, "having received them and worshipped them with highest veneration, he said to his captains and soldiers: 'These are sons of our God Viracocha'" (Part 2, Book I, Chapter XIX, vol. 1, 57).[71] The identification of the conquerors with the god Viracocha dominates the earliest chapters of the Second Part, and, rather curiously, there is not a single mention of Pachacámac when the Spaniards are being "worshipped" as Cápac Viracochas. The very first mention of Pachacámac in the Second Part occurs in Chapter XX of Book I, just a few short phrases after Atahualpa marks the moment as a pachacuti by saying "the state of the republic will be turned to a better lot" (*el estado de la república se trocará en mejor suerte*). He then calls the Spaniards "sons of our great God Viracocha *and* messengers of Pachacámac" (*hijos de nuestro gran Dios Viracocha* y *mensajeros del Pachacámac*; my emphasis), which is then repeated in ensuing chapters. Although these titles appear to be synonymous, they are not. Considering that the encounter is a moment of indigenous uncertainty regarding the true nature of the invaders as well as a pachacuti, the separation of the "sons of our God Viracocha" from the "messengers of Pachacámac" feeds into the eventual clarification of the markedly different actions of the new Viracocha Incas and Viracocha zupaycuna. The behaviors that signal the difference are destruction and punishment. As Atahualpa puts it rather directly: "either your prince and all of you are tyrants who are destroying the world, taking away the kingdoms of others, killing and robbing those who have done you no harm and owe you nothing, *or you are ministers of God, whom we call Pachacámac, who has selected you for our punishment and destruction*" (Part 2, Book I, Chapter XXIV, vol. 1, 70).[72] Whereas Apu Inti, the resplendent Lord Sun symbolizing the majesty and power of the Incas at their height, fathers the Spanish Cápac Viracocha Incas, the dark, angry god Pachacámac, whose very words can destroy the entire world, engenders the Spanish Viracocha zupaycuna as his messengers of doom.

With Pachacámac on the ascent, trouble abounds for the Incas. Accordingly, the presence of the Devil and his ministers increases (Part 2, Book II, Chapter VI and Book III, Chapter XIX). If appeals must be made and prayers offered to Pachacámac in order to avoid disaster, then we should expect to hear his name more frequently from this point forward. This is precisely what happens. In the First Part, indigenous references to god almost always take the form "our Father the Sun" (*nuestro padre el sol*), and we have been duly warned that the name Pachacámac was uttered only when Indians were forced to do so (Part 1, Book II, Chapter II, vol. 1, 70). Following Atahualpa's execution, indigenous references to Pachacámac not only increase, but eventually subsume *all references* to the god Viracocha. Moreover, when Pachacámac's name is invoked it is either in the context of violence or in anticipation of a defeat. At the execution of Sancho de Cuéllar, the Indians announce, "The Pachacámac bids this *auca* [tyrant, traitor] to be hanged" (*A este auca manda el Pachacámac que ahorquen*) (Part 2, Book II, Chapter VI, vol. 1, 123). Before requesting restoration of the empire from Francisco Pizarro, Manco Inca says of the Spaniards, "perhaps, since they say they are messengers of the God Pachacámac they will fear him," and then continues by making the distinction, "if they are true sons of the Sun, as we believe, they will act like Incas" (Part 2, Book II, chapter XI, vol. 1, 136).[73] Of course, Manco Inca is never properly restored to the throne in the *Royal Commentaries*, and his invocation of Pachacámac therefore carries fear, violence, and loss. In fact, it is shortly after Manco Inca's rebellion in Cuzco, in which the miraculous appearance of St. James the Apostle accounts for the indigenous failure, that all explicit references to the god Viracocha cease. The Indians call St. James "a new Viracocha, who carried illapa [lightning, thunder, thunderbolt] in his hands" (*un nuevo Viracocha, que traía illapa en las manos*) (Part 2, Book II, Chapter XXV, vol. 1, 178). Yet we have already seen that the second or "new" name given to the Spanish Viracochas was Viracocha zupay, some of whom carried illapa in the form of artillery and harquebuses and were agents of destruction (Part 2, Book I, Chapter XL, vol. 1, 107). Quite appropriately, before abandoning Cuzco and in reflecting on his failed uprising, Manco Inca says, "it appears to me that the Pachacámac has visibly opposed this," and again, "all of which, properly considered, clearly tells us that these are not the works of men, but rather of Pachacámac" (Part 2, Book II, Chapter XXIX, vol. 1, 196–97).[74] Although repeated incessantly throughout Book 1 of the Second Part, in the over six hundred pages, or approximately two-fifths, of the *Royal Commentaries* that remain, *not once* does the phrase "our God Viracocha" (*nuestro dios Viracocha*) reappear. Pachacámac and his "messengers" have taken over.

It is primarily the indigenous association of Pachacámac with darkness, destruction, and the threat of loss, therefore, for which he is invoked in moments of anxiety, tension, humiliation, and defeat through the rest of the Second Part. When Sairi Túpac Inca departs from his mountain retreat for Lima at the behest of Viceroy Mendoza, the Marquis of Cañete, to receive a grant of land in the Yucay valley, the Inca's advisors worry about the prospects of the meeting. They suggest that nothing will change, that his vassals will weep on seeing him exiled and poor, and that, if the gift fails to conform to his rank, it would be better for him to die in the mountains than take the journey and suffer humiliation. Sairi Túpac was determined to go because "the Pachacámac and his Father the Sun had ordered him to do so" (*el Pachacámac y su padre el Sol se lo mandaban*). The Indians celebrated him on his journey, "but their celebrations were more for weeping than enjoyment, due to *the misery of the present compared with the greatness of the past*."[75] The juxtaposition of Pachacámac with the "Father Sun" corresponds rather precisely, once again, with the "misery of the present" and the "greatness of the past." Sairi Túpac was indeed humiliated by the grant, which he compared to a single thread from a tablemat, the whole of which was rightfully his (Part 2, Book VIII, Chapter X, vol. 3, 210–11). On the scaffold of his execution, Túpac Amaru, the last Inca, challenges the charge of treason of which he had been accused and convicted by Viceroy Toledo. He calls the charge a lie and in his last words he says, "I call upon Pachacámac, who knows that what I say is true" (*Yo llamo al Pachacámac, que sabe que es verdad lo que digo*). To this Inca Garcilaso adds, "with this the ministers of justice proceeded" (*Con esto pasaron adelante los ministros de la justicia*) (Part 2, Book VIII, Chapter XIX, vol. 3, 249). The terrible silence of Túpac Amaru's execution follows.[76]

Yet if Pachacámac is the god of darkness, loss, and suffering for the Incas and some of the Spaniards are legitimately included within their ranks by Inca Garcilaso, then this god should hold a similar power over the Spanish Incas as well. In the battle of Chupas, in which the royalist forces of Licentiate Pedro Vaca de Castro squared off against those of the mestizo rebel, Diego de Almagro the Younger, this is exactly what occurs. Since Almagro the Younger was held responsible for the assassination of Francisco Pizarro, a number of Pizarristas, i.e., those whom Inca Garcilaso calls first conquerors and Incas, fought for the royalists. To no surprise, the battle occurs *at night*. Moreover, "Both sides fought so obstinately that, although the sun had set and night settled in, they did not stop, even without knowing the ones from the others except by their names, with the ones saying 'Chile!' and the others 'Pachacámac!' in place of Almagros and Pizarros, for these names were also given to the factions" (Part 2, Book III, Chapter XVII, vol. 1, 294).[77] The forces of Pachacámac, the Pizarros, and Vaca de Castro win the "night" over the Chilean Almagros, and Almagro the Younger is captured and executed. Though the Pachacámac-Pizarro contingent appears victorious, in fighting for the royalists they lay claim to a Pyrrhic victory. For directly following Almagro the Younger's execution (Part 2, Book III, Chapter XIX), Inca Garcilaso announces the promulgation of the New Laws, in which *all* of the conquerors who engaged in the civil wars, regardless of whether they had been Pizarristas or Almagristas, were stripped of their encomiendas (Part 2, Book III, Chapter XX). Just as he does for their indigenous brethren, the nocturnal god Pachacámac doles out defeat to the Spanish Incas.

I hope to have sufficiently established that Inca Garcilaso selected Pachacámac for a number of simultaneous reasons and among them are the associations of darkness and destruction Pachacámac had in Andean contexts. Moreover, through a very complicated series of symbols, Inca Garcilaso simulates a cyclical, indigenous structure of history in which partial aspects of the deity Pachacámac, from very early in the *Royal Commentaries*, are generalized to project the image of a dark god of violence and defeat over the Incas, both indigenous and Spanish Viracocha Incas alike. Pachacámac's permanent ascendancy over the traditional high god of the Incas and his other "face," Viracocha, therefore represents a pachacuti in and of itself; a turning of the world for the worse, in which the natural movements of the Sun and Earth have stalled. It should not be forgotten, however, that Inca Garcilaso is quite explicit about equating Pachacámac with the Christian god and, in fact, he declares that there is no other word for the latter in Quechua (Part 1, Book II, Chapter II, vol. 1, 72). Yet this equation appears to open up an ambiguity that Inca Garcilaso may or may not have intended. For if Pachacámac is characterized as a vengeful, punishing god who is the *same* as the Christian god, then it seems to follow that the Spanish arrival, the ascendancy of Pachacámac, and the advent of Christian institutions and government in Peru necessarily mark a period of woe for indigenous Andeans. It did, of course, and Inca Garcilaso was not only fully aware of this, but the symbolization he has deployed seems to express as much to Andean readers. Nevertheless, as a "Catholic Christian Indian" (*indio cristiano católico*), condemning Catholicism is certainly not a message he was trying to convey. Rather, and in a very clever way, Inca Garcilaso is highlighting the relationship between political and military supremacy and religious belief for his Andean readers so that they might realize both the necessity and social benefits of accepting Catholicism. His message, instead, appears to be an allegory for indigenous conversion and the possibility of social renewal in the present, in which the open-endedness of "matters of importance" turning for the better or worse weighs in the balance.

This is most clearly seen in the *sole instance* in which Pachacámac's presence does not spell disaster in the *Royal Commentaries*. This is during the conquest of the Pachacámac valley, the location of the Yunga temple to Pachacámac, during the reign of Inca Pachacútec, which, in order to further diminish Inca Pachacútec's contributions to Inca history in favor of Inca Garcilaso's own panaca, is attributed to General Cápac Yupanqui (Part I, Book VI, Chapters XXX–XXXI). Above all else, it should be pointed out that Cápac Yupanqui's conquest of the valley of Pachacámac is portrayed as a *peaceful* conquest achieved through negotiating with the *curaca* (local lord) Cuismancu. The main reason for the lack of bloodshed, according to Inca Garcilaso, is that Cápac Yupanqui and Cuismancu realized they both worshipped the same deity as their highest god, the "sustainer of the world universe" Pachacámac. For although "the Inca Kings of Peru, with the natural light God gave them, realized that there was a Maker of all things, called Pachacámac," the doctrine that had originated with the Incas "spread throughout their realms, both before and after they were conquered" (Part I, Book VI, Chapter XXX, vol. I, 392).[78] The Neoplatonic underpinnings are rather explicit: through natural reason (*lumbre natural*) alone, it was quite possible for indigenous Andeans to glean the existence of the one, true God. Cuismancu and his followers were concerned, however, that the Incas worshipped the Sun, which they themselves did not. The Yungas did not want to be ruled by the Incas and "they did not want to repudiate their gods, which were very great" (*no querían repudiar sus dioses, que eran muy principales*). When General Cápac Yupanqui arrived, therefore, Cuismancu met him with a great army and the Yungas prepared to defend themselves. But Cápac Yupanqui illustrated his prudence: "The General Cápac Yupanqui sent word to him to understand that *they should not fight until they had spoken at greater length about their gods* because he should know that the Incas, beyond worshipping the Sun, worshipped Pachacámac as well . . . since the ones and the others worshipped the same god, there was no reason they should quarrel or fight, but rather they should be friends and brothers" (Part I, Book VI, Chapter XXXI, vol. I, 395).[79] After "they had spoken at greater length about their gods," there was no longer any reason for animosity between the two sides and they agreed to terms for peace in which Cuismancu retained his sovereignty within the Inca imperial system.

This meeting of indigenous minds over theological and political disputes occurs in the very seat of Pachacámac's preeminence, yet he does not stir. The potential violence and upheaval are avoided, and Pachacámac is either appeased or the equilibrium of his intrinsic duality—as both "sustainer" and "shaker" of the world-universe—is restored because the parties involved conduct themselves civilly, rationally, and peacefully. In more pointed terms, they all act like Incas. The allegorical relevance to the turmoil of the Andean present is clear. According to Inca Garcilaso, Pachacámac *is* the Christian god. Social amelioration remains, therefore, a possibility in the present and future through conversation and dialogue in which indigenous and Spanish Peruvians come more fully to know each other by speaking "at greater length." This allegory, furthermore, is Inca Garcilaso's argument to Andeans about the potential social and political benefits, i.e., peace and the restoration of their former status, to be won by joining the Catholic fold. To this argument Inca Garcilaso adds the specific, practical recommendations he thinks would further this end, which will be taken up in chapter 6. For now it is enough to say that, although matters of importance generally proceed from good to bad, they can also turn from worse to better. Just as the first Incas arose from the darkness of the First Age, so too might a new Peruvian society emerge from the darkness of the present.

Inca Garcilaso's postcolonial vision of Peru, then, is based upon the idea of an alliance and coordination of interests between past and present "Incas," beginning with the panaca of his ancestors as well as the first conquerors and encomenderos and extending to their common descendants. The character of the political arrangements envisioned by Inca Garcilaso for a renewed Peru is discussed in chapter 5. Before that, however, we must first explore the moment of uncertainty and conflict that lies at the very center of the work: the Spanish arrival and conquest. For, if the Incas and some of their conquerors were implicit kinsmen and brothers, both of whom had been divinely appointed in their own ways for the benefit and perfection of Peru, then why did their first interactions bring about such ruin? It is to the promise and pitfalls of Francisco Pizarro's meeting with Atahualpa that we turn in the following chapter.

4
AUCA
To Kill a Tyrant

Perhaps the most astonishing event of the Spanish conquest of Peru was one of the very first, the initial meeting between Francisco Pizarro and the Inca ruler Atahualpa at Cajamarca on November 16, 1532. Notwithstanding its significance as a triumphal note in the overture of Spanish expansion in the Andes region, this infamous encounter between Adelentado Pizarro and the Inca potentate has been imbued with a symbolic import that well surpasses the limits of its historical post; it has spawned numerous legends of intercultural misunderstanding and confrontation, of diplomacy and conquest, of greed and loss. In many ways, this singular event encapsulates the anxiety and miscomprehension that permeated the early years of the conquest and the violence that almost invariably attended the encounters of Europeans and indigenous peoples in the New World. In a setting electrically charged as it was, what under different circumstances might have been construed as simple acts of misrecognition, such as the mishandling of precious articles or lapses of decorum, rapidly devolved into pretenses for armed conflict and slaughter. For example, Pedro Pizarro, the younger cousin of the famed conquistador who was present at the fateful meeting in Cajamarca, relates that after Dominican Friar Vincente de Valverde had delivered the *requerimiento* (requirement) to

Atahualpa, instructing the latter in the faith and ordering him to submit obedience to the Pope and Emperor, Valverde presented the Inca with a bible or breviary, which Atahualpa promptly cast upon the ground, enraged that he could not open it (Pizarro 1921: vol. 1, 181–83).[1] In a different account dictated about the same time by Titu Cusi Yupanqui, the son of Manco Inca and a leader of Inca resistance in Vilcabamba, we are told that Atahualpa's rejection of the breviary was spurred by Spanish clumsiness in a solemn Inca ceremony when the Spaniards inadvertently dropped a golden chalice of *chicha* (a beverage of fermented maize) offered to them in a gesture of welcome (Cusi Yupanqui 1985: 2). Regardless of which breach of etiquette occurred first, this awkward engagement triggered the onrush of a Spanish ambush that issued in Atahualpa's capture by Governor Pizarro, brought forth an enormous ransom to Spanish coffers, and culminated in Atahualpa's execution on July 26, 1533 (Hemming 1970: 23–85; Lockhart 1972; Elliott 1987: 1–58).

While Atahualpa's capture by Pizarro and his staggeringly outnumbered troops was a startling military feat that earned him the praise of many of his contemporaries, his subsequent execution of Atahualpa sullied the glory that could have been his and contributed to a changing tide of Spanish opinion against the conquistadors. As Carlos Noreña has noted, "Spain was both amazed and shocked at the exploits of Pizarro in Peru" (Noreña 1975: 97): amazed by not only the stunning and rapid victory over such a vast empire but also the seemingly endless river of wealth that began to flow into the ports of Seville; and shocked by the utter audacity and brazen disrespect for indigenous sovereignty displayed by Pizarro in his dispatch of the Inca ruler. In fact, the very legitimacy of Spanish dominion in Peru seemed to hinge upon whether the episodes with Atahualpa could be justified. The more strident proponents of Spanish imperialism tended to agree with the assessment made by Hernando Pizarro's secretary, Francisco de Jerez, when he claimed, "it was wonderful to see so great a lord taken prisoner in so short a time" (Jerez 1921: 56). Others, such as Dominican theologian and head of the University of Salamanca, Francisco de Vitoria, expressed their doubts. In a letter to Miguel de Arcos, Vitoria wrote, "as far as I understand from the eyewitnesses who were personally present during the recent battle of Cajamarca, neither he nor any of his people had ever done the slightest injury to the Christians, nor given the least grounds for making war on them" (Vitoria 1991: 332). Vitoria's fellow Dominican, Bartolomé de Las Casas, who devoted his life to reforming the Spanish conquest and improving the plight of New World indigenous peoples, had no doubt that Pizarro's actions were as nefarious as they were unforgivable. Las Casas charged Pizarro with having falsely accused Atahualpa of treason in order to do away with him, and the friar openly fumed that Pizarro's cruelty and wickedness were of such proportions that only in the Last Judgment would a full reckoning be possible (Las Casas 1992: 107–09).

Las Casas's unflinching description of the atrocities in the New World stirred controversy throughout Europe and provided fuel for the anti-Spanish "Black Legend" propaganda of the English and Dutch. Although the interventions of Las Casas on behalf of the Indians contributed to both the growing European criticism of Spanish conquest and to a gradual alteration of the moral and political justifications of Spanish imperialism, the restoration of indigenous sovereignty for which he called was never implemented.[2] While the debates in Europe were heating up, the legitimacy of the conquest, rather ironically, became an increasingly moot question to the Spanish crown. Shortly after Las Casas's death in 1566, Philip II turned his interest more toward securing the territories in Peru rather than returning them to the semi-autonomous Inca heirs residing in their fortified retreats. In order to consolidate the political and economic administration of the territories and to extirpate the resilient religious practices of indigenous Andeans, Philip appointed Francisco de Toledo the fifth Viceroy of Peru, with the latter arriving in Lima in 1569 and serving until 1581. Part of Toledo's project of comprehensive reform was an unprecedented and systematic collection of information about the Andes from indigenous witnesses through a series of *visitas* (visitations). This information, which Toledo used to support his programs, was submitted in a report to Phillip II in 1572 called *Informaciones acerca del señorio de los Incas* (Information about the Kingdom of the Incas). The report, in addition to reviving Sepúlveda's neo-Aristotelian arguments regarding the natural inferiority of the Indians, declared that Philip II held legitimate and undisputed title to Peru on the grounds that the Incas had been recent conquerors who brutally subjugated the inhabitants of the Andes by means of relentless warfare and oppressive tyranny (Brading 1991: 128–46). As a result, the Toledan school, which included the historical works of Juan de Matienzo and Captain Pedro Sarmiento de Gamboa, provided a new justification of the Spanish conquest in which the Incas and the *curacas* (local ethnic lords) became the tyrants and the Spaniards the liberators (Zamora 2010a: 121–23). Against the "chaos and confusion of ignorance on the subject" to which he claimed Las Casas and others had succumbed, Sarmiento de Gamboa wrote to Philip II in his *Historia Indica* (History of the Indies, 1572) explaining the "signal service" proposed by Toledo in the matters of Peru. According to Sarmiento de Gamboa, this service lay chiefly in undeceiving "all those in the world who think that the Incas were legitimate sovereigns and that the curacas were natural lords of the land." Instead, Sarmiento de Gamboa called the rule of the Incas a "terrible, inveterate, and horrible tyranny" from which the Spanish invasion and Toledo's reforms were "emancipating and freeing them [Indians] . . . and finally giving them a rational life" (Sarmiento de Gamboa 1999: 5–9).[3] Pizarro's execution of Atahualpa, perpetrated against a tyrant, had gone from an inexcusable crime to an act of Christian liberation.

Like the commentators who preceded him, Inca Garcilaso was avidly concerned with the legitimacy of the conquest. As a native Peruvian and the mestizo scion of an Inca princess and a Spanish conquistador, however, he was much less interested in the rights of the Spanish crown than the fortunes of his contemporary and future Peruvian compatriots. At the very center of his reconstruction of Inca civilization and Spanish conquest lies his treatment of the "axial figure" of Atahualpa, whose tyrannous rise to power and violent death at the hands of Pizarro are the thematic bridges that connect the end of the First Part with the beginning of the Second.[4] Seen in the context of his broader political project, Inca Garcilaso had to maneuver very delicately around the issue of Atahualpa's execution in order to provide a historically plausible justification of the conquest upon which the descendants of Incas, conquerors, and *encomenderos* (Spaniards rewarded for their services with *encomiendas*, a grant of Indian labor) could reconcile the conflicts in their social interests.

It is well to remember with David Brading that the "chief target" of Inca Garcilaso's attack "was not the Spanish conquest, of which he was a child, but rather the imperial regime inaugurated by Philip II and his viceroys" (Brading 1991: 256). That being the case, neither of the most prevalent stances on these events was adequate for Inca Garcilaso's political aims: the Lascasian defense of indigenous sovereignty carried with it a stinging condemnation of the conquistadors; and the Toledan defense of the conquest transformed the Incas into tyrants. As such, Inca Garcilaso constructed his own version of this pivotal moment in Peruvian history, and the tale he weaves oscillates between justification and condemnation. His justification of the conquest hinges upon Atahualpa's tyranny, the state of Inca politics at the moment of Spanish arrival, and the inability of Spaniards to fully comprehend their surroundings. He attempts to exonerate Pizarro by portraying him as a tyrannomach in order to set the stage for a potential alliance between Pizarro and members of Huáscar's *panaca* (royal kinship group). This justification, however, is laced with Inca Garcilaso's criticisms of both the manner in which the conquest was conducted as well as its results. In particular, he focuses on the motives behind Spanish expansion and the problem of factionalism in Inca politics. When all is said and done, we come to find that Atahualpa's execution was not only warranted, but also an essential precondition for the possibility of restoring Inca sovereignty to its rightful heirs and establishing peaceful coexistence between Incas and Spaniards in Peru. The problem represented by the conquest for Inca Garcilaso, therefore, is not Atahualpa's death. Rather, the major difficulty for which he needed to account was why the first encounters between Incas and Spaniards produced such a spectacular failure. Moreover, he had to do so in such a way that would be comprehensible to both European and Andean audiences.

From the early moments of the First Part of the *Royal Commentaries*, the shadow of a tyrant is cast over Tahuantinsuyu (the four corners of the world); Inca Garcilaso spares neither time nor ink draping the villain's cloak over Atahualpa's shoulders. For instance, when Inca Garcilaso recounts the mythical origin of the semi-divine Manco Cápac, he also introduces the "cruelty and tyranny of Atahualpa" as both a segue and foil to the founder of the Inca dynasty (Part 1, Book I, Chapter XV, vol. 1, 39). Nearly every detail of the First Part demonstrates that the contrast between the archetypal Inca and Atahualpa could not be greater. Whereas the benevolent Manco Cápac was ordered by the Sun to deliver the Andeans of the First Age from their primitive savagery by inducing them through rational persuasion and moral example to accept the benefits of civilization (Part 1, Book I, Chapters XV–XXV), Atahualpa was the belligerent, bastard son of Huayna Cápac who practiced dissimulation, incited a fratricidal civil war with his half-brother Huáscar, and callously murdered innocent women, children, and servants in his groundless attempts to procure and maintain the scarlet fringe of Inca sovereignty (Part 1, Book IV, Chapter X and Book IX, Chapters XXXII–XXXIX). If Manco Cápac's words and deeds were the very foundation of the Inca empire, which all his successors and subjects earnestly sought to imitate (Part 1, Book I, Chapter XIX), then Atahualpa was an anomalous Inca indeed.

Atahualpa's character is further elaborated in Inca Garcilaso's treatment of the Inca civil war and by way of comparing the former to Huáscar. We are told that the twelfth Inca Huayna Cápac, influenced by the prophecy of Viracocha

Inca, broke with Inca tradition and entrusted the recently conquered Quito to his favorite son Atahualpa (Part 1, Book V, Chapter XXVIII and Book IX, Chapter XV). In so doing, Huayna Cápac transgressed the Inca law of succession (Part 1, Book IV, Chapter X) by promoting his illegitimate son Atahualpa, the product of the union between Huayna Cápac and the heiress of Quito, over his legitimate son Huáscar, who was of the royal lineage in Cuzco. Doubly emboldened by his father's favor and the scepter of Quito, his possession of which resulted in an unprecedented division of the empire, Atahualpa planned to overthrow Huáscar in Cuzco and to unite the severed realms under his power following their father's death. A protracted civil war ensued from which Atahualpa emerged victorious, and with just title to neither Quito nor Cuzco according to Inca law, the new emperor initiated a series of purges to secure his precarious rule (Part 1, Book IX, Chapters XXXII–XXXIX). The wretched Huáscar managed to escape with his life for the time being, but his kingdom had been lost. Atahualpa, on the other hand, was honored by his subjects for his usurious and ruthless deeds with the epithet *auca*, "tyrant, traitor" (Part 1, Book II, Chapter XV, vol. 1, 105).[5]

In this tale we are presented not only with the substance of Atahualpa's tyranny but also with the ruinous and chaotic condition of the Inca empire at the moment of Spanish arrival, which Inca Garcilaso uses to partially explain its defeat (Part 2, Book I, Chapter XL). The above account, however, is the result of partisan political maneuvers in an Andean frame of reference by the mestizo historian that can easily go unnoticed. In the first place, while Inca Garcilaso presents the civil war between Atahualpa and Huáscar as an aberrant occurrence in Andean history, ritual wars of succession following the death of a ruler were part and parcel of Inca political life. This was known by some of Inca Garcilaso's contemporaries, including Pedro Sarmiento de Gamboa, who described many of the factional struggles in his *Historia Indica*.[6] The wars of succession pitted the leading candidates from rival panacas in combat and coalition for the throne. The matrilineal character of the panacas meant that the claimants were all sons of the Inca from his numerous wives, and legitimacy or fitness to rule was determined in the outcome of the conflict and not through primogeniture as Inca Garcilaso suggests (Rostworowski 1983: 167–83). In this sense, these battles were as much for family as for regional or political supremacy, and Franklin Pease has suggested that the purported legitimacy of neither Atahualpa nor Huáscar can be accepted uncritically (Pease 1981: 63–96).

For our purposes, it is well to remember the central role that women played in determining one's panaca and how this relates to Inca Garcilaso's version of the events. Inca Garcilaso credits his mother Chimpu Ocllo, her brother Don Fernando Huallpa Túpac Inca Yupanqui, and their uncle Cusi Huallpa as being his primary oral sources of information about Inca civilization (Part 1, Book IX, Chapter XIV). All these were members of Túpac Inca Yupanqui's panaca, and knowing this sheds considerable light on Inca Garcilaso's account. Atahualpa and Huáscar were half-brothers of the same father, Huayna Cápac, but from different mothers belonging to rival panacas of the Inca elite. Atahualpa's mother was from the panaca of Pachacútec Inca, the ninth ruler, with links to a military faction in Quito, while Huáscar's mother (like Inca Garcilaso's) was a member of Tupac Inca Yupanqui's panaca, the tenth Inca, with religious functions in Cuzco. When the ritual war of succession arose after Huayna Cápac's death, the panaca of Túpac Inca Yupanqui supported the forces of Huáscar and the panaca of Pachacútec Inca supported Atahualpa. Atahualpa's forces prevailed in capturing Cuzco, thus solidifying victory, and proceeded to slaughter Huáscar's remaining supporters, starting with the panaca of Túpac Inca Yupanqui. Against the backdrop of the ritual wars of succession in Inca politics, Inca Garcilaso's insistence on Atahualpa's illegitimacy and cruelty bears the stamp of his own personal connection to Inca royalty. Inca Garcilaso not only champions the perspective and interests of the panaca from which his mother descended, but he also restores Huáscar as the "legitimate" and victimized heir to the throne. Although his account is regionally biased toward Cuzco and projects the political priorities and interests of one faction of Inca nobility to the exclusion of others, it would have been recognizable to Andean publics, the oral histories of which were family-oriented, selective, and encomiastic.

Furthermore, in applying the appellation auca to Atahualpa, Inca Garcilaso anticipates both the justice of the treatment the tyrant will receive from Pizarro as well as how it will be viewed by Huáscar's supporters. Inca law, according to Inca Garcilaso, was both prudent and strict, with the slightest infraction earning the transgressor's death (Part 1, Book II, Chapter XIII). Not content with demonstrating the righteous severity of Inca legal doctrines, he adds that the Incas themselves were subject to the very laws they upheld. Although he tells us that any such occurrence was vehemently denied by indigenous Peruvians, an Inca who committed a crime was disavowed of the prestigious title, expelled from the royal blood, and subject to the grimmest of punishments (Part 1, Book II, Chapter XV, vol. 1, 104). In the eyes of those who had survived Atahualpa's atrocities, Pizarro's execution of Atahualpa was not only justified but welcomed, "they said that the Spaniards had killed the tyrant as punishment and to avenge the Incas" (Y dijeron que los españoles habían muerto al tirano en castigo y venganza de los Incas) (Part 1, Book V, Chapter XXI, vol. 1, 300). Or, more specifically, in speaking of the Spaniards the Indians said, "they had been sent from heaven to avenge Huáscar and all of his followers, and to punish Atahualpa" (*los había enviado del Cielo para que vengassen a Huáscar y a todos los suyos, y castigassen a Atahualpa*) (Part 2, Book I, Chapter XL, vol. 1, 107).

To an Hispano-European audience of the time that was entirely unacquainted with the intricacies of political structures and conflicts in the Andes, Inca Garcilaso's reconstruction of the late Inca dynasty around the Cuzco-centric oral histories of Túpac Inca Yupanqui's panaca would most certainly have been lost. By accentuating Atahualpa's illegitimacy and the relentless ferocity with which he pursued and consolidated his power, however, Inca Garcilaso was able to provide a profile of the indigenous ruler that was familiar to Europeans as well. At least since Plato, there has been a long and venerable tradition in Western political thought that has devoted its attention to elucidating the moral character and ruling practices of tyrants. In Plato's *Republic*, the tyrant is characterized as the very antithesis of the wise and benevolent philosopher king; he is a man of exorbitant and insatiable passions unchecked by reason who is given over to lawlessness and vice and rules for his own benefit rather than the common good. The tyrant is licentious, essentially unjust, friendless, dissembling, cruel, and his regime is nothing short of slavery (Plato 1991: Books VIII and IX, 564a–92b, 242–75). Whereas Plato argued that tyranny necessarily arose from democracy, in his *Politics*, Aristotle pointed out that, in addition to unscrupulous demagogues, ambitious kings who overstepped the limits of their powers were equally tyrants (Aristotle 1993: 1310b14–19, 130 and Book V, Sections 10–11, 1310a40–1315b10, 129–40). Moreover, Aristotle claimed that "any one who obtains power by force or by fraud is at once thought to be a tyrant," and that a tyrannical constitution was either no constitution at all or at least the very worst imaginable (Aristotle 1993: 1313a10, 135; 1266a3, 32).

For those who believed that the perfection of human capacities and the cultivation of virtue were inextricably linked to action, as did Aristotle, and specifically to public action in the service of the state, as did Cicero, the presence of a tyrant in the public domain was absolutely intolerable; his behavior destroyed the very ground upon which mankind's pursuit of its highest ends was based. Aristotle agreed with Plato that a tyrant would "lop off those who were too high" and "put to death men of spirit," and in securing his rule he would invariably humiliate his subjects, sow mistrust among them, and render them completely incapable of action (Aristotle 1993: 1313a40, 135; 1314a13–29, 137). The realization that a tyrant would actively persecute men of virtue enraged Cicero, for exemplary citizens were the very heart and life-blood of the state. Given the primacy he placed on the moral obligations owed to the *patria*, it was then easy for Cicero to conclude that killing a tyrant was the veritable patriotic duty of a committed citizen. The Roman republican completes this line of reasoning in *On Duties*: "we have no ties of fellowship with a tyrant, but rather the bitterest feud; and it is not opposed to Nature to rob, if one can, a man whom it is morally right to kill;—nay, all that pestilent and abominable race should be exterminated from human society . . . those fierce and savage monsters in human form should be cut off from what may be called the common body of humanity" (Cicero 1997: III.vi.32, 299).

Although it would take us too far afield to review in detail the positions of the numerous thinkers who contributed to the development of the doctrine of tyrannicide, such as St. Augustine's views on "just war" in *City of God* (Book IV, Chapter 15 and Book XIX, Chapter 7), which were accepted by the Catholic church, Aquinas's endorsement of tyrannicide in *Commentaries on the Sentences of Peter Lombard* (Book II, Dist. 44, Question 2, Article 2), or the works on tyranny by Bartolus of Sassoferato and Coluccio Salutati (Emerton 1925), to name but a few, it is sufficient to note that the general profile of the tyrant etched in antiquity continued to hold sway relatively unchanged through the Middle Ages and into the Renaissance. This was particularly the case in the avalanche of advice manuals and "mirror for princes" books published throughout the sixteenth century. These works, two of the most popular being Erasmus's *The Education of a Christian Prince*, dedicated to the princeling Charles V in 1516, and Antonio de Guevara's *Reloj de los principes* (Dial of Princes, 1529), attempted to educate rulers in the princely and cardinal virtues as the essential fundaments of good government (Skinner 1978: vol. 1, 211–43). In order to more vividly illustrate the extent to which the paths of Christianity, virtue, justice, and the common good were to be kept by a ruler at all times, it was customary for authors in this genre to juxtapose the image of the "true prince" against his loathsome alter-ego. The depictions of tyrants to be found in such works, often supported by a litany of history's most infamous characters and their calamitous ends, faithfully rehearse the commonplaces established by Plato, Aristotle, et. al.: the tyrant is completely self-interested, irascible, and violent; he revels in sowing discord and in persecuting outstanding citizens; he humiliates and enslaves his subjects; and rather than being the shepherd of his flock, he is their devourer (Erasmus 1997: 27–37). "Just as there is no more honorable title than 'prince,'" Erasmus sums up, "so there is no term more detested and cursed on every score than 'tyrant'" (Erasmus 1997: 25).

As an avowed pacifist and one who was more concerned with educating legitimate princes to avoid degenerating into tyrants than explaining the rights of subjects against their oppressors, conspicuously absent from Erasmus's treatise is an explicit statement on the legitimacy of tyrannicide. The same could be said of Jesuit Pedro de Ribadeneira's *Tratado de la religion y virtudes que debe tener el príncipe cristiano* (Treatise on the Religion and Virtues of the Christian Prince), which falls within the same genre of writing and was published in 1595. This is not the case, however, with the work of Ribadeneira's compatriot and fellow Jesuit, Juan de Mariana. The ostensible targets of both Ribadeneira's *Tratado* and Mariana's *De rege et regis institutione* (The King and the Education of the King) published in 1599, are the twin "heresies" of Machiavellian "reason of state" politics and Protestant absolutism. Both Spanish Jesuits believed that good government, meaning monarchy, could only be built and maintained on a solid foundation of orthodox Christian morality, which had been betrayed by Machiavellians and Protestants in their own ways, thereby accelerating the breakdown of Christian unity in Europe. Similarly, both included extended, though conventional, comparisons of the "true king" with the tyrant to remind their readers that rulers who flagrantly disregarded ethical norms to secure the welfare of their states, as Machiavelli had suggested in *The Prince*, were, in the words of Ribadeneira, "ministers of Satan" (Ribadeneira 1952: 453; my translation).[7] Weaned as they were on Cicero and Aquinas, one might expect both to endorse tyrannicide, as did their intellectual role models and many other members of the Society.[8] Ribadeneira, however, is rather ambiguous on the issue. Whereas his treatise contains countless historical examples of tyrants coming to "disastrous ends" (*desastrados fines*), he also quite explicitly states that tyrants are a necessary part of God's inscrutable providence who are sent to punish and purify evildoers and are then punished in turn, both in this life and the next, when they have outlived their usefulness (Ribadeneira, 1952: Book II, Chapter XL, 577–79). While Ribadeneira tends toward quietism, Mariana goes for the jugular:

> Both philosophers and theologians agree that if a prince rises to power in a republic through force of arms, without any reason or right whatsoever, without the consent of the people, he can be deprived of his crown, his government, and his life by anyone; that being a public enemy and provoking all manner of evils in the patria and proving himself to be truly deserving of

> the name tyrant through his character, he can not only be dethroned, but it can be done with the same violence with which he snatched the power that belongs to none but the very society he oppresses and enslaves. (Mariana 1961: vol. 1, Book I, Chapter VI, 109–10; my translation)

The differences between Ribadeneira and Mariana on this point are important, for as José Durand's research has shown, Inca Garcilaso had direct knowledge of both authors' works, most likely through his Jesuit companions, and his political thought travels along similar lines (Durand 1976: 108–09). And, as we have seen, Inca Garcilaso presents Atahualpa as the very blueprint of tyranny (rivaled perhaps only by Tiberius, Nero, Caligula, and the like), whose outline would have been clearly recognizable to Mariana, Ribadeneira, and the rest of their European contemporaries. It is frequently assumed, however (and Durand's comments are a case in point), that what Inca Garcilaso shares with Mariana, through their reading of Ribadeneira, is simply an allergic reaction to "reason of state" politics.[9] To be sure, Inca Garcilaso uses language that could very well have come from Ribadeneira when he refers to proponents of that "new teaching . . . called reason of state" as "ministers of the Devil" (Part 2, Book V, Chapter XXIX, vol. 2, 232). Nevertheless, it is more likely that Inca Garcilaso found in Mariana a justification for Atahualpa's execution which then informed his treatment of the events in the Second Part of the *Royal Commentaries*. For, in portraying Atahualpa as a tyrant, Inca Garcilaso has engaged in a discourse that can either endorse his execution in siding with Mariana or retreat from it in siding with Erasmus or Ribadeneira. The difficulty in this case is that Inca Garcilaso never explicitly endorses either position, and in fact appears to oscillate between them, both in his version of Atahualpa's trial and in the two alternative courses of action he proposes in the chapters following Atahualpa's execution. As we shall see, one of these options states that Atahualpa's death was counterproductive to spreading the gospel and therefore plays up the imprudence of his execution. The other option, however, is predicated upon Atahualpa's death in that it argues for the restoration of Inca sovereignty to a legitimate heir. For reasons that will be made clear below, Inca Garcilaso favors the latter alternative, indicating that his portrayal of Atahualpa's tyranny was intended to legitimate his execution and advance a specific political agenda.

For the moment, however, it is enough to say that Inca Garcilaso's intercultural account of Atahualpa's tyranny opens the possibility of his legitimate removal in the eyes of Andeans and Spaniards alike. With such accounts, he is able to achieve three very important, if only implicit, results. First, he reinforces the perspective of the first chronicles of the Peruvian conquest, which extolled the deeds of the conquerors and claimed that the execution of Atahualpa was justified due to his cruelty and treachery. In comparing these chronicles to Inca Garcilaso's version, however, one finds that he has shrewdly toned down the supposed threat of indigenous reprisal surrounding the conquistadors. For instance, Francisco Pizarro's secretary, Pedro Sancho, had it that Spanish hands were forced in dealing with Atahualpa because, "fifty thousand men of Quito . . . were coming to kill all the Christians" (Sancho de la Hoz 1917: 16). Las Casas held this to be a bold-faced lie that revealed "only too clearly the pretext upon which this 'just war' was conducted" (Las Casas 1992: 109). Like Las Casas, Inca Garcilaso maintained that the Incas had offered no resistance to the Spaniards, as the Incas had themselves prophesied the Spanish arrival and ordered the latter to be obeyed by their subjects. In this sense, Inca Garcilaso sides with Las Casas in denying that the conquest of Peru could be seen as a "just war," yet, he nevertheless assuages some of the damage the conquerors' image had suffered from Las Casas's pen by claiming that, in the end, they had merely executed a dreaded tyrant.

This brings us to the second point, because it now appears that Inca Garcilaso is somewhat closer to the perspective of Viceroy Toledo and his colleagues who argued that the conquest was a "just war" against the Inca despots. The idea of "just war," however, is one that Inca Garcilaso was anxious to avoid due to what it entailed in practice. Sarmiento de Gamboa appealed directly to the authority of Francisco de Vitoria on what constituted a just war (Sarmiento de Gamboa 1999: 11), and Vitoria's *De Indis* (On the Indians, 1539) was in fact one of the best known and most influential documents on the law of nations, the justice of warfare, and the legitimate grounds of conquest throughout the sixteenth century. For our purposes, we need only consider that when a war was entered for legitimate reasons, according to Vitoria, "all rights of war" could then be exercised against the wrongdoers and aggressors, "including plunder, enslavement, deposition of their former masters, and the institution of new ones" (Vitoria 1991: 283). As a staunch proponent of Inca sovereignty, it is all too obvious that Inca Garcilaso could not permit Atahualpa's execution to be seen as a consequence of just war by the Spaniards because, according to the rights of such warfare, this would allow the Incas to be legitimately deprived of their rule. Inca Garcilaso was able to offer a response to the official reports of Viceroy Toledo, however, by shifting the discourse away from just war to its kindred doctrine of tyrannicide, and he thereby conceded the strongest claim of the Toledan school that there indeed had been tyranny in Tahuantinsuyu. The major difference is that the *Toledistas* argued that *all* of the Incas were tyrants, that there was not a legitimate ruler or heir to be found in the lot of them, and that, therefore, taking over their empire and extinguishing the Inca line were perfectly warranted.[10] For his part, Inca Garcilaso admits the presence of a tyrant, albeit a *single* tyrant who was in no way indicative of the Inca dynasty as a whole, and then counters the Toledan school by suggesting that the anomalous presence of Atahualpa was remedied, in part, by his execution.

Finally, what Inca Garcilaso is doing is changing the focus of the European discourse on the legitimacy of the conquest away from the sphere of Spanish foreign policy and the rights of the crown derived from international law to the venue of domestic Inca politics. As the legitimate "natural lords," political authority in Peru flowed through the Inca dynasty, making the rights of the Spanish monarchy at best a tangential concern for Inca Garcilaso. None other than Atahualpa voices this perspective in his reply to the garbled and poorly translated requerimiento delivered by Valverde at Cajamarca.[11] After lamenting their lack of a common language, Atahualpa illustrates that he has perfectly understood the demand to cede his power to King Charles V, saying: "if this Charles is Prince and lord of the whole world, what necessity did he have for the Pope to give him a new concession and donation to make war on me and usurp these kingdoms? And if he had need of it, is not the Pope a greater lord than he, and more powerful, and Prince of all the world?"[12] Atahualpa continues by denying any obligation to pay tribute to Charles, but he recognizes that tribute might be more properly owed to God, Jesus, and the pope, "who can give and concede my kingdoms and my person to others" (*que puede dar y conceder mis reinos y mi persona a otros*). Of course, obligations to God, Jesus, and the pope were only incurred after one had actually entered the congregation of the faithful, which reiterates the point that the Spanish presence in the Andes depended upon their mission as proselytizers. As Atahualpa points out concerning his obligations to church authorities, "but if you say I owe these nothing, I owe less to Charles, who was never lord of these regions nor has he ever seen them" (Part 2, Book I, Chapter XXIV, vol. 1, 71).[13]

Atahualpa's argument on indigenous sovereignty is reinforced and overlapped by the prophecy Inca Garcilaso uses repeatedly to explain and justify the conquest to an Andean public. During the same speech to Valverde, Atahualpa declares, "my vassals and I offer ourselves to die or anything else you wish to do with us, not out of fear of your arms and threats, but to fulfill what my father Huayna Cápac left as a mandate at the hour of his death."[14] We are reminded that Huayna Cápac ordered his subjects to serve and honor a bearded people who had a better religion and better customs and were wiser and braver than the Incas. For this reason the Spaniards were called "Viracochas" after the Inca who had inaugurated the prophecy, and, as "messengers of the great god Viracocha," the Incas expected the Spaniards to "act like divine messengers and ministers" (Part 2, Book I, Chapter XXIV, vol. 1, 71). Through recourse to this indigenous imperial mandate, Inca Garcilaso makes the conquest appear, at least in principle, as within the evolution and progression of the Inca dynasty.

Atahualpa's invocations of indigenous sovereignty, providential mission, and Inca prophecy do nothing, however, to offset the charge of tyranny leveled against him. Rather, Inca Garcilaso situates these justificatory reminders at the very outset of the conquest to set the stage for a potential alliance between the legitimate heirs of Huáscar's *panaca* and Atahualpa's executioner, Francisco Pizarro. Such an alliance, according to Inca Garcilaso, would have righted the injustices caused by Atahualpa's tyranny, restored the Inca throne to its "legitimate" heirs, brought the spiritual benefits of Christianity to Peru, and justified the Spanish conquest to Andeans as a fulfillment of Inca prophecy. More importantly, Inca Garcilaso focuses our attention on the relevant context in which the legitimacy, justice, and utility of the conquest should have been gauged, which is the *indigenous* context and not that of the foreign invaders. Of course, Las Casas and other like-minded reformers of the conquest had attempted to suggest something similar in their respective works. The *Royal Commentaries*, however, provides a plausible, historical description of how the events should have played themselves out given specific and prior conditions in Inca politics.

Having prepared potential audiences from different cultural backgrounds with a multifaceted and in many respects unmistakable presentation of Atahualpa's tyranny, one might expect the treatment of Atahualpa's trial in the Second Part (Part 2, Book I, Chapter XXXVII) to make the argument explicit and cinch the case. There is no such payoff. Instead, one encounters passages that seem to portray those *opposed* to the results of the proceedings in the most favorable light, and which end on an ironic note. At the moment of truth, Inca Garcilaso vacillates, and some have taken this to mean he condemned the manner of Atahualpa's death (Brading 1991: 411). For reasons already mentioned, however, interpreting the *Royal Commentaries* as a flat condemnation of Atahualpa's execution misses the mark. Further, in the chapters leading up to Atahualpa's trial and execution, we are reminded that he had ordered the brutal murder of his brother, the Inca and "natural King," Huáscar, which stood as "the greatest of his cruelties" (Part 2, Book I, Chapter XXXIII, vol. 1, 89). In the following chapter, Inca Garcilaso tells us that Atahualpa's machinations had ultimately failed to secure his empire, liberty, or even his life, and of the last he would shortly be deprived. For, "it is a very ordinary punishment from heaven against those who trust more in their cunning and tyrannies than in reason and justice. And in this way God permits them to fall into these and even worse punishments, as we shall see" (Part 2, Book I, Chapter XXXIV, vol. 1, 90).[15]

When we turn to Atahualpa's trial (Part 2, Book I, Chapter XXXVII), it becomes evident that Inca Garcilaso's intent in these passages is not to defend Atahualpa, but rather to defray the guilt attributed to some of the conquistadors. First and foremost, those who object to Atahualpa's death sentence in Inca Garcilaso's account are all members of the first conquerors (those who arrived in Peru with either Francisco Pizarro or Diego de Almagro the Elder), and the general tendency of the *Royal Commentaries* is to exonerate and valorize the first conquerors in order to provide a critique of Las Casas as well as to forward Inca Garcilaso's own conciliatory political project. These men of "generous and pious spirit" (*ánimo generoso y piadoso*) argued that it was impermissible to kill a king (*no se permitía matar un Rey*) who had received them so courteously and had caused them no harm, that killing the imprisoned king (*Rey prisoniero*), who had made good on the better part of the ransom he had offered for his freedom, constituted a breach of the promises the Spaniards had made to him, and that they should send Atahualpa to Charles V rather than execute him, because they had no jurisdiction to constitute themselves as judges over him (*no se hiziessen juezes contra un Rey, que no tenían juridición sobre él*). Compared to Atahualpa's advocates, his prosecutors appear far less principled. The moral character of these men receives no praise, and they are given instrumental arguments to the effect that their sole duty is to increase the territories of their Emperor and King, and that by executing the tyrant (*aquel tirano*) they would assure the conquest of the Inca empire and safeguard their own lives, both of which would be lost if Atahualpa were suffered to live. Against the respect for indigenous sovereignty evinced by the arguments of Atahualpa's defenders, the justifications offered by Atahualpa's executioners ring of the very crudest "reason of state" politics, proponents of which, as we have seen, Inca Garcilaso scorns as "ministers of the Devil" (*los ministros del demonio*) (Part 2, Book V, Chapter XXIX, vol. 2, 232). The dispute between the two parties ends when Atahualpa's defenders are reminded that they are outnumbered by a count of 350 to 50, and the critical intent of the passages is rendered explicit when Inca Garcilaso asserts, "with these threats and good reasons" (*con estas amenazas y buenas razones*), Atahualpa's defenders were placated. The prisoner was baptized, then garroted. Although Francisco Pizarro presided over the trial and authorized the execution, he is nevertheless partially absolved because the men who were directly under his command fought the battle of substantive moral justice against the avaricious "ministers of the devil" and were defeated.[16]

Despite the stark portrayal of Atahualpa's tyranny and the ironic tone that pervades Inca Garcilaso's account of the trial, the question whether the execution is condemned or condoned in the *Royal Commentaries* is far from resolved. More pointedly, if Pizarro's men, the first conquerors, had been correct in arguing as they did, then their subsequent actions were flagrantly criminal and could never be justified. The question turns away from Atahualpa's tyranny—his character has been firmly established and is maintained throughout—instead, the question becomes whether Pizarro and his men can be redeemed from their knowing participation in regicide.

For Pizarro and his men to have been culpable of such a charge, they would have had to have known that Atahualpa was in fact a legitimate sovereign and then intentionally acted against him nonetheless. There is ample ground in the *Royal Commentaries*, however, for the suggestion that, due to their linguistic differences and the Spaniards' concomitant lack of specific knowledge about Inca civilization, those who defended Atahualpa as if he were a "king" (*Rey*) had made a crucial, if understandable, error in judgment. From the very opening moments (in fact, before the narrative begins in the First Part, "Preface to the Reader" and "Warning"), Inca Garcilaso dons the cap of the Quechua philologist and explains how Spanish histories of Inca civilization are strewn with corrupted words and poorly interpreted phrases because Spanish historians were ignorant of indigenous languages. This theme winds through both parts of the *Royal Commentaries*, and first resurfaces in this case in Inca Garcilaso's account of the encounter between Friar Vincente de Valverde and Atahualpa. Their encounter is a travesty of mutual miscomprehension caused by the absence of a common language and the incompetent performance of the Indian translator Felipillo (Part 2, Book I, Chapters XXIII–XXIV). Further, the same dilemma is present when Hernando de Soto and Pedro del Barco come across the despondent and despoiled Huáscar, who had been imprisoned by Atahualpa's men after the civil war. Huáscar informs them of Atahualpa's usurpations and implores them for assistance because he fears that Atahualpa's guards are going to kill him. Instead of remaining with him and defending him, Soto and Barco continue on their journey to Cuzco, inadvertently causing Huáscar's death, for "what they said to one another was not understood" (*lo que hablaron no se entendío*) (Part 2, Book I, Chapter XXXI, vol. 1, 84). Next, Atahualpa, desiring to sound out Francisco Pizarro's reaction to his planned murder of Huáscar, feigns a terrible sadness and informs Pizarro that he had just received news of his beloved brother's execution. Pizarro consoles him rather than interrogating him and at this mild reaction Atahualpa sends out the order to have Huáscar undone. Pizarro misinterprets Atahualpa's actions as a sign of mourning rather than a cunning ploy, and Inca Garcilaso remarks that had Pizarro replied, "'You had him killed: I shall investigate and punish your crime as it deserves!' the murder would certainly not have been committed" (Part 2, Book I, Chapter XXXIII, vol. 1, 89).[17] Finally, Felipillo, the interpreter who had so terribly botched the translation between Valverde and Atahualpa in their first encounter, is charged with translating the responses of the Indian witnesses during Atahualpa's trial (Part 2, Book I, Chapters XXXVI–XXXVII). Time and again, on numerous occasions when life and death hang in the balance, the Spanish foreigners are presented as failing to fully comprehend their surroundings.

So that Inca Garcilaso's readers could see that an error of this sort was understandable, even in a matter as important as Atahualpa's true position in the Inca hierarchy, he inserted an anecdote in the penultimate chapter of the First Part to prepare the ground for this interpretation. The anecdote involves the death of Atahualpa's son, Don Francisco Atahualpa, who died shortly before Inca Garcilaso left Peru for Spain.[18] Before the funeral, many of Inca Garcilaso's Indian relatives came to visit his mother, Chimpu Ocllo, and among them was the aged Cusi Huallpa. Instead of offering condolences (after all, Chimpu Ocllo had just lost a relative, the son of her cousin), Cusi Huallpa congratulated her and asked Pachacámac to preserve her long enough to see the death of all her enemies. Upon hearing this, the young mestizo asked his uncle, "Inca, why should we rejoice over the death of Don Francisco, who was so closely related to us?"[19] This question sent Cusi Huallpa into a rage whereby he replied, "Do you want to be the relative of an auca, the son of another auca (which is 'tyrant traitor'), who destroyed our empire?"[20]

After expressing his desire to eat Don Francisco "raw without pepper," Cusi Huallpa returned to Atahualpa: "If he had been an Inca, he not only would not have committed the cruelties and abominations he did, but never even imagined them."[21] Cusi Huallpa concludes his scolding of the young mestizo by saying, "Do not say that one who was so against all our ancestors is our relative. See that you offend them and us and yourself in calling us relatives of a cruel tyrant, who from kings he made servants those few of us who escaped his cruelty" (Part 1, Book IX, Chapter XXXIX, vol. 2, 645).[22] Although similar sentiments are expressed in numerous places throughout the *Royal Commentaries*, what stands out about these remarks is that Inca Garcilaso portrays *himself* as having made a mistake very similar to the one Pizarro and his men committed. These passages reiterate not only the enduring animosity between rival panacas in Inca political life, but also, and more importantly, that even one with "expert" knowledge of Inca culture, such as Inca Garcilaso, had to be carefully instructed and reminded of the severity of Atahualpa's transgressions. Inca Garcilaso had learned his lesson about the word *auca*: it was "so evocative of tyrannies, cruelties, and evils," that is was a "proper title and mantle for those who earned it" (Part 1, Book IX, Chapter XXXIX, vol. 2, 645).[23]

Returning once again to Atahualpa's trial, we find that Inca Garcilaso has provided his readers with far more information concerning Atahualpa's character than the conquerors were able to realize on their own. Even if one had not read the First Part of the *Royal Commentaries*, Inca Garcilaso informs us in the opening sentence of the Second Part that his previous book had ended with "the fierce King Atahualpa so content and smug in thinking that with his cruelties and tyrannies he had secured his empire" (Part 2, Book I, Chapter I, vol. 1, 19).[24] As John Hemming has pointed out, Inca Garcilaso was not the first historian of the Peruvian conquest to portray the execution of Atahualpa as the result of legal proceedings. His account is unique, however, in that it is by far the most elaborate (Hemming 1970: 82–83). Armed with the knowledge of Atahualpa's illegitimacy, his murderous propensities, and the cloud of ignorance surrounding the conquerors, what becomes the most striking element of Atahualpa's trial are the questions that are put to Indian witnesses during the proceedings. No fewer than half of these dozen questions are directly related to Atahualpa's political status: was Huáscar the legitimate son and Atahualpa a bastard; did Atahualpa inherit the kingdom or usurp it; had Huáscar been deprived of the kingdom; had Atahualpa ordered Huáscar's death; had Atahualpa waged unjust wars (*guerras injustas*) and killed many people in the course of them; and had Atahualpa both depleted the Royal treasury by making gifts to relatives and friends and wasted the public granaries (Part 2, Book I, Chapter XXXVII)? Inca Garcilaso has provided answers to these questions for the benefit of his readers, all of which constitute a resounding indictment of the defendant. Yet the ensuing argument between Spaniards, as we have seen, is as much about whether Atahualpa is a tyrant as it is about what should be done with him. His defenders declare him a king and favor his removal to Spain; his prosecutors emphasize his tyranny and demand his death. Although the arguments of the first conquerors in opposition to Atahualpa's execution are morally salutary, in that they demonstrate respect for Inca sovereignty and prefer peaceful measures to violence, they are misplaced. Without doubt, Atahualpa was an auca, not an Inca.[25]

The reasons for these divagations on Inca Garcilaso's part are somewhat easier to see at this point. He attempts to exonerate the first conquerors through two separate means. First, their ethical character is vindicated insofar as they forward arguments that occupy a rather unambiguous moral high ground. Second, given that, in Mariana's words, "anyone" could legitimately kill a tyrant, it could be said that in going along with Atahualpa's execution they had done nothing wrong, whether they, or other Europeans, realized this or not. By suggesting this second line of defense, however, Inca Garcilaso brings up the crucial question of the motives behind the judicial murder and hence the Spanish conquest, which he has characterized as being of the basest sort. Atahualpa's prosecutors were solely concerned with establishing territorial control and, worse, filling their purses. When Pizarro's partner, Diego de Almagro, received news of Atahualpa's capture and the dazzling ransom in gold and silver he had offered in exchange for his life, Almagro hastened to join his companion in Cajamarca to split the booty as per their contract. Almagro and his men were soon disillusioned by their more fortunate comrades-in-arms, who said that, since the former were not present during the capture, they had no claim to the flood of riches before their eyes. At this, the *Almagristas* "began to say that they should kill the Inca so that they could have their share of what was won afterward. To this demand and to their good reason they added others as weak and weaker. But such as they were, they were sufficient to kill a prince as great as Atahualpa, who was in great fear of his death, seeing the discontent and acrimony that the Spaniards caused one another, and the many disputes, yelling and shouting from moment to moment and hour to hour, there were between them" (Part 2, Book I, Chapter XXXIV, vol. 1, 91).[26] It was conflicts such as these, over the division of spoils and the ambition to rule, that caused the outbreak of civil wars among the Spaniards, impeded the conversion of the Indians to Christianity, and hurtled Peru into chaos (Part 2, Book II, Chapter VI). Whereas Las Casas had imputed these motives to Pizarro, his men, and for that matter all the other conquerors, Inca Garcilaso pluralized the field and allowed a few of the conquistadors to stand apart from the insatiable lust for power and wealth driving the others.

The problems of intercultural uncertainty and sinister motivations, however, are not relegated solely to the invaders. At first, and due to the prophecy of Viracocha Inca and Huayna Cápac, the Incas believe that the Spaniards are Viracochas, "sons of our great god Viracocha" (Part 2, Book I, Chapter XX, vol. 1, 60). Nevertheless, the Incas are both unsettled and disconcerted by the violence and destruction wrought by those who were their potential kinsmen. As seen in Chapter 3, due to the murders and looting caused by the Spaniards and the threat of further bloodshed contained in the requerimiento, Atahualpa tells the strangers "either your prince and all of you are tyrants who are destroying the world, taking away kingdoms of others, killing and robbing those who have done you no harm and owe you nothing, or you are ministers of God, whom we call Pachacámac, who has selected you for our punishment and destruction" (Part 2, Book I, Chapter XXIV, vol. 1, 70).[27] It was this indigenous belief, of the common solar descent and implicit kinship between Incas and Spaniards, according to Inca Garcilaso, that kept the Indians from offering any resistance to the conquerors. And although the Incas would shortly be undeceived of their error, their inability to grasp the true character of the majority of the strangers in their lands directly contributed to their downfall.

With regard to motivations, the Indian translator Felipillo stands accused of intentionally providing false information during Atahualpa's trial to further his own ends. Inca Garcilaso makes the point by quoting a chapter from Francisco López de Gómara's *Historia de las Indias y México* (The History of the Indies and Mexico, 1552), which states:

> The death of Atahualpa was plotted whence it was least expected, for Felipillo, the interpreter, fell in love with and befriended one of Atahualpa's wives, in order to marry her if he died. He told Pizarro and the others that Atahualpa was gathering men in secret to kill the Christians and free him. As this began to resound among the Spaniards, they started to believe it; and some said that they should kill Atahualpa for the security of their own lives and those kingdoms, and others that they should send him to the Emperor and that they should not kill so great a prince, whatever his guilt. (Part 2, Book I, Chapter XXXVI, vol. 1, 94)[28]

This illustration of Felipillo's ulterior motives and their immediate impact further expiates the conquerors, because in addition to miscomprehending their surroundings they had been actively misled to believe, perhaps to their own convenience, that they were in eminent danger. Inca Garcilaso resolutely holds to the claim that the Incas did not resist, as we have seen, in order to avoid portraying the conquest as a "just war." He therefore offers Felipillo as a scapegoat to explain why some Spaniards mistakenly argued, with ultimately self-serving intentions, that their lives were in peril of being lost.

It now appears that the Spanish adversaries in Atahualpa's trial were *both* arguing from false premises. The one party, seeking to uphold justice and protect the integrity of the indigenous sovereign, thought that Atahualpa was the rightful king and defended him accordingly. The other, more numerous party was already possessed of crude desires and used the misinformation provided by Felipillo as a pretext for their actions. The whole atmosphere created by Inca Garcilaso is one of intercultural confusion and conflict, where it seems impossible for the Spaniards to adequately recognize and resolve the problems before them. What almost leaps out from the text, moreover, is the Spanish failure to attend to and accurately gauge the intentions and interests of indigenous actors, which in turn signals the miscarriage of their actions.

For Inca Garcilaso, the best interests of indigenous Peruvians appear to be rather straightforward: they lacked only the revealed truths of Christianity. Glaringly absent from the heated debate during Atahualpa's trial is any mention whatsoever of this all-important consideration. Inca Garcilaso raises the issue two chapters later, as he sums up the "Discourse that the Spaniards made over the events" (Part 2, Book I, Chapter XXXIX). Here we are presented with three Spanish explanations of the conquest. The first, which Inca Garcilaso claims was put forward "with boasting and without due consideration" of Inca prophecies, attributed the conquest solely to Spanish military prowess, "valuing only themselves." Others, "better considered and zealous of God's honor and the augment of the Holy Catholic faith," held that the conquest was nothing short of a miracle worked by divine providence for the propagation of the Word. The final group went further and said that since Atahualpa had been baptized it would have been better "for the peace of the kingdom and the augment of the Catholic faith" (*para la quietud del reino y para el aumento de la fe católica*) if he had been allowed to live. He could have issued an official edict in favor of Christianity, thereby converting the entire empire virtually overnight.[29] To this Inca Garcilaso adds his firm assent: "It is certain," he writes, "without any doubt, that everyone would have been baptized" (*Es cierto, sin duda ninguna, que bautizaran todos*), and for this he adduces the following reasons. The mandate of the Inca was taken to be divine law by his subjects; the Indians were by nature obedient to their kings; the example of the king was always followed by Indians; and they sought above all to comply with the prophecy of Huayna Cápac, which for Indians was the "most obligatory and strongest" reason. Inca Garcilaso admits that this would have been a great advantage to indigenous conversion, "but Our Lord God, in his secret wisdom, permitted events to succeed as they did" (Part 2, Book I, Chapter XXXIX, vol. 1, 104–05).

This, then, closes the book on Atahualpa's execution. Or does it? Perhaps the "secret wisdom" of providence is not as enigmatic as it first appears. These passages once again underscore and challenge the extent to which the conquerors had actually concerned themselves with spreading the faith. Had this been their primary motivation, they would have used Atahualpa to help them do so. Inca Garcilaso has already made very similar points, several times in fact, and these statements serve to sharpen their focus. In so doing, he is able to illustrate just how ineffective the providential justification and evangelical ideals behind the conquest proved to be *in practice*, despite the fact that these were the only justifications he was willing to allow. This, therefore, stands as his most devastating critique of the conquest, in that it exposes the hypocrisy of imperial agents and apologists who invoked Christian principles for what Inca Garcilaso considered to be incontrovertibly un-Christian ends.

More problematic for the interpretation that Inca Garcilaso favored Atahualpa's execution are the statements concerning why a living Atahualpa would have been more useful than an executed one. It should be noted, however, that the reasons he provides merely reassert the moral and political authority of the Incas and reiterate that they would have played an indispensable role—the familiar role of *praeparatio evangelica*, in fact—in peacefully bringing Christianity to their subjects. Such is Inca Garcilaso's argument throughout the *Royal Commentaries*, and these statements offer nothing new on this score. Conspicuously novel, however, are the suggestions that Atahualpa possessed the same power and authority as previous Incas and that his conversion, had he lived, would have been a tremendous and efficacious stimulus for his subjects to follow suit. This suggestion places Inca Garcilaso in an obvious contradiction: the certitude of Atahualpa's tyranny in the *Royal Commentaries* clashes noisily with the certitude that the entire empire would have obeyed and imitated his example had he been allowed to rule as a Christian. More specifically, Inca Garcilaso's own panaca, whose perspective and interests he nearly univocally champions when treating indigenous subjects, was so revolted by Atahualpa that they celebrated when his *children* died, decades after the purges he had unleashed on them had passed. Perhaps this is why Inca Garcilaso's assent to the Spanish opinion that saving Atahualpa's life for *both* the peace of the realm and the augment of the faith mentions *only* baptism and not political stability. However that may stand, Inca Garcilaso has provided ample evidence to question, if not completely undermine, the conclusion he draws about Atahualpa's usefulness, and particularly so when one considers the specific, indigenous perspective he projects in his texts.

Why, then, does Inca Garcilaso appear to side with the panaca of Pachacútec Inca and Atahualpa, the bitter rivals of his own lineage? The answer can only be found in Inca Garcilaso's treatment of indigenous politics, for he realized quite clearly that the descendants of Atahualpa's own panaca considered him the legitimate ruler. In a chapter somewhat innocently titled, "De las Gallinas y Palomas" (Of Hens and Doves), Inca Garcilaso makes the case. Starting from the usual perspective of Huáscar's partisans, the full inventory of Atahualpa's irredeemable behavior is briefly summarized, and we are told that not only did the Indians think that the Spaniards had come to punish the tyrant, but that they continued to abominate his memory by crying "Atahualpa!" every time a rooster crowed, once the latter had been introduced from Spain. He goes on to tell us, on the authority of mestizo Jesuit Blas Valera (who hailed from Chachapoyas, Atahualpa's sphere of influence), that Indians in the vicinity of Quito engaged in a similar practice, yet they cried "Atahualpa!" with solemnity and mourning in remembrance of their executed "natural king" (*rey natural*). Valera's version came from Atahualpa's vassals in Quito, while Inca Garcilaso heard his account in Cuzco, and upon this he concludes with one of his most memorable phrases, "each one says of the fair how it goes for him in it" (*Cada uno dice de la feria como le va en ella*) (Part 1, Book IX, Chapter XXIII, vol. 2, 613). This attests to the regional and political partialities of the historical accounts passed down in Andean oral traditions. But it also suggests that the alternative to Atahualpa's execution, which would have enabled him to continue as head-of-state with the purpose of facilitating indigenous conversion, was a *partial* solution at best. Somewhat like their Spanish conquerors, indigenous opinion was firmly divided over the question of Atahualpa's status: one party saw him as a tyrant, the other as a king.

The problem signaled here is the very same that Huayna Cápac's decision to cede the kingdom of Quito to Atahualpa instigated in the first place, the age-old political problem of factions. Prior to that moment, and with exception of the Chancas revolt (Part 1, Book IV, Chapters XXIII–XXIV and Book V, Chapters XXVII–XXX), both the functioning and succession of the Inca dynasty are presented as fluid and seamless, everything afterward is tumult and bloodshed. The division of the empire resulted in the emergence of royal factions, according to Inca Garcilaso, which became a permanent problem in indigenous politics following the deaths of Atahualpa and Huáscar. The same chapter in which he presents the Spanish explanations of the conquest and concludes with his defense of Atahualpa's utility for spreading the faith begins with a clarification of this predicament. Now that their kings were dead, "the Indians of one band and the other," Inca Garcilaso writes: "were like sheep without a shepherd, with no one to govern them in peace or in war, neither for their own benefit nor against the pain received from others. Rather, the supporters of Huáscar retained their enmity against Atahualpa's supporters, and for the ones to prevail over the others, everyone in each band attempted to serve and ingratiate themselves with the Spaniards and bring them to their side against their opponents" (Part 2, Book I, Chapter XXXIX, vol. 1, 104).[30] Indigenous resistance is mentioned at this point as something to follow precipitously, and unsurprisingly it is fomented by two of Atahualpa's captains, Quizquiz and Rumiñaui. The first passage of the succeeding chapter reiterates the point that "the war between the brother Kings, Huáscar and Atahualpa, was the total destruction of the Empire, which facilitated the entrance of the Spaniards so they could win it with the ease with which they did" (Part 2, Book I, Chapter XL, vol. 1, 106).[31] In the next sentence, he goes on to remind us that God had allowed this to happen so that the Gospel could enter Peru. Strikingly, however, Inca Garcilaso adopts the formulaic structures of the simulated indigenous voice that he deploys as a stylistic device throughout the *Royal Commentaries* to establish his authority before a prospective indigenous audience.[32] "But Our Lord God, having pity on their paganism, permitted the discord between the two brothers, so that the preachers of His Gospel and Catholic Faith could enter with greater ease and less resistance" (Part 2, Book I, Chapter XL, vol. 1, 106).[33]

The shift in style calls our attention to the likelihood that Inca Garcilaso wanted potential indigenous readers to consider this explanation in particular. And the point he wanted them to take was that the animosities between the partisans of Huáscar and Atahualpa, respectively, had served an essential, historical purpose (i.e., allowing for the entrance of the Gospel). Once that purpose had been achieved, however, there was no longer any need for the rivalries to continue. In fact, Inca Garcilaso says that it was precisely this infighting among indigenous factions that had enabled the Spaniards to become "absolute lords" (*absolutos señores*) of both Quito and Cuzco (Part 2, Book I, Chapter XXXIX, vol. 1, 104).[34] His diagnosis of the ruinous consequences of faction for indigenous politics and his self-conscious recognition of the extent to which he was reconstructing events still hotly contested by indigenous Peruvians led him to partially defend Atahualpa. Read in the broader context of the passages surrounding this alternative to Atahualpa's execution, however, it becomes evident that Inca Garcilaso was providing an example of how to transcend the partisan character of Inca politics in the interests of a unified indigenous front. The first proposed alternative does not constitute what he considered the best solution. It is an olive branch stretched out from one *panaca* to another; it recognizes Atahualpa's power and prestige in certain sectors of indigenous society and validates the anger and discontent his descendants inherited as a result of his execution.

Such a gesture of reconciliation on Inca Garcilaso's part toward the panaca of his adversaries was to a certain measure necessary if they were to accept as plausible the second alternative to Atahualpa's execution. It is of central importance that this solution is both formulated and proposed by Inca Titu Atauchi, who is portrayed as Atahualpa's full brother (Part 2, Book I, Chapter XVII).[35] Shortly after the execution, Atahualpa's captain, Quizquiz, had managed to capture a number of Spaniards in an ambush as the latter were departing Cajamarca. Among the Spaniards taken were Sancho de Cuéllar, the scribe who had announced Atahualpa's sentence, Francisco de Chaves, and Hernando de Haro, two of those who were credited with having defended Atahualpa during the trial (Part 2, Book II, Chapter VI). After conducting an investigation of their own, the Indians decided that Cuéllar, for having dared to sentence their king, was to suffer the same fate. In pronouncing Cuéllar's sentence, we finally come to know the punishment accorded to tyrants in the Inca empire, "'Pachacámac orders this auca to be hanged, and all those who killed our Inca'" (Part 2, Book II, Chapter, VI, vol. 1, 123).[36] Although Inca Garcilaso claims that the Indians appropriated the practice of publicly declaring criminal sentences from the Spaniards, insofar as the sentence itself is applied to the auca Cuéllar for the death of "our Inca" from the perspective of Atahualpa's supporters, it is equally applicable to Atahualpa from the perspective of Huáscar's supporters. That this *auca* could be legitimately executed as recompense for the death of an Inca mirrors and completes Inca Garcilaso's numerous statements to the effect that "the Spaniards had killed the tyrant

[Atahualpa] as punishment and to avenge the Incas" (*los españoles habían muerto al tirano en castigo y venganza de los Incas*) (Part 1, Book V, Chapter XXI, vol. 1, 300), or to "avenge Huáscar and all of his followers" (*vengassen a Huáscar y a todos los suyos*) (Part 2, Book I, Chapter XL, vol. 1, 107). With this single act of vengeance, moreover, the other Spanish prisoners are redeemed, particularly Chaves and Haro, who had argued on Atahualpa's behalf.

Cuéllar's death leads to a number of capitulations negotiated by Titu Atauchi with Chaves and Haro, and these represent Inca Garcilaso's views on what should have happened following Atahualpa's execution. The seven principal terms of the agreement are as follows: (1) that all past injuries on both sides will be forgotten; (2) that there shall be peace between Indians and Spaniards; (3) that the Spaniards will not resist the return of the imperial crown to Manco Inca, the legitimate heir; (4) that Indians and Spaniards will behave like friends in their dealings and contracts and assist one another; (5) that the Spaniards will remove the shackles from Indians so held and quit that practice in the future; (6) that the laws of the Incas compatible with the Christian faith will remain in effect and be enforced; (7) that Francisco Pizarro will travel to Spain forthwith and confirm the points of this treaty with Charles V (Part 2, Book II, Chapter VI). Chaves agreed to these terms and made two requests of Titu Atauchi, which were granted. These were that the Incas would wholeheartedly embrace the Christian faith, and, since the Spaniards were foreigners in that land, the Incas would provide them with provisions and Indian servants.

That all of the foregoing was perhaps completely fabricated by Inca Garcilaso should provoke neither surprise nor concern, for it is in the elaboration of such scenarios that he reveals his political thought.[37] These capitulations, fanciful as they may seem, tie up all the loose ends: indigenous sovereignty is respected and maintained; Atahualpa's tyranny and Huáscar's death are avenged for members of Huáscar's panaca; Atahualpa's panaca partially redresses their ruler's execution through the death of Cuéllar; Christianity is accepted by the Incas and their subjects; an alliance between Pizarro and Huáscar's panaca is created through Atahualpa's execution and Manco Inca's return to the throne as legitimate heir; and the terms for political coexistence and economic cooperation between all parties are established. The comprehensiveness of this plan dwarfs the earlier recommendation to keep Atahualpa on the throne to spread the Catholic faith; it achieves not only the religious goals of the conquest, but also suggests the practical measures to be taken for the necessary reform of indigenous politics. Furthermore, for this solution to have been a possibility, Atahualpa's execution was absolutely necessary, for Manco Inca, one of Huayna Cápac's sons with family ties to Cuzco (Regalado de Hurtado 1993: 106), is presented as the legitimate heir, once again illustrating Inca Garcilaso's preference for his own panaca.[38]

It finally appears that Atahualpa's execution was not only warranted and justified from the perspectives of European political thought and Huáscar's panaca, but that the tyrant's death was actually in the best interests of all parties involved in the conquest. Francisco Pizarro is more than partially absolved for his involvement in Atahualpa's murder, he is completely redeemed for his actions when we come to find that among the Spaniards there were many who favored the full implementation of these capitulations, "and the Governor himself was one of them" (*y el mismo governador era uno dellos*) (Part 2, Book II, Chapter VI, vol. 1, 124). Both Aquinas and Mariana argued that killing a usurper was an entirely justifiable course of action, yet each was careful to point out that in so doing one should attend to strengthening the public good to avoid further disturbances or unwittingly allowing another tyrant to take the place of the first (Mariana 1961: vol. 1, 110–15; Aquinas 1988: 267–71).[39] With these well-known doctrines of tyrannicide as a subtext, Pizarro's support of the capitulations presents him as looking after the public good, indigenous and Spanish alike, despite Inca Garcilaso's suggestion that neither he nor his men were fully aware that they were killing a tyrant when they did so. Pizarro can now be styled as a tyrannomach, and his desire for an alliance with Manco Inca, whose supporters were the loudest claimants for Atahualpa's death, reinforces this characterization.[40]

Realizing, however, the offense Atahualpa's supporters certainly would have taken at finding a member of Huáscar's panaca put forward as the sole legitimate heir, Inca Garcilaso appealed to the broader interest of indigenous unity to smooth over his obvious reversion to a partisan solution. Quite provocatively, Inca Garcilaso claims that Atahualpa's party, despite their recent enmity, was willing to agree to Manco Inca's enthronement as "supreme lord of the entire empire" (*supremo señor de todo aquel Imperio*) as a defense initiative: "They agreed, with sound military counsel, to restore the Empire to whom it legitimately belonged, so that all the Indians would be as one to resist and snatch the kingdom from the Spaniards, or to live together with them, for in this way they would be more esteemed and feared for not being divided in bands and factions" (Part 2, Book II, Chapter VII, vol. 1, 126).[41] This is not the only instance in which Inca Garcilaso suggests a show of indigenous military strength would have captured the attention of their Spanish invaders.

For when Manco Inca is preparing to request restoration and the fulfillment of the capitulations from Pizarro, Quizquiz recommends preparation for war. Manco Inca does not follow the counsel of Quizquiz; instead, he claims, "Let us act in reason and justice, let them act as they would" (*Hagamos nosotros lo que es razón y justicia, hagan ellos lo que quisiera*) (Part 2, Book II, Chapter XI, vol. 1, 137). Acting in "reason and justice" gets Manco Inca nowhere. It leads to his imprisonment and, desperate and enraged by Pizarro's interminable delays, he eventually leads a failed uprising in Cuzco (Part 2, Book II, Chapter XXII–XXV). Of course, Inca Garcilaso's hands were significantly tied in his representations of Manco Inca's rebellion and other numerous instances of indigenous resistance, because he had to present them as having been egregiously provoked and hence completely victimized in order to avoid the waging of a "just war" against them in response.[42] Furthermore, in order to maintain the legitimacy of claims for restoration pressed by the descendants of the Incas (such as himself), indigenous martyrdom was a more secure representational strategy, and one more amenable to the Catholic sensibilities of his day, than righteous insurgency. Nevertheless, given the cataclysmic unfolding of events in the Second Part for indigenous Peruvians, from the failure of the capitulations to the execution of Tupac Amaru, it is clear that Inca Garcilaso thought that a coordinated military alliance among the Inca elite would have been a more prudent course for all of the panacas rather than the factionalism, sedition, and martyrdom he frequently portrays.

At least three interrelated problems, according to Inca Garcilaso, accounted for the abysmal failure of the Spanish conquest. The first was the inability of Spaniards and Incas to understand each other, particularly the Spaniards, for if they had understood what was going on around them, they would have realized that Atahualpa was a usurper and they might have been able to prevent Huáscar's death. Inca Garcilaso suggests that there was a ready-made solution to the legitimation problems that arose from the conquest of Peru, and had Pizarro been able to more adequately capitalize on the situation in which he had thrust himself, he would have executed Atahualpa and returned the empire to Huáscar or a member of his panaca. Pizarro's actions could have then been justified before Europeans as tyrannicide (rather than through recourse to the doctrine of just war) and before Andeans as a fulfillment of the prophecy that held the invaders to be sons of Viracocha Inca. Although Atahualpa was indeed dispatched, the Spaniards had improperly assessed indigenous sentiments and politics, and the judicial murder was carried out for all the wrong reasons. The latter represents the second problem of the encounter: Inca Garcilaso maintains that most Spaniards involved in the conquest (the count of 350 to 50 at Atahualpa's trial is symbolic) were callously self-interested, and through their actions they put the lie to the Christian ideals behind Spanish imperialism. Allowing such unscrupulous men to win the day at Atahualpa's trial simply increased their desires and set off a disastrous train of events, which accounted for the failure of the capitulations, the Indian uprisings, and the warfare among Spaniards that loomed on the horizon. This situation was so dire and all-encompassing that Inca Garcilaso said it must have been provoked by none other than "the Devil, the enemy of human kind . . . with the help and sound diligence of his ministers, the seven deadly sins" (Part 2, Book II, Chapter VI, vol. 1, 125).[43] For their part, indigenous Peruvians began to realize that the strangers among them were not, in fact, heirs apparent to Inca greatness. Because their behavior was so inexplicably cruel and so unlike what was expected from Incas, the newcomers were no longer honored with that title. Instead, they were called "*zupay*, which is 'demon'"(Part 2, Book I, Chapter XL, vol. 1, 107). As culpable as certain Spaniards were and as nearly ubiquitous as diabolical intervention becomes in the Second Part, Inca Garcilaso nevertheless suggests that had indigenous Peruvians overcome the third problem, the feuds between panacas that began with Atahualpa's rise to power, they might have been able to resist the imposition of foreign rule or, failing that, at least press their claims more effectively on the battlefield. An inter-panaca military front, however, never materialized. Instead, according to Inca Garcilaso, the Indians remained divided among themselves and tried to enlist the service of their conquerors against one another, thereby worsening their collective plight. It was these all-too-human failings that turned what should have been one of history's most glorious moments into a complete and utter disaster.

Of course, with the Spanish conquest of the Incas we arrive at the climactic midpoint of the *Royal Commentaries*, and the story Inca Garcilaso has to tell is far from over. As I argued in Chapter 3, furthermore, Atahualpa's execution and the failure of the capitulations are but one *pachacuti*, or world reversal, in a cyclical series that runs through and connects both parts of the work. Having isolated the main reasons for the initial failure of a peaceful, dynastic succession and cultural fusion between Incas and Spaniards, Inca Garcilaso has illustrated from the very earliest moments of encounter forward just how difficult the realization of Peru's veritable providential destiny has been and, hence, will be. Both the Devil and the angry face of Pachacámac ascend over the Andes, and in the *Royal Commentaries* the Peruvian civil wars turn us further and further from the resplendence of the Inca past toward the darkness of a violent and tumultuous colonial society tearing all its diverse members to shreds. Given, then, what Inca Garcilaso portrays as the very dire consequences of a botched encounter, one can ask if it is possible to right the course of Peru toward the ideal of a just, intercultural society forwarded by the mestizo historian. This ideal is without doubt the central element of the *Royal Commentaries'* utopian promise, but the utopian spur driving Inca Garcilaso, despite the Stoic remove from the vanities of the world implied by his posture of being undeceived (*desengañado*) throughout the Second Part, is that he never completely gives up the hope of its possibility. Where and how, in the darkest of times, can a historical opportunity for the perpetuation and possible realization of this hope be found? For Inca Garcilaso, it is in Gonzalo Pizarro's rebellion, to which we turn in the next chapter.

5
"DIE A KING"

Gonzalo Pizarro's Rebellion

On November 20, 1542, the provisions of the New Laws were sent forth from Barcelona by order of King Charles V to regulate the conduct of Spanish conquistadors, administrators, clergy, and settlers in the Spanish overseas territories. Inspired in part by the tireless lobbying of Bartolomé de Las Casas, the principal intent of the laws was to provide for the "conservation and increase of the Indians" and to ensure that indigenous populations were both instructed in the Catholic faith and treated as "free persons" and "vassals" of the Spanish crown. Among the forty-plus stipulations were those that forbade further enslavement of Indians under any pretense, strict limitations on the amount and kind of tribute that could be exacted from Indians held in *encomiendas* (a grant of labor) (which completely ruled out personal service to *encomenderos*, Spaniards rewarded for their services with encomiendas), prohibitions against the grant of encomiendas to colonial administrators and clergy, a moratorium on the creation of new encomiendas, and the elimination of the succession of encomiendas through inheritance.[1]

The storms of protest following the arrival of the New Laws in many ways exposed the underlying intent of the monarchy—to diminish the threat to regal authority posed by the growing political and economic power base of the encomenderos and secular clergy in the New World. Such royal efforts to safeguard and indoctrinate indigenous vassals and to neutralize, if not outright dispossess, the conquerors were nothing new; religious, economic, and political motivations intermingled in Spanish expansion from the very beginning. In the preceding fifty years there had been numerous attempts by both the Spanish crown as well as high-ranking religious officials to protect indigenous peoples from the abuses of their new masters, some of the most notable being Queen Isabella's prohibition of Indian slavery in 1500, the Laws of Burgos in 1512, and the 1537 bull, *Sublimus Deus*, by Pope Paul III, which included Amerindians within the brotherhood of humanity redeemable through Christ (Hanke 1974: 7–21). While the crown was solidifying its stance toward the treatment of indigenous peoples, it was also beginning to exhibit a pattern in its pragmatic policies toward the conquerors and settlers of the new realms. In general terms, the Catholic Kings Ferdinand and Isabella, and later Charles V, were often very generous in granting broad powers, titles, estates, pensions, and tax exemptions to the most promising explorers and then slowly tightening the reins, thereby undermining the previous grants, to establish a state-controlled, bureaucratic regime once the territories had been subdued. Despite vociferous petitions and litigation on their own behalf, this was the treatment respectively accorded to such notable figures as Christopher Columbus and his son Diego, Hernán Cortés, and Francisco Pizarro.[2]

Although immediate opposition to the New Laws percolated throughout the Spanish possessions, the attempts to defuse the potentially explosive consequences of the legislation in Mexico and Peru marked a somewhat drastic turn in the respective trajectories of these colonial centers. While Viceroy Antonio de Mendoza and Royal Inspector Francisco Tello de Sandoval were able to avoid catastrophe in New Spain by suspending the application of the laws and striking a compromise with the interests of encomenderos and the secular clergy (Haring 1975: 51–53), Peru erupted. The latter was particularly hard-hit by the ordinances in the first place due to its higher concentration of encomenderos. James Lockhart, for instance, has estimated that the roughly 480 encomenderos represented anywhere from one-eighth up to one-fourth of the total Spanish population in Peru in the early 1540s (Lockhart 1968: 12). Further, the laws found Peruvians in a precarious state of mind as they were just limping away from yet another internal convulsion. On September 16, 1542, two short months before the New Laws were signed, the mestizo rebel Diego de Almagro the Younger had been defeated in the bloody battle of Chupas by the forces of Licentiate Cristóbal Vaca de Castro. Almagro's defeat and execution carried the hope of respite from five years of intermittent fratricidal conflict between the Spaniards, which (among scores of Spaniards and Indians alike) had accounted for the deaths of the two leading Peruvian conquerors, Diego de Almagro the Elder and Francisco Pizarro. Instead of easing these social tensions, however, the New Laws curtly revoked the encomiendas of all those who had participated in the Peruvian civil wars, regardless of whether they had been *Pizarristas* or *Almagristas*, royalists or rebels (Konetzke 1953: vol. 1, 216–20). The rule of Licentiate Vaca de Castro (1541–1544), moreover, brought little salve to the fresh wounds of the fledgling realm. Although he had received very explicit directives and powers from Charles V to attend to governance, he expended a great deal of his energies looking after his own purse, and particularly in devising ways to profit from the vast holdings of the Pizarro estate (Varón Gabai 1997: 94–97). The final insult, however, arrived with the first Viceroy of Peru Blasco Núñez Vela (1544–1546). Whereas Mendoza and Tello de Sandoval appear to have proceeded with discretion in Mexico, Núñez Vela, who has since become notorious for his ill-temper, not only insisted upon full, immediate, and rigorous implementation of the laws, but also refused to hear any petitions against them (Vargas Ugarte 1966: vol. 1, 184–190). Núñez Vela's impertinence was more than the encomenderos, nearly all of whom stood to lose their Indians to the crown, could suffer. Although the laws were retracted by royal decree on September 20, 1544 (Lohmann Villena 1977: 13), news of the suspension reached Peru too late. On October 23, 1544, the Audiencia of Lima appointed Gonzalo Pizarro (Francisco's youngest half-brother) Governor, General Procurator, and Captain General of Peru.[3] The following day Gonzalo took the appropriate oaths and Peru was in revolt.

As Guillermo Lohmann Villena has suggested, Gonzalo Pizarro's victory over the hapless Núñez Vela at the battle of Iñaquito on January 18, 1546 profoundly disturbed His Cesarean Majesty Charles V, perhaps even more than the revolts of the *comuneros* in Castile (1520–1521), the upstart *Germanías* (brotherhoods) of Valencia, and the social conflicts incited by the Protestant Reformation (Lohmann Villena 1977: 11). There was good reason for the emperor's concern, for in the tumult at Iñaquito, Viceroy Núñez Vela, theoretically an extension of the king's very person, had been decapitated. At that moment Gonzalo had effectively removed not only Peru but also the enormous silver mines of Potosí, recently discovered in 1545, from monarchical control. Gonzalo, with his outnumbered troops guided by the brilliant military strategies of the corpulent octogenarian Francisco de Carvajal, once again defeated the forces of Charles V led by Diego Centeno at Huarina on the shores of Lake Titicaca on October 21, 1547, further entrenching his position. Nevertheless, his rebellion and reign lasted less than a half-year from this climactic victory, in which, rightly or wrongly, Inca Garcilaso's father, Captain Sebastián Garcilaso de la Vega, was inculpated over the dicey issue of a horse. Lured by promises of pardon and reward offered by the king's minister, Licentiate Pedro de la Gasca, Gonzalo's company was diminished through desertion and succumbed to La Gasca's royalists under Diego Centeno at the battle of Sacsahuana outside Cuzco on April 8, 1548. Gonzalo Pizarro and his military leader, Francisco de Carvajal, whose actions were generally considered seditious, were charged with high treason and executed in Cuzco the following day, signaling the end of this dramatic chapter in early Peruvian history.

Born on April 12, 1539, Inca Garcilaso (as yet still called Gómez Suárez de Figueroa) was three days shy of his ninth birthday when he witnessed the hanging and beheading of Gonzalo Pizarro and Francisco de Carvajal (Part 2, Book V, Chapter XXXIX). His treatment of Gonzalo's rebellion in the Second Part of the *Royal Commentaries* is correspondingly filled with vivid boyhood recollections from those stormy years. Inca Garcilaso was somewhat more than a youthful eyewitness, however, as his own life appears to have been endangered on more than one occasion thanks to the skirmishing and the apparent inconstancy of his father's loyalties. For instance, Captain Garcilaso is listed among those who immediately, yet secretly, protested and repented of Gonzalo's election to Captain General as well as General Procurator in Cuzco to appeal the New Laws, for he realized that a heavily armed Gonzalo would be tempted to rebel (Part 2, Book IV, Chapter VII). Captain Garcilaso was also among the first, along with the chroniclers Pedro Pizarro, Diego de Trujillo, and Diego de Silva, to abandon Gonzalo's cause and seek alliance with Viceroy Núñez Vela (Lohmann Villena 1994: 264–65). For this betrayal, Pedro de Puelles sacked and threatened to burn the home of Captain Garcilaso, causing the young Inca Garcilaso, his mother, sister, and the rest of the household to flee for their lives, and Hernando Bachicao routinely cannonaded the house from across the plaza in Cuzco (Part 2, Book IV, Chapter X). This was only the beginning of the bizarre relationship between the rebel leader and the captain, the two of whom had previously been closely aligned and had undertaken the successful conquest of the Charcas together, that unfolded through the course of the rebellion. Captain Garcilaso became the nominal prisoner of Gonzalo despite the fact that the two continued to dine at the same table and sleep in the same field tent. Moreover, during this time Gonzalo loaned 800 pesos to Captain Garcilaso, which allowed the latter to purchase the famous Peruvian steed, Salinillas. Of course, this is the very same Salinillas that would later undermine the sincerity of Captain Garcilaso's royal sentiments in the eyes of some Spanish officials and prove disastrous during Inca Garcilaso's petition to the crown in Madrid in 1563. The testimonies of historians Francisco López de Gómara, Agustín de Zárate, and Diego Fernández the Palentine credit Captain Garcilaso with having given this horse and, hence, the victory to the fallen Gonzalo during the battle of Huarina (see chapter 1). Inca Garcilaso dedicated an entire chapter in the Second Part to restoring his father's reputation from the slanders of previous historians, and he claims that this one incident had forced him into the "corners of solitude and poverty" (*los rincones de la soledad y pobreza*) from which he wrote, having done penance for the sin of his father, a sin that had never been committed (Part 2, Book V, Chapter XXIII, vol. 2, 216). Yet, the destruction of their home, the enduring suspicion of his father, and his own failure at court were not the only losses suffered by the de la Vega family during the revolt. Juan de Vargas, Captain Garcilaso's youngest brother and Inca Garcilaso's uncle, received four fatal harquebus wounds at Huarina fighting for the king (Part 2, "Prologue").

Considering, then, the negative consequences of Gonzalo's rebellion on the mestizo historian's childhood and early adulthood, one might expect Inca Garcilaso's portrayal of the last, youngest, and perhaps most audacious of the Pizarro brothers in Peru to balance the scales for the considerable harm caused to the author and his family. This, however, is not the case. Both Gonzalo and Carvajal are not only remembered fondly by Inca Garcilaso, but he also explicitly defends and, as far as possible, exalts them. For instance, according to Inca Garcilaso, the ones who knew Gonzalo best saw that "he was a man of sufficient understanding, neither quarrelsome nor deceptive, neither of false promises nor double words, but rather a simple man of truth, kindness and nobility, trusting in his friends, who destroyed him" (Part 2, Book IV, Chapter XLI, vol. 2, 137).[4] And to fill out the portrait: "Gonzalo Pizarro had the build of a gentleman, with a very fine face, good health, and great endurance for hardships, as our history has shown. An elegant rider on horseback in both saddles; a skillful harquebusier and crossbowman, with an arc of clay pellets he could paint anything he desired on a wall. He was the best lance to have come to the New World according to the conclusion of all those who have spoken of the famous men who have gone there" (Part 2, Book V, Chapter

XLIII, vol. 2, 278–79).[5] As for Francisco de Carvajal, Inca Garcilaso assures us that he would have been known as the "flower of the Peruvian militia" if he had served the King (Part 2, Book V, Chapter XVIII, vol. 2, 199), and for those who knew him (among whom the mestizo historian numbers himself) many said that not since Julius Caesar had there been another soldier such as he (Part 2, Book IV, Chapter XXVI, vol. 2, 89). Above and beyond his prowess in the field, however, it was Carvajal's unswerving loyalty and feral military discipline that caused him to respond so mercilessly to the rebellion's "weavers" (*tejedores*), whose allegiances passed to and fro like the spindles of a loom (Part 2, Book IV, Chapter XXVIII, vol. 2, 98). Such weavers provoked Carvajal's wrath and more often than not earned themselves a wage of exemplary execution in return for their lack of resolve (Part 2, Book IV, Chapter XXIX). The ostensible cruelty of these spectacles, which according to Inca Garcilaso were as understandable as they were excessive, was the main reason why Carvajal's character had been so thoroughly misunderstood and misrepresented. Finally, Inca Garcilaso devotes no fewer than two full chapters to Carvajal's wry witticisms and gallows humor (Part 2, Book V, Chapters XLI–XLII), and perhaps these stand as the clearest evidence of the historian's fondness for the aged warrior. For, in the entirety of the *Royal Commentaries*, the hardened veteran of countless wars in the Old World and the New is paid the high compliment of being the most consistently and intentionally funny of any person to appear in the texts.

These vindications of Gonzalo and Carvajal once again propel the craft of Inca Garcilaso's narrative into troubled waters. For in the published record of the time (the works of López de Gómara, Zárate, and Fernández mentioned above), Gonzalo was generally portrayed as a dimwitted traitor to the crown and a tyrant whose bellicose transgression of royal privilege duly warranted his execution.[6] Francisco de Carvajal fared even worse. While all agreed that the wily Carvajal was perhaps the greatest military commander to set foot in the New World, his callous indifference to human life and his appetite for butchery earned him the sobriquet "Devil of the Andes." López de Gómara suggested that of the four hundred needless executions of Spaniards after Viceroy Núñez Vela's arrival in Peru, Carvajal and his four African guardsmen were responsible for nearly all of them (López de Gómara 1941: vol. 2, 179–80). In speaking so highly of Gonzalo and Carvajal, Inca Garcilaso was defending sordid characters indeed.

Added to these difficulties, Inca Garcilaso had a strong personal stake in the events. Captain Garcilaso, as we have seen, suffered the guilt of his mere association with the rebels, regardless of his true loyalties and what may or may not have occurred in the heat of battle. In order to restore his father's reputation, Inca Garcilaso had two rhetorical strategies open to him: first, to deny that the gift of Salinillas to Gonzalo at the battle of Huarina had occurred in the way previous historians suggested; and, second, to transform the act, regardless of when or how it occurred, into an expression of his father's nobility. Inca Garcilaso pursues both strategies, yet it is the second that most jeopardizes the authority and veracity of his narrative. For if the donation of Salinillas to his friend Gonzalo in a harrowing moment of pitched battle displayed the "spirit, strength, and bravery" (*ánimo, esfuerzo, y valentía*) of Captain Garcilaso, then, within the standards of rank, nobility, and gallantry of the day, the recipient of such a gift would have to have been worthy of receiving it (Part 2, Book V, Chapter XXIII, vol. 2, 216). This, of course, veritably *requires* a reestimation of Gonzalo's worth and status, for no nobleman deserving of the title would shirk his duty to his king to aid and abet a criminal. Yet, insofar as Gonzalo's treachery and tyranny were widely accepted among his contemporaries, Inca Garcilaso's positive reappraisal of the rebel's character threatened to raise serious concerns about the mestizo historian's partiality, understood here in terms of doling out excessive praise or blame in accordance with his own personal interests. Attesting to this predicament, Inca Garcilaso claims that he had long ago lost hope of benefiting from the truth of these matters (Part 2, Book V, Chapter XXIII), and on more than one occasion he goes so far as to say that previous historians had impugned both Gonzalo and Carvajal out of their desire to flatter the powers that be, i.e., the Spanish monarchy (Part 2, Book V, Chapter XLIII). Finally, in a clear allusion to Tacitus's mantra *sine ira et studio* ("without ire or interest") (Tacitus 1996: 32), Inca Garcilaso restates his obligation as historian to relate the truth of events in his own time to "the whole world . . . without passion or partisanship" (Part 2, Book V, Chapter XXXIX, vol. 2, 263).[7]

Needless to say, abundant complications attended Inca Garcilaso's treatment of Gonzalo Pizarro's rebellion, which in many respects represents the most difficult historical revision undertaken in the *Royal Commentaries*. And while Inca Garcilaso's desire to vindicate the memory of his father certainly contributed to his assessment of Gonzalo's character and actions, that motivation on its own fails to grasp the full significance of this reconstruction.[8] For at stake in his portrayal of Gonzalo's rebellion is nothing less than Inca Garcilaso's espousal and endorsement of a political perspective vehemently opposed to the absolutism of the Spanish monarchy and viceregal regime.

Inca Garcilaso not only favored an independent Peru, but he used the events of Gonzalo's rebellion, and particularly the character of Francisco de Carvajal, to suggest the kind of government a liberated Peru should adopt. This government was to be a monarchy with a system of corule between Incas and Spaniards and an advisory court comprised of a landed aristocracy from the leading cities. The mestizo polity Inca Garcilaso envisioned was not only in direct opposition to the bureaucratic, state-controlled, viceregal regime of the Spanish empire, but, by defending the rights and characters of those who rebelled against it, he also opened the discursive possibility of an antiabsolutist, antiviceregal, and potentially revolutionary ideology in Peru.[9]

Before turning to his political recommendations and the champion of this perspective, Francisco de Carvajal, it is best to review how Inca Garcilaso authorizes Gonzalo Pizarro's character and deeds for his Andean readers. As I argued in chapter 3, Inca Garcilaso transforms some of the first conquerors and encomenderos of Peru into Viracocha Incas in order to establish the newcomers as implicit kinsmen and, therefore, legitimate heirs to the Inca dynasty. Gonzalo, one of the four Pizarro brothers explicitly lauded as divine emissaries at the outset of the Second Part (Part 2, Book I, Chapter II), reaps the benefits of this association. Moreover, Inca Garcilaso draws a series of parallels between the eighth ruler, Viracocha Inca, and Gonzalo through which the latter's defeat by La Gasca's troops at Sacsahuana is the mirrored inverse of the former's victory over and restoration of the empire from the rebelling Chancas on the same site (Part 1, Book V, Chapter XVII). The treatments of both figures, occurring as they do in Books IV and V of their respective parts, represent equally climactic moments of the narrative. The major difference between the two is that whereas Viracocha Inca's victory rescued the empire from the invaders and Inca Yáhuar Huácac's flight, thereby representing a *pachacuti*, a turning of the world for the better (Part 1, Book V, Chapter XXVIII), Gonzalo's defeat by the royalists represents the opposite: it is a pachacuti for the worse.

Gonzalo's geographical movements during his campaign likewise duplicate and invoke the route of the culture-hero cum deity Viracocha in Andean myths (Mazzotti 1996a: 293–322; 2008: 248–77). For instance, in many of the Inca myths of origins, the god Viracocha arises from Lake Titicaca in the region of Tiahuanaco, proceeds on a diagonal journey in a northwesterly direction to Cuzco, during which he calls various tribes into being, and continues along this path until he departs over the sea at either Pachacámac or Puerto Viejo.[10] As Henrique Urbano has demonstrated, two of the major components of the Viracocha myth-cycle are "codes of kinship" and "codes of space," which are distinct yet inseparable elements expressing crucial ideological aspects of a broader sociopolitical worldview. In this sense, the very movements or route of the god Viracocha had a profound social significance for indigenous Andeans, and his diagonal trajectory (southeast to northwest) was inextricably bound to his manifestation as Viracocha Pachayachachi, the organizing and civilizing agent of the world (Urbano 1981: XXXII–XXXIII).

After his defeat of Viceroy Núñez Vela outside Quito, Gonzalo eventually heads toward Collao in order to confront the royalist troops of Diego Centeno. Gonzalo's surprising triumph over Centeno at Huarina is fought on the shores of Lake Titicaca, and in order to recall Viracocha, in the twofold sense of recalling the deity and his relation to the Spaniards signaled earlier (Part 2, Book I, Chapter XL), Inca Garcilaso reminds us that Gonzalo's outnumbered band was victorious thanks to their "*illapas*, which, as I have said, means lightning, thunder and thunderbolts in the language of the Indians, and such were the harquebuses to General Diego Centeno's most noble and splendid army . . . [that] almost all of them perished in that unfortunate and cruel battle" (Part 2, Book V, Chapter XX, vol. 2, 206).[11] When Gonzalo arrives in Cuzco shortly thereafter, his abbreviated itinerary coincides with what José Antonio Mazzotti has identified as "the route of Viracocha," and he is received with all the pomp and ceremony of the former rulers, even to the extent that the Indians were "hailing in loud voices, calling him Inca, and other majestic titles that they used to say to their natural Kings in their triumphs" (Part 2, Book V, Chapter XXVII, vol. 2, 213).[12] At this moment in the text, the return of Viracocha is actualized in the person of Gonzalo Pizarro, and his role as a potential restorer of the Inca empire is authorized for Andean readers through his emulation of the ancient deity (Mazzotti 1996a: 311–14; 2008: 266–69).

If we remember with Franklin Pease that Andean originary myths were not myths of creation in the Judeo-Christian sense, but rather tales of founding and ordination (Pease 1995: 152), then the resemblance between the god Viracocha, the ruler Viracocha Inca, and Gonzalo Pizarro forwards the encomendero rebel as a refounder of the Inca empire to Andean readers. At this point it is therefore necessary to explore what kind of social and political restructuring the arrival of the new Inca promises for Peru. The first response is obvious enough: Gonzalo's victory promises the end of the viceregal regime, for after defeating Viceroy Núñez Vela, Gonzalo almost immediately turns to governing in the best interests of both Indians and Spaniards: "Gonzalo Pizarro endeavored to make laws and ordinances for the good government of the land, for the peace and benefit of Indians and Spaniards, and for the augment of the Christian religion" (Part 2, Book IV, Chapter XXXV, vol. 2, 119).[13]

This, however, is just the beginning of a more detailed plan for restoring indigenous sovereignty and creating a new mestizo polity through the political alliance and intermarriage of encomenderos and Incas. This proposal is voiced by Francisco de Carvajal in a speech advising Gonzalo of the best way to secure his rule (Part 2, Book IV, Chapter XL). As David Brading points out, a letter by Carvajal is mentioned by other historians, but its supposed contents are recorded only in the Second Part of the *Royal Commentaries*, illustrating that its message is Inca Garcilaso's own creation (Brading 1986: 19).[14] It should be added that, throughout the Second Part, Inca Garcilaso includes numerous, often very long, quotations from other historians (principally López de Gómara, Zárate, and Fernández) to support his views, and this practice is most certainly related to the precarious status of his narrative, which seeks to valorize the characters and actions of rebels. In this case, as in many others, there is no external corroboration for the text of Carvajal's speech via citation of other authors, and in nearly all similar cases Inca Garcilaso's conspicuous omission of references corresponds with the articulation of his own views.[15] Carvajal's advice is worthy of a lengthy quotation:

> Sir, when a viceroy is killed in battle and his head is cut off and placed on a picket and the battle was against the standard of His Majesty . . . there is no hope for pardon from the King nor any other agreement whatsoever, even though Your Lordship provides sufficient excuses and remains more innocent than a suckling babe, nor can you trust their promises and words, no matter the assurances that come with them, unless Your Lordship were to rise up and call yourself King, and, instead of depending on foreign hands, take the government and mandate for yourself and place a crown on your own head and allot the vacant lands to your friends and supporters; and what the King gives temporarily for two lives, will be given by Your Lordship in perpetuity, along with the titles of dukes and marquises and counts, as there are in all the kingdoms of the world, so that in order to sustain and defend their own estates they will defend that of Your Lordship.
>
> Establish military orders with the names and titles of those in Spain or of other saints, their patrons, with the insignias you find fitting; and for the

knights of such habits assign rents and pensions so they can eat and enjoy throughout their days, as military knights do in all parts. With what I have said in brief, Your Lordship will attract all the Spanish gentlemen and nobility in this Empire to your service, and it will fully reward those who conquered it and served Your Lordship, which is not the case for them now. And to attract the Indians to your devoted service, so that they will die for Your Lordship with the same love they held for their Inca Kings, Your Lordship should take for his woman and spouse the princess among them who is closest to the royal family-tree, and send your ambassadors to the mountains where the Inca, heir to this Empire, is enclosed, and bid that he come forth to restore him in his majesty and greatness, and that by his hand give to Your Lordship for your wife any daughter or sister he may have, for Your Lordship well knows how much the prince will esteem your kinship and friendship, and more than winning the universal love of all the Indians with the restitution of their Inca, Your Lordship will gain their becoming truly willing to do what their king should order of them in your service . . . in short, all the Indians will be on your side, for if they do not help Your Lordship's adversaries with supplies and carrying cargoes, your enemies can neither prevail nor even be part of this land; and the prince will content himself with the title of King and with his vassals obeying him as they did before, governing his Indians in peace as his ancestors did, and Your Lordship and your ministers and captains will govern the Spaniards, administering that which pertains to war, requesting of the Inca that he order the Indians to do and fulfill what Your Lordship orders and mandates. . . .

More than this, Your Lordship will receive from the Inca not only all the gold and silver the Indians obtain in this Empire, for they have never regarded it as treasure or riches, but also all the treasure of the Kings, their ancestors, that they have hidden (as is notorious), for they will give and deliver all of it to Your Lordship, as much for your kinship as for restoring the Inca's majesty and greatness; and with this much gold and silver as fame relates, Your Lordship can buy the whole world if you desire to be its lord; and Your Lordship should pay no heed to those who say you act treacherously toward the King of Spain; you do not, because, as the refrain goes, no king is a traitor. This land belonged to the Incas, its natural lords, and since it has not been restored to them, Your Lordship has more right to it than the King of Castile, because you won it in person, at your own cost and risk, together with your brothers; and now, in restoring it to the Inca, you are doing what you should by natural law, and in wanting to govern and control

> it yourself as its conqueror and not as the subject or vassal of another, you are also doing what you should for your own reputation, for whoever can be King by the valor of his arm, there is no reason for him to remain a servant through weakness of spirit: everything hangs on taking the first step and making the first declaration. . . . and in conclusion I say that, no matter what happens, Your Lordship should crown yourself and call yourself King, for no other name befits him who has won [an Empire] with his arms and valor; die, Your Lordship, a King; and many times I repeat, die a King and not a subject, for whoever consents to being wronged deserves worse. (Part 2, Book IV, Chapter XL, vol. 2, 133–35)[16]

The plan, expressed by way of Carvajal's visionary cynicism, incorporates not only a full restoration of the Incas and the seedlings of a mestizo ruling class, but also the desire of the conquistadors/encomenderos to be fully remunerated for their efforts by becoming lords of vassals on feudal estates. For the moment, there are at least two elements of the platform that should be noticed. The first is its decidedly medieval slant, which can be seen most clearly within the notion of fiefdoms with vassals, the granting of titles of high nobility, and the establishment of Peruvian military orders of knighthood (Mazzotti 1996a: 317–18; 2008: 272–74). Second, and a bit more confusing from a purely European perspective, is the idea of the restored Inca governing the Indians in peace while Gonzalo simultaneously governs the Spaniards and oversees matters pertaining to warfare. Although it is not explicitly stated, what Inca Garcilaso certainly has in mind here is the duality, or corule, endemic to political structures throughout the Andes. As María Rostworowski de Diez Canseco succinctly states, "Every chiefdom within the Inca state was divided into two moieties corresponding to the native concept of *hanan* and *hurin* (upper and lower) or *ichoq* and *allauca* (left and right). Each moiety was governed by a chief . . . [and] one of the chiefs of the two moieties was always subordinate to the other, although this dependence might vary, sometimes the upper half (as in Cusco) being more important and in others, the lower (as in Inca)" (Rostworowski 1999: 144). Contained within Carvajal's advice, then, is an interplay between Inca and Spanish rulers in which the two participate in government with their own distinct functions, i.e., peace and war, yet are connected through corule and kinship. Whether alluding as he does to the European standards of natural law or traditional indigenous practices, Carvajal has exposed the illusory claims of the Spanish crown and realized that there can be no legitimate government in Peru without alliance and political coordination between conquistadors/encomenderos and Incas, which is precisely Inca Garcilaso's point.

As complete as it seems, there is a substratum of argumentation directly related to this political program that expands and fills out Inca Garcilaso's views. Again, Francisco de Carvajal plays the role of Gonzalo's advisor as well as Inca Garcilaso's mouthpiece, but this time his advice is in response to Licentiate Pedro de La Gasca's offer of pardon to Gonzalo and his band (Part 2, Book V, Chapter V). Shortly before this, Inca Garcilaso describes the "absolute power in everything" (*absoluto poder en todo*) granted to La Gasca by Charles V, including the power to revoke the New Laws, to dispose of the viceroy if necessary, to make grants of encomiendas and *repartimientos* of Indians, to administer government and justice, and to pardon all crimes (Part 2, Book V, Chapter II, vol. 2, 146). The ability to revoke the New Laws and to grant a general pardon, according to Inca Garcilaso, was the most important of La Gasca's powers, for it was these promises that actually "fought the war with Gonzalo Pizarro and gave the Empire to Licentiate la Gasca" (Part 2, Book V, Chapter IV, vol. 2, 154).[17] Inca Garcilaso also praises La Gasca primarily for being a tactful and forthright negotiator and for being able to earn the respect of fire-hardened adventurers and soldiers despite his uncomely appearance and disproportionate body (Part 2, Book V, Chapter II).

Chapter IV in Book V of the Second Part finds Gonzalo in Lima, shortly before he will march toward Collao to square off with Centeno at Huarina, and it is in Lima that La Gasca's messenger, Pedro Hernández Paniagua, presents Gonzalo with two letters, one from Charles V and one from La Gasca. The gist of the two letters is much the same. In the emperor's letter, which Inca Garcilaso credits Zárate with having provided, the king tells Gonzalo that he has heard of the disturbances in Peru and he is confident that neither Gonzalo nor his followers had the slightest intention of disobeying him, they simply wanted relief from the "harshness and rigor" (*aspereza y rigor*) of Viceroy Núñez Vela. He then instructs Gonzalo to heed the instructions of La Gasca for the benefit of all. La Gasca's letter is longer, but he too offers excuses for Gonzalo's behavior: "His Majesty and the rest of Spain have understood [your actions] neither within the scope of rebellion nor as infidelity against your King, but rather as a defense of your just rights through the appeal which had been sent to your Prince" (Part 2, Book V, Chapter IV, vol. 2, 156).[18] Then, as in the king's letter, Gonzalo is assured that his services to the crown will be remembered and rewarded and that in return he owes obedience to his king.

La Gasca rounds out the letter with appeals to Gonzalo's natural duty to his king, his honor as a noble gentleman, and the strength of the king's forces in Europe in order to entice the rebel to come to terms. Inca Garcilaso cuts the letter short at this point, saying that a longer version is available in the works of other historians and that the rest, a mere catalogue of Charles V's victories over his many foes, was intended "to persuade Gonzalo Pizarro to surrender and submit to his Prince, against whom [Gonzalo] could not have the forces to resist" (Part 2, Book V, Chapter IV, vol. 2, 157).[19] Of course, in the short run, Inca Garcilaso's sounding out of the emperor's and La Gasca's none-too-subtle threats proves them to be mistaken, for as we have seen, Gonzalo roundly and precipitously defeats the royalists at Huarina (Part 2, Book V, Chapter XIX–XX).

In any event, both of these letters are important for they equally express the royal desire to negotiate with and even pardon Gonzalo. More important, however, is Carvajal's reaction to these communiqués, for in an apparent volte-face of his earlier and unequivocal recommendations, he tells Gonzalo and Licentiate Diego de Cepeda "these are very good bulls, and it seems to me there is no reason why Your Lordship should fail to take them, and all of us should do the same, because they carry great indulgences" (Part 2, Book V, Chapter V, vol. 2, 157).[20] Odd advice indeed from one who has recently urged Gonzalo to die a king and has warned him not to trust the promises and words of royal administrators regardless of the assurances that accompany them (Part 2, Book IV, Chapter XL). Carvajal's reasons for accepting the offer, however, let us know what Inca Garcilaso has in mind:

> Sir, they [the bulls] are very good and very cheap, since they offer us the revocation of the ordinances and a pardon for all the past, and *for the future the orders and opinions of the city assemblies are to be taken, so as to order that which is agreed upon* for the service of God and the good of the land and the benefit of its settlers and residents, which is all we have desired and can desire, because with the revocation of the ordinances our Indians are secured for us, which is what forced us to take up arms and place ourselves in danger of losing our lives, and with the pardon of the past our lives are secured, and *with the order that is to be held from this moment forth, in which the land will be governed by that which is agreed upon with the opinion and council of the city assemblies, we are made lords of the land, since we have it to govern ourselves.* For all these reasons, I am of the opinion that the bulls should be accepted and that new ambassadors should be elected to go to the President with our reply,

and have him carried aloft into this city and pave the streets upon which he comes with silver railings and gold rings, and make the greatest possible fuss over him, in thanks for bringing us such a great message, and to oblige him to treat us as friends in the future so we can discover if he carries the great faculty and power of giving Your Lordship the government of this Empire, which I do not doubt he has, for, since he has matched stakes with us from the first move, it is a sign that he has more to bid. Bring him here as I have said, for, if we do not find his arrival fortunate, then we can do with him what we please. (Part 2, Book V, Chapter V, vol. 2, 158)[21]

Carvajal notices that the rebels can enter negotiations with La Gasca from their current position of power and that they should capitalize on this advantage to obtain the governance of Peru for Pizarro and themselves *legally* or, failing that, possibly dispose of La Gasca, take the country, and call the king's bluff. In this sense, everything Carvajal advised Gonzalo to do earlier is implicitly carried over: Gonzalo will still rule and the alliance with the Incas will both legitimate and strengthen the new government. Carvajal does not, therefore, change his counsel, but rather, sensing their advantage, he proposes that the rebels should shift the venue of their resistance from the battlefield to the negotiating table. Yet in the passages italicized above we can see that the government described by Carvajal will allow some form of encomendero representation, in which the opinions and agreements of the "city assemblies" (*regimientos de las ciudades*) partake at some level in political authority and administration. This appears to be a rather interesting interpretation on the part of Carvajal, for in the letters of Charles V and La Gasca there is not the slightest mention, as one might imagine, of their endorsement of an arrangement of this sort. But this seems to be Carvajal's and Inca Garcilaso's point, because if Gonzalo had managed to take control of Peru, whether by force or through royal concession, he then would have been able to construct a government more or less of his choosing, a government that promoted rather than paralyzed encomendero interests.

It should be pointed out that Carvajal's statements on city assemblies and their role in colonial government are primarily based on the customary political practices of Spanish settlers in Mexico and Peru, and should not be understood as a gesture by Inca Garcilaso toward a more democratic or republican form of government. The *cabildo* or municipal corporation was the fundamental unit of local politics in the Spanish overseas territories, and it was comprised of either elected or appointed (most usually the latter) members on the pattern of the Castilian system of *cortes*, or municipal courts (Haring 1975: 147–51).[22] That the cabildos, which in the first decades of Spanish expansion in Peru were dominated by encomenderos, were what Inca Garcilaso had in mind can be seen in the following description:

> in Mexico as well as Peru it was then customary, and still was when I left there in 1560, that since offices were not perpetual, in every Spanish town they elected four of the most principal gentlemen, those with the most credit and confidence they could find, to be officials of the royal patrimony and to keep the fifth of gold and silver taken from the entire land. . . . In addition to these officials, each year in every Spanish town they elected two ordinary municipal justices, a magistrate and a deputy magistrate, and six or eight or ten representatives, more or less according to the size of the town, and along with these the rest of the offices necessary for the good government of the republic. (Part 2, Book IV, Chapter IV, vol. 2, 16)[23]

The above description of the cabildos follows shortly after the announcement of the New Laws, Viceroy Núñez Vela's arrival, and a drubbing of Las Casas, both for his anti-encomendero sentiment and his disregard for the practical consequences of the ordinances he proposed to Charles V (Part 2, Book II, Chapter XIX–XX and Book IV, Chapters I–III). It supports Inca Garcilaso's negative assessment of the impact that the New Laws had on Peru, particularly the provision that revoked the encomiendas of those who had held public offices, by suggesting that, inasmuch as these rather typical Spanish institutions gave no cause for alarm, penalizing those who had simply participated in colonial government was unjustifiable.

Moreover, Inca Garcilaso is careful to point out, contrary to popular opinion at the turn of the seventeenth century, that the cabildo government of the encomenderos was not only capable of looking after the "good government of the republic," but also was supportive of royal interests in Peru. For instance, after Francisco Pizarro's assassination by the supporters of Diego de Almagro the Younger (Part 2, Book III, Chapter VII), Captain Garcilaso de la Vega's cousin, Gómez de Tordoya, calls for an election of new officials to confront the rebels on the king's behalf. "Many gentlemen equal in quality and merits" (*mucho caballeros iguales en calidad y méritos*) from Los Charcas, Arequipa, and Cuzco convened in the capital city, held an election, and declared war on Almagro. Inca Garcilaso adds, "those in the city could do this with just title, because in lacking a governor named by His Majesty, the council of Cuzco (as the head of that Empire) could nominate ministers for war and justice during the interim in which His Majesty had named none" (Part 2, Book III, Chapter XI, vol. 1, 273).[24] Although it should be kept in mind that the conflicts between *Pizarristas* and *Almagristas* were factional struggles for supremacy in Peru conducted with little regard for the desires of the distant monarch, Inca Garcilaso asserts the legitimacy of political and military initiatives taken by the city assemblies to defend both their own and royal interests. This line of argumentation becomes important later, when Gonzalo is elected general procurator, governor, and captain general in Cuzco at the beginning of the rebellion. For, in applying the New Laws so strictly and immediately, it is Viceroy Núñez Vela who jeopardizes royal interests in Peru by denying the encomenderos' legal rights to petition against the legislation:

> The rigid character of the viceroy increased this scandal and fear, along with his not wanting in particular to hear the appeal of any city over the ordinances, but rather to have them applied with full rigor. As such, the settlers of the four cities, which are Huamanca, Arequipa, Chuquisaca, and Cuzco, in which the Viceroy had not yet been acknowledged, decided that electing a general procurator to speak for all four and the entire kingdom, because being elected by Cuzco, which was the head of that Empire, was seen as being elected by all of it, could remedy the injury they feared. (Part 2, Book IV, Chapter VII, vol. 2, 28)[25]

As we shall see, Inca Garcilaso uses arguments derived from the comunero revolution in Spain (1520–1521), which incorporate a distinction between domestic Peruvian and foreign Spanish (monarchical and viceregal) rule, to defend the rights of Gonzalo's band to resist and rebel against the rigidity and ignorance of Viceroy Núñez Vela. For the moment, however, it should be kept in mind that Carvajal's comments regarding city assemblies invoke the cabildo system in early Peru and not a broader republican ideal. Moreover, Inca Garcilaso's description of the procedures of local election and appointment to public office in Peruvian municipal corporations prior to his leaving Peru in 1560, mentioned above, conceal an element of critique. For, after the financially strapped prince ascended to the throne in 1556, Phillip II introduced the practice of auctioning public offices in Peru to the highest bidder in order to increase royal revenues. This replaced the former procedures with a system of private purchase that, by the turn of the seventeenth century, had made many municipal offices in Peru proprietary, hereditary, and, in Inca Garcilaso's words, "perpetual" (*perpetuado*) (Part 2, Book IV, Chapter IV, vol. 2, 16) (Haring 1975: 154–55).

By way of examining both of Carvajal's counsels, then, we see that the promise of Gonzalo's rebellion in the *Royal Commentaries* is the creation of an independent Peruvian monarchy that includes restoration, intermarriage, and corule with the Incas and advisory courts of seigniorial encomenderos. Further, Cuzco, which had been displaced by Lima, will be restored as the "head of the Empire," and as per the earlier capitulations between Titu Atauchi, Chaves, and Haro, it appears that the new Inca, Gonzalo, may enforce all the Inca laws compatible with Christianity (Part 2, Book II, Chapter VI). The government's dual structure, based upon the indigenous categories hanan and hurin, and its incorporation of Spanish institutions, such as aristocratic fiefdoms, military orders, and advisory courts, give it a distinctively mestizo flavor in that it fuses together practices from Andean and Spanish political culture. Inasmuch as Carvajal's recommendations to Gonzalo, the new Viracocha Inca, attend to fully rewarding and remunerating the conquistadors for their efforts in winning the territories as well as restoring the Incas, the former "natural lords," to power, the rebellion carries with it the possibility of establishing domestic peace and justice in Peru.

Having examined the character and social organization of the independent Peru promised by Gonzalo Pizarro's rebellion, we can turn our attention to the arguments Inca Garcilaso uses to defend the encomenderos' right to resist the New Laws and the Spanish viceroyalty. As stated briefly above, Inca Garcilaso makes his case by referring to an earlier precedent in Spanish history of popular resistance to a monarchy primarily controlled by foreign ministers. By attending to this subtext we will not only be able to see how Inca Garcilaso justifies the actions of the Peruvian rebels, but also, in comparing his views to elements of the political ideology he borrows for these events, we will gain a better understanding of the specific political sensibility informing the *Royal Commentaries*.

The precedent to which Inca Garcilaso is cautiously alluding in his portrayal of Gonzalo's rebellion is the comunero revolt in Castile (1520–1521) against the newly crowned King of Spain and Holy Roman Emperor Charles V. When the Flemish Charles succeeded to the throne of Castile in 1516, Castilians were faced with the prospects of being ruled by a foreign king ignorant of their language, culture, and politics who, in addition, would most often rule in absentia due to his imperial duties (after 1519). Moreover, through his appointment of equally foreign courtesans and advisors, chief among them being the Lord of Chièvres William of Croy and Adrian of Utrecht, to the most powerful and lucrative posts in the Spanish realm, a system of corruptive abuse replaced the normal flow of government in Castile, which Charles's new subjects found intolerable. As John Lynch puts it, "Castilians were kept at a distance from their king and were forced to watch offices and sinecures invaded by newcomers and the national wealth plundered by foreigners who neither understood nor cared for the problems of Spain" (Lynch 1991: 51; Elliott 1963: 144–51; Espinosa 2008: 35–46). In order to voice their grievances with the new government, Castilians turned to the cortes (courts), which were representative bodies in each city composed of members elected from each of the three estates (nobility, clergy, and commons). In existence since the Middle Ages, the cortes had not traditionally been regularly convening deliberative assemblies with legislative powers, but rather generally lent prestige and credibility to, without being able to restrict, royal prerogatives (Lynch 1991: 10–11, 65; Espinosa 2008: 46–65). Despite their practical powerlessness, the cortes also functioned as the institutional locus in which protests against royal injustices were lodged. According to A.W. Lovett, "by the sixteenth century a living and long established tradition maintained that the cities had the right to petition against misrule; and if remedy were not forthcoming, many thought that their inhabitants were authorized to take whatever action was required, including resistance to the king, or his representative" (Lovett 1986: 34). In general terms, this is what transpired in fourteen of the eighteen *ciudades* (cities) of Castile: representatives were elected; formal petitions against misrule were submitted; and when it became clear that no remedy could be expected from the monarchy, Castile revolted.

With its initial critical mass located in Toledo and Salamanca, the short-lived rebellion, which lasted from May 1520 until the comuneros' lopsided defeat at Villalar on April 23, 1521 (Elliott 1963: 151; Espinosa 2008: 71–82), represented not only a profound rejection of Charles V, but also a socially diversified, geographically extensive, and primarily urban social movement with an explicitly revolutionary agenda. As Aurelio Espinosa has argued, what began as a tax revolt against the foreign patronage system of an absent king, "developed into a political experiment; city-states, or *comunidades*, were realizing their potential to rule without a monarchy . . . and the tax revolt became a struggle for a representational form of government" (Espinosa 2008:

71–72).[26] The twin bases of comunero political thought were the Aristotelian and neo-Scholastic notion that the comunidad, and its synonymous ciudad (polity), was an associative agreement among a multitude for the common good, on the one hand, and the principle from Roman law *quod omnes tangit, ab omnibus debet approbari*, "that which touches all must be agreed to by all," on the other (Maravall 1970: 201).[27] In this sense, the city or community was not only a moral entity composed of distinct yet interdependent members (i.e., the corporate union and partnership of the three estates) but also the ultimate source of political power. As Maravall explains, for the comuneros "the *comunidad* was never simply the urban conjunction, considered physically, or an informal mass of materially adhering inhabitants, but rather the moral and political body that constituted those integrated within it" (Maravall 1970: 103; my translation). Their program for structural reform centered on increasing the power of the *cortes* as representative, deliberative, and legislative bodies that actively participated in national politics in order to limit and render accountable royal power, particularly in the realm of judicial appointees, while stressing the need for a mixed constitution with republican institutions anchored in an active citizenry on the model of the Italian city-states (Pérez 1998: 539–45). The underlying vision, as Maravall again points out, was of confederated city-states "with their own governments, not subjected to a superior lord, that is, cities governed by councils, in terms of magistrates elected by the community" (Maravall 1970: 194; my translation). Comunero goals, which explicitly proposed a more inclusive, diverse, and ultimately proto-nationalist conception of the common good, were a direct and drastic challenge to Charles's views on royal sovereignty, which were founded on the idea of dynastic privilege and denied the very possibility of either conflict or contradiction between dynastic interests and those of subjects (Maravall 1970: 110–16; Pérez 1998: 558–59; Espinosa 2008: 71–82).[28]

The defeat of the comunero movement demonstrated not only the power of the Spanish nobility's coalition in favor of the king, but it also spelled the end of any republican pretensions of potential city-states on the peninsula while further enhancing and consolidating monarchical rule (Espinosa 2008: 88–89, 91).[29] Spanish historians of the sixteenth century were certainly not oblivious to this point, as the words of Francisco López de Gómara attest, "the comunidades began in Castile, which from a good beginning achieved a bad end, and, wanting to humble the king, they made him greater than he was before" (López de Gómara 1912: 201; my translation). Moreover, the failure of the *comuneros* elicited a generalized rejection of the representative and republican ideals of the movement throughout Spain. The accomplished humanist and Charles V's royal historian, Pedro de Mejía, with whose other works Inca Garcilaso was well familiar, scorned the comuneros for having made bold to demand that Charles should establish "such order in the government that part of it would be given to the cities of the realm," and that such a demand made "a minor and a pupil of the king, and them his tutors" (Mejía 1945: 136 and 187).[30] In his *Apologética historia summaria*, Bartolomé de Las Casas illustrated his opposition to the comuneros by placing them within his first two classes of barbarians, which included "whichever Christian nations transgress the bounds of reason by way of their cruel, harsh, ferocious, and disorganized works or through their furious impetuosity for frightful opinions, as is clearly seen in Castile in the year 1520 in the time of the comunidades" (Las Casas 1992: vol. 8, "Epílogo," 1590; my translation). The stain associated with comunero involvement and ideology endured through the end of the sixteenth century and beyond; so much so, in fact, that in 1578 the Admiral of Castile complained "everything is in the hands of lowly and vindictive people, many of whose fathers were comuneros." Philip II, whose government the admiral was criticizing and who never seemed to forget any insults against the royal person of either his father or himself, at least agreed with the admiral's evaluation of the rebels. For as late as 1591, seven decades after the fact, the Prudent King was still referring to Juan Padilla, one of the comunero leaders, as a "tyrant" (Kamen 1998: 177, 228).

The first point to be made about the foregoing is that Inca Garcilaso implicitly suggests not only a similarity between the comunero revolt and Gonzalo's rebellion, but also alludes to the former to justify the latter. In so doing, however, he proceeds both cautiously and indirectly, for he was well aware of the disrepute in which the comuneros were held in his day. To sympathize openly with the comuneros or even the semblance of their political views was to compromise one's own name, all the more so if one were a mestizo who had family ties to Inca resistance in Vilcabamba until 1572 and whose mestizo friends and classmates had planned an unsuccessful rebellion in Peru in 1567 (see chapter 1). If, for some reason, an inquisitive censor had been provoked by the *Royal Commentaries* to delve into Inca Garcilaso's personal life, he would have found the historian's connections to these Inca and mestizo "rebels," the printed rumors regarding his father's relationship with the rebel Gonzalo, and, rather surprisingly, at least three relatives who had actually participated in the Castilian revolt. The first, the Golden Age poet, Garcilaso de la Vega, whose name Inca Garcilaso de la Vega shares, provides no cause for concern:

he fought on behalf of the king; suffered a facial wound in the comunero advance on Toledo in August 1520; and was named *regidor* of Toledo for his faithful service to the crown (Pérez 1998: 365, 648). Don Pedro Laso de la Vega, the poet's older brother and a former student of humanist Peter Martyr Anghiera, however, was not only one of the most notable and admired members of the movement, but also one of its instigators (Pérez 1998: 476, 621–22).[31] Don Pedro's involvement is mentioned in Mejía's *Historiador del Emperador Carlos Quinto* (History of Emperor Charles V) as having been the elected, chief representative of Toledo who brought the comunero grievances before the king (Mejía 1945: 134).[32] Maravall has added that Don Pedro entered the negotiations hoping for peaceful arbitration, but was fully prepared to take up arms "for the defense of our liberties" (Maravall 1970: 184; my translation). This he did, but he eventually abandoned the enterprise in February 1521 and fled upon Charles's return to Spain in 1522 to Portugal, where he remained until 1526 (Pérez 1998: 478, 585). Charles was so angered by Don Pedro's leadership, he who came from one of the most well-known and respected families of the Castilian aristocracy, that he excluded him from the general pardon of 1522 and would have had his head were it not for the protection he received at the court of King João in Portugal (Seaver 1928: 353–54; Pérez 1998: 614–17).[33] So also did Gómez de Tordoya y Vargas, first-cousin to Inca Garcilaso's father whom the mestizo historian claims wore the habit of the Knights of Santiago (Part 2, Book VIII, Chapter XII), provoke the wrath of the king. As John Varner points out, before sailing for the New World, Gómez de Tordoya had been sentenced to death in Spain for his actions on behalf of the comuneros, and years later a royal order dated February 13, 1541 officially banned him from all realms under Spanish jurisdiction (Varner 1968: 31, 47). This is the same Gómez de Tordoya, perhaps not so coincidentally, that Inca Garcilaso credits with having called the legitimate election in Cuzco after Francisco Pizarro's assassination, mentioned above (Part 2, Book III, Chapter XI). With so many personal connections to comunero and Peruvian antagonists, all of whom had openly resisted royal interests, it would have been at the very least imprudent, if not extremely dangerous, for Inca Garcilaso to link his defense of Gonzalo Pizarro's rebellion explicitly to the earlier revolution.[34]

It should be emphasized at this point that Gonzalo Pizarro's rebellion in Peru was not, although it attempted to appropriate similar justifications, a movement with the same diversified scope and revolutionary political goals as the *comunero* revolt in Castile, as Guillermo Lohmann Villena's study on the legal and political thought of Gonzalo's rebellion amply demonstrates.[35] Nevertheless, similarities between the two were both noted and recorded in varying degrees by New World historians of the sixteenth century, and it is through his citation of other authors that Inca Garcilaso transfers the *comunero* defense of their right to resist to Gonzalo.[36] In Chapter VII, Book V of the Second Part, Gonzalo is elected in Cuzco, and Inca Garcilaso quotes Agustín de Zárate for the arguments in favor of allowing Gonzalo to travel to Lima with an armed guard. Inca Garcilaso cuts off Zárate's passage following this statement:

> There was no lack of lawyers who established and made understood that in all of this there was no disrespect, and that they had the right to do so, and that force can and should be repelled by force, and that the judge who proceeds de facto can be resisted de facto. And in this way they resolved that Gonzalo Pizarro should raise his standard and enlist men, and many of the residents of Cuzco offered him their persons and properties, and some even said that they were willing to lose their souls for their demands. (Part 2, Book IV, Chapter VII, vol. 2, 30)[37]

Thanks to Zárate, Inca Garcilaso establishes the right of encomenderos not only to appeal, but also to resist Viceroy Núñez Vela and the New Laws with force, on the grounds that Núñez Vela had violated legal procedures by disallowing encomendero petitions against the ordinances: "the judge who proceeds de facto can be resisted de facto." The same argument is extended in the following chapter, in the words of Francisco López de Gómara who, as the chaplain and historian of Hernán Cortés, was the most sympathetic to Spanish conquistadors and encomenderos of any of the writers cited by Inca Garcilaso in the Second Part. Again, the passage concerns the arguments forwarded by the encomenderos to justify their actions, and amongst those enumerated we find the following:

> others [said] that they could defend their vassals and privileges with arms, as the *hidalgos* [a Spanish contraction for "*hijo de algo*," meaning "the son of something"] *of Castile had defended their liberties*, which they held for having helped the Kings win their kingdoms from the power of the Moors, just as they had won Peru from the hands of idolaters; in the end they all said that they would not fall into trouble for appealing the ordinances, and many [said] that they would not even if they opposed them, since *they were not obliged until they had consented to them and acknowledged them as laws.* (Part 2, Book IV, Chapter VIII, vol. 2, 31)[38]

Inca Garcilaso explains, to clear up any possible discrepancies between previous accounts, that in the beginning the "true intention of the four cities" (*verdadera intención de aquellas cuatro ciudades*) was not to rebel, but to "send representatives with sufficient powers" (*embiaron sus procuradores con poderes bastantes*) to peacefully petition against the ordinances as "loyal vassals who had won the Empire for the augment of the Spanish crown" (*vasallos leales que habían ganado aquel Imperio para aumento de la corona de España*). Although he sticks rather closely to the procedures of the Spanish legal system and downplays the option of force at the outset, Inca Garcilaso selects as the "true intention" of the rebellion the one that López de Gómara explicitly links to the "hidalgos of Castile," and which invalidates legislation that has not received the consent of the citizens. This was the rebels' intention, according to Inca Garcilaso, because "they trusted that if they were justly heard, they could not be denied, even by a tribunal of barbarians" (*fiaban que si les oyessen de justicia, no se la habían de negar, aunque fuese en tribunal de bárbaros*). Although the encomenderos had justice on their side, it was the "terrible harshness of the viceroy's character" that made a peaceful appeal and resolution impossible and caused Gonzalo to take up arms (Part 2, Book IV, Chapter VIII, vol. 2, 32).

Inca Garcilaso's invocation of the comunero movement to defend the initial moments of Gonzalo's rebellion come well before the announcements of Carvajal's political recommendations. His use of comunero arguments, however, is directly related to the latter for the obvious reason that, regardless of what he portrays as the desirability and justice of Carvajal's proposals, he still needed to justify Gonzalo's actions in the first place. In simpler terms, Inca Garcilaso needed a strong argument for the right to resist and even take up arms against monarchical and viceregal abuses, which he found in the comunero revolt. Just as important, furthermore, it is very likely that Inca Garcilaso found a ready-made critique of the Peruvian viceroyalty in the comuneros' rejection of Charles V's foreign ministers. Viceroy Núñez Vela's actions are representative of precisely the kind of problems that frequently attended the appointment of native Spaniards to the highest offices in Peruvian government. The idea here, which is an undercurrent running throughout the Second Part, is not simply that the conquistadors had not been properly rewarded for their services to the crown, but that giving charge of Peru to those who were completely unfamiliar with local politics inevitably opened the door to unnecessary and often systematic abuses for which there was insufficient remedy. Again, on Inca Garcilaso's view, Núñez Vela's ill-temper and imprudence are extreme examples, as is the "absolute power" (*poder absoluto*) later wielded by the fifth viceroy, Francisco de Toledo (Part 1, Book VI, Chapter XXXVI, vol. 1, 409). Theoretically, and if the Spanish monarchy had actually been concerned with the general welfare of its Peruvian subjects, this should not have been so often the case, given the normal procedures and institutions of Spanish constitutionalism. That the Spanish monarchy, and therefore the ministers and functionaries appointed by the monarchy, was more interested in exploiting rather than benefiting Peru, however, is a point Inca Garcilaso makes bold to relate. In concluding the chapter in which he tabulates the amount of Atahualpa's ransom, he writes "these were sent by my country to Spain and the rest of the Old World, showing herself to be a cruel stepmother to her own sons and a devoted mother to those of foreigners" (Part 2, Book I, Chapter XXXVIII, vol. 1, 103).[39] Somewhat like the comuneros, then, Inca Garcilaso suggests that the rule of an absent king through "foreign" peninsular ministers is prejudicial to just governance in Peru, which in turn supports his argument that Gonzalo was well within his rights in resisting it.

Although Inca Garcilaso deploys some of the terminology associated with the *comuneros*, which can be seen most clearly in the passages cited above in his rather precise use of such terms as *ciudad, tierra, buen gobierno, bien común* (city, land, good government, and common good),[40] and relies upon the movement's ideology to defend Gonzalo, there is a major and telling difference between his position and that of the Castilian revolutionaries. As Pérez and Maravall have meticulously demonstrated, the comuneros' notions of republican liberty were rooted in a robust understanding of popular sovereignty, which, from the first, flirted with the democratic and then veered heavily in that direction when the comunero extremists (i.e., those who held strongly antiseigniorial and even communist views) coopted leadership of the movement in its later stages (Pérez 1998: 451–502, 532–62; Maravall 1970: 181–218).[41] Although this democratic sensibility was couched in corporate terms and translated institutionally into electing representatives from the three estates (nobility, clergy, and commons), it was present in greater or lesser degrees throughout the movement.

Comparatively, by no stretch of the imagination can Inca Garcilaso's views be called democratic. As we have seen in preceding chapters, for Inca Garcilaso political authority in the Peruvian context derives from the coordination and alliance of very specific social interests, in particular the authority, nobility, and virtues of his Inca *panaca* and the leading conquerors and encomenderos. Much to the credit of his thinking, his notions of sovereignty are not only broad enough to include but also adamantly insist that legitimate government in Peru requires the participation of both Incas and Spaniards in a system of corule that integrates the interests of a culturally diverse aristocracy. In this way, and within certain limits, he embraces an inclusive, because culturally plural, idea of political authority somewhat different from other political thinkers in his day. Nevertheless, through Carvajal's suggestions to establish landed grandees and military orders of knighthood, we have likewise seen that Inca Garcilaso's vision of Peru maintains a caste system of privileges and entitlements as well as a preeminent status for Cuzco as "the head of that empire." Moreover, insofar as Inca Garcilaso recognizes and stresses the importance of kinship (*ayllus* and panacas) in indigenous politics and represents the leading conquerors as the symbolic brothers, i.e., Viracocha Incas, of the Inca dynasts (see chapter 3), his political sensibility is not only thoroughly aristocratic and Cuzcocentric, but also tends toward the oligarchic.

Inca Garcilaso's preference, furthermore, for a ruling system stemming from the leading Inca and encomendero sectors carries with it a distrust of the "lower" social groups. Although his suspicion of lower castes is counterbalanced by his belief that virtue is a product of actions rather than birth or blood, neither curacas (local ethnic chiefs) nor plebian Spaniards play much of a role in his political thought for different reasons. The curacas, on the one hand, are marginalized in favor of cultural, which is to say religious, concerns. As Inca Garcilaso explains in his criticism of the New Laws, abolishing the encomienda system would greatly hamper indigenous conversion to the faith: "since it was notorious that what they [Spaniards] most preached was that the Indians should be Christians, this could not be achieved if they were left in the power of their *caciques* (chiefs). Especially as it was very clear that if an Indian became a Christian and returned to the power of his cacique, he would be sacrificed to the Devil" (Part 2, Book IV, Chapter I, vol. 2, 8).[42] Inca Garcilaso's similar distrust of plebian Spaniards and foot soldiers, on the other hand, is illustrated first in his crediting the anonymous mass of soldiers, driven by their greedy impatience, with instigating the slaughter at Francisco Pizarro's initial confrontation with Atahualpa in Cajamarca (Part 2, Book I, Chapter XXV). It is more clearly seen, however, in his treatment of Francisco Hernández Girón's rebellion during the viceroyalty of Don Antonio de Mendoza (Part 2, Book VII), which challenged on the battlefield the interests of Cuzco's *vecinos*, i.e., those Spaniards who had allotments of Indians (Part 1, "Warning"), among whom Inca Garcilaso's father was still numbered at the time. Inca Garcilaso looks unfavorably on Girón's uprising, which pitted the impoverished commoners against the propertied encomenderos, and for our purposes all we need consider is the following remark. According to Inca Garcilaso, Francisco Hernández Girón "had much communication and friendship with soldiers, and none with the vecinos, which is a sufficient indication to suspect badly of his intentions and spirit" (Part 2, Book VII, Chapter I, vol. 3, 94).[43] As such, the mestizo polity forwarded by Inca Garcilaso does not partake of the more democratic inclinations of the comuneros, but rather prefers a hierarchically ordered system of quasi-oligarchic municipal corporations with the Inca and encomendero elite in Cuzco jointly embodying the common good of all.

The defense of Gonzalo Pizarro's rebellion and the blueprint of a Peruvian mestizo polity advanced in the *Royal Commentaries* should therefore neither be interpreted as the result of a democratic impulse in Inca Garcilaso's thinking nor the germ of a nascent bourgeois consciousness in the mestizo historian's work.[44] Nor, inasmuch as he harkens back to traditional practices of Incas and Spaniards alike, can Inca Garcilaso's view be called "modern." For him, of the utmost importance was illustrating that Inca and conquistador/encomendero interests were not necessarily irreconcilable, on the one hand, and demonstrating through Gonzalo's rebellion how they could have come together to form a mutually beneficial and independent government, on the other. What is rather daring about his treatment of these events, however, is the argument running throughout that Peruvians actually had the right to take up arms against the viceregal government, given both the injustice and unresponsiveness of the viceroyalty toward indigenous and settler interests. On Inca Garcilaso's view, as expressed in Carvajal's counsels to Gonzalo, both Incas and encomenderos had been wronged by the actions and agents of the Spanish monarchy. It is therefore fair to conclude that Inca Garcilaso saw the policies of the Spanish monarchy and the colonial bureaucracy as major obstacles to social justice, which, as these institutions became more entrenched, made the conditions in Peru increasingly worse. Writing over half a century after Gonzalo's rebellion, Inca Garcilaso knew that substantive reform in favor of the groups he championed had not and for their mestizo descendants most likely would not occur. Drastic measures were perhaps the only means remaining to realize the kind of society he favored. This much, at any rate, is suggested by Carvajal's unequivocal admonition to Gonzalo to establish an independent Peru, "many times I repeat, die a king and not a subject, for whoever consents to being wronged deserves worse" (Part 2, Book IV, Chapter XL, vol. 2, 135).

For all their idiosyncrasies and conservative orientation, there are at least two elements that make Inca Garcilaso's views distinctive. The first is that, in supporting and defending Gonzalo Pizarro's rebellion, Inca Garcilaso is the first writer both to consider seriously and argue for the possibility of an independent Peru freed from the direct control of the Spanish monarchy. Inasmuch as Inca Garcilaso is also the first native-born and self-identified person of indigenous descent to publish texts about the New World in the Old, one can legitimately push this point a bit further and say that he is the first American thinker to see armed insurrection in the service of independence as an alternative to colonial rule.

Second, and despite the fact that his views are aristocratic and elitist, Inca Garcilaso suggests that the best approach to government in Peru is one that coordinates and aligns the leading sectors of indigenous and Spanish society and combines institutions and practices of both. Although his notion of *mestizaje* is rooted in the interests of his own panaca and the encomenderos in and around Cuzco, both his political sensibility and recommendations are quite different from others voiced in his day. For instance, the strongest champion of indigenous rights and sovereignty, Bartolomé de Las Casas, despised the Spanish conquistadors and encomenderos for the callous and shocking destruction their presence and actions wrought upon the New World. Las Casas wanted this group of Spanish settlers completely excluded from colonial politics, so much, in fact, as colonial situations worsened and his thought progressed over the years, that he began leaning more and more toward a defense of monarchical absolutism. As Las Casas states in *Las doce dudas* (The Twelve Doubts, 1564), written two years before his death, "If, when the King of Spain should restore the Kings of Peru to their realms, the encomenderos should rebel against the King of Spain, refusing thereby to give up what they gave each other, then the King of Spain is obliged to make war on them, and die in war if that is what it takes to free those innocent peoples the Spaniards hold in subjugation" (Las Casas 1995: 349). By contrast, Inca Garcilaso portrays the Spanish monarchy and its agents as impediments to rather than reliable instruments for social and political justice in Peru.

The other figure with whom Inca Garcilaso's views can be compared is his indigenous Andean compatriot and a marvel of intercultural hybridity in his own right, Guaman Poma de Ayala. In his *Nueva corónica y buen gobierno*, Guaman Poma de Ayala's criticisms of the Spanish viceroyalty are both scathing and condemnatory, and his knowledge of, respect for, and solidarity with indigenous traditions outside the Inca hierarchy are obviously and understandably profound. Nevertheless, while he recognizes the permanence of the Spanish presence and would have Spaniards and Andeans interact culturally, primarily through the Catholic religion, his vision of Peru is a separatist one. The past and present have taught Guaman Poma that it would be best if the natives and newcomers left each other alone (Guaman Poma 1980: vol. 3; Adorno 1986: 7). Had he actually been living in Peru at the turn of the seventeenth century, like Guaman Poma, who knows what Inca Garcilaso would have thought. Yet, perhaps through his distance from Peru and the sense of intercultural, aristocratic entitlement he inherited from both his family lines, Inca Garcilaso realizes that Andeans and Spaniards are indeed forced into cohabitation, but he also maintains that there had been ways in the past that may apply to the present through which the two could come together socially, culturally, and politically for their mutual benefit. This is the utopian ideal and progressive postcolonial hope of the *Royal Commentaries*, for which Inca Garcilaso uses both Gonzalo Pizarro's rebellion and Carvajal's independent mestizo polity as exemplars, perhaps to be imitated in the future.

6
JESUIT AMAUTAS

Prejudice, Preaching, and Pedagogy in Peru

Much has been written on the utopian and idealized flavor of Inca Garcilaso's depiction of Inca civilization and Peruvian history in the *Royal Commentaries*. As Margarita Zamora has noted, "the suggestion that there is an affinity between the *Royal Commentaries* and Thomas More's *Utopia* threatens to become a critical commonplace," and "practically all studies of the Inca's work have taken up the novelesque or fictional qualities of the *Comentarios reales*" (Zamora 1988: 129). Students of Spanish and Spanish American literature realize that the impetus for approaching the *Royal Commentaries* in this way, particularly the First Part, is attributable to the assessment of the famous literary historian and critic Marcelino Menéndez y Pelayo.[1] To be certain, it would be quite inaccurate to assert that Erasmian humanism, as both filtered through and found within the priorities and perspectives of Spanish Jesuit humanists at the turn of the seventeenth century, neither influenced nor informed Inca Garcilaso's work. It is also the case that until recently attempts to detail, document, and interpret the Hispano-European roots of the *Royal Commentaries* have frequently shied away from exploring the Andean contexts and meanings suggested by the texts. As a result, and as my position has been throughout this investigation, fully comprehending both the historical specificity and importance of the political interventions within the *Royal Commentaries* requires an interrogation of both Andean and European contexts.

The emphasis placed on the similarities between the *Royal Commentaries* and utopian literature of the Renaissance as well as the recent tendency to view the former as a species of creative literature has had an additional consequence.[2] By stressing the artistic and imaginative aspects of Inca Garcilaso's intervention, potential questions regarding the practical implications of the *Royal Commentaries* have received less treatment than one might expect. This is not to suggest that students and scholars of Inca Garcilaso's work have somehow overlooked the general political intent of his defense of Incas, conquistadors, *encomenderos*, mestizos, and Indians found both in his masterpiece and in *La Florida del Inca*, for there is broad consensus in the secondary literature regarding the extent to which these texts bear witness to the political orientation of the mestizo historian's efforts. It *is* to suggest, however, that if we approach Inca Garcilaso first and foremost as a political thinker, it may be of interest and importance to turn our attention toward his treatment of and response to some of the more specific political issues of his day.

Since the primary political intent of the *Royal Commentaries* is to move a diverse and conflicted Peruvian society toward political and cultural integration, one might expect that, in addition to illustrating the exemplary historical figures to be imitated by posterity, there may be proposals within the texts that aid potential readers to link the moral and political lessons of the past to their present circumstances. This chapter will therefore consider the question of whether the *Royal Commentaries* contains any specific recommendations for colonial reform. In order to do so, we must first address the prevalent view that, at the level of practical politics, Inca Garcilaso favored the Lascasian recommendation of indigenous restitution.[3] For instance, Inca Garcilaso records the attempts of mestizos from the Inca elite, such as Don Melchor Carlos Inca, and other descendants of the last Inca, Huayna Cápac, to petition the Spanish crown for privileges and titles (Part 1, Book IX, Chapters XXXI–XL). As for Don Melchor Carlos Inca's request (grandson of Paullu Inca and son of Inca Garcilaso's schoolmate Don Carlos Inca), Inca Garcilaso informs us that through his petition he received a perpetual annuity of 7,500 ducats, the habit of the Knights of Santiago, and a subsidy to move his wife and household from Peru to Spain. The theme of restitution through legal means is picked up again at the end of the Second Part in the example of Ana María Lorenza de Loyola,[4] the daughter of Inca princess Beatríz Clara Coya and Governor of Chile, Martín García de Loyola. Ana María was created the Marquess of

Oropesa by Philip III, which gave her the distinction of being the first Peruvian to receive a noble title as well as a hereditary fief in Peru with full jurisdiction (Hemming 1970: 457–73). On reporting this news, Inca Garcilaso claims to have been gratified when he heard that "the First Part of our *Comentarios* was of no little service in this, by reason of the successive relation given of the Inca kings" (Part 2, Book VIII, Chapter XX, vol. 3, 254).[5]

There can be little doubt, then, that Inca Garcilaso suggests the pursuance of political reform in Peru and at least partial restoration for the would-be heirs of dispossessed Incas and encomenderos through the use of legal channels.[6] In a political culture as obsessed with legality as sixteenth-century Spain, it cannot be said, however, that Inca Garcilaso's recommendation was an original one. Following rapidly upon the conquest, the judicial apparatuses of Peru and Spain had experienced a constant deluge of petitions for recognition, restitution, land and labor rights, and exemption from tribute from nearly every segment of colonial society: conquistadores, encomenderos, Incas, and *curacas* (local ethnic lords). With regard to restitution for indigenous Andeans, two of the most notable cases were the petition brought by Dominican Friar Domingo de Santo Tomás to the Council of Indies with a handsome financial offer on behalf of a group of Peruvian curacas to abolish the embattled *encomienda* system in 1560, and the *probanza* (legal evidence or proof) drawn up in Cuzco in 1569 by the members of Túpac Inca Yupanqui's *panaca* (royal kinship group) requesting *mercedes* (grants) from the Spanish crown.[7] Like countless others of the time, nothing came of these two actions, yet the incessant litigation throughout Peru at one point caused Viceroy Francisco de Toledo to remark, "in these parts . . . it seems people are more accustomed to lawsuits than are people anywhere else." As a result, in the ordinances for the city of Cuzco in 1572, Toledo mandated the peaceful resolution of disputes and the avoidance of courts (Niles 1999: 25–29n).

By the time Inca Garcilaso was writing the *Royal Commentaries* at the turn of the seventeenth century, there had already been a half-century tradition, as it were, of resistant legal action by Inca elites, Spanish encomenderos, and their mestizo descendants in Peru. Yet the stark reality was that, despite the best efforts of Bartolomé de Las Casas and his sympathizers to convince Charles V and Philip II of the alternatives, restitution of indigenous territories and titles in anything more than a piecemeal and politically motivated fashion was simply out of the question and had been for quite some time. This was realized by even some of the earliest commentators on the Spanish conquest, such as Dominican theologian Francisco de Vitoria. In *De Indis* (On the Indies, 1539), where he laid out the legitimate titles for Spanish conquest and occupation of the New World, Vitoria concluded that if the conditions for just war were inapplicable to Spanish endeavors in the West Indies, then "*the whole Indian expedition and trade would cease*, to the great loss of the Spaniards. And this in turn would mean a huge loss to the royal exchequer, which would be intolerable" (Vitoria 1991: 291). If this was apparent to Vitoria, who was writing a mere six years after Atahualpa's execution by Francisco Pizarro in 1533, it must have been doubly so six years later when the silver mines of Potosí, which became so important and then so disastrous to the Spanish economy, were discovered in Peru in 1545. Three decades later, after the Peruvian civil wars had been snuffed out and Viceroy Toledo had begun his monumental program of reform, Jesuit José de Acosta, one of the most influential writers of the late sixteenth century and an erudite scholar who knew Vitoria's work well, voiced a similar concern (Pagden 1982: 147ff.; Burgaleta 1999: 88–89; Hosne 2013: 14). In *De procuranda indorum salute* (On Procuring the Salvation of the Indians), written in Lima in 1577 and published in Seville in 1588, Acosta argued it was pointless to worry whether the conquest of the New World was or had ever been justifiable. Such disputes were not only harmful to the increase of the Catholic faith, but they also failed to consider the practical dilemmas of restoring the territories to their previous rulers. Even if one conceded that the Spaniards had "seriously erred in usurping the dominion of the Indians," restitution would still be impossible because "there was no one to whom to make restitution nor a means of affecting it" (Acosta 1987: Book 2, Chapter 11, 333). The only necessary titles, according to Acosta, were the special rights of the Catholic church to evangelize and the evident fact of Spanish territorial control or prescription. After all, he asked, has not every government originated in violence (Acosta 1987: Book 3, Chapter 3, 397–401)?

In many respects, Acosta's assessment was right on the mark. After the death of Las Casas in 1566, Spanish proponents of indigenous restitution found themselves without their greatest and most outspoken champion, and in Peru the colonial regime was about to experience a profound transformation in the person of the fifth Viceroy, Francisco de Toledo (1569–1581). Certainly there were some, such as the first Jesuit Visitor from Rome, Juan de la Plaza, who still agonized over the justice of the Spanish presence in the New World. Yet persons such as he either had their consciences consoled, were simply outnumbered by "realists" like Acosta, or were harassed by the more extreme members of Toledo's administration (Martín 1968: 21–25). The time had come for the consolidation of political power in Peru, the increase of the colony's economic productivity, and programmatic evangelization. Toledo was the man appointed to achieve these goals (Hemming 1970: 392–456).

A huge leap toward the achievement of these ends was taken during the capture and execution of the last heir to the Inca throne, Túpac Amaru, in September 1572. In one fell swoop Toledo was able to put an end to the tradition of Inca resistance at Vilcabamba, which had been both an embarrassment and a threat to his authority, and to undermine the "insurrectionary idolatry" of indigenous Andeans for which he thought the Incas were primarily responsible.[8] Toledo confiscated the remainders of traditional Inca lands and "reduced" or forcibly resettled Inca aristocrats beyond the outskirts of their homes in Cuzco (Urteaga 1931: 229–35). These heavy-handed measures were criticized by members of the religious orders, especially the Jesuits, and even Acosta, who at first had shown himself able to compromise with Toledo over the issue of *doctrinas* (Indian parishes), called the viceroy's attempt to justify his actions by claiming he had liberated the Indians from the tyrannical Incas "ridiculous" (Acosta 1987: Book 3, Chapter 3, 40). So when Acosta wrote in 1577 that there was "no one to whom to make restitution nor a means of affecting it," he appears to have neatly summed up the events of the preceding years.

In the early seventeenth century, therefore, both political officials and prominent members of the religious orders in Peru had distanced themselves from the Lascasian ideal of indigenous restitution. For Toledo and the historians whose work he commissioned, such as Pedro de Sarmiento de Gamboa and Juan de Matienzo, there could be no question of restoration because the Incas, as ruthless conquerors and tyrants, had never had any rights of which to speak (Brading 1991: 128–46). For Acosta the point was simply moot: the chief concern of the Spanish in the New World was, as it had always been, converting the Indians to Christianity and instructing them in the faith. For Inca Garcilaso, however, who saw the Incas as legitimate rulers, whose Inca relatives had suffered malfeasance and dispossession, and who had personally experienced the failure of his own petition to the crown in 1563 (Part 2, Book V, Chapter XXIII), some form of restitution through legal appeal still seemed a strategy worth considering. He does not, however, appear to have been overly optimistic about the possible results. His personal experiences alone had taught him to be skeptical about the justice of colonial courts, and perhaps the severity of the abuses meted out to his Inca forebears had led him to conclude that there could be no adequate remuneration. In discussing the petition of Don Melchor Carlos Inca mentioned above, Inca Garcilaso tells us that in 1602 Don Melchor was currently in Valladolid, "awaiting the grants he is to receive," and adds, "however great they are he is owed better" (Part 1, Book IX, Chapter XXXVIII, vol. 2, 640).[9] The same point is more vividly rendered in an exchange between Sairi Túpac Inca, son of Manco Inca, and Archbishop of Lima Don Jerónimo de Loaisa. According to Inca Garcilaso, Viceroy Don Andrés Hurtado de Mendoza had offered Sairi Túpac Inca a grant of lands in the fertile Yucay valley in exchange for the latter's pledge of obedience to Philip II and for ending his resistance from Vilcabamba. The Inca traveled to Lima, where he dined at Loaisa's table. Near the end of the meal, the documents of the grant were explained to Sairi Túpac. Then: "Having heard and understood them [the terms] the prince took the tablemat he had in front of him, which was velvet and trimmed in silver silk, and, pulling out a silver thread, with it in his hand, he said to the Archbishop: 'This whole cloth and its trimming was mine, and now they give me this little thread to sustain myself and my entire household'" (Part 2, Book VIII, Chapter X, vol. 3, 211).[10] Finally, at the conclusion of the Second Part of the *Royal Commentaries*, Inca Garcilaso reports the failure of the petition of Huayna Cápac's other descendants, those who were not direct heirs to the throne. Here he suggests that it was none other than Don Melchor who "did not want to present the papers so as not to confess how many persons there were of the royal blood, for it seemed to him that if he did this he would lose many of the grants and honors he claimed and hoped to receive, and so he did not speak in favor of his kinsmen" (Part 2, Book VIII, Chapter XXI, vol. 3, 255).[11] Seen in the context of recent changes in Peruvian politics, Inca Garcilaso thus leads his readers to believe that the inconstancies and parsimoniousness of the colonial system as well as potential antagonisms between indigenous claimants made restitution through legal means a tactic that receives his qualified endorsement at best.[12]

There are, however, additional recommendations that can be taken from the *Royal Commentaries* that critically appraise Spanish missionary practices and educational institutions in Peru, and encourage Incas and mestizos from Cuzco to claim (or reclaim) their roles in shaping Peruvian culture. If it is recalled, as argued in chapter 3, that the *Royal Commentaries* contains an allegory for indigenous conversion, in which the possible rebirth of a new society from the chaos and darkness of the Andean First Age (revived in the present thanks to the policies of Viceroy Francisco de Toledo) may be realized by devotees of Pachacámac conversing "at greater length about their gods" (Part 1, Book VI, Chapter XXXI) vol. 1, 395), then it appears that a significant portion of the texts' dual structure itself points toward a set of issues regarding religion and intellectual exchange. We should not be surprised to find, therefore, that the crux of Inca Garcilaso's most specific proposals concerns the implementation of Jesuit missionary practices in Peru at the end of the sixteenth and early seventeenth centuries. More specifically, in the Jesuits' emphasis on mastering indigenous languages and their policies regarding the admission of Creoles, mestizos, and Indians into their ranks, Inca Garcilaso saw both possibilities and problems that he alternately endorses and criticizes. As he advances his criticisms and correctives, which are both principally and implicitly aimed at the work of Spanish Jesuit José de Acosta, he directs the attention of Andean readers toward the benefits to be gained by entering the colleges of the Society of Jesus. Given Inca Garcilaso's realizations that the opportunity for an independent Peru through Gonzalo Pizarro's rebellion had long since passed, that restitution was both an unlikely and highly uncertain strategy for reform, and that the religious and political institutions of the Spanish colonial regime were now permanent features of the Peruvian social landscape, he suggests that Indian and mestizo descendants of the Incas could improve their marginal positions through education and by aligning themselves with the Jesuits. In order to illustrate how the *Royal Commentaries* forwards these views, we shall first turn to a brief consideration of Jesuit missionary practices in Peru, followed by a return to Inca Garcilaso's texts.

Led by Father Jerónimo Ruiz de Portillo, the first Jesuits set sail for Lima in the closing months of 1567 at the request of Philip II to fulfill the urgent need for a stronger missionary presence in Peru. To the frustration and dismay of colonial administrators and clergy, the religious and cultural practices of indigenous Peruvians had proven much more recalcitrant to Spanish conversion efforts than they had perhaps anticipated. This was no doubt in part due to the continuing presence of Inca resistance between the retreats of Vitcos and Vilcabamba, which lasted from the late 1530s until the capture and execution of Túpac Amaru in 1572 (Kubler 1947). Another grave illustration of the inadequacy of Spanish proselytizing was the pan-indigenous religious revival of the mid-1560s called *Taki Onqoy*, which means "dancing sickness." This indigenous millenarian movement of religious and political revolt prophesied that a coalition of Andean deities would rise up and defeat the Christian God by visiting untold calamities and scourges on both Christians and their sympathizers. Although the movement was led primarily by local ethnic chiefs or curacas, Peruvian officials thought that it had been instigated by Titu Cusi

Yupanqui, the Inca ruler in exile. In any event, the existence of a hounded yet semi-autonomous Inca state and the undercurrent of indigenous backlash against their Spanish rulers revealed a profound renunciation of colonial policies that terrified Peruvian officials (Duviols 1977: 133–45; MacCormack 1991: 181–204; Stern 1993: 51–79).[13] It was these disruptive indigenous movements that the Jesuits, known for their unparalleled commitment to education, were sent to address.

Following the work undertaken by previous Peruvian missionaries, such as Dominican Friar Domingo de Santo Tomás, who had published the first Quechua grammar and dictionary in Valladolid in 1560, the Jesuits made it their top priority to master native languages to better instruct Indians in the ways of the faith. What was most essential for evangelists, according to Jesuit José de Acosta (1540–1600) who had arrived in Lima in 1571 and was both the intellectual and administrative engine driving Peruvian reforms, was a thorough knowledge of the languages of those to whom they were preaching (Acosta 1987: Book 4, Chapter 6, 49–51). Experience had shown that forcing indigenous peoples to learn Spanish in order to comprehend the faith was a counterproductive strategy, for the already difficult and mysterious doctrines of Christianity had been explained to potential indigenous converts and novices in a foreign tongue, thereby compounding rather than reducing their confusion (Acosta 1987: Book 4, Chapter 3, 17–23). Instead, Acosta was "completely persuaded" that the "most efficacious" and "most certain" way to proceed in the "business of saving the Indians" was by accommodating missionary methods to the rational capacities and customs of indigenous peoples, and this meant, above all else, their language (Acosta 1987: Book 4, Chapter 6).

Acosta, then acting as Provincial, spearheaded the Provincial Congregation of 1576, which mandated compulsory courses in native languages for all Jesuit missionaries in Peru. Further, with the assistance of accomplished indigenous linguists, such as Peruvian mestizo Jesuit Blas Valera and Spanish Jesuit Alonso de Barzana, the Congregation developed two grammars, two dictionaries, and two catechisms in Quechua and Aymara. These resources were intended to help missionaries bridge the linguistic, cultural, and communicative divides between Spaniards and Andeans by first standardizing the two primary native languages and codifying them in a form that facilitated the learning habits of Europeans, and then by providing missionaries with an efficient means of instructing the rudiments of Catholic doctrine to the Indians. The Congregation additionally proposed the establishment of *colegios de caciques y curacas* ("colleges for chiefs and local lords"), based upon Acosta's realization of the centrality of *ayllus* (extended kinship units) to the organization and function of indigenous social life (Martín 1993; Huys 1997). In these colleges the children of Inca aristocrats and local elites were to be instructed in Spanish, music, and catechism, with the possibility of the most outstanding students attending the regular cycle of courses in grammar, humanities, and rhetoric offered to the Spaniards (Acosta 1987: Book 5, Chapter 10, 259–71; Santos Hernández 1992: 309–11). The emphasis of these policies, as Acosta makes clear in the systematic *De procuranda* that accompanied the Congregation, was placed squarely on education, and not only for Indians: the Jesuits saw the need for linguistic training to communicate with and ultimately convert the native inhabitants of Peru, and they initiated the steps to institutionalize this curriculum for their members.

These new procedures, which were at the very core of Jesuit missionary practices, reversed the policies of Charles V during the 1550s that had prohibited preaching to indigenous peoples in their own languages, for the latter were seen as inadequate vehicles for expressing Catholic doctrine whose use would only result in dissonance and confusion (Harrison 1989: 34–40). This view began to change with the work of Dominican Friar Domingo de Santo Tomás who, in the prologue to his *Lexicon o vocabulario de la lengua general del Perú* (Lexicon or Vocabulary of the General Language of Peru, 1560), defended the expressiveness and elegance of what he named the "Quechua" language (Santo Tomás 1951: 5–16). The Jesuits took the next logical step; they not only believed that Catholic doctrine could be adequately communicated in indigenous languages (despite their lack of essential terms, such as a word for God), but also that it was in the best interests of Christianity to do so. This shift in perspective and practice, however, did not bring with it a wholesale appreciation for the intrinsic value of indigenous cultures. To the contrary, with the lingering memories of Taki Onqoy as a reminder, certain members of the religious orders held indigenous Peruvian culture to be inundated with the false beliefs and vicious customs characteristic of the lowest forms of polytheistic idolatry, which had to be extracted from their roots.[14] In fact, with the arrival of Viceroy Toledo, the writings of Acosta, and the policies established by the Provincial Congregation of 1576, which were later reinforced by the Third Council of Lima (1582–1583), the epoch of "extirpation of idolatry" began Peru (Duviols 1977: 168ff).

Ironically, the extirpation campaigns took part of their basis and rationale from the very group of intellectuals and administrators who, while emphasizing the value of indigenous languages in facilitating communication between

Spaniards and indigenous Peruvians, nonetheless attempted to put an end to the long-standing debate over the natural inferiority of the Indians. Once again the work of Acosta is exemplary in this regard. In both *De procuranda* and his *Historia natural y moral de las Indias* (Natural and Moral History of the Indies, 1590), Acosta summarily dismisses the view associated with the works of the Spanish humanist and jurist Juan Ginés de Sepúlveda that indigenous peoples of the New World were biologically defective creatures analogous to Aristotle's "natural slaves" (Pagden 1982: 109–18; Sepúlveda 1984).[15] As he rather forcefully states in *Historia natural y moral*, Acosta's intention was to "confute that false opinion many do hold of them [Indians], that they are a grose and brutish people, or that they have so little understanding, as they scarce deserve the name of anie." He continues by saying, "I find no better meanes to confound this pernicious opinion, then in relating their order and manner, whenas they lived under their own laws, in which, although they had many barbarous things, and without ground, yet had they many others worthy of great admiration, whereby wee may understand, that they were by nature capable of receiving any good instructions." Compared with the "ignorant and presumptuous" who had insisted upon the natural inferiority of the Indians, Acosta concluded, "the most grave and diligent, which have searched and attained to the knowledge of their secrets, customs, and ancient government, hold another opinion, and admire the order and discourse that hath been betwixt them" (Acosta 1921: Book 6, Chapter 1, 390–91).

At the same time, however, Acosta was just as careful to avoid the conclusions reached by Bartolomé de Las Casas who, in defending the Indians and arguing for their restitution as well as their peaceful conversion through rational persuasion, idealized both their rational capacities and cultural practices to the point of justifying indigenous rituals of human sacrifice.[16] Acosta, who endeavored to tell the whole truth about the Indians by giving praise where it was warranted and rebuking sins as needed, not only disagreed with Las Casas on the question of restitution, as we have seen, but also on the methods to be used in converting Indians (Acosta 1987: Proemio, 55–59). For Las Casas, the Dominican Friar and first Bishop of Chiapas, there was but one universally valid method of converting peoples with no prior exposure to the Catholic faith: rational persuasion and good works free from all coercion.[17] Acosta agreed with Las Casas that this particular method was the most perfect and most desirable, as it had been sanctioned by none other than Christ and the first Apostles. The "Apostolic" method, however, could not be used in the New World, and not because the native inhabitants intrinsically lacked reason. Rather, the Apostolic method was to be reserved, according to Acosta, for the first class of barbarous peoples in his tripartite, hierarchical, and evolutionary scale of pagan cultural development (Pagden 1982: 146–97; Acosta 1987: Proemio, 61–67). In the first class of barbarians were the Chinese, and perhaps the Japanese and some East Indians, who, although errant on some important questions of right reason and natural law, possessed stable government, public laws, fortified cities, and a well-established use of letters. Societies such as these, which had attained the very height of non-Christian cultural advancement, could be brought into the faith with the Apostolic method as the ancient Greeks and Romans had been. The great empires of the Americas, such as the Inca and Mexica, however, belonged to the second and slightly less advanced class of barbarians. These societies, although they possessed notable political capacities and religious ceremonies of some solemnity, had strayed further from right reason and natural law than those of the first class, and they lacked knowledge of the philosophical and civil sciences as well as the all-important art of writing. For barbarians such as these, a "new method" of conversion amenable to their rational capacities and backward customs was needed, a strategy that combined elements of rational persuasion and good works with a modicum of punitive force (Acosta 1987: Book 2, Chapter 8, 303–11; Chapter 12, 339–41). To the third class belonged the majority of Amerindians, people without laws or rulers, with no fixed homes or settlements, and who were susceptible to the most "unnatural" of human vices, such as cannibalism and sodomy. Although there were some in this category who were more peaceful than cruel and illustrated rudimentary forms of government, it was nevertheless acceptable to reduce them to civil behavior and Christianity through the use of force. Like the good Aristotelian he was, Acosta saw the Incas as a mean between the very worst sort of barbarians, who were little more than packs of roaming beasts, and the most civilized barbarians, i.e., the Chinese and Japanese, who could be dealt with more gently (Acosta 1987: Proemio, 59–61). Unlike Las Casas, Acosta argued that a different evangelical method was required for each cultural type; that is, if the missionary did not want to "err seriously" in his efforts (Acosta 1987: Proemio, 69).[18]

In laying out these new methods, Acosta managed to redirect the terms of debate regarding the indigenous inhabitants of the New World away from their supposed natural or biological inferiority toward their *cultural* inferiority. As he succinctly notes, "in this rudeness of mind and cruelty of Indian customs, factors such as birth, origin or natural climate do not intervene in any way, rather [it is] an inveterate education and certain customs which differ little from the lives led by beasts" (Acosta 1987: Book 1, Chapter 8, 149). Having dispensed with the biological argument, Acosta concluded that it was indigenous culture itself that was responsible for the false beliefs and depraved practices of Indians, such as their numerous forms of idolatry and rituals of human sacrifice (Acosta 1921: Book 5, Chapter 19, 344–45). To be sure, insofar as Indians were rational beings, they had the potential for civilized existence and eternal salvation if they could but be instructed to understand that the beliefs and practices impressed upon their minds since birth and to which they had become habituated were severely mistaken. As Anthony Pagden has pointed out, Acosta held that some of these errors stemmed simply from the fact that even the most advanced Amerindian societies were at a lower level of cultural evolution and development than their Christian European counterparts (Pagden 1982: 191–92). More importantly, however, and as Acosta emphasizes in *Historia natural y moral*, Indians had to learn that the errors in their conventional understandings of natural, political, and religious phenomena had been the result of satanic manipulation. The Devil, through his "pride and presumption" as well as the hatred he holds for mankind, always "seekes and strives to be honored as God" (Acosta 1921: Book 5, Chapter 1, 298). As such, he both opposes God and deceives human beings in their natural tendency to worship by establishing perverse imitations or counterfeits of the true church. Acosta explains, "there is scarce any thing instituted by Jesus Christ our Saviour in his Lawe of his Gospel, the which the Divell hath not counterfeited in some sort," including sacrifices, priests, and holy sacraments (Acosta 1921: Book 5, Chapter 11, 324–25). Toward the end of his discussion of Inca and Mexica religious practices in Book 5 of the *Historia natural y moral*, Acosta assures his readers that any resemblance between indigenous practices and orthodox Catholicism is not the effect of a correspondence between customs established by natural reason and those mandated by divine revelation, but is rather a product of diabolical perversion: "And although it seeme that many of their ceremonies agree with ours, yet differ they much for the great abomination they mingle therewithall." Because Satan deceived mankind into revering that which is lower in nature rather than higher, it was common for indigenous ceremonies "to have usually one of these three things, either cruelty, filthiness or slouth . . . for in all his illusions we finde a mixture of these three, or at least one of them." Since Acosta saw religion as humanity's teleological goal and highest cultural achievement and because religious observance was tied to political organization, he could then conclude, "and whereas the temporall power was greatest, there superstition hath most increased, as we see in the Realmes of Mexico and Cusco" (Acosta 1921: Book 5, Chapter 27, 370–71). Thus, Indians were no more defective than the broader patterns of socialization in which their customs and beliefs were formed. These patterns did in fact bear witness to the rational capacities of Amerindians, but they had been distorted by the Father of Lies nonetheless.[19]

If the first end of evangelization was saving mankind from sin and eternal perdition by imparting knowledge of and faith in Christ through preaching (Acosta 1987: Book 5, Chapter 1, 177–81), the second end was the reformation of indigenous customs, whereby infidels and recent converts would be removed from the darkness of their ways and placed in the admirable light of honorable living (Acosta 1987: Book 5, Chapter 9, 247). In this regard, the most important task, according to Acosta, was completely eradicating or extirpating the love of idols displayed by both recent converts to the faith as well as those who were shortly to become so. There were two main difficulties in accomplishing this task. The first was that there were three forms of idolatry, which, taken together, covered a broad spectrum of superstitious beliefs and practices. The first kind of idolatry centered on the worship of natural elements and celestial bodies, as the Chaldeans had done. In the second class of idolatry, practiced by the ancient Greeks, belonged forms of ancestor worship and the deification of human beings. The final and worst type of idolatry had been practiced by the Egyptians and included veneration of vile and sordid animals and even inanimate objects such as rocks and hills (Acosta 1987: Book 5, Chapter 9, 249–51).[20] "Our Peruvians," explains Acosta, exhibited all three types of idolatry: the Incas reserved their greatest veneration for the Sun, followed by lightning, the moon, and stars; they deified their kings and ancestors and had cults of mummies; and in their *huacas* (cults or shrines) they exhibited the tendencies of the Egyptians to worship the basest of creatures and objects. Although Acosta argued that some of the beliefs underpinning these practices might be removed from the hearts of Indians through the use of simple arguments, the second difficulty to be encountered by the missionary was the sheer pervasiveness of idolatry in indigenous life. He states the problem thus: "Neither in peace nor in war, neither at rest nor at work, neither in public life nor in private are they capable of doing anything without first consulting the superstitious cult of their idols." The Indians celebrated some "pagan sacrilege" at weddings and funerals, before leaving their homes or commencing work. In short, every facet of their lives was "completely overrun by idolatrous sentiments." Idolatry, the beginning and end of all evil, was a "plague" (*peste*) and a "hereditary sickness" (*enfermedad idolátrica hereditaria*) that Indians had contracted from their mother's milk, which had grown in them through the examples of their fathers, and had been reinforced by custom and the authority of the public laws (Acosta 1987: Book 5, Chapter 9, 247–55). Continuing with the medical metaphor, Acosta warns that if left untended, these diseases were lethal; yet if medicines were applied, they could be cured (Acosta 1987: Book 5, Chapter 10, 271).

The full implications of Acosta's views on Jesuit missionary practices and the "extirpation" policies established at the time can be fairly summarized as follows. The major impetus for learning indigenous languages was to aid Europeans in their efforts to understand, and hence control, the traditional beliefs and conventional understandings of Indians in order to direct them to civility and true religion. Indigenous peoples were rational beings, at least in potentia, but their cultural development had stalled at an intermediary, albeit somewhat sophisticated stage of evolution toward civility and truth. Although Acosta argued for the conservation of indigenous practices that were contrary to neither Christianity nor justice, he likewise maintained that such tolerance would allow the Spaniards to rule more effectively (Acosta 1987: Book 3, Chapter 24, 587–93). In other words, the outward trappings of indigenous cultures were allowed to remain if the deeper meanings of those practices could be transformed to correspond with Catholic doctrine and European ways of living. Both the political utility of and social urgency for this conceptual translation were reinforced by Acosta's diagnosis of the satanic intervention at the root of the epidemic of idolatry plaguing Peru. The "false beliefs" and impious worship of indigenous Peruvians were seen as forms of social contamination that had not only saturated Amerindian life and thought, but also threatened to spread if not quarantined and treated. As a result, *anyone* who had been raised in or had prolonged contact with an indigenous milieu could become stricken and polluted by errors in thought and behavior. For these reasons, the Indians, mestizos, and criollos who had endured the longest exposure to these contaminants were looked upon as culturally backward beings who, though they could be saved with the appropriate methods, were to be handled with kid gloves.[21]

As David Brading has argued, Inca Garcilaso's *Royal Commentaries* can be seen as a sustained attack on the entire tradition of Spanish colonial historiography in the sixteenth century (Brading 1986: 3). Yet as he and other commentators have also pointed out, a central element of Inca Garcilaso's broader intervention is his rigorous yet implicitly stated critique of Acosta's views (Zamora 1988: 85–120; MacCormack 1991: 332–82). As we have seen, Acosta was not only one of the key administrative agents during a period of comprehensive reform in colonial Peru; his written works also provided the intellectual foundation and systematic justification for a series of new missionary policies and procedures. Although the works of both authors have taken on a more general significance stretching across modern academic disciplines, Inca Garcilaso's confrontation with Acosta is first and foremost a local struggle over Jesuit missionary and educational policies in colonial Peru.

The crux of Inca Garcilaso's dispute with Acosta revolves around the latter's insistence that the Incas were culturally inferior beings, as evidenced by the many forms of idolatry they practiced, and who, in the final analysis, had been deceived by the Devil. Against this view, Inca Garcilaso places the Incas in a privileged position with respect to other indigenous Andean ethnic groups by first separating pre-conquest Peruvian history into two ages: a barbaric First Age, in which many of the superstitious beliefs and inhuman practices that Acosta describes were rampant; and a Second Age brought about by the Incas who, in turn, had eradicated the former evils, civilized pre-Hispanic Peru, and instituted natural religion. Although Inca Garcilaso admits that "in the First Age and ancient gentilism there were some Indians who were little better than tame animals and others much worse than wild beasts," that their gods "were of a piece with the simplicity and stupidity of the times" (Part 1, Book I, Chapter IX, vol. 1, 28), and then goes on to describe in graphic detail the idolatry, sacrifices, tyrannical government, incest, and cannibalism of these hapless beings (Part 1, Book I, Chapters X–XIV), he stresses the need to maintain both the temporal and cultural distinction between pre-Inca and Inca periods.[22] The distinction drawn by Inca Garcilaso, which can also be seen in the works of authors with diametrically opposed views on the nature of the Incas, such as Las Casas and Sarmiento de Gamboa, applies equally to the condition of Peru before the Inca empire as it does to those ethnic groups in the present who were never conquered by it. In the latter case, the characteristics of the First Age could be seen in the present day, because peoples such as the Cape Passau Indians and Chirihuanas had never come under the civilizing influence of the Incas, therefore making it easy to conflate their radically divergent behavior with the epoch and actions of the emperors (Part 1, Book I, Chapter XXII). In this way, Inca Garcilaso challenges Acosta's analysis of Inca religion as being based on a chronological error, which in turn led to conceptual and cultural confusion.[23]

Further, although both Acosta and Inca Garcilaso saw history as the unfolding of divine will in time—the Augustinian *operatio Dei*—Inca Garcilaso likewise rejected Acosta's suggestion that Satan was the motivating force behind Inca beliefs. Like Las Casas and Jerónimo Román who had argued that the Inca empire was an essential precursor to the arrival of the Christian gospel in the New World and had paved the way for evangelization by bringing the essential benefits of civilization to Peru, Inca Garcilaso portrays the Incas in the divinely ordained role of *praeparatio evangelica* (Zamora 1988: 110; MacCormack 1991: 234). Instead of groping through the darkness of diabolical manipulation, the first Inca, Manco Cápac, was appointed by God as a "morning star" to bring the light of natural law and civilization to the "savages" so that when God "saw fit to send forth the light of His divine rays upon those idolaters, it might find them no longer in their first savagery, but rendered more docile to receive the Catholic faith and the teaching and doctrine of our Holy Mother the Roman Church" (Part 1, Book I, Chapter XV, vol. 1, 39). In this way, and with a strong Neoplatonic bent, Inca Garcilaso presents the central tenets and core practices of Inca civilization as being based not on an abysmal error, but rather on the partially revealed truths of divine grace grasped through the use of natural reason. Whereas Acosta places the Incas on the outer margins of Christian history, Inca Garcilaso uses this providentialist and universalist view to cast the Incas as central to the destiny of the Catholic church in America.[24]

To these two argumentative strategies Inca Garcilaso adds another and more damaging critique. As Margarita Zamora has demonstrated, Inca Garcilaso's philological exegesis of Quechua religious terms, such as *apachitas*, *huaca*, *Pachacámac*, *Viracocha*, and *Tangatanga*, corrects the linguistic errors made by Acosta in his use of these words in the *Historia natural y moral* (Zamora 1988: 117–20). Of course, Acosta explains the meaning of these terms in order to demonstrate the depth and precise nature of Peruvian idolatry as well as the clear relationship between Inca religious practices and the counterfeit Church of Satan. Inca Garcilaso argues, however, that it was a lack of facility with native languages which caused Spaniards to misinterpret and misrepresent the very beliefs and practices they criticized. As he explains in a celebrated chapter on the multiple meanings of the word *huaca*: "The Spaniards attribute many other gods [beyond Pachacámac and the Sun] to the Incas because they do not know how to divide the times and idolatries of the First Age from those of the Second. And also, for not knowing the propriety of the language in asking for and obtaining information from the Indians, their ignorance has given birth to attributing to the Incas many or all of the gods the latter removed from the Indians they subjected to their empire" (Part 1, Book II, Chapter IV, vol. 1, 76).[25] Inca Garcilaso goes on to say that whereas Spaniards took the word *huaca* simply to mean "idol," it had numerous meanings in the general language of Peru depending upon variations in pronunciation and the context in which it was uttered. For instance, *huaca* could mean idol but not the verb "to idolatrize"; it could mean sacred article, temple, sanctuary, offering, oracle, or anything that stood out from the ordinary due to its novelty, beauty, or ugliness. If the last syllable was pronounced in the back of the throat, *huaca* could mean "to mourn." Yet "of this pronunciation—and all the others this language has—the Spaniards pay no attention at all, however inquisitive they may be (no matter how concerned they are with knowing them), because they do not exist in the Spanish tongue" (Part 1, Book II, Chapter V, vol. 1, 79).[26] Of course, Acosta is not the only Spanish commentator being criticized in these remarks, and in fact his name is conspicuously absent from the several chapters in which Inca Garcilaso challenges the prevailing accounts of Inca religion. Instead, Inca Garcilaso refers to "one author," a "certain historian," "Spanish historians" or the generic "Spaniards" when upbraiding Acosta. Nevertheless, when Inca Garcilaso wrote with regard to Inca religious practices that "Spaniards . . . have no certain account for what they say" (*los españoles . . . no tuvieron cierta relación para lo que dicen*) (Part 1, Book II, Chapter I, vol. 1, 69), it would have been all too obvious to anyone familiar with Acosta's *Historia natural y moral* that this applied to his work as well.

The multiple arguments used by Inca Garcilaso to correct and emend Acosta's estimation of Inca civilization have only been touched on briefly here because they have received detailed treatment by authors cited above. But even in this quick overview we can see how Inca Garcilaso continually redeploys the major themes and arguments of his work to achieve various discursive ends. Perhaps the single and most important of Inca Garcilaso's arguments, the one for which he is arguably most well known, concerns Spanish ignorance of indigenous languages. This argument is particularly poignant, moreover, when viewed in light of Inca Garcilaso's ingenious critique of Acosta in the context of Jesuit missionary practices in Peru. We have already seen that two of Acosta's major themes in *De procuranda* and *Historia natural* are (a) the need for missionaries to master indigenous languages and (b) his location of Inca idolatry between the least and most civilized barbarian cultures which, in turn, required a new or mixed evangelical approach. A third theme in Acosta's work, which has not been mentioned thus far, is his stress on personal experience and observation in discerning the truth about the New World. In the sixteenth century, knowledge was based primarily on the interpretation of authoritative texts, for instance, the Bible and Roman Canon Law (Foucault 1994: 17–44). Yet when Europeans were confronted with the diversity of New World geography, flora, fauna, and indigenous peoples, try as they might, they often found insufficient conceptual coverage or correspondence between what they encountered and what was contained in the works of traditional authorities (See Chiapelli 1976; Grafton, Shelford, and Siraisi 1992; Pagden 1993; Kupperman 1995). Acosta was by no means the first either to notice or attempt to negotiate this divide between the traditional foundations of knowledge and the challenges brought to those foundations through personal experience of the New World. Yet he did attempt, as Las Casas had before him (Pagden 1982: 109–45), to raise the empirical data collected through personal observation to a new level of intellectual and analytical sophistication. Acosta did not just describe the natural and cultural phenomena of the New World, he offered explanations, and it was the combination of his personal experience of the absurd conclusions postulated by ancient thinkers who obviously lacked any knowledge of the Americas and his formidable erudition that allowed him to suggest a comparative, historical framework with all the trappings of philosophical and theological rigor (del Pino-Díaz, 1978; Pagden 1982: 151–57).[27]

When Inca Garcilaso suggests, through his philological analysis and restoration of Quechua terms, that Acosta's knowledge of indigenous languages is at best faulty if not substandard, he catches the theologian with his frock up. The same author who had argued for the essential connection between mastery of indigenous languages and the reformation of indigenous cultures as well as the demonstrative value of personal experience in properly understanding the truth of indigenous matters was the very same one who had failed to understand some of the most basic words in the general vocabulary of indigenous Peruvians. According to Inca Garcilaso, Acosta, like so many other Spaniards before him, compounded his error by using his faulty knowledge of Quechua to then evaluate the nature of Inca culture in its entirety. As a result, with regard to Inca religious practices and terminology, Inca Garcilaso points out, "the Spanish Christians abominate them all as works of the Devil, and neither do the Spaniards trouble to ask for clear information about them, but rather dismiss them as diabolical, as they imagine" (Part 1, Book II, Chapter

II, vol. 1, 72).[28] The immediate implication of this critique, as we have seen, is that Inca Garcilaso can then claim Spanish historians and observers have "no certain account for what they say" because "the Spaniard who thinks he knows the language best is ignorant of nine-tenths of it" (*Que el español que piensa que sabe más de él ignora de diez partes nueve*) (Part 1, Book I, Chapter XIX, vol. 1, 50). As if to further illustrate the point, Inca Garcilaso manipulates Acosta's *Historia natural y moral*, arguably the most read and respected work on the New World in seventeenth-century Europe, by citing it only in those instances in which Acosta appears to sanction Inca Garcilaso's own perspective (Zamora 1988: 107).[29]

Acosta's analysis of Inca idolatry is thus neutralized, but Inca Garcilaso does not go so far as to explicitly challenge the former's comparative, evolutionary framework of pagan cultural development. Rather, Inca Garcilaso's thorough reevaluation of Inca culture in the First Part of the *Royal Commentaries* strongly suggests that certain elements of Acosta's framework have been inappropriately applied to the Incas. What Acosta saw as the worst form of Inca idolatry, Inca Garcilaso attributed to the primitive First Age of Andean civilization. Acosta found these types of superstitious beliefs particularly contemptible because they took creatures and objects clearly below the dignity of humankind as worthy of veneration. Inca Garcilaso, however, maintained that things could have been much worse, and that indigenous Peruvians should have been congratulated rather than admonished for having remained free from other, more serious vices: "In their [Incas] idolatry—and in that which preceded them—the Indians are greatly to be esteemed, both in the Second Age as well as the First. Since among such diversity and such foolishness of gods as they possessed, they never adored pleasures and vices like those in the ancient gentilism of the Old World—who adored confessed adulterers, murderers, drunkards (and above all Priapus), while being people who presumed so much of their letters and knowledge, and these other people [Indians] were so far from all good learning" (Part 1, Book II, Chapter V, vol. 1, 80).[30] In addition to attempting both to diffuse the stigma that had been attached to the Andean huacas and distancing the Incas from their worship, Inca Garcilaso further insists that the Incas "excelled in moral philosophy, as well in teaching it as in the exercise of the laws and the customs they observed . . . [and] in the exercise of this science they were so vigilant that their place cannot be exaggerated" (Part 1, Book II, Chapter XXVII, 134).[31] Further, in a discussion of Inca laws that Inca Garcilaso quotes at length from Jesuit Blas Valera, we are told, "[in their laws] the Incas of Peru should be preferred not only to the Chinese and Japanese and East Indians, but also to the gentile natives of Asia and Greece" (Part 1, Book V, Chapter XI, vol. 1, 274).[32] These remarks are specifically directed at Acosta's claim in *De procuranda* that the Incas were barbarians of the second class who lacked knowledge of the civil sciences (Acosta 1987: Proemio). If, as Acosta argued, religious beliefs and political institutions were two of the primary measures by which one could gauge the cultural sophistication and moral character of a people, then it was only too clear, according to Inca Garcilaso, that the Incas had climbed to the very summit of civility, and they had done so without the aid of writing and without explicit knowledge of divine revelation.

The overall effect of these arguments is to move Inca culture *up* the civilizational scale, as it were, into the first class of barbarians as described by Acosta and perhaps slightly above all other non-Christian peoples. Although Inca Garcilaso admits being "well aware that gentilism is a sea of errors" (Part 1, Book 1, Chapter 19, vol. 1, 50), he redescribes Inca religious practices so they appear more familiar and, hence, acceptable to European readers. The Incas are presented as having achieved the very epitome of just monarchism, knowledge, and inward worship of the "unknown god" Pachacámac, similar to that of the Athenians (Acts 17:22–33), outward worship of the Sun as the visible manifestation of Pachacámac, and adoration of their leaders and ancestors as "Children of the Sun" in appreciation for all the social benefits they had provided (Part 1, Book II, Chapters I and IV). As Acosta had argued in *De procuranda*, these forms of idolatry, the worship of natural elements and ancestors, were much less objectionable and much easier to uproot through rational persuasion than the third class of idolatry. As we have seen, Inca Garcilaso disputes the extent to which Acosta's third type of idolatry (worship of low animals, objects, and man-made images) applies to the Incas, and he goes even further by flatly contradicting Acosta's account of Inca rituals of human sacrifice (Acosta 1921: Book 5, Chapter 19, 344–45).[33] Once again, Inca Garcilaso places human sacrifice in the First Age of Peruvian history, appeals to Pedro de Cieza de León's *Crónica del Perú* (Chronicle of Peru, 1550) for corroboration, and sternly warns, "such an inhuman accusation should not be made unless it is known for certain" (Part 1, Book II, Chapter X, vol. 1, 94).[34] Although Inca Garcilaso altered both the form and content of certain Andean religious practices, these alterations were in some sense necessitated by his attempt to portray the Incas in the role of praeparatio evangelica. A privileged pagan civilization that had been divinely selected to prepare the way for the gospel would have to resemble or contain in embryonic form orthodox Christian norms, and the Incas of the *Royal Commentaries* appear to be the very embodiment of Christian cultural ideals.

This obviously idealized representation of the Incas, although clearly influenced by Renaissance *philosophia christi* and Neoplatonism, has a very practical, political intent. By moving the Incas to the summit of pagan cultural development and portraying the guiding principles, core beliefs, and institutional structures of Inca civilization as having a high level of correspondence with Christianity, the First Part of the *Royal Commentaries* reiterates, with copious historical examples and argumentation, both the priority and applicability of the Apostolic method of conversion through rational persuasion in Peru. It was this method, according to Acosta, that had accounted for the "thousands of marvels" the Company of Jesus had thus far achieved with the Chinese, Japanese, East Indians, Ethiopians, Persians, Arabs, and so on, but which had been "condemned for its extreme stupidity" in the New World, and "not without reason" (Acosta 1987: Book 2, Chapter 8, 307). Acosta indeed recognized that the opportunity for using this method in the Americas had been missed due to the violence of the conquest, the frustrating inability of present-day missionaries to perform miracles (to which he devotes two full chapters), and the fact that many of the Incas had already been converted and placed under Christian rulers (Acosta 1987: Book 2, Chapters 8–11, 303–37). Nevertheless, it was his variable assessment of Amerindian cultures that provided the foundation for the new methods. So, in correcting Acosta's evaluation of Inca culture, which Inca Garcilaso suggests is imagined and without authority, and replacing it with a more positive one, Inca Garcilaso creates ample discursive space for a corresponding shift in the evangelical practices at the very least toward the "patient and gradualist tradition" within Jesuit proselytism in Peru, if not all the way back to the Lascasian ideal.

Further, Inca Garcilaso uses Acosta to launch a polemic against other Spanish colonial historiographers and clergymen concerning the precise kind of personal experience required for the proper comprehension and evaluation of Amerindian cultures. From the very opening pages, he continually faults Spaniards for their ignorance of indigenous languages. He is just as adamant to remind his readers that he is a native Quechua speaker, that he is a Peruvian "natural son," an Inca, Indian, mestizo, and that he has intimate, first-hand knowledge of Inca culture through his "mother's milk," prolonged contact, and privileged access to indigenous oral traditions and ways of life. In light of the context in which he was writing, such statements certainly help to authorize his work for a European readership through the criteria of personal experience and eyewitness observation prevalent in colonial historiography (Mignolo 1981). Inca Garcilaso's repeated use of these common places, however, transforms them into a rather resounding valorization of a dual linguistic and cultural perspective. It was precisely Inca Garcilaso's ability to see things "with the ones and with the others" (*yo la miraba con los uno y los otros*) (Part 1, Book VIII, Chapter XXIV, vol. 2, 553) that previous Spanish observers had lacked and which, therefore, signaled the inadequacy of their accounts.

This inadequacy was not only a product of linguistic ignorance and inaccurate information, it was also, according to Inca Garcilaso, evidence of a serious ethical failing. For instance, in an anecdote inserted in the chapters in which his critique of Acosta is at its height (Part 1, Book II, Chapters I–X), Inca Garcilaso compares the differences between Inca and Spanish processes of examining witnesses and providing testimony in judicial proceedings. Under the Incas, after a witness had promised to tell the truth, it was required that he say "what he knew of both sides, whether for or against." By contrast, after the Spaniards had conquered Peru there was a murder trial in which the deposition of a curaca was taken. After having the witness promise to tell the truth, the judge asked him what he knew about the murderers. The judge asked nothing of the victims, who had been the aggressors, and the curaca asked "to be allowed to say all he knew about the case, for he understood that if he told one side and was silent about the other it was lying, and he would not have told the whole truth as he had promised" (Part 1, Book II, Chapter III, vol. 1, 75).[35] The placement of this anecdote within Inca Garcilaso's assault on Spanish misinterpretations of Inca religion results in a harsh indictment. Due to their ignorance of indigenous languages, Spanish historians could not tell both sides of the story and arrive at the truth. Moreover, they were caught in a double bind: if they tried to tell both sides they would misconstrue the indigenous one; and if they did not try to tell both sides they would inevitably lie.

Inca Garcilaso's valorization of an intercultural, mestizo perspective and his idealization of Inca civilization act in tandem as corrosive agents applied to the prejudicial slant of Spanish colonial historiography. In some instances at least, the critique tends toward an outright denial of Spanish pretensions to any meaningful knowledge about indigenous Peruvian civilization. This, however, is the argument at its most extreme, and it should be remembered that Inca Garcilaso's intent was to reconcile the social antagonisms in colonial Peru rather than exacerbate them. Instead, his arguments probe and dissect the claims upon which the stigma that had been attached to indigenous Peruvians and their descendants was based by Spanish observers and administrators. The idea that Amerindians were naturally inferior, as we have seen, had been rejected in favor of the view that cultural differences could be better comprehended as being representative of lower or earlier stages of historical evolution and, therefore, cultural inferiority when compared to European standards. Although the latter view certainly went a long way toward relativizing cultural differences (albeit in a hierarchical and teleological framework), it nevertheless adhered to conceptual and rhetorical structures of what Stephen Greenblatt has called "blockage"; in other words, "the social imposition of an imaginary order of exclusion" (Greenblatt 1991: 121). In this case, the order of exclusion constructed by Acosta was maintained through the purported deficiencies of Inca culture, most notably their idolatry and their lack of writing (Acosta 1921: Book 6, Chapter 4, 396–98). To be sure, insofar as he viewed indigenous peoples as rational beings potentially capable of moral improvement, education, and salvation, Acosta did not erect an absolute structure of difference or exclusion. Yet he explicitly linked supposed cultural deficiencies with truncated intellectual development, the stain of diabolical collusion, and the metaphors of pollution, contamination, and disease.

Inca Garcilaso clearly understood the problematic nature and practical consequences of this system of associations, and it should hardly be surprising that he consistently eschews the language of sickness when discussing Inca religion. Even in his description of the idolatry of the pre-Inca age he uses words such as "darkness," "illusion," "error," "folly," and "deception," but never "plague" or "infirmity." The only notable exception in this regard is his description of the Inca purification ritual, Citua; but here the purpose is to illustrate that the Incas understood the relationship between illnesses (*enfermedades*) and sorrows (penas) and had their own methods of alleviating them (Part 1, Book VII, Chapters VI and VII). Metaphorically speaking, the *Royal Commentaries* works to sanitize and purify the uncleanliness attributed to Incas, mestizos, and criollos in order to provide members of these groups with a counternarrative capable of allowing them not only to take pride in their heritage, but also to confront the charges against them with a stockpile of effective arguments. As he explicitly states in a chapter discussing the racial categories of the New World, "mestizo," although used as an "insult" (*menosprecio*) in the Indies, was a word and condition Inca Garcilaso had embraced: "I call myself it [mestizo] with a full mouth, and honor myself thereby" (Part 1, Book IX, Chapter XXXI, vol. 2, 627).[36]

The general significance of Inca Garcilaso's intervention in the Spanish discourse regarding the cultural inferiority and limited intellectual capacities of native Peruvians hardly needs more comment at this point. The practical recommendations he appends to this intervention, however, do. As argued above, despite the priority the Jesuits placed on mastering indigenous Peruvian languages in facilitating conversion, their policies were implemented in an atmosphere of profound suspicion regarding the people they were ostensibly to benefit. This suspicion translated into a deep ambivalence and an ongoing dispute over who could be admitted to the Society of Jesus in Peru. The main tension, which in many respects mirrored the ambivalence regarding indigenous culture seen in Acosta's published works, arose from the realization of religious administrators that criollos and mestizos displayed a much greater facility with indigenous languages than either Spanish or European missionaries, but as they were also the ones who had experienced the longest exposure to Indian culture, their moral characters and loyalties were forever in question.[37] In 1555, for instance, the religious orders of Mexico prohibited ordaining men of indigenous descent, including mestizos, a policy reiterated by the Third Provincial Council of Mexico in 1585 (Hyland 1998: 434). As for Peru, the usual refrain from the late 1560s onward was that it was "undesirable to trust people from here" (*no conviene confiar en la gente de acá*), and the religious orders in general moved with extreme caution in admitting "*naturales*" (Lavallé 1985: 137–53).

Interestingly enough, Acosta was part of a liberal minority who thought that admitting criollo priests was a "very useful" policy due to their language abilities; that is, if the applicants could be shown to be men of moral virtue and solid character. He likewise held the Society should neither "loathe nor injure" the mestizos, among whom they might find another Timothy, the son of a Greek man and a Jewish woman, as St. Paul had (Acts 16:1–3). Of course, as Acosta notes in *De procuranda*, with mestizo applicants there was need for even greater vigilance than with criollos, because the former "ordinarily maintain the bad habits of the Indian condition and customs, with whose milk and dealings they have been raised" (Acosta 1987: Book IV, Chapter III, 67–69), but the door should not be closed to them due to the mere fact of their mestizaje, in any event.[38]

The guarded optimism of some of the early Jesuits was nevertheless short lived. By 1582 the Society had voted unanimously to exclude all mestizos from its ranks, a vote in which Acosta participated, although the prohibition was overruled by the Archbishop of Lima St. Toribio Alfonso de Mongrovejo.[39] Mongrovejo's counterpolicy, however, restricted those mestizos the Society did admit to pastoral duties in Indian doctrinas, "usually the poorest, most isolated and least influential parishes in which a priest could serve in colonial Peru" (Hyland 1998: 439, quote on 444). In 1588 Philip II rescinded his earlier ban on mestizos from the priesthood (1576) by issuing a decree that enabled archbishops and bishops in the New World to ordain mestizos as long as diligent investigations into the life, character, habits, extent of educational training, prior religious instruction, and legitimate birth of each candidate were undertaken prior to admission. Yet even this decree was indicative of the antagonisms surrounding the question of criollo and mestizo initiates: what seemed like a potential opening tended in practice to bar a large number of potential candidates from the priesthood, as illegitimate birth was common among mestizos (Konetzke 1946b: 215–37; Hyland 1998: 444–54). Although there were a few mestizos who not only managed to break into the religious ranks but were also ordained as full priests, such as Mercedarian Francisco de Ribera and Jesuit Blas Valera, both their numbers and status remained low (Hyland 1996: 454; Lavallé 1994: 141, 146), and after his visitations of 1599–1602, Provincial Rodrigo de Cabredo recommended that the Society further restrict the admission of mestizos due to the bad examples he had seen and the many novices whom he had been forced to expel (Santos Hernández 1992: 82)

If one believed, however, that Indians, mestizos, and criollos were neither naturally defective nor morally suspect due to cultural contamination, then there could be no sufficient reason for excluding them from positions in the religious orders or for that matter the political hierarchy. Furthermore, if the goal of converting and civilizing indigenous Peruvians was to be realized through an efficiently structured program of education that emphasized a mastery of indigenous languages, then why not allow native speakers to be more active in the process? Inca Garcilaso adopts this position, and the *Royal Commentaries* can easily be read as advocating both the utility and necessity of providing Peruvians of indigenous descent with the training, opportunity, and authority to function in such capacities. This, at any rate, is what he seems to suggest through the example of Father Diego de Alcobaza, the mestizo son of Juan de Alcobaza and an Inca woman and one of Inca Garcilaso's childhood friends from Cuzco. Of Alcobaza, who was a "vicar and preacher to the Indians in many provinces," he writes, "his prelates have moved him to many places, because, as a mestizo native of Cuzco, he knows the language of the

Indians better than others who are not natives of this land. And his work is more fruitful" (Part 1, Book III, Chapter I, vol. 1, 145).[40]

Inca Garcilaso's proposal is stated more explicitly later in the work, although somewhat indirectly. In fact, and as is usually the case with his most controversial views, Inca Garcilaso refrains from making the argument himself. Instead, he allows one of the first Peruvian mestizo Jesuits, Blas Valera, to act as his spokesman. Valera was not only Inca Garcilaso's favorite written source on Peru, he was also an associate of Acosta's who had been personally involved with translating and codifying Quechua and Aymara for the evangelical purposes of the Provincial Congregation and was stationed at the Jesuit college in Cuzco in 1576.[41] Valera is cited often in the *Royal Commentaries* with high praise, and juxtaposed to the argumentative treatment Acosta's work often receives, it could be said that part of Inca Garcilaso's intention in the *Royal Commentaries* was to substitute the authority of Europe's best-known commentator on Peru and the New World for that of an unpublished and unknown mestizo.[42]

However that stands, Valera's views on education are presented during two continuous chapters on the general language of Peru that are little more than an extended quotation from his tattered manuscript, which Inca Garcilaso had received from Jesuit Pedro Maldonado de Saavedra from Seville (Part 1, Book I, Chapter VI). In these pages we are told that the Incas gave various orders for the good of their subjects, yet none so important as establishing an official language, the general language of Cuzco, to overcome the "confusion and multitude of tongues" in their empire. For this they sent natives of Cuzco to each newly conquered territory where official language instructors were given houses and lands so they and their children could settle and teach permanently. This practice, whereby "the vassals of various tribes behaved like brothers, for they all spoke the same tongue," had been neglected after the conquest because "it never occurred to anyone to see to a thing so suited and necessary for the preaching of the Holy Gospel." In fact, the old diversity of languages had resurfaced and been exacerbated by "a certain viceroy" who had reduced small Indian villages into larger ones, bringing members of many different tribes together in the same place. In so doing, the viceroy (Toledo) had disregarded the point that "the similarity and conformity of words almost always helps to reconcile men and bring them to true union and friendship." The measure to be taken by viceroys and other governors to reverse this trend was to order "the children of the language teachers appointed by the Incas to resume teaching the general language to the rest of the Indians (as they did before)" (Part 1, Book VII, Chapter III, vol. 2, 420–22). The quotation of Valera continues uninterrupted into the next chapter, and includes praise for the general language of Peru, which "has the same value to Peruvian Indians as Latin to us," commendation of the Incas for their prudent diligence in this regard, and concludes with a call to governors to "affect this simple measure." To this Inca Garcilaso simply adds, "up to this point is Father Blas Valera, and for appearing to me to be a thing so necessary for teaching the Christian faith I have included it here" (*Hasta aquí es del padre Blas Valera, que parecerme cosa tan necesaria para la enseñanza de la doctrina cristiana lo puse aquí*) (Part 1, Book VII, Chapter IV, vol. 2, 425).

The *Royal Commentaries* thus urges Peruvian missionaries and administrative personnel to do two things: to employ the Apostolic method of preaching through persuasion and good works when dealing with the descendants of the Incas and their former subjects; and to enlist native Quechua speakers from Cuzco as teachers, both as a means toward conversion and to restore a common language and a sense of communal identification to indigenous Peruvians. These reforms receive Inca Garcilaso's strongest endorsement, and he realized rather clearly the extent to which both the European discourse of Indian inferiority as well as the concomitant stigmatization of native-born Peruvians effectively thwarted the kind of cultural rapprochement he desired. In this sense, Inca Garcilaso admonishes Peruvian missionaries for perpetuating an atmosphere of suspicion and exclusion in their evangelical practices, in their written works, and within their ranks, and he proposes reforms to make the essential processes of education and proselytism (neither of which he challenges) more effective, more inclusive, and more humane.

It appears, then, that Inca Garcilaso was not only fully aware of the approaches to education and evangelization being taken by the Jesuits in Peru and their attendant barriers at the turn of the seventeenth century, but that he also saw certain of those policies, if reformed and extended, as providing an opportunity for the mestizo and Indian descendants of the Incas to play an active role within colonial institutions and cultural life. Yet it remains to be seen how he signaled this to a potential Andean audience, the latter of whom had every reason for holding their own misgivings and suspicions about colonial administrators and missionaries, given their experiences of the conquest, the abuses of the Toledan regime, and the extirpation campaigns. The challenge for Inca

Garcilaso in this regard was to persuade Andean readers to view the Jesuits with trust from within the operative normative framework of the indigenous past, and he attempts to do so by creating a series of overlaps or resemblances between the practices of the Jesuits and the Incas.

In the first instance Inca Garcilaso calls the attention of his readers to the Society of Jesus and their commitment to the Quechua language, and from the very opening of the *Royal Commentaries* the Jesuits are singled out among all other religious orders for praise. In the *Advertencia* (Warning) to the First Part, Inca Garcilaso remarks, "the fathers of the Holy Society of Jesus have worked a great deal at it [the general language of Peru] . . . so as to know how to speak it well. And with their good example (which is what matters most) they have greatly advanced the instruction of the Indians" (Part 1, "Warning").[43] He later calls them "Apostles among the Indians," whose experiences with the indigenous peoples of Peru are a "summary argument" for just how worthy and capable of salvation the latter are (Part 2, "Prologue"). Between and beyond the prefatory statements to the First and Second Parts, the Jesuits are mentioned on numerous occasions, which reiterate how these Fathers are "so inquisitive in everything," how "much they labor in the language to indoctrinate the gentiles" (Part 1, Book IV, Chapter XI, vol. 1, 222), and how everyone alive "should give thanks to God for sending them the Society of Jesus, in which there is such an abundance of all sciences and all good teaching" (Part 1, Book II, Chapter XXVIII, vol. 1, 140).[44] In addition to his continued use of Jesuit sources, Inca Garcilaso early and often establishes the exemplary character of Jesuit pedagogy as well as the extent to which they complement and reinforce their educational efforts with good works.

In so doing, Inca Garcilaso is able to create a resemblance between the missionary practices of the Jesuits and the civilizing mission of the first Incas, Manco Cápac and Mama Ocllo Huaco. Inca Garcilaso calls the deeds of Manco Cápac "the beginning and foundation of our history," because all the Incas, "whether kings or not kings, prided themselves on imitating in every way the character, works, and customs of the first prince" (Part 1, Book I, Chapter XIX, vol. 1, 50). For our present purposes, what is most notable about Manco Cápac and Mama Ocllo Huaco is their role as teachers: they civilized the barbarians of the First Age by instructing them in all the arts and crafts necessary for civil life, justice, and brotherhood by persuading them through reason to conform to natural law (Part 1, Book I, Chapter XXI). Further, they maintained a scrupulous correspondence between their words and their deeds that, along with the many benefits they provided, confirmed the fable of their divine origins (i.e., being children of the Sun) in the eyes of their subjects. Indians accepted this providential genealogy because "these people are attentive to nothing as much as observing whether what their teachers do conforms with what they say, and finding conformity between life and doctrine, no arguments are necessary to convince the Indians to do what the teachers wish" (Part 1, Book I, Chapter XXV, vol. 1, 61–62).[45] Although the correspondence of word and deed was an ideal of Renaissance philosophia christi, Inca Garcilaso attributes the same rationale to the Incas to create an overlap between the former's role as praeparatio evangelica and the mission of the Jesuits. In this way, the Jesuits can be viewed by Andeans as following Inca precedent.

Continuing with this theme of Inca precedent, Inca Garcilaso informs us that the Incas had their own philosophers, *amautas*, who were experts in moral philosophy and who amplified the information contained in the *quipus* (knotted cords) into historical narratives and allegories, and their own poets, *harauicus*, who composed comedies and tragedies (Part 1, Book II, Chapter XXVII). Next we learn that "some studious religious of various orders, principally from the Company of Jesus" began to write comedies in indigenous languages to induce a feeling for the mysteries of the faith in their pupils based upon their realization that the Indians had performed plays in the time of their Inca kings (Part 1, Book II, Chapter XXVIII, vol. 1, 138). The Jesuits, then, not only appear to conduct themselves in the same altruistic spirit as the first Incas and are sensitive to their practices, but they also provide instruction in the same language, in "traditional" subject matter, and in the familiar roles of amautas and harauicus.

The Jesuits are not only made to resemble the intellectuals of the Inca regime, but another set of associations links the former to a symbolic location. We are first told in Book V, Chapter X of the First Part that the Jesuits, who established a college in Cuzco in 1571, had taken up residence in the district of Cuzco named Amarucancha, meaning the district of *amarus*, or large snakes. In Andean religions amarus were considered sacred animals or huacas (Part 1, Book II, Chapter IV), and they were also part of the insignia of Inca *panacas*. What seems like a trivial or thin association is further elaborated by Inca Garcilaso when he explains that Amarucancha, "Palace of the Serpent," was also the palace of the last ruler, Inca Huayna Cápac, and that upon the death of a king his royal palace was considered a "sacred place" (*lugar sagrado*), in other words, a huaca. Huayna Cápac was not only the last Inca, but, more importantly, he was also responsible for publicizing the prophecy of Viracocha Inca, which held that after the reign of twelve kings a new race of men with invincible arms and a better law would come to Tahuantinsuyu (the four corners of the world united) and that the Indians should obey them in everything (Part 1, Book IX, Chapter XV). Inca Garcilaso uses this prophecy to account for the defeat of the Inca empire by the Spaniards, to explain why the first Spanish conquerors of Peru were called "Viracocha Inca" by indigenous peoples (Part 1, Book V, Chapter XXI, vol. 1, 300), and it is one of the major strategies he uses to suggest the *translatio imperii* from Inca rule to that of the conquistadors and encomenderos (see chapter 3).

For the moment, however, it is more important to follow the progression of the palace/district of Amarucancha through the course of the *Royal Commentaries*. After the Spanish invasion, the palace serves to house Hernando de Soto and Pedro del Barco when they first arrive in Cuzco, because "as divine people they had been given the house of the greatest and best loved of the Incas." Here the prophecy of Huayna Cápac is reiterated, which announces not only the coming of the Spaniards, but also the "preaching of the Holy Gospel in Peru" to substantiate the claim that "the Indians therefore worshipped the Spaniards as gods," as they had the Incas (Part 2, Book I, Chapter XXXII, vol. 1, 87). When Cuzco is divided among the conquerors, the palace of Amarucancha becomes the residence of Hernando Pizarro, the brother of Francisco Pizarro, who at one point is called "Cápac Inca Viracocha" by an Inca princess (Part 2, Book I, Chapter XIX, vol. 1, 58). Both the progression of the sacred location (huaca) and the prophecy carry strong religious connotations, and both are "completed" and reinforced each time Inca Garcilaso reminds his readers that the palace belonging to Huayna Cápac had first passed to the "new" Viracocha Incas (i.e., the first conquerors), and had now become the enclave of the Jesuits/amautas. This set of associations and process of transfer are repeated no fewer than seven times throughout both the First and Second Parts of the *Royal Commentaries*, making it a recurring theme, and suggesting it was a continuity that Inca Garcilaso intended his readers to accept.[46]

Before moving on to a final piece of evidence, it should be noted that Inca Garcilaso appears once again to have once altered the indigenous record in order to create these associations. According to Pedro Sarmiento de Gamboa, Amarucancha was built by and belonged to Huascar, Huayna Cápac's son and the imperial claimant who had been defeated by his rival half-brother Atahualpa in the battle of succession for the Inca throne following Huayna Cápac's death (Niles 1999: 76, 79; Sarmiento de Gamboa 1999: 170). That Amarucancha was in fact Huáscar's palace seems to be a piece of information

Inca Garcilaso would have known given that both his mother and uncle were members of the same *panaca* as Huáscar, the *panaca* of Túpac Inca Yupanqui, from whom he claims to have received his version of the Inca past (Part 1, Book IX, Chapter XIV). The omission or alteration of this information, however, allows Inca Garcilaso to maintain the continuity between the actions and prophecy of the eighth ruler, Inca Viracocha, and the ensuing transmission of authority from Huayna Cápac to the first conquerors and on to the Jesuits. For, since Huáscar had lost the ritual war of succession to Atahualpa, his status before an Andean public would have been severely compromised, and his very presence in the royal oral traditions would have been erased beyond the surviving members of his own kinship group (Rostworowski 1999: viii–ix). Inca Garcilaso avoids this difficulty by making Amarucancha the palace of the last *undisputed* Inca, Huayna Cápac, and by transferring the royal symbol belonging to Viracocha Inca, the amaru or serpent, to the former as well.[47] In this way, Inca Garcilaso is able to maintain the link with the Inca past through an authoritative symbolization and to partially restore his own panaca to prominence by illustrating the importance of Huáscar's palace to contemporaries.

Finally, there is a curious piece of linguistic evidence that both encourages the association of Jesuits with amautas and marks the Jesuit college in Cuzco as a place for positive interaction and perhaps social transformation. According to Inca Garcilaso, the sixth emperor, Inca Roca, founded schools in Cuzco, where the amautas and harauicus, "the sages and teachers" (*sabios y maestros*) lived and taught to the children of the royal blood. At this point, Inca Garcilaso claims to have forgotten the name of the district in Cuzco where the schools were located; however, he writes, "we can call it 'the ward of the schools'" (*podrémosle llamar "el barrio de las escuelas"*) (Part 1, Book VII, Chapter X, vol. 2, 441). He then provides the Quechua term for school, *yachahuaci*, which he defines as "house of teaching" (*casa de enseñanza*). The chapter continues with brief descriptions of three royal palaces, Coracora, Cassana, and Amarucancha, during the last of which we are reminded, "it was the palace of Huayna Cápac: it now belongs to the holy Society of Jesus" (*Fueron casas de Huaina Cápac, ahora son de la santa compañia de Jesús*) (Part 1, Book VII, Chapter X, vol. 1, 442). Inca Garcilaso has already suggested the similarity between the amautas, harauicus, and the Jesuits much earlier in the work, and by juxtaposing the location of the Cuzco schools with descriptions of royal palaces he is able to recall it. Yet it should be remembered that Inca Garcilaso has cautioned several times that Quechua words have multiple meanings, and, in addition to being a central element of his critique of Spanish historians, these reminders serve as an invitation for Quechua speakers to amplify or elaborate such terms, as he maintains the amautas had done when allegorizing the condensed information contained in the quipus (Part 1, Book VI, Chapter IX). If one accepts Inca Garcilaso's invitation and searches for alternative meanings to the Quechua word for school, *yachahuaci*, such an alternative is found in Diego González Holguín's dictionary, *Vocabulario de la lengua general del todo Peru* (Vocabulary of the General Language of All Peru), published in Lima in 1608. In particular, one finds the phrase "*yachacuna huaci*," which Holguín translates as "*la casa donde va bien y se hace; o ha bien en ella*": the house where things go well and are made; or in which there is good (González Holguín 1952: 362; my translation). Since the suffix *cuna* attached to *yacha* simply denotes plurality (González Holguín 1952: 54), we come to find that the word Inca Garcilaso used to refer to "school" also contained a decidedly positive connotation for indigenous Peruvians in the early seventeenth century. The implication to be taken is that, in the schools or houses of teaching run by Jesuit *amautas* in Cuzco, there is something good to be found for the descendants of the Incas and, further, perhaps something good to be *made*.[48]

Taken all together, these associations portray the Jesuits as amautas, the teachers and philosophers of the former empire. It may also be the case that Inca Garcilaso constructed this image of Jesuit amautas in order to liken them to "Incas by privilege": an honorific title and official position conferred by Manco Cápac on people outside the royal lineage who had performed notable service to the state; who were most amenable to his teaching; and who had dutifully labored to bring the Indians to the benefits of Inca civilization (Part 1, Book I, Chapter XXIII, vol. 1, 57). For included under the heading of "Incas by privilege" were the "priests and servants" (*sacerdotes y criados*) of the religious temples (Part I, Book III, Chapter XXII, vol. 1, 194), and this nexus of pedagogical and religious functions strongly suggests that Inca Garcilaso intended the Jesuit *amautas* to be accepted as the new functionaries in these traditional indigenous offices.[49]

As we have seen, Inca Garcilaso was also aware that the Incas and the Jesuits had already joined in an alliance through marriage: Don Martín García de Loyola, grandnephew of Saint Ignatius of Loyola, founder of the Jesuits, was not only the governor of Chile but had also captured Túpac Amaru in Vilcabamba, brought him to Viceroy Toledo in Cuzco, and later married Beatríz Clara Coya, the daughter of Sairi Túpac Inca.[50] As mentioned earlier, Inca Garcilaso alludes to this union by noting the noble status conferred by Phillip

III upon the mestiza daughter of García de Loyola and Beatríz Clara Coya, Ana María Lorenza de Loyola, in the Second Part of the *Royal Commentaries* (Book VIII, Chapter XX), in which his work had assisted. In this way, the authority of the Jesuits before an Andean public is based upon their conformance to traditional Inca norms, their possession of sacred Inca symbols and locations, and ayllu or panaca kinship. The Christian faith can then be presented as the culmination and perfection of the natural moral philosophy introduced and institutionalized by the former rulers of Peru, and Jesuit missionary efforts receive legitimation from the practices of Manco Cápac, the educational institutions of Inca Roca, and the prophecies of Viracocha Inca and Huayna Cápac. In the *Royal Commentaries*, the pedagogical practices of the more tolerant, or at least "patient and gradualist" flank of the Society of Jesus, particularly their commitment to indigenous languages and the instruction they provided in the humanities and catechism, do not constitute a radical break from indigenous traditions, but rather the perpetuation and possible renewal of those traditions in the present.

As is characteristic of his thought and writing, Inca Garcilaso's practical recommendations for reform in colonial Peru branch off in two directions with two corresponding series of arguments. In the first argument directed toward Spanish Peruvian missionaries, one finds Inca Garcilaso's critique of imperial historiography, and in particular his critique of the account of Inca religious practices given by José de Acosta. By demonstrating that previous Spanish historians were ignorant of indigenous languages and that this ignorance caused them to misrepresent the essential nature of Inca culture, Inca Garcilaso is able to engage religious practitioners in ongoing debates over the proper methods to be used in converting indigenous Peruvians to the Catholic faith as well as the admission of native Peruvians to the religious orders. Inca Garcilaso argues for a shift toward the "Apostolic" method of rational persuasion in indigenous languages reinforced by the good works and moral virtue of the preacher and for a more liberal policy of inclusion within the religious ranks. These arguments are against the "new" or "mixed" evangelical method proposed by Acosta in *De procuranda*, on the one hand, and the restrictive policies regarding the admission of criollo and mestizo candidates to the Society of Jesus in late-sixteenth-century Peru, on the other. In so doing, Inca Garcilaso attempts to alleviate the stigma of cultural inferiority and the suspicion of contamination with which native Peruvians were viewed, and suggests that a more authentic understanding of the relationship between Inca and Hispano-European cultures is to be had through an intercultural or mestizo perspective. Inca Garcilaso's second argument establishes the authority of Jesuit missionaries and educators for his Andean readers by likening them to amautas, imbuing them with sacred symbols and locations, portraying their pedagogical practices and their commitment to Quechua as based on Inca precedent and prophecy, and cementing all of this with ties of kinship. The Jesuit amautas and "Incas by privilege" become the inheritors of traditional Inca norms and practices and can thus be viewed by indigenous Peruvians as providing a link to their past as well as the possibility of meaningful interaction in the present and future.[51]

Numerous studies within the past decade have convincingly demonstrated how indigenous elites early grasped the central importance of writing under Spanish rule and dedicated themselves to learning how to read and write, many serving as scribes or notaries (Charles 2010a; Burns 2010, 2014; Rappaport and Cummins 2012; Ramos 2014; Ramos and Yannakakis 2014). Their pursuit of writing and induction into literate culture inevitably led them to greater contact with the religious orders, and as Jean-Jacques Decoster puts it: "Part of this population used religion to improve their condition and situate themselves in the new colonial society. This class better positioned to take advantage of the new social conditions was the indigenous political and social elite, principally the Incas, because they already had more mobility within their own society and also because they received privileged treatment from the conquistadors themselves" (Decoster 2002: 281; my translation).[52] Education for the indigenous elite, as Monique Alaperrine-Bouyer explains, represented "a privilege equivalent to the recognition of their nobility. It was the only way to a hypothetical integration in the Peruvian society that was hostile to them but still needed them" (Alaperrine-Bouyer 2002: 162; my translation).[53] With this in mind, it perhaps comes as little surprise that in 1601 a group of "principal Incas" (*Ingas principales*) in Cuzco petitioned the crown for the construction of the college for Incas and curacas that had been promised during Toledo's viceroyalty, but had still not materialized (Alaperrine-Bouyer 2002: 157, 2007: 66; Dueñas 2010: 16).

That college would in fact arrive in Cuzco in 1621, with the founding of San Francisco de Borja, more commonly known as Colegio de San Borja (College of San Borja), five years after Inca Garcilaso' death in 1616 (Alaperrine-Bouyer 2007: 72–75; Charles 2010b: 61; Dueñas 2010: 16).[54] Although he did not live to see the college admit its first students, Inca Garcilaso was keenly aware of the obstacles and difficulties indigenous Andeans faced while trying to educate and better themselves within the Jesuit-run system at the turn of the seventeenth century. Acosta's "mixed" method had been stretched and deformed by extirpators to include wholesale destruction and mass burning of indigenous artifacts, public floggings, fines, Inquisition-like interrogations, and imprisonment for the lack of strict conformity to Christian dogma. Inca Garcilaso also appeared to be well versed in the reluctance of Andeans to submit themselves to corporal punishment and other forms of abuse as the price of an education within the new colonial culture. Guaman Poma, for instance, sketched two scenes depicting the violence that indigenous Andeans suffered at the hands of priests: one of a priest "cruelly punishing" (*castiga cruelmente*) boys between the ages of five and seven for learning improperly (ironically implying that the priest is teaching incorrectly due to his brutality); and another that shows a priest flogging a naked, badly flayed man, to which is appended the word *verdugo*, which means "executioner" (Guaman Poma 1980: vol. 2, 550–52, f. 583[597], 554–56, f. 586[600]; Dean 2002: 170–71).

As if speaking to these very worries, Inca Garcilaso has recourse to two of his highest authorities, Inca Viracocha and Blas Valera, as the latter reports the *only* saying attributed to the former. The chapter is titled "The death of Inca Viracocha; the author saw his body," drawing Inca Garcilaso himself tightly into the web of associations that links Inca Viracocha and Blas Valera within the *Royal Commentaries*.[55] The passage concerns the rearing of children, wherein Inca Viracocha, who had been treated severely by his own father Yáhuar Huácac in Inca Garcilaso's account, advises:

> 'Fathers [los padres] are often the cause of their children being lost or corrupted by the bad habits they allow them to form in childhood. Because some raise them with excessive indulgence and too much softness, and some, enchanted by the beauty and tenderness of children, allow them to have their own way without looking to what will happen to them, when they are men. There are others who raise them with too much harshness and punishment, which also destroys them. Because too much indulgence weakens and diminishes the forces of body and soul while excessive punishment discourages and blunts their wits, in such a way that they lose hope of learning and hate education. And those who fear everything cannot strive to do anything worthy of men. The arrangement that should be kept is to raise them a middle way, so that they emerge strong and brave in times of war and wise and prudent

> in times of peace.' With this saying Father [padre] Blas Valera completes the life of this Inca Viracocha. (Part 1, Book V, Chapter XXIX, vol. 1, 323)[56]

The ambiguity between the use of the word *padres*, meaning "parents" or "fathers," and *padre* to refer to Blas Valera, meaning both "father" and "priest," appears intentional, as if to emphasize Inca Garcilaso's point. He may or may not have fully sanctioned Acosta's "mixed" or "middle" method of instructing indigenous Andeans, but he appears cognizant of what Indian and mestizo descendants of Incas and caciques were likely to confront in the course of their education, and he uses Inca Viracocha, Blas Valera, and himself to encourage them to be brave, to endure, and to educate themselves anyway.

It stands to reason, as a mestizo, a humanist, a historian, a Jesuit, and a Catholic, that Inca Garcilaso's main focus would be on education itself, in religion, humanities, and indigenous culture. Yet his intercultural pedagogy is forever double-edged: he lectures Europeans on the destructive hypocrisy involved in manipulating the discourse of Inca history and culture to serve their own economic and political ends; and he implores his Peruvian compatriots to accept the responsibilities and personal risks of reclaiming their own history from those who had neither understood nor esteemed it. The dual structure of the *Royal Commentaries*, Inca Garcilaso's arguments, and his suggestions for pedagogical reform in Peru orient us toward this conclusion, a conclusion drawn in the following lines from the "Prologue" to the Second Part, which in light of the above, may perhaps strike an even more personal note regarding its author. Speaking to and about the indios, mestizos, and criollos of Peru, Inca Garcilaso writes:

> Thus for their keen and subtle wits, fit for every sort of letters will serve the vote of Doctor Juan de Cuéllar, Canon of the Holy Cathedral Church of Imperial Cuzco, being the teacher of those of my age and sort, with fresh tears he used to tell us, "O, sons! How I wish to see a dozen of you at the university of Salamanca!": appearing to him: would the new plants of Peru flourish in that garden, and orchard of learning. And it is certain a land so fertile with rich minerals, and precious metals, was the reason veins of generous blood swelled there, and mines of understanding for all arts and faculties awakened. For which the natural Indians do not lack the ability; and a surplus of capacity the Mestizos, children of Indian mothers, and Spanish fathers, or Spanish mothers and Indian fathers. And the native Creoles, those born and raised there. To all of whom, like brothers, and friends my kin, and

> Lords, I do plead and beseech, take heart and press forward in the exercise of virtue, study, and the art of war, turning to yourselves and to your good name, to that which will make you famous on earth and eternal in heaven. And on the way it would be well to understand the Old World and politics, that the New World (regarding its barbaric appearance) neither is barbaric nor ever has been but for the lack of culture: Of the sort that in antiquity the Greeks and Romans, for being the cream, and flower of knowledge, and power, in comparing other regions to themselves, called barbarous: Including in this list the Spanish, not because of any defect of nature, but rather due to a lack of the artificial. . . .[57]

Not only does Inca Garcilaso encourage his diverse Peruvian readers to press forward in their study of "every sort of letters," but he also reminds them that the haughtiest of Spaniards, so certain of their superiority, had once been barbarians in the eyes of their own ancient rulers. Moreover, and most importantly, Inca Garcilaso has underscored for all his readers the relationship between the relative artifices of culture and politics, or in his own words "knowledge and power" (*saber y poder*). Given what he portrays as the dearth of opportunities for substantive change in the chaos of the Peruvian present, Inca Garcilaso suggests that the quest for social justice can be kept alive by politicizing and therefore transforming the terrain of culture itself. In order to achieve this, native Peruvians would need to continue to develop the intercultural intellectual skills to negotiate the difficulties of confronting Spanish agents on their own terms while simultaneously restoring what remained of their indigenous cultural inheritance. For this task the *Royal Commentaries* provides abundant evidence, pointed arguments, and an outstanding example. But the *Royal Commentaries* also does a bit more than this. It suggests that speaking within and between different languages and cultures may not only be possible, but that it may also be done critically, creatively, and elegantly, that a history of political loss, dissent, and resistance can be also be a work of art. And for this contribution to the political thought of the early Americas, Inca Garcilaso de la Vega's legacy endures in the present.

APPENDIX

Prologue to the Indians, Mestizos, and Creoles of the Kingdoms and Provinces of the Great and Most Rich Empire of Peru, El Ynca Garcilasso de la Vega, Your Brother Compatriot and Fellow Countryman, Health and Happiness.

TRANSLATED BY JAMES W. FUERST

This translation of Inca Garcilaso's "Prologue" was rendered from a photocopy of the first edition of the Second Part of the *Comentarios reales*, titled *Historia general del Perú*, published by the press of Doña Lucía de Leries in Córdoba in 1617. In the main, I have tried to do two things. First, I have attempted to make as literal a translation as possible, and, second, I have endeavored (as far as this could be done) to retain the sentence structures, paragraphs, and punctuation of the original. Although Inca Garcilaso's winding periods, multiple clauses, and erratic punctuation may make the prose seem a bit choppy or difficult to follow in places, my intent was to reproduce as much of the form and content of the piece in English as I could, without modernizing it unduly.

For three reasons among others, my gentlemen and brothers, have I written the First, and do write the Second Part of the Royal Commentaries of the Kingdoms of Peru. The first is to make known to the universe our *patria*, people, and nation, no less rich at the present with the treasures of the wisdom, and science of God, of His faith and evangelical law, than she has always been due to the pearls, and precious stones of her rivers, and seas, her mountains of gold, and silver, fine furnishings, and her roots which contain the roots of her riches: nor less noteworthy for being conquered by the mighty, noble, and valiant Spaniards, and subject to our Catholic Kings: Monarchs of the most and best of the Globe, than for having been possessed, and governed by her ancient princes, the Incas, Peruvians: Caesars in felicity and fortitude. And because by virtue, arms, and letters lands are customarily esteemed, inasmuch as they imitate Heaven: For these three gifts may ours be praised, giving to God the thanks, and glory, since her inhabitants are by their nature docile, with vigorous souls, sharp wits, and volitions moved to piety, and religion, since the Christian religion possesses their hearts, changed by the hand of the most high: trustworthy witnesses of which are the annual letters of the fathers of the Company of Jesus, who have performed the duty of Apostles among the Indians, they experience their singular devotion, reform of customs, frequency of sacraments, alms, and good works: a summary argument for the estimate and appraisal of their salvation. In faith of which these Apostolic noblemen testify, that their faithful Indian parishioners, with the first fruits of the spirit, provided those from Europe with nearly the advantage, that those of the primitive church provided the Christians of our age when the Catholic faith exiled from England and the Netherlands[1] its ancient colony leaves one pole for the other, to reside with the antipodes. Of whose valor and boldness I have made large mention in the first volume of these Royal Commentaries, giving account of the glorious undertakings of the Incas who could have competed with the Dariuses of Persia, the Ptolomeys of Egypt, the Alexanders of Greece, and the Scipioes of Rome. And of the Peruvian arms, more deserving of praise than the Greeks, and Trojans, I will give a brief description in this book, citing the deeds, and exploits of some of their Hectors and Achilleses: And that which they have given will suffice as a testimony of their powers and strength, by which is understood the invincible Castilians: Conquerors of both worlds. Thus for their keen and subtle wits, fit for every sort of letters will serve the vote of Doctor Juan de Cuéllar, Canon of the Holy Cathedral Church of Imperial Cuzco, being the teacher of those of my age and sort, with fresh tears he used to tell us, "O, sons! How I wish to see a dozen of you at the university of Salamanca!": appearing to him: would the new plants of Peru flourish in that garden, and orchard of learning. And it is certain a land so fertile with rich minerals, and precious metals, was the reason veins of generous blood swelled there, and mines of understanding for all arts and faculties awakened. For which the natural Indians do not lack the ability; and a surplus of capacity the Mestizos, children of Indian mothers and Spanish fathers or Spanish mothers and Indian fathers. And the native Creoles, those born and raised there. To all of whom, like my brothers, and friends my kin, and Lords, I do plead and beseech, take heart and press forward in the exercise of virtue, study, and the art of war, turning to yourselves and to your good name, to that which will make you famous on earth, and eternal in heaven. And on the way it would be well to understand the Old World and politics, that the New World (regarding its barbaric appearance) neither is barbaric nor ever has been but for the lack of culture: Of the sort that in antiquity the Greeks and Romans, for being the cream, and flower of knowledge, and power, in comparing other regions to themselves, called barbarous: Including in this list the Spanish, not because of any defect of nature, but rather due to a lack of the artificial, whereas since then with the art they have given heroic natural displays of talent in letters, of bravery in arms, and on both accounts they shone rays of light in those days in the Roman Empire, with the Wise Senecas of Cordoba, flower of learning and chivalry, and with the most August Trajans and Theodosiuses of Italy. O Seville! Key to the treasures of the Occident: already lifting your head among your rival nations: and above them, that in this way you give the prize and palm to ours who were previously unlearned, today through you I am educated, and from the forest of gentilism and idolatry emerges a Christian Paradise from which redounds no small glory to Spain, the Almighty having hidden it with a dividing wall: in order to illuminate with the light of faith the regions, that slept in the shadow of death: because truly the Spanish people, like the very inheritance of the Son of God, inherited from the Eternal Father, who says in a psalm of David: *Postula a me; et dabo tibi gentes hereditatem tuam, et possessionem tuam terminos terrae.*[2] He divides the Celestial estate of the faith, and gospel with the Indians with a free hand, like with younger brothers; to whom the paternal blessing of God is extended; and although they come to the vineyard of his church at the eleventh hour, by fortune the same wage and equal pay will fall to their lot as to those who *portarunt pondus diei, et aestus.*[3]

The second consideration and motive for writing this history was to celebrate (if not honorably, at least appropriately) the greatness of the heroic Spaniards who won with their valor and military science, for God, for their King, and for themselves this rich Empire, whose names, worthy of Cedars, live in the book of life, and will live forever in the memory of mortals. For three ends are the heroic deeds of men in peace, and letters, or in arms, and remarkable wars eternalized in writing. To reward their merits with perpetual fame; to honor their *patria*, the illustrious honor of which resides in her outstanding citizens and residents; for the example, and imitation of posterity, who revive the passage of events in the pose of antiquity, following their battles; to secure their victories. To this end, by the laws of Solon and Lycurgus, Legislators of fame, the republics of Athens and Lacaedemonia made their Heroes quite famous. I believe and hope all three ends will be secured with this history, because in it there will be prize winners of honor and praise, the prize worthy of virtue alone, for its own resplendence, the brilliant conquerors of the New World, who are the delight, and Crown of Spain, mother of nobility, and Lady of the power, and assets of the world: which together will be enlarged and exalted, as the mother and mistress of such, so many and so great sons, suckled at her breasts with the milk of faith and fortitude, better than Romulus, and Remus. And finally the hidalgo bosoms of the descendants, and successors, never familiars of cowardice they will whet their points with new dash and daring, to follow in the footsteps of their elders: undertaking Mergrandiose feats in the militia of Pallas, and Mars, and in the school of Mercury, and Apollo, not degenerating from their most noble family and ancestry, without advancing the good of their lineage, which seems to take its origin from Heaven; where like the proper and true *patria*, they must take leave of this exile, and valley of tears, and turning their eyes to the crown of glory for which they hope, aspiring to remove themselves to it, entering with pikes and lances, overcoming difficulties and dangers: so that just as with their virtue they have leveled the passage, and opened the door to the predication, and true evangelical in the kingdoms of Peru, Chile, Paraguay, and New Spain, and the Philippines, so shall they in Florida, and the Magellanic lands below the Antarctic Pole, and having victory over the unfaithful enemies of Christ, surrounding the Emperors, and Roman consuls, may the Spaniards enter triumphantly with the trophies of the faith in the Imperial Capitolio.[4]

The third cause for having given my hand to this work, has been to sufficiently occupy the time with an honorable occupation, and not waste it in idleness, mother of vices, step-mother of virtue, root, fount, and origin of a thousand evils, which can be avoided with the honest labor of study; employment worthy of the fine-witted, the noble-souled, for these to entertain themselves nobly according to their quality, and spend their days in laudable exercises; and in that business to nourish their delicate taste in the pastures of wit and to advance the abundance in the refinements of wisdom, the rents of which amount to and yield more to the soul, than the body or even the annuities of pearls from the Orient or the silver from our Potosí. For this reason I wrote the chronicle of *La Florida*, of the true Florida not with my dry style, but with the flowers of Spain, which transplanted in that uncultivated wasteland, could bear the blessed fruit, leveling with force of arms the evil blaze of paganism and planting with the dew from Heaven the tree of the Cross and the standard of our Faith, the Flowered staff of Aaron and Jesse.[5] Also in order to profit by the years of my age, and serve the studious I translated from the Italian into Castilian romance the philosophical dialogues between Philo and Sophia, a book entitled León Hebreo, which has been translated in all languages, even in the Peruvian language (so that where it is seen it reaches the curiosity, and studiousness of our people) and in Latin it runs through the Latin world with the acceptance, and judgment of the Wise, and lettered, who appreciate, and esteem it, for its high style, and the delicacy of its material. For the latter of which with just accord, the Holy and General Inquisition of these Kingdoms, in the last Expurgation of Prohibited Books, not forbidding it in other languages, ordered it collected in our vernacular, because it was not for the vulgar; and since this much is clear from its prohibition, it is well that the cause is known although afterward I have heard it said around here that there has been a dispute over it, and because it is dedicated to the King, our Lord Don Philip the Second, whom God holds in his glory, there is reason to bring to light the dedication, which is as follows:

HOLY CATHOLIC,
Royal Majesty,
Defender of the Faith.

It cannot be denied that my boldness is most great in imagining to dedicate to Your Catholic Royal Majesty this translation from Tuscan into Spanish of the three Dialogues of Love by the most learned Master León Hebreo, so little and lacking are my merits. But many just causes concur in favoring this my daring, which force me to place myself before the exalted throne of Your Catholic Majesty and to invoke them on my behalf.

The first and most principal, is the excellence of he who composed them, his discretion, talent, and wisdom; it is meet and right that his work be consecrated to Your Holy Majesty.

The second is, to my understanding, and if I am not deceiving myself, that these are the first to be offered to Your Royal Majesty of that which in this kind of tribute you are owed by your vassals, the natives of the New World, especially by those from Peru, and more particularly by those from the great city of Cuzco, head of those Kingdoms and provinces where I was born. And as the first-born, or birth right, it is just, although unworthy on my part, that they are offered to Your Catholic Majesty, as to our King and Lord to whom we are obliged to offer all that we are.

The third, that since in my youth I spent the military part of my life in the service of Your Holy Majesty, and in the rebellion in the Kingdom of Granada, in the presence of the most serene Don Juan of Austria, who is in glory, your most dignified brother, I served you in the rank of captain, although undeserving of your stipend: it is just and necessary in my mature age that what has been worked on, and acquired in the exercise of reading and translation, is not divided from the first intent: so that the sacrifice of the entire discourse of my life I offer to Your Royal Majesty may be complete, as much the time as that which has been done therein with the sword and with the pen.

The fourth and final cause is that it has fallen to my lot, to be of the family and blood of the Incas, who Reigned in those Kingdoms before the most felicitous empire of Your Holy Majesty. That my mother the Palla Doña Isabel was the daughter of Inca Huallpa Túpac, one of the sons of Túpac Inca Yupanqui and Palla Mama Ocllo his legitimate wife, parents of Huayna Cápac Inca, the last King of Peru. I say this, sovereign Monarch and our lord, not for my own vainglory, but rather for your greater majesty, because one may see how much more we now possess being your vassals, than we did when we were being ruled by others because that liberty and dominion was without the light of the evangelical doctrine, and this servitude and vassalage is with it. Through the invincible arms of the Catholic Kings of glorious memory your progenitors, and from the Emperor, Our Lord and yours, was communicated to us, through His mercy, the most high and true God, with the faith of the Holy Mother Roman Church at the end of so many thousands of years, to those nations, so numerous and so great, who remained in the sorrowful shadows of their gentilism. The benefit we have now is far better, as much as the spiritual is greater than the temporal. And to such ones, Holy Majesty, it is permissible for us (as the proper servants we are, and the more favored as we should be) to bring ourselves with greater spirit and confidence to your clemency and piety to offer you, and present to you our pittances and pains, works of our own hands and talent. Additionally for the part of Spain I am the son of Garcilaso de la Vega your servant, who was a conqueror, and settler of the kingdoms and provinces of Peru. He journeyed to them with Adelentado Don Pedro de Alvarado, in the year 1531. He found himself in the first general conquest of its natives, and in the second of their rebellion, without other particulars that he accomplished in new discoveries, going to them as Captain and leader of Your Catholic Majesty. He lived in your service in those parts, until the year 1559, when he left this life, having served your Royal crown in everything concerning Peru that was offered to him; including; in peace administering justice, in war, against the tyrants, who arose at different times, fulfilling the offices of captain and soldier. I am, at the same time, the nephew of Don Alonso de Vargas, brother of my father, who served Your Holy Majesty thirty-eight years in war, never failing to attend your commission, not even a single day in all that time. He accompanied your Royal person from Genoa to Flanders, together with Captain Aguilera, who were the two captains of the guard for that voyage who were elected by Our Lord the Emperor: He served in Italy, France, Flanders, Germany, in Corón, in Africa, in everything that your service offered him, in the expeditions which in those times were made against the Heretics, Moors, Turks, and other nations, from the year 1517, until 1555, when his Imperial Majesty gave him license to return to his homeland to rest from the past labors. Another brother of those already named, called Juan de Vargas, died in Peru from four harquebus wounds which were delivered to him in the battle of Huarina in which he entered as a captain of Your Catholic Majesty's infantry. These ever so sufficient causes give me spirit King of Kings (since today all of the inhabitants of the land give you obedience, and recognize you as such) to whom in the name of the great city of Cuzco, and all of Peru, I dare to present myself before Your August Majesty, with the poverty of this first, humble, and small service, although for me very great, respecting how much time and work it cost me: because neither the Italian language in which it is written, nor the Spanish in which I have put it, is my native language, nor in the schools in which I was placed in my boyhood did I acquire more, than an Indian born between the fire and furor of the cruelest civil wars of his *patria*, between arms and horses, and raised in the exercise of them; because in her there was nothing else then: until I traveled from Peru to Spain to better myself in everything, serving much closer to your Royal person. Here it will be seen, defender of the Faith, how love is. How universal her Empire! How high her genealogy! Receive her Sovereign Majesty as she wishes and as you are, imitating the omnipotent God whom you so much attain in imitating, who holds in higher regard two copper coins from a poor little old woman, for the spirit with which they are offered, than the large presents of the rich: in whose semblance in everything, I offer this ever so small one to Your Holy Majesty. And the mercy that your clemency and piety deign to do me in receiving it with the kindness and affability for which I hope, it is certain that the most extensive Empire of Peru, and that great and most beautiful city its head, they will receive it, and hold it as the highest and universal favor:

because I am their son, and of those whom she raised with more love, for the causes stated above. And although this pittance of a service is of no moment to Your Royal Majesty, to me it is of great importance: because it is a sign and example of the most affectionate feeling I have always had, and do have for your Royal person and service: that if I managed to achieve what I desire, you will be satisfied with my service. But with my little powers, if I am not lacking divine favor and that of Your Majesty, I hope, for a better indication of this emotion, I will offer you shortly another similar, which will be the expedition that Adelantado Hernando de Soto made to Florida: that as late as today is buried in the shadows of oblivion. And with the same favor I intend to forge ahead and summarily treat the conquest of my land, enlarging upon her customs, rites, and ceremonies, and in her antiquities: of which, as her own son I will be better able to speak, than another who is not, for the glory and honor of our Lord God, that from his heart of mercy, and from the merits of the blood and passion of his only begotten Son, moved with pity in seeing us in such poverty and blindness, tried to communicate to us the grace of his Holy Spirit, reducing us to the light and doctrine of his Roman Catholic Church, under the Empire and protection of Your Catholic Majesty. That afterward, we have this for the first mercy from His divine hand, which guards and exalts the Royal person and August offspring of Your Holy Majesty with long life, and increase of Kingdoms and Empires, as we your servants desire. Amen. From Montilla, 19 January 1586 years.

Holy Catholic, Royal Majesty, defender of the Faith.

I kiss the Royal hands of Your Catholic Majesty, your servant,

Garcilasso Ynca

de la Vega.

In addition to this dedication I wrote another for a new manuscript: which was given to his Majesty by a gentleman and great lord of mine, with a book from those of our translation: which is the one that follows, in which, due to the pragmatic regarding courtesies at this time, there was no other title used:

Lord.

Having said in the dedication to Your Catholic Majesty I made in this book, everything it was suitable for me to say, I will not repeat it in this: only will it serve to beg Your Majesty as my King and lord to be so good as to order the reading, and hearing of it, that only this favor do I desire, and seek for gratification, as much for the labor of my study, as for the spirit for your Royal service I have always had. The work, as Your Majesty can see is prolix, although the greatness of its author deserves whatever mercy Your Majesty may do him. For my part there is nothing worthy of taking into account, if it were not for the boldness of an Indian in such an enterprise, and the desire I had of giving with it an example to those of Peru, where I was born, of how they should serve Your Catholic Majesty in every kind of duty. With this same desire and pretension I am occupied in tidying up the account being prepared for Your Catholic Majesty about the discovery, your Governor; and Captain General Hernando de Soto made in Florida, where he traveled more than four years. The work will be of importance for the augment of the most felicitous crown of Spain (which may God exalt, and place in the highest Monarchy with the long life of Your Majesty) because with the news of such, and so fine provinces like the ones this Captain discovered, which are even now unknown, and having seen their fertility and abundance your servants, and vassals will be compelled to conquer, and settle them, increasing their honor and profit in your service. At the conclusion of this account, I intend to give another of the customs, rites, and ceremonies, that in the gentilism of the Incas former lords of Peru, were kept in their Kingdoms: so that Your Majesty may see them from their origin and principle, written with somewhat more certainty and propriety, than that which until now has been written. To Your Catholic Majesty I beg that with the clemency so typical of your Royal person you condescend to receive the spirit of this small service, which in the name of all Peru I have offered and do offer. And the favor for which I aim and hope, is that all of those from this Empire, as much Indians, as Spaniards, in general, and in particular may enjoy it together with me, that each and every one of them may take it as their own: because from both nations I have ties that oblige them to participate in my successes and failures: which are my father having been a conqueror, and settler of that land, and my mother her native, and myself having been born, and raised between them. And because my hope is in conformity with my faith, I cease, begging Our Lord God may keep Your Catholic Majesty as we your servants desire, Amen. From Las Posadas, jurisdiction of Cordoba, 7 November 1589.

The Catholic Majesty, having read the one, and the other, called for his jewel keeper and said to him: Protect this book for me, and when we are in the Escorial, remind me that you have it, put it in writing: do not forget.

When the jewel keeper arrived at Escorial, he reminded the King of how he had the book there: and His Majesty called for the prior of the royal convent of St. Jerome and said to him, "Look at this book Father, to see what you think of it: see that it is the new fruit from Peru."

It is also much to be esteemed, the appraisal that our León Hebreo had from the most illustrious lord Don Maximillian of Austria, who died Archbishop of St. James of Galicia, a noble man no less distinguished in valor, and prudence, than in blood.

His Lordship sent me a letter of approbation for my translation with which I was obliged to dedicate its Prologue to him. And for his assessment will suffice that which was given by the gentleman Don Francisco Murillo Schoolmaster, and dignitary of the Holy Church Cathedral of Cordoba, because for more than twenty-five years now, after I had newly arrived to live in this city, have I had acquaintance, and friendship with Licentiate Agustín de Aranda, one of the priests of the church office, to whom I gave one of these books, and he gave it to the Schoolmaster: whose confessor he was. The Schoolmaster, who had been the general inspector of His Majesty's armies, and armadas, having seen the book said to his confessor, that he wanted to meet me, and the confessor told this to me, once, twice, and three times: I, a foreigner, did not dare to place myself before so great a personage. Finally due to the pestering of Licentiate Aranda, I went to kiss the hands of the gentleman Schoolmaster, and I brought him one of these books finely embroidered, and gilded: he showed me great favor in everything although he was in bed crippled with gout. And the first words, with which he greeted me, were these: "An Antarctic, born in the New World, down there below our hemisphere, and who drank the general language of the Indians of Peru with his mother's milk, what does he have to do with being an interpreter between Italians, and Spaniards? and since he has already presumed to be one, why did he not take whichever book, and not the one Italians esteemed most, and Spaniards knew least?" I replied that it had been the brashness of a soldier, that their best deeds were set upon in this way, and if they emerge with victory they are considered brave men, and if they die they are considered crazy. He laughed quite a bit at the response, and in other visits I repeated it many times. Nor is it of lesser justification for the quality of our León Hebreo in romance, what was given in praise of it by His Father the most Reverend Father Friar Juan Ramírez of the Seraphic Order of St. Francis, who assessed it by order of the Holy Office of Cordoba. I do not wish, gentlemen, to have exhausted your graces, whose rest I want more than my own, because my only desires are to serve you, which is the aim of this Chronicle, and its Dedication, in which she and her author dedicate themselves, who in everything, and for everything desire to please, and honor, recognize, and make known. And in this way I do plead and request that you do me the great favor of accepting this little present, with the intention, and spirit, with which it is offered which has always been to illustrate our *patria* and parents, natural right, and by a thousand titles owed by law to son, to mother, and Palla and Peruvian princess (daughter of the last Lord and gentile Prince of those opulent provinces) and Spanish Father, noble in blood, character, and arms Garcilasso de la Vega my lord, may he be in glory. And may it please the King of glory that your graces attain eternal Heaven, and here that which they deserve, and I intend to give them in this their history since so much is owed to them by title of their nobility founded in the virtue of their ancestors, and ennobled by their own in arms, with which surpassing the labors, of Hercules, they have labored valiantly, and courageously in so many struggles, turning their cheeks to the blows of fortune; in liberal arts, and mechanics, in so many of which they have advanced, principally in Astrology and seafaring, with which they peruse the Heavens, and navigate this Ocean to Islands, and lands never known before; also in Agriculture, with which they cultivate the fertile soil of Peru, transforming it into the most fertile, for everything human life can crave. I say nothing of the domestic arts of regaled food, although regulated, and suits of clothing, tailored to size of which the attire of a native Peruvian woman would be an admirable and enjoyable example that was given to be seen, and admired in this city of Cordoba, in a tourney celebrated during the festival of beatification of the blessed St. Ignatius Patriarch of the Sacred Company of Jesus, whose outline, and natural form I gave to Father Francisco Castro, and if passion has not blinded me it was the most lustrous and celebrated stall, which won the eyes of all for its novelty, and curiosity: blessed be God: may He by His kindness and clemency reward, and remunerate the merits of your graces with His glory, to you who possess action, and right by your Christianity, and the Celestial virtues of Faith, love, justice, mercy, and religion with which you have been endowed, as pledges of the gifts of glory, where you may enjoy it for an eternity after many, and long years of prosperity health, and life.

El Ynca Garcilasso
de la Vega.

NOTES

INTRODUCTION

1. The vast majority of scholarship on Inca Garcilaso is in Spanish, but there are invaluable books and essay collections first published or now rendered in English, such as Margarita Zamora's *Language, Authority and Indigenous History in the Comentarios Reales* (1988); *Garcilaso Inca de la Vega: American Humanist. A Tribute to José Durand*, edited by José Anadón (1998); *Beyond Books and Borders: Garcilaso de la Vega and La Florida del Inca*, edited by Raquel Chang-Rodríguez (2006); *Incan Insights: Inca Garcilaso's Hints to Andean Readers* (2008), a translation of José Antonio Mazzotti's earlier text *Coros mestizos del Inca Garcilaso* (1996a); and the recent collection of cutting-edge approaches found in *Inca Garcilaso and Contemporary World-Making*, edited by Sara Castro-Klarén and Christian Fernández (2016). If one were to add Julia Fitzmaurice-Kelly's *El Inca Garcilaso de la Vega* (1921), Frances G. Crowley's *Garcilaso de la Vega: El Inca and his Sources in the Comentarios Reales* (1971), and Jonathan D. Steigman's *La Florida del Inca and the Struggle for Social Equality in Colonial Spanish America* (2005) to the others listed above, one would have the complete list of full-length studies and essay collections dedicated to Inca Garcilaso in English. Other indispensable sources include José Durand's essay, "Garcilaso between the World of the Incas and That of Renaissance Con-

cepts," Pierre Duviols's "The Inca Garcilaso de la Vega, Humanist Interpreter of the Inca Religion," both from 1964; David Brading's essay "The Incas and the Renaissance. The *Royal Commentaries* of Inca Garcilaso de la Vega" (1986) and the chapter on Inca Garcilaso in his *First America* (1991: 255–272); and Sabine MacCormack's chapter on Inca Garcilaso in *Religion in the Andes* (1991: 332–382), the several exegetical sections throughout her last work, *On the Wings of Time* (2007), and her essay in Anadón's anthology (1998), noted above, in addition to the many other essays, articles, and chapters cited throughout this work and listed in the bibliography.

2. *Empire and Modern Political Thought* (2012), the anthology edited by Sankar Muthu in which Pitts's above-cited essay appears, marks a clear signpost in the study of political theory regarding the host of new research across a wide spectrum of issues related to imperialism and colonialism in the modern era (ca. 1492–1900) that has been published since the turn of the twenty-first century. Himself an early and influential advocate for this new agenda—see, for instance, *Enlightenment against Empire* (2003)—Muthu nevertheless notes in his introduction that although "the emphasis in this book is on European thinkers of the modern period, one hope that underlies this volume is that the many connections and tensions among European and non-European thinkers' perspectives about conquest, occupation, and imperial rule can be researched and investigated in ways that will be enhanced by the following chapters" (3). This "hope," however, is perhaps emblematic of ongoing debates regarding which thinkers and writers are involved in political conversations surrounding the making of the modern world. Consequently, a reasonable response to the above might suggest that many of the most central "connections and tensions among European and non-European thinkers" have already been researched and published in different fields but will remain undertheorized and underdeveloped in political thought as long as they continue to be left aside for another conversation, presumably to be held some other time.

CHAPTER 1: BECOMING AN INCA

1. For the date of Shakespeare's death, see Shakespeare (1997: 3390); for Cervantes's see Ledesma (1973: 350); and for Inca Garcilaso's see Varner (1968: 371–72n26), although Harold V. Livermore qualifies that all three "possibly" died on the same day, and Christian Fernández reminds us that the date of Inca Garcilaso's death is alternately listed as April 22, 23, and 24 in various documents and plaques, making the actual date uncertain (Livermore 1966: xxv; Fernández 2016: 31n11).

2. Mestizo (feminine: mestiza) was the Spanish word for people who were half-Spanish and half-Indian. Creole (criollo/criolla in Spanish), originally an African word, referred to people born in the New World whose parents were of the same, nonindigenous racial/ethnic background. Indian (*indio/india*) referred to all indigenous peoples.

   Diego Valadés (1533–1582?), born in Tlaxcala, New Spain, merits the distinction of being the first American to break into European letters with his *Rhetorica cristiana*, published in Perugia, Italy in 1579. While Rappaport and Cummins contend that he was "probably a mestizo," they also observe that Valadés never identified himself as mestizo or Tlaxcalan, which Don Paul Abbotts suggests is likely a consequence of having to suppress his mixed parentage and probable illegitimacy in order to join the Franciscan order (Rappaport and Cummins 2012: 6 and 42; Abbott 1996: 41–59).
3. Because a general portrait of Inca Garcilaso's life appears in numerous works dedicated to him, I have stayed close to the principal biographical sources. While Aurelio Miró Quesada's (1971) and John Grier Varner's (1968) biographies remain the most complete, essential information and analyses are also to be found in Julia Fitzmaurice-Kelly (1921); José de la Torre y del Cerro (1935); Miró Quesada (1948); Eugenio Asensio (1953); Raúl Porras Barrenechea (1955); Donald G. Castanien (1969); and José Durand (1976).
4. In keeping with the theme of this chapter, which attempts to highlight the political events that contributed to Gómez Suárez de Figueroa's becoming El Inca Garcilaso de la Vega, I have opted to maintain the names by which he was known in different moments of his life. This may be a bit confusing for those who are less familiar with his life and work, but happily there are only three names to keep an eye on: Gómez Suárez, Garcilaso, and Inca Garcilaso. My intention is to underscore the extent to which "Inca Garcilaso" came into being, as it were, through a conscious choice, which implicitly links him not only to the Renaissance tradition of self-fashioning and to the nascent tradition of self-naming and self-creation endemic to the Americas, but also indigenous traditions of taking new names during rites of passage at different stages of life. For a similar understanding of Inca Garcilaso's dual processes of self-naming, see Fernández (2004: 59–94), in which he makes a compelling case that Inca Garcilaso's chosen Andean name was Amaru. For an account of Inca Garcilaso's life with a comparable structure, see Chang-Rodríguez (2006b).
5. Quechua term used by the Incas to refer to their empire meaning "the four corners of the world united." "World" and "earth" are generally interchangeable in the translation of Quechua terms. For instance, the word *pacha* can be rendered as

"earth," "world," and even "world universe," so both world and earth are often used for Tahuantinsuyu.

6. Unless otherwise noted, the dates regarding Peruvian history in this chapter come from Hemming's timeline (1970: 501–05). A brief and lively account of Inca Garcilaso's life against the backdrop of historical events can be found in Spalding (2006). Regarding Inca Garcilaso's biography, publication histories, and critical reception of his work, the chronologies of Raquel Chang-Rodríguez (2006: 33–40), Mercedes López-Baralt (2011: 305–16), and Hernán Amat Olazával (2012: 121–51) are also very helpful.
7. The other was named María Pilcocissa, with whom Captain Garcilaso had a mestiza daughter, Francisca de la Vega (Varner 1968: 107).
8. Sebastián Garcilaso de la Vega and Luisa Martel had Blanca de Sotomayor and Francisca de Mendoza. Chimpu Ocllo and Juan del Pedroche had Ana Ruiz and Luisa de Herrera (Varner 1968: 201 and 189). Fermín del Pino-Díaz suggests that Captain Garcilaso may have been forced to marry a Spaniard for being considered "dangerous—due to personal disloyalty" to the crown thanks to his role in Gonzalo Pizarro's rebellion, and that this circumstance may have accounted for Gómez Suárez's rejection by the Council of Indies in 1563 (del Pino-Díaz 2011: 12–13).
9. All quotations of the First Part of the *Royal Commentaries* are from Carlos Araníbar's two-volume edition of the *Comentarios Reales de los Incas* (Garcilaso de la Vega 1991).
10. All quotations of the Second Part of the *Royal Commentaries* are from Ángel Rosenblat's three-volume edition of the *Historia general del Perú. Segunda parte de los Comentarios Reales* (Garcilaso de la Vega 1944).
11. Fernández proposes "it is fair to say that he [Gómez Suárez] probably was bilingual since very early in his childhood," as he was raised in the households of both his mother and father (2016a: 21).
12. The petition of the *encomenderos*, which was brought to Charles V in 1555, offered the King 7,600,000 pesos should the request be granted. The petition of the *curacas* promised to exceed the highest offer of the encomenderos by 100,000 ducats (Hemming 1970: 386–89).
13. For the actions of Captain Garcilaso as Corregidor see Miró Quesada (1948: 60–61).
14. Del Pino-Díaz estimates that this sum, 4,000 pesos, was equivalent to more than *ten times* the worth of Alonso de Vargas's home, the uncle with whom Gómez Suárez would eventually live in Montilla, a sizable inheritance indeed (del Pino-Díaz 2011: 14).

15. For the treatment of mestizos in the religious orders in Peru, see Hyland (1998).
16. That Inca Garcilaso falsely identifies the *mallquis* has been pointed out by María Rostworowski (1999: 32–34). However, Paul Firbas observes that Inca Garcilaso does not himself identify the mallquis incorrectly but rather reports what Indians said (*decían los indios*) of them without either confirming or denying those reports (Part 1, Book V, Chapter 29, vol. 1, 320). Nevertheless, Firbas also contends that Inca Garcilaso was aware of the misidentification through his personal association with Ondegardo and his reading of Acosta's *Historia natural y moral de las Indias* (Natural and Moral History of the Indies, 1590) (Firbas 2009: 43–44). In this instance, as is so often the case in Inca Garcilaso's work, the precision of his language is telling. For the mallquis of Inca Viracocha and Túpac Inca Yupanqui, he has "decían los indios" and "decían" (Indians said, they said), respectively, while in naming the third male mallqui, he has "El tercero *era* Huaina Cápac" (the third *was* Huayna Capac; my emphasis). The last identification is presented as his own and is definitive, which stands to reason given that the embalmed corpse of Huayna Cápac was perhaps the most celebrated mallqui in Ondegardo's possession (Firbas 2009: 44).
17. For *limpieza de sangre*, see Elliott (1963: 107, 220–24, 308–10); Kamen (1997: 230–54); and Zamora (2016).
18. Upon his retirement from military service, Alonso de Vargas was granted an annuity of two hundred pesos on properties in Badajoz and tax exemptions (Varner 1968: 157).
19. Gómez Suárez de Figueroa, the fifth Count of Feria (later, first Duke of Feria) and fourth Marquis of Priego, was a close confidant of Philip II's (Kamen 1997: 72, 132, and 181).
20. For the *encomienda* system and the New Laws, see Zavala (1943: 69–92) and Hanke (1965: 83–105).
21. Varner has correctly suggested that Captain Garcilaso's "captivity" to Gonzalo Pizarro was either feigned or at the very least has never been satisfactorily explained, *if* one is to believe that he somehow remained loyal to the crown while hardly ever leaving Pizarro's side during the latter's rebellion. Captain Garcilaso did finally desert Pizarro at the battle of Sacsahuana, as did many others, yet Captain Garcilaso's loyalties, whether to Pizarro or the King, remain questionable (Varner 1968: 60–97).
22. Inca Garcilaso steadfastly maintained that Captain Garcilaso gave his horse to Gonzalo Pizarro only *after* the battle had been won by the latter and not during (Part 2, Book V, Chapter XXIII).
23. While Gómara names Captain Garcilaso, "Pizarro would have been in peril had

not Garcilaso given him a horse" (1941: vol. 2, Chapter 181), Zárate does not (1991: Book VII, Chapter 3).

24. This process began as soon as Francisco Pizarro arrived in Peru and continued well into the seventeenth century, see Espinoza Soriano (1973).

25. In the chapter in which his meeting with Las Casas is recounted, Inca Garcilaso includes a scathing portrait of Las Casas's own involvement in the conquest, from which he distances himself by claiming that he heard it from others (Part 2, Book IV, Chapter III).

26. According to José Luis Rivarola's research, the marginalia in a shared copy of López de Gómara's *Historia general de las Indias y conquista de México* shows that the collaboration between Silvestre and Inca Garcilaso generated not only *La Florida del Inca* but also the *Royal Commentaries,* see Rivarola (2011).

27. *Hidalgo* is a Spanish contraction for "*hijo de algo*," meaning "the son of something." Although its cultural significance is difficult to render into English, in sixteenth-century Spain it was a term of respect used to refer to lesser nobles or men from lower social classes who had distinguished themselves in some way (Hemming 1970: 88n; Lockhart 1972: 31–33).

28. Inca Garcilaso, *La traduzión del Indio,* Letter to Don Maximiliano, September 18, 1586. For similarities in Inca Garcilaso's and Hebreo's biographies as well as a critical analysis of Inca Garcilaso's translation, see Novoa (2006).

29. The first eight Jesuits landed at Callao, Peru, at the end of March 1568 as a response to Philip II's request for additional evangelization. They were followed by another twelve in 1569 (Campbell 1921: 55–56).

30. Durand suggests that Garcilaso made the acquaintance of Juan de Ávila the Apostle of Andalusia, who was residing in Montilla at the time, had been a personal friend of St. Ignatius of Loyola, and preached at the dedication ceremony of the Jesuit college there (Durand 1964: 24–26).

31. For a description of the intellectual milieu in Andalucía at the time, see del Pino-Díaz (2011: 16–23).

32. For the Alpujarras revolt, see Elliot (1963: 235–41).

33. Chimpu Ocllo's will is transcribed in Miró Quesada (1948: 245–53).

34. Inca Garcilaso did, however, dedicate the First Part of the *Royal Commentaries* to his mother's memory (Part 2, Book VIII, Chapter XXI).

35. Titu Cusi Yupanqui became violently ill in Puquiura, neighboring Vitcos, in about May 1571. The Indians suspected that he had been poisoned by Martín Pando, Titu Cusi's mestizo secretary, and Augustinian Friar Diego Ortiz. Both Pando and Ortiz balanced the ledger of those suspicions with their lives (Hemming 1970: 417–18).

36. Francisco de Vitoria, *De Indis* (1539) (Vitoria 1991: 231–92); Bartolomé de Las Casas, *In Defense of the Indians* (1552) (Las Casas 1992); and Juan Ginés de Sepúlveda, *Democrates secundus o de las justas causas de la guerra contra los Indios* (Sepúlveda 1984).
37. The fact that the *Royal Commentaries* end with these incidents as well as the unmistakable enmity Toledo receives in the Second Part of the text make this a point worth considering (Part 2, Book VIII, Chapters XIX–XXI).
38. The *Segunda parte de los comentarios reales* (Second Part of the Royal Commentaries), in which these events are treated, was published posthumously in 1617.
39. The full title of the work is *La traduzión del indio de los tres diálogos de amor de León Hebreo hecha de Italiano en español por Garcilaso Inca de la Vega natural de la gran ciudad del Cuzco, cabeza de los reinos y provincias del Perú. Dirigidos a la Sacra Católica Real Majestad del Rey Don Felipe Nuestro Señor* (The Indian's translation of the three dialogues of love of León Hebreo done from Italian into Spanish by Garcilaso Inca de la Vega native of the great city of Cuzco, capital of the kingdoms and provinces of Peru. Directed to the Sacred Catholic Royal Majesty of King Philip our Lord).
40. For the inadequacy of his education see *La traduzión*, Letter to Don Maximillian of Austria, March 12, 1586; the letter to Juan Fernández Franco, December 31, 1592, in Asensio (1953); *La Florida*, "Preface," Book II, Part I, Chapter XXVII, and Part 1, Book II, Chapter XXVII of the *Royal Commentaries*. For the interruptions brought by war and his poverty see *La Florida* ("Preface") and Garcilaso de la Vega (1951b).
41. Appended to the text there are two letters to Don Maximiliano de Austria, one dated March 12, 1586 and the other September 18, 1587, and two letters to Philip II bearing the dates January 19, 1586 and November 7, 1589. Also included is Don Maximiliano de Austria's return letter to Inca Garcilaso, dated June 19, 1587. In the first letter to Don Maximiliano, Inca Garcilaso mentions his desire to conclude the history of Florida as having slowed his redaction of the translation. Similarly, in both letters to Philip he announces his account of Soto's Florida expedition and reveals, for the first time, his intention to write a history of the conquest of the Incas. In the second letter to Don Maximiliano, however, Inca Garcilaso explicitly requests the abbot to act as guardian of the text and to use his influence to bring it to the attention of the king. It seems that he had not yet given up hope of receiving some recognition by the crown.

    For an illuminating reconsideration of the chronologies of Inca Garcilaso's works that gives his translation of the *Dialoghi* a more central and simultaneous role within his historiographical and philosophical project, see Castro-Klarén (2016a: 198–205).

42. Alonso de Vargas held an encumbrance on the estate of the Marquis of Priego that was to be paid to his widow, Luisa de Ponce, until her death, at which time it would pass to Inca Garcilaso. With the advent of the new Marquis, Pedro Fernández de Córdoba y Figueroa, Inca Garcilaso experienced prolonged difficulties collecting the amounts owed and was eventually forced to take legal action (Castanien 1969: 40–41).
43. The November 7, 1589 letter to Philip II in *La traduzión del Indio* was actually sent by Inca Garcilaso from Las Posadas.
44. Inca Garcilaso never reveals the source of *La Florida*, yet José de la Riva-Agüero appears to have been the first to identify him as Gonzalo Silvestre due to internal textual evidence (Riva-Agüero 1910: 43; Miró Quesada 1971: 145; Hilton 1982: lxxxix–xcvii).
45. Inca Garcilaso consulted the brief and disorganized accounts of the Florida expedition by Alonso de Carmona, native of Priego, and Juan Coles, native of Zafra, both of whom had survived the ordeal (*La Florida*, "Preface"). It is possible that he also used the anonymous Portuguese account by the "Gentleman of Elvas" published in Lisbon in 1577 under the title *Relaçam verdadeira dos trabalhos que ho gobernador dom Fernando de Souto e certos fidalgos portugueses passaron no descubrimiento da provincia de Florida. Agora novamente feita per hun fidalgo Delvas* (True account of the hardships which the Governor Fernando de Soto and certain Portuguese gentlemen suffered in the discovery of the province of Florida. Now newly done by a gentleman of Elvas), yet, as Inca Garcilaso was usually quite conscientious about naming his written sources, this hypothesis seems unlikely. Be that as it may, Rolena Adorno has demonstrated his indebtedness to and use of Cabeza de Vaca's *Naufragios* (Adorno 2006).
46. There is evidence to suggest that Inca Garcilaso had finished a first draft as early as 1592, and that by 1599 he was already making plans for its publication (Asensio 1953: 587–88; Durand 1976: 144). However that stands, we do know that Jesuit Juan de Pineda extolled *La Florida del Inca* as the "very delightful and very truthful" history of the "noble García Laso Inga" in the second volume of *Commentariorum in Job* (1601), four years before *La Florida* was published (Durand 1979: 36).
47. Inca Garcilaso's *Relación de la descendencia del famoso Garcí Pérez de Vargas* (1596) was originally intended to be the preface of *La Florida del Inca*. He later decided to omit it, and the piece remained both unfinished and unpublished.
48. All quotations of *La Florida del Inca* are from Sylvia-Lyn Hilton's edition (Garcilaso de la Vega 1982).
49. *La traduzión del Indio*, Letter to Don Maximiliano, September 18, 1586. Also see Miró Quesada (1971: 165–90).

50. Listed in the book catalog copied at Inca Garcilaso's death was a Greek dictionary and a French translation of Hebreo's *Dialoghi d'Amore* (Durand 1948: 239–64).
51. See Appendix.
52. The works for which Ambrosio de Morales is generally known are *Discurso sobre las antigüedades de las ciudades de España* (Discourse on the Antiquities of the Cities of Spain, 1575) and *Discurso sobre la lengua castellana* (Discourse on the Castilian Language, 1585). See Sánchez Alonso (1944: vol. 2, 25–30), Mora (2010a), del Pino-Díaz (2011), and Serna (2011).
53. For the sack of Cadiz, see Kamen (1997: 306–08).
54. A Spanish translation of Castro's dedication can be found in Porras Barrenechea (1955: 260–263). Also see José Rico Verdu (1973: 103–04).
55. In August 1597, Inca Garcilaso is identified as "cleric" in a transaction document between himself and the great Baroque poet, Luis de Góngora y Aragote (Varner 1968: 320n15).
56. For Inca Garcilaso's use of Tacitus, see Brading (1991: 255–72).
57. For Las Casas on Florida, see Las Casas (1992: 102–04).
58. For Soto, see Book V, Part I, Chapter VII; Book VI, Chapter XI, and for Silvestre see Book IV, Chapter XIV; and Book V, Part II, Chapter VIII, among others.
59. For example, compare the speech of Calgacus, chief of the Britons, in Tacitus's *Agricola* with the speech delivered by the cacique Acuera in Book II, Part I, Chapter XVI of *La Florida del Inca*. For Calcagus's speech, see Tacitus (1970: 80–83).
60. Published under the full title *Primera Parte de los Comentarios Reales, que tratan del origen de los Yncas, Reyes que fueron del Peru, de su idolotría, leyes, y govierno en paz y guerra: de sus vidas y conquistas, y de todo lo que fue aquel Imperio y su República, antes que los Españoles passaron a él* (First Part of the Royal Commentaries, which treats of the origin of the Incas, former kings of Peru, their idolatry, laws, government in peace and war: their lives and conquests, and everything relating to that Empire and Republic before the arrival of the Spaniards), the manuscript was submitted for the Inquisition's approval in 1604, was licensed in 1605, and finally published by Pedro Crasbeeck in Lisbon in 1609.
61. For Inca Garcilaso's account of the naming of Peru, see Part 1, Book I, Chapters IV–VI.

CHAPTER 2: MESTIZO RHETORIC

1. Both refer to Inca Garcilaso's authority on the etymology of the word "Peru" (Durand 1976: 138–60 and 1979; Mora 2010a; Serna 2011: 156–57).
2. For more on the reception of the *Royal Commentaries* in Spain, see Pérez de Tudela (2010).

3. Carmen de Mora states that "the first translator of the Inca Garcilaso's work was the Frenchman Jean Baudoin," a claim that still holds true if it is understood to mean the first translator of a complete edition of the *Royal Commentaries* submitted for publication, which Hakluyt's unpublished excerpts collected by Purchas were not (Mora 2006: 165).
4. In Part 1, Chapter 12 of *Leviathan*, Hobbes writes "the first king and founder of the kingdom of Peru pretended himself and his wife to be the children of the Sun" (Hobbes 1968: 177), a clear reference to Inca Garcilaso's claim that Manco Cápac and Mama Ocllo Huaco created the "fable" of their divine descent from the Sun in Book 1, Chapter 25 of the First Part of the *Royal Commentaries*, which itself is an allusion to Plato's "noble lie" in *The Republic*. For Locke's citation and use of Inca Garcilaso, see Fuerst (2000: "Epilogue" and 2016); for Defoe, see Leckie (1908), Mesa Gisbert (2008) and Voigt (2009: 91–97); and for Swift, see Potter (1999). Hume cites Inca Garcilaso in the essay "Of Interest," see Hume (1985: 305), and for Jefferson see Montiel (2010: 114 and 128). For Stuart/Cugoano, see Gates (1988: 146–52).
5. On Ávila's library and its contents, see Hampe-Martínez (1993: 10–11).
6. For Oliva's praise of Inca Garcilaso, see Guibovich (2016: 133–35).
7. A longstanding complaint of *garcilacistas* is that there has been no textual evidence of the earliest reception of Inca Garcilaso's work by indigenous Andeans, see for instance Mazzotti (1998: 101–02). Some have then gone on to interpolate the probable dissemination of the *Royal Commentaries* to indigenous Peruvian audiences through the common sixteenth-century Spanish practice of holding public readings for the illiterate, see Frenk (1982: vol. 1, 101–23), or to follow the "trail of Garcilaso" in the art and iconography of early Peruvian painting, along the lines of Buntix and Wuffarden (1991). To my knowledge, however, Juan de Cuevas Herrera's "Cinco memoriales" stands as the earliest documented instance of an indigenous reception of the *Royal Commentaries* yet to surface, giving credence to the notion that the *Royal Commentaries* did in fact enjoy currency within elite indigenous and mestizo circles from its first arrival in Peru. In addition to the well-known examples of Don Felipe Guaman Poma de Ayala and Joan de Santacruz Pachacuti Yamqui Salcamaygua, a recent wave of historical studies has buttressed this point by documenting literacy among the indigenous and mestizo elite in the viceroyalty of Peru, subverting the prevailing image of a colonial society full of illiterate Indians. See Burns (2010 and 2014); Charles (2010a); Rappaport and Cummins (2012); Ramos (2010: 120–21 and 2014); and Ramos and Yannakakis (2014).
8. From the original: "los Comentarios de un auctor libre de toda sospecha, mayor

de toda excepción de la Sangre Real de los Reyes Yncas Garcilaso de la Vega" (my translation). Cuevas Herrera's condensed account equates Pachacámac with the Christian God, features a phantasm that appears to Inca Viracocha, who had previously been banished from Cuzco by his father Yáhuar Huáca (Yavarvacac), to whom the phantasm offers a prophecy about the coming of new, white, bearded people with the true religion, a prophecy that is repeated and publicized by Huayna Cápac, and which in turn accounts for Atahualpa's and Manco Inca's defeat by the Spaniards, in accordance with Pachacámac's will. As we shall see in chapter 3, these elements are not only specific to Inca Garcilaso's version of Inca religion and dynastic history, but also constitute rhetorical and ideological maneuvers that he made in an Andean field of reference to appeal to the common understandings of potential indigenous readers of his work. It appears that Cuevas Herrera not only fastened onto but also accepted, reiterated, and disseminated the very rhetorical moves that Inca Garcilaso had intended for potential Andean readers. As a final, tantalizing note, Cuevas Herrera suggests that, beyond reading the *Royal Commentaries*, skeptics of Philip IV's just title to Peru should "come, communicate, and ask the few branches that have remained of the Royal Trunk of the Yncas: *they would find that same teaching and tradition*" (*vengan, communiquen, y pregunten a las ramas que han quedado del Tronco Real delos Yncas:* hallarian esa misma doctrina y tradición; my emphasis), implying that Inca Garcilaso's account of Inca history was prevalent among indigenous and mestizo descendants of the Incas across Peru in the mid-seventeenth century (Cuevas Herrera 1650, 220).

9. For the classic and still invaluable study of this transatlantic debate see Gerbi (1973).
10. Also see Varner (1968: 378–84) and Brading (1991: 483–91).
11. For *limpieza de sangre*, see Elliott (1963: 107, 220–24, and 308–310) and Kamen (1997: 230–54). For racial theories of the sixteenth century, see Zamora (2010b and 2016).
12. For Fray Calixto, see Dueñas (2010: 65–78 and 212–14).
13. For the genre of commentaries in the sixteenth century, see Foucault (1994: 40–42), for the type of commentary Inca Garcilaso may have taken as the model for his work, see Fernández (2004: 23–55), and for a new approach to the title of the *Royal Commentaries*, see Rodríguez Garrido (2010).
14. For Neoplatonism in Inca Garcilaso's works, see Iberico (1939), Arocena (1949), Martí-Abelló (1950), Durand (1964 and 1976: 32–46), Miró Quesada (1971: Chapter 5), Durán Luzio (1976), Pupo-Walker (1982), Jákfalvi-Leiva (1984: 3–33), Zamora (1988: 58–61), MacCormack (1991: 332–64), Sommer (1996a, 1996b), Maz-

zotti (2006), Benand (2010), Lebsanft (2011), and Castro-Klarén (2016a), among others.

15. From the original: "una verdad no puede ser contraria a otra verdad, es necesario dar lugar a la una y la otra, y concordarlas."
16. Appendix.
17. For instance, one author writes that although Inca Garcilaso was "agonizingly aware that he was the issue of two cultures," he nevertheless "wrote not as a European apostle to the other but, instead, as a mestizo missionary to the land of his father" (Abbott 1996: 79). In fairness, however, this is just one of the many studies of Inca Garcilaso's work that confines itself to European audiences, intellectual traditions, and modes of expression and that predominate in the scholarly literature.
18. In a more recent work, Zamora posits that in the *Historia general del Perú*, otherwise known as the Second Part of the *Royal Commentaries*, Inca Garcilaso "conceived of the *Historia* as his service to a specific readership comprised of the Indians, Mestizos, and Creoles of Peru, with whom he identified and to whom he dedicated the work." She goes on to say, "one of the most unique and important aspects of the text may well be the prescient anticipation of a racially diverse colonial community of readers united by affective ties to a common homeland, a shared history, and a lettered cultural tradition that could facilitate precisely the kind of critical reflection on Peru's past and future that the *Historia* models" (Zamora 2010a: 120). I would only add that this idea holds for *both* parts of the *Royal Commentaries*, taken as a whole, not simply the Second Part.
19. María Antonia Garcés published an early and still important investigation of Quechua as a "subtext" in the *Royal Commentaries* (Garcés 1991), but the groundbreaking, full-length work in this regard is José Antonio Mazzotti's *Coros mestizos del Inca Garcilaso, resonancias andinas* (1996a), revised and translated into English as *Incan Insights: Inca Garcilaso's Hints to Andean Readers* (2008). Since, there have been a number of new studies exploring Andean as well as European contexts in Inca Garcilaso's work, such as Fernández (2004, 2016b), Mazzotti (1996b, 2006), Romiti (2009), Fuerst (2010), Millones (2010), Ossio (2010), and López-Baralt (2011), among others.
20. I have used the Spanish translation of "La Dedicatoria del Arte de Retorica de Francisco de Castro al Inca Garcilaso" in Porras Barrenechea (1955: 260–263). For Castro's vita, see Rico Verdu (1973: 103–04).
21. Also see Asensio (1953), Durand (1949: 278–90 and 1976: 138–48), Araníbar (1991: vol. 2, 693, 701–02 and 785–86), Mora (2010a), and del Pino-Díaz (2011).
22. On the founding of the college see Ribadeneira (1952: 142). On Catalina Fernández de Córdoba's relation to Inca Garcilaso, see Varner (1968: 160), and for Inca Gar-

cilaso's milieu in southern Spain more generally, both familial and intellectual, see del Pino-Díaz (2011).

23. Inca Garcilaso de la Vega, *La traducción del Indio*, Letter to Don Maximiliano, September 18, 1586.
24. Second Part of the *Royal Commentaries*, "Aprovación" (Garcilaso de la Vega 1944: vol. 1, 3–4).
25. Menéndez y Pelayo held that the First Part of the *Royal Commentaries* was not a work of history, but rather a "utopian novel" akin to the works of More, Campanella, and Harrington (Menéndez y Pelayo 1948: vol. 2, 73–77). Carmelo Saenz de Santa María was among the first to challenge this approach to Inca Garcilaso's work, arguing for a critical appraisal that took into consideration his affinities with his intellectual contemporaries (Saenz de Santa María 1965).
26. For the influence of Erasmus on the founders of the Society, see O'Malley (1993: 243–63 and 1990: 471–87). For an opposing view, see Bataillon (1991: 771–72).
27. On the role of eloquence in Jesuit education, see Höpfl (2004: 12–13), and for their practice of rhetoric in Europe and the New World at the turn of the seventeenth century, see Abbott (1996: 102–20).
28. Inca Garcilaso's relation to Ciceronian humanism and historiography has been discussed most explicitly by Arocena (1949), Avalle-Arce (1970), and Pupo-Walker (1982). As all three interpret Inca Garcilaso exclusively from the perspectives of European humanism and historiography (Arocena and Avalle-Arce) or creative literature with a strong autobiographical bent (Pupo-Walker), it is necessary to cover this ground again to highlight not only what Inca Garcilaso's conceptions of history and style owe to humanism, but also the elements of both that cannot be reduced to European antecedents.
29. For the pervasiveness of this view of history in Spanish political thought at the end of the sixteenth century, see Fernández-Santamaría (1983: 157–66).
30. For Petrarch's views on Cicero, see Petrarch (1948: 47–133). For the influence of Cicero on the political thought of the Italian Renaissance, see Skinner (1978: vol. 1, 84–112).
31. Rhetoric was composed of five techniques—invention, arrangement, style, memory, and delivery—each of which was to be mastered by the speaker (Cicero 1976: I.vii.9). Further, Roman theories of rhetoric followed Aristotle in distinguishing between three types of oratory: deliberative, which dealt with deciding on a future course of action; judicial, which concerned accusation and defense in legal proceedings; and epideictic or demonstrative, which dealt with praise and blame (Aristotle 1991: 1358b–1359a, 47–49). Literature, broadly defined, was seen as a species of epideictic speech.

32. Also see the pseudo-Ciceronian, *Rhetorica ad Herennium* (1989: I.viii.13) and Quintillian (1989: II.iv.2).

33. Likewise, Quintillian advised the rhetorician not only to begin with historical narrative, but also to retire at the height of his career and dedicate himself to writing the history of his own time (Quintillian 1989: II.iv.2–3 and XII.xi.4).

34. According to Höpfl, sixteenth-century Jesuits understood the relationship between rhetoric and history in the same way. He writes: "The study of rhetoric . . . a Jesuit *forte*, not only dealt with techniques such as *inventio*, *dispositio*, and the enthymeme, but was also the site in the academic curriculum for the study of rhetorical exemplars (notably Cicero) and the classical historians, as well as poets. History, in turn, was the indispensable complement to practical experience in the cultivation of prudence, the political virtue *sans pareil* for reason of state, and the use of historical *loci* and model instances was its characteristic mode of argument" (Höpfl 2004: 22).

35. For the influence of rhetoric on Italian humanist historiography, see Gilbert (1965: 203–301), Struever (1970), and Cochrane (1981: 15ff); for French historiography, see Kelley (1970) and Franklin (1963); for Spanish historiography, see Sánchez Alonso (1944: vol. 2); and for New World historiography, see Mignolo (1981: 358–402).

36. For Ciceronianism in the historical conception of Pedro Cieza de León, Agustín Zárate, and Bartolomé de Las Casas, all of whom Inca Garcilaso had read, see Mignolo (1981: 380–386).

37. Cochrane differentiates "literary historians," who were primarily concerned with the ethical, formative, and stylistic elements of history, from "research historians," who busied themselves in archives and antiquarian compilations, and places the Jesuits in the former category. Anthony Grafton suggests a similar distinction stemming from the fifteenth century between "pedagogical" humanists, whose scholarly aim was the formation of moral character, and "scientific" humanists, whose goal was attaining precise information and developing more powerful intellectual techniques. Grafton, however, is careful to stress that these different methods and aims often existed simultaneously in the same group of scholars (Grafton 1991: 23–46).

38. "The good doctor Luis Vivas" is mentioned in *La Florida del Inca* (Book II, Part I, Chapter XXV, 78v) and his works are among those listed in Inca Garcilaso's library at the time of his death, see Durand (1948: 239–264). Inca Garcilaso calls Guicciardini "the great doctor of both laws and the great historian of his own times and great gentleman of Florence . . . worthy son of such a mother," in the Second Part of the *Royal Commentaries* (Part 2, Book I, Chapter II, vol. 1, 22). Jean Bodin's *Six*

Books on the Commonwealth is cited by Inca Garcilaso in the chapter following his praise of Guicciardini (Part 2, Book 1, Chapter 3, vol. 1, 23).

39. As Cicero has Crassus remind us, "every speech consists of the matter and the words, the words can have no place if you take away the matter, nor the matter receive any illustration if you take away the words" (1997b: III.v.19).
40. The analysis in this paragraph is indebted to A.J. Woodman's insightful study, *Rhetoric in Classical Historiography* (1988: 70–116).
41. The full discussion of propriety as a moral duty can be found in Cicero's *De Officiis* (1997a: I.xxvii.93ff).
42. Quentin Skinner has argued, however, that humanist inheritors of Roman rhetoric focused above all on *ornatus* due to the power of amplification to sway the emotions of an audience (Skinner 1996: 138–39).
43. Cicero says that one way to persuade is to conciliate the audience (1997b: II.xxvii.115), which can be achieved through the dignity of the speaker, his deeds, and the opinion the audience forms of his life. He suggests that orators should attempt to "paint their character in words" through their style (1997b: II.xliii.182–184). For the importance of the historian's character in Greek and Roman historiography, see Marincola (1997: 128–174).
44. Also see O'Gorman (1972b); Elliott (1970); Pagden (1982); and Grafton, Shelford and Siraisi (1992).
45. Missionaries, of course, also wrote histories of the New World. Moreover, their close contact with indigenous peoples and their knowledge of native languages contributed to the gradual refinement and sophistication of New World historiography.
46. This letter is included in Inca Garcilaso's "Prologue" to the Second Part. See the Appendix.
47. Inca Garcilaso almost wholly avoids the words "pagan" and "paganism" (*pagano* and *paganismo*) when describing the religious condition and practices of indigenous Americans in order to avoid the connotative stigma of idolatry and cultural inferiority attached to these terms in his day. Instead, he prefers the word "gentilidad," which I have translated with the archaic "gentilism," because it emphasizes Amerindians' status as gentiles; in other words, the extent to which indigenous peoples were ignorant of Christianity and therefore outside the church, not out of any malice or defect on their part, but simply due to the fact that they had no prior contact with Catholic doctrine. In this sense, Inca Garcilaso's view of indigenous peoples corresponds with Las Casas's.

    Somewhat unfortunately, however, Livermore consistently uses "paganism," "heathenism," or "heathens" for *gentilidad* in his English edition of the *Royal Com-*

mentaries, thereby obscuring Inca Garcilaso's meaning. For an example, see Garcilaso de la Vega (1966: vol. 1, 4).

48. The second letter is also included in the "Prologue" to the Second Part. See the Appendix.
49. Eduardo Hopkins Rodríguez argues that Inca Garcilaso's intended audience in *La Florida* is broader and more diverse: "The receptor in *La Florida del Inca* is multiple and complex. It encompasses the King, nobles, gentlemen [caballeros], and in general, Spaniards and people of the New World" (Rodríguez 2011: 60).
50. For Inca Garcilaso's "discursive strategies" in *La Florida*, see Mora (1994), and on combating Hispano-European prejudice toward Amerindians, see Steigman (2005) and Chang-Rodríguez (2006b).
51. For more on this point and particularly Inca Garcilaso's use of sources in *La Florida*, see Rodríquez Vecchini (1982: 587–620).
52. Also see Castro-Klarén (2016a) for the overlapping chronology of Inca Garcilaso's written works.
53. Hayden White has argued that "a preface is, by its very nature, an instruction on how to read the text that follows it and, by the same token, an attempt to guard against certain misreadings of the text, in other words, an attempt at control" (White 1987: 201).
54. From the original: "Aunque ha habido españoles curiosos que han escrito las repúblicas del nuevo mundo, como la de México y la del Perú y las de los otros reinos en aquella gentilidad, no ha sido con la relación entera que de ellos pudiera dar" (all quotes from the Preface are on page 4).
55. From the original: "Que lo he notado particularmente en las cosas que del Perú he visto escritas, de las cuales como natural de la ciudad del Cuzco (que fue otra Roma en aquel imperio) tengo más larga y clara noticia que la que hasta ahora los escritores han dado."
56. From the original: "Pero escríbenlas *tan cortamente* que, aun las muy notorias para mí, *de la manera que las dicen*, las entiendo mal" (my emphasis). Also see Garcés (1991: 125–151).
57. Cicero extends this point in his discussion of Caesar's commentaries, to which Inca Garcilaso's commentaries allude and which Cicero claims were "plain, correct, graceful, and divested of all ornaments of language, so as to appear . . . in a kind of undress." Commentaries, as records of first-hand experiences, were the raw materials for histories properly so-called and required stylistic elaboration. Further, Cicero criticizes the earliest Roman historians, for they did "not understand the adornment of composition," and, "so long as their narrative is understood, they regard brevity (*brevitatem*) as the historian's single merit" (1997b: II.xii.53–54).

These deficiencies are juxtaposed to the accomplishments of Herodotus and Thucydides, both of whom are praised for their eloquence (1997b: II.xiii.55–56). In addition to their relationship to Caesar's commentaries, Christian Fernández argues convincingly that Inca Garcilaso's were most likely influenced by St. Jerome's commentaries in *Contra Rufinum* (Fernández 2004: 23–55).

58. Inca Garcilaso's "Preface" may be an allusion to Titus Livy's "Preface," in which the Roman historian says revisionist historiographers usually justify their work through the promise of more accurate information or a finer style: "each succeeding writer thinks he will either bring greater accuracy to the facts or surpass his unpolished predecessors in artistry and style" (Livy 1998: 3). Lacking in Inca Garcilaso's "Preface," however, is the playful, self-deprecating irony apparent in Livy's.

59. For an overview of the clash between European and Andean concepts in early Peruvian historiography, see Pease (1995: 121–136).

60. In the "Author's Preface," Cieza de León puts his *excusatio* this way: "And if this history is not written with the gentleness that science gives to letters nor with the required ornaments, it is at least full of truths, and to each is given its own with brevity, and the deeds poorly done are reprehended with moderation" (*Y si no va escripta con la suavidad que da a las letras la sciencia ni con el ornato que requería, va a lo menos llena de verdades, y a cada uno se da lo que es suyo con brevedad, y con moderación se reprenden las cosas mal hechas*) (Cieza de León 1984: 67–68; my translation).

For more on the relationship between personal experience as the guarantor of veracity in New World historiography, see Mignolo (1981: 386–392). Additionally, in the sixteenth century there were various subgenres of writing, such as the letter, chronicle, and relation that were often assimilated under "history" without fulfilling all of the latter's requirements. For the distinctions between these forms and history properly so called, see Mignolo (1992: vol. 1, 57–116).

61. From the original: "Que mi intención no es contradecirles sino servirles de comento y glosa y de *intérprete* en muchos vocablos indios que, *como extranjeros en aquella lengua*, interpretaron *fuera la propriedad de ella*" (my emphasis).

62. A royal decree of 1556 placed all works relating to America under the official jurisdiction and review of the Council of Indies, and in 1571 Philip II created the post of Official Cosmographer and Chronicler of the Indies, which was first occupied by Juan López de Velasco and later by Antonio de Herrera. See Haring (1947: 226–227) and Elliott (1970: 38).

63. Las Casas explains the "mystical body of Christ," following Augustine, as those members of every earthly nation who have been preselected by divine providence to be among the Elect at the Last Judgment. He continues, "divine Providence

must have naturally disposed these people for indoctrination and divine grace . . . appointing a time for their calling and glorification, and since we do not know who these might be, we must esteem and judge all men, trying to help them inasmuch as we desire salvation" (Las Casas 1971: 6–7).

64. The appeal to the "mystical body of Christ" and Christian piety resonates with the moral attitude and conduct prescribed by Neoplatonic philosophies of love, such as Hebreo's. As José Durand put it, "the abandonment of *hatred* thus becomes, for the Inca, an explicit norm for his ethics as an historian" (Durand 1964: 24).
65. From the original: "Espero que se recibirá con la misma intención que yo la ofrezco porque es la correspondencia que mi voluntad merece, aunque la obra no lo merezca."
66. Similar claims of the representative character of Inca Garcilaso's persona and work can be found in the "Preface" to *La Florida*. He asks his readers to "favor in me (although I may not deserve it) all the mestizo Indians and Creoles of Peru" (*favorecer en mi* [*aunque no lo merezca*] *a todos los Indios mestizos y criollos del Peru*).
67. From the original: "Esto es no contradiciendo a los que dicen que las dicciones bárbaras se han acentuar en la última, que lo dicen por no saber la lengua" (all quotes from the Warning are from pages 5 and 6).
68. Antonio de Nebrija is hailed by Inca Garcilaso as "the great master Antonio de Lebrija, to whom all good Latinists in Spain today are indebted" (Part 1, Book IX, Chapter XXXI, vol. 2, 628).
69. From the original: "Y, como los indios no las tienen, comúnmente pronuncian mal las dicciones españolas que las tienen."
70. From the original: "Para atajar esta corrupción me sea lícito, pues soy indio, que *en esta historia yo escriba como indio con las mismas letras* que aquellas tales dicciones se deben escribir" (my emphasis).
71. From the original: "Y no se les haga de mal que las leyeren ver la novedad presente en contra del mal uso introducido, que antes debe dar gusto leer aquellos nombres en su *propriedad y pureza*" (my emphasis).
72. Gonzalo Lamana similarly argues that writing like an Indian is at the heart of Inca Garcilaso's political project (Lamana 2016).
73. From the original: "Otras muchas cosas tiene aquella lengua diferentísimas de la castellana, italiana y latina, *las cuales notarán los mestizos y criollos curiosos*, pues son de su lenguaje" (my emphasis).
74. This is not the only instance in which Inca Garcilaso indirectly adds information intended for native Peruvians. When listing the territories conquered by the second Inca, Sinchi Roca, Inca Garcilaso writes, "naming the provinces in such specificity is for Peruvians, for it would be an impertinence for those from other king-

doms: Pardon me, for I desire to serve all" (*nombrar las provincias en tan particular es para los del Perú, que para los de otros reinos fuera impertinencia: perdóneseme, que deseo servir a todos*) (Part 1, Book II, Chapter XVI, vol. 1, 108). Further, in describing the *corequenque* feathers adopted by the Incas as part of their insignia and lamenting how this fashion had been appropriated by even the lowest of Indians after the conquest, Inca Garcilaso remarks, "This notice, although it is of little or no importance to Spaniards, I have decided to include as having belonged to the former kings" (*Esta noticia, aunque es de poca o ninguna importancia a los de España, me pareció ponerla por haber sido cosas de los reyes pasados*) (Part 1, Book VI, Chapter XXVIII, vol. 1, 388). These seemingly innocuous asides have the same tangential character as the statement in the "Warning," yet they clearly demonstrate that Inca Garcilaso was in fact considering diverse Peruvians when he wrote the *Royal Commentaries*.

75. From the original: "Que yo harto hago en señalarles con el dedo desde España los principios de su lengua para que la sustenten en su pureza, que cierto es lástima que se pierda o corrumpa."
76. *Tahuantinsuyu* is the Quechua word used by the Incas to refer to their empire meaning "the four corners of the earth" (Part 1, Book I, Chapter V, vol. 1, 17). See chapter 1, note 5.
77. The separation of Andean history into different epochs is not Inca Garcilaso's invention, rather it is also found in other European sources as well as in the works of indigenous Andeans such as Guaman Poma de Ayala and Juan Santacruz Pachacuti. See also Ossio (2010: 66–67).
78. From the original: "más dóciles para recibir la fe católica y la enseñanza y doctrina de nuestra santa madre Iglesia Romana."
79. For more on this theme in Inca Garcilaso's work, see MacCormack (1998: 3–31; 2007), del Pino-Díaz (2011), and Campos-Muñoz (2013). Comparisons of Mexica and Inca civilizations with Rome were commonplace in Spanish imperial historiography, and Inca Garcilaso was by no means alone in drawing out the similarities. See Jaime González (1981).
80. Inca Garcilaso identifies his source as Cusi Huallpa in Book IX, Chapter XIV of the First Part (vol. 2, 594). On how Inca Garcilaso attempts to "recover the lost indigenous voice, especially that of his uncle Cusi Huallpa," see No (1999).
81. From the original: "Inca, tío: pues no hay escritura entre vosotros, que es la que guarda la memoria de las cosas pasadas, qué noticia tenéis del origen y principio de nuestros reyes?"
82. From the original: "pues estamos en la puerta de este gran laberinto, será bien pasemos adelante a dar noticia de lo que en él había" (39).

83. Elena Romiti points out that in sixteenth-century Peru historical *quipus* were often described by Spanish observers as "labyrinths," and that as Inca Garcilaso embarks upon the origins of the Incas, "the semantic axis of labyrinth-quipus unfolds before the reader," thereby creating an analogy between his account of Inca oral history and Inca quipu traditions (Romiti 2009: 83).
84. From the original: "Después de haber dado muchas trazas y tomado muchos caminos para entrar a dar cuenta del origen y principio de los Incas, reyes naturales que fueron del Perú, me pareció que la mejor traza y el camino más fácil y llano era contar lo que en mis niñeces oí muchas veces a mi madre y a sus hermanos y tíos y a otros sus mayores acerca de este origen y principio. Porque todo lo que otras vías se dice de él viene a resolverse en lo mismo que nosotros diremos. Y será mejor que se sepa por las propias palabras que los Incas lo cuentan, que no por las de otros autores extraños."
85. From the original: "La cual yo he procurado traducir fielmente de mi lengua materna, que es la del Inca, en la ajena, que es la castellana."
86. From the original: "Empero bastará haber sacado el verdadero sentido de ellas, que es lo que conviene a nuestra historia."
87. It should also be pointed out, as Juan M. Ossio has observed, that Inca Garcilaso's version of the Inca myth of origins is not found in any other contemporary chronicle of the Incas or other indigenous Andeans (Ossio 2010: 69).
88. The "lower" half was called Hurin Cuzco (Part 1, Book I, chapter XVI, vol. 1, 43). The duality and complementarity of opposites were fundamental principles of social and spatial organization throughout the Andean world. Franklin Pease has argued that the division of Cuzco into the upper and lower halves of Hanan and Hurin, respectively, is a manifestation of the symmetrical interrelationship of inseparable conceptual pairings (e.g., high/low, right/left, male/female) contained within the Andean notion of *yanantin* (Pease 1995: 104–105).
89. From the original: " . . . todas las cosas que consistían en cuenta de números, hasta poner las batallas y reencuentros que se daban, hasta decir cuántas embajadas habían traído al Inca y cuántas pláticas y razonamientos había hecho el rey."
90. From the original: "Porque las letras son las que perpetúan los hechos, mas como aquellos Incas no las alcanzaron valiéronse de lo que pudieron inventar. Y *como si los nudos fueran letras* eligieron historiadores y contadores (*que llamaron quipucamayu, que es 'el que tiene cargo de los nudos'*), para que por ellos—y por los hilos y los colores de hilos y con el favor de los cuentos y de la poesía—*escribiesen y retuviesen* la tradicíon de sus hechos. *Esta fue la manera de escribir que los Incas tuvieron en su república*" (my emphasis).
91. From the original: "Y el indio que no había tomado de memoria por tradición las

cuentas (o cualquier otra historia que hubiese pasado entre ellos) eran tan ignorante en lo uno y lo otro como el español o cualquier otro extranjeros."

92. From the original: "Yo traté los quipus y nudos con los indios de mi padre y con otros curacas cuando por san Juan y Navidad venían a la ciudad a pagar sus tributos."

93. For more on the numerical and positional logics of *quipus* as an Andean subtext within the *Royal Commentaries*, see Romiti (2009: 77–97).

94. For the full discussion see Mazzotti (1996a: 101–171; 2008: 79–139).

95. For instance, in Chapters XV–XVII in Book I of the First Part, in which the origin of the Incas, the foundation of Cuzco, and the first subjects brought under Inca rule are described, the narrative alternates as a series of quotations within a quotation between five distinct "voices": Inca Garcilaso as narrator; Inca Garcilaso as a youth; Cusi Huallpa; the Sun; and Manco Cápac. The superposition of perspectives in this "choral writing" (*escritura coral*) need not blend into or be reduced to a single, harmonious voice (Mazzotti 1996a: 98–101 and 2008: 83–93).

96. There are at least three such formulas corresponding to different political acts: a formula of foundation, in which the Sun, as the first cause of the Inca empire, orders Manco Cápac and Mama Ocllo Huaco to imitate his example; a formula of requirement, used to justify the civilizing mission of the Incas to their eventual subjects; and a formula of validation, employed for reporting outside voices, including written authorities or the direct speech of important persons (Mazzotti 1996a: 127–152; 2008: 93–122). To give an example, the first formula of foundation occurs when the Sun authorizes the Incas to bring the people out of their primitive existence of the First Age. As Cusi Huallpa relates, "Our father the Sun, seeing men such as I have told you, felt sorry and took pity on them and sent from heaven to earth a son and daughter of his so that . . ." (*Nuestro padre el sol, viendo los hombres tales como te he dicho, se apiadó y tuvo lástima de ellos y envió del cielo a la tierra un hijo y una hija de los suyos para que . . .*) (Part 1, Book I, Chapter XV, vol. 1, 41). Generically, the formal structure of this passage is a subject followed by an adverbial phrase that begins with a gerund, which in turn is followed by a verb (Subject + Adverbial Phrase + Verb). When Manco Cápac and Mama Ocllo Huaco found Cuzco in the next chapter with Cusi Huallpa still narrating, we find the same linguistic structure introducing their deeds: "Our princes, seeing the many people gathered there, ordered that . . ." (*Nuestros príncipes, viendo la mucha gente que se les allegaba, dieron orden que . . .*) (Part 1, Book I, Chapter XVI, vol. 1, 43). Inca Garcilaso reclaims narration in Chapter XX of Book I in the First Part, and in the next chapter he continues recounting the deeds of Manco Cápac in this way: "The Inca Manco Cápac, settling his people along with teaching his vassals to

cultivate the earth and build houses and draw irrigation and do all the other things necessary for human life, continued instructing them . . ." (*El Inca Manco Cápac, yendo poblando sus pueblos juntamente con enseñar a cultivar la tierra a sus vasallos y labrar las casas y sacar acequias y hacer las demás cosas necesarias para la vida humana, les iba instruyendo* . . .) (Part 1, Book I, Chapter XXI, vol. 1, 52). In this instance the adverbial phrase is longer, but the general structure is identical to its predecessors. Again, this is but a single, serial iteration of one of the three major formulas and their numerous repetitions in the *Royal Commentaries*.

A final caveat. Livermore's translations of *The Royal Commentaries* and *The General History of Peru* retain almost nothing of the aforementioned grammatical structures. The only formula that appears consistently in Livermore's editions is the formula of validation, which generally ends Inca Garcilaso's direct quotation of other authors, such as in the following examples: "Up to here is from Father Acosta, taken word for word" (*Hasta aquí es del padre maestro Acosta, sacado a la letra*) (Part 1, Book I, Chapter III, vol. 1, 14), or "Up to here is from López de Gómara, taken word for word" (Hasta aquí es de López de Gómara, sacado a la letra) (Part 1, Book I, Chapter V, vol. 1, 19). Livermore has "This, word for word, is from Padre Acosta," and, "This extract is taken word for word from López de Gómara," respectively. See Garcilaso de la Vega (1966: vol. 1, 14, 18). The point is not to impugn Livermore's translations or to undermine the enjoyment of his editions. Rather, it is to bring attention to the fact that the interpretation presented here will find little to no confirmation for those who approach Inca Garcilaso's work solely through the English versions.

97. From the original: "todos ellos generalmente, así los reyes como los no reyes, se preciaron en imitar en todo y por todo la condición, obras y costumbres de este primer príncipe Manco Cápac."

98. For a detailed exposition and analysis of Inca Garcilaso's "intellectual alternativity" (*alternatividad intelectual*), see Mabel Moraña (2010).

CHAPTER 3: THE MANY FACES OF VIRACOCHA AND THE TURNING OF THE WORLD

An abridged and edited version of this chapter was published as "'El Dios no Conocido' y la Vuelta del Mundo en los *Comentarios reales*," in *Renacimiento mestizo: Los 400 años de los Comentarios reales*, edited by José Antonio Mazzotti. See Fuerst (2010).

1. For instance, see José de la Riva Agüero (1944: xliv–xlix).

2. Part of the temptation to view the *Royal Commentaries* as separate works undoubt-

edly stems from the erroneous title, *Historia general del Perú* ("General History of Peru," 1617), imputed to the Second Part. If one reads the printer's pages, the censor's approbation, and Inca Garcilaso's "Prologue" to the Second Part, however, one finds that the manuscript is only referred to as the *Segunda parte de los Comentarios reales* (Second Part of the Royal Commentaries). The other title of the work, by which the text is most commonly known, is obviously the product of an editorial decision that probably occurred between Inca Garcilaso's death in 1616 and the publication of the Second Part/General History of Peru in 1617. The reasons for this change have never been discovered, yet all the evidence attests to the fact that it was not of Inca Garcilaso's doing. Also see No (2010a: 97).

On this point Christian Fernández cautions, "Considering this fact, it can be affirmed that both parts of the work form an inseparable unity and whatever study that is made on this theme in particular ought to proceed taking into account this undeniable fact, otherwise we would be falling into the same error in which earlier critics have fallen" (Fernández 2004: 35; my translation).

3. From the original: "'Cuitados de nosotros, que perecemos afanando por ganar imperios y reinos estraños, no para nosotros ni para nuestros hijos, sino para los ajenos!'"
4. The events surrounding Francisco Pizarro's capture and execution of the Inca Atahualpa are related in Book I of the Second Part.
5. From the original: "Y para interpretarlo en toda su significación, quiere decir 'hombre de la sangre real.'"
6. From the original: "mandó que ellos y sus descendientes para siempre se llamasen Incas sin alguna distinción ni diferencia unos a otros."
7. From the original: "todos son descendientes por línea masculina, que de la femenina (como atrás queda dicho) no hicieron caso los Incas si no eran hijos de los españoles conquistadores y ganadores de la tierra (porque a estos también les llamaron Incas, creyendo que eran descendientes de su dios el sol)."
8. Cf. Sabine MacCormack, "It was surely by no unintended irony that the invaders of the Andes appear in Inca Garcilaso's history of Inca and Spanish Peru as descendants or semblances of an Inca ruler's phantasm, as 'sons of the imagined god Viracocha'" (MacCormack 1991: 363–64).
9. José Antonio Mazzotti was first to suggest the possibility of dual historical schemas in the *Royal Commentaries*. See Mazzotti (1996a: 175–202; 2008: 141–69).
10. In his philosophical excavation of the "Andean ghost" Viracocha, Francisco A. Ortega arrives at a similar conclusion from a different analytical perspective, maintaining that the Viracocha "ghost complex" at once appears in the *Royal Commentaries* as "the result of an unknown loss" and "the repository of historicity,

the remainder of historical possibilities—that is to say, tacitly the locus for renewal and reconstitution" (Ortega 2016: 245).

11. Inasmuch as Inca Garcilaso credits Blas Valera with providing both the Quechua poem relating Pachacámac and Viracocha (Part 1, Book II, Chapter XXVII, vol. 1, 132–33) as well as first-hand testimony from Cajamarca regarding Atahualpa's capture and execution (Part 2, Book I, Chapter XVIII, vol. 1, 56), it may be the case that Inca Garcilaso's knowledge of the various Andean identifications between Pachacámac and Viracocha derived from this source.
12. From the original: "Pero si a mí, que soy indio cristiano católico por la infinita misericordia, me preguntasen ahora: 'Cómo se llama Dios en tu lengua?,' diría 'Pachacámac.' Porque en aquel lenguaje general del Perú no hay otro nombre para nombrar Dios sino este."
13. The war with the Chancas and their subsequent defeat mark one of the seminal moments in Inca history. Before this victory the Incas were one of many ethnopolitical groups in the Cuzco valley vying among one another for supremacy. According to modern research, the eighth ruler, Viracocha Inca, was the first to permanently settle the regions around Cuzco that had been subdued by the Incas, yet their acquisitions encompassed a relatively small geographical radius of approximately 50 miles from the city. Although shrouded in indigenous myth, the defeat of the Chancas opened the way for the veritable blitzkrieg of Inca expansion that lasted approximately one century (ca. 1438–1532) and which began under the ninth dynast, Pachacútec Inca Yupanqui. From Pachacútec Inca Yupanqui's reign onward, the Incas extended their territorial lands around Cuzco into an enormous empire that stretched from modern-day Ecuador to Chile and beyond. John H. Rowe was the first contemporary scholar to argue for the explosive and short-lived character of Inca dominance in two articles written in the 1940s, and his findings have since become fundamental to anthropological, ethnohistorical, and archaeological investigations in the Andes region. See Rowe 1946: 200–09) and Murra (1986). For more on the Chanca war, see Rostworowski (1999: 22–36).
14. Both Betanzos and Sarmiento de Gamboa mention Cusi Yupanqui's vision of Viracocha; Cieza de León does not.
15. Zamora claims that "strictly aesthetic considerations" before an audience of "Christian Europeans" were the determining factors for Inca Garcilaso in this instance (Zamora 1988: 126).
16. The common denominator of both studies, however, is Neoplatonism. Zamora stresses Inca Garcilaso's "Neoplatonic theory of language" (Zamora 1988: 84) and MacCormack emphasizes his use of "Platonist theology" (MacCormack 1991: 352).

    Inca Garcilaso's familiarity with Las Casas's views most likely stems from his reading of Augustinian Friar Jerónimo Román y Zamora's *Repúblicas de las Indias Occidentales* ("Republics of the West Indies," 1595). Román's account of the Incas is copied directly from Las Casas's *Apologética historia sumaria* (1560), whose other publications—the *Apologética historia* had *not* been published under Las Casas's own order—had been collected and banned in Peru by Viceroy Francisco de Toledo. See Adorno (1992).

17. Citing Rostworowski, MacCormack mentions the same point without developing it further (MacCormack 1991: 353n20).

18. The English translation of Rostworowski's comments is taken from Duviols (1998: 57). Elsewhere Rostworowski has argued that these same motives caused Inca Garcilaso to intentionally alter the identities of the Inca mummy bundles (*mallquis*) shown to him by Polo de Ondegardo in Cuzco (Part 1, Book V, Chapter XXIX), despite having read the works of Cieza de León and Acosta in which the mallquis are properly identified (Rostworowski 1999: 32–34). Furthermore, Mazzotti has demonstrated that Inca Garcilaso's description of the fortress of Sacsahuaman on a hilltop just north of Cuzco (Part 1, Book VII, Chapter XXVIII) misconstrues the zigzag configuration of the outer walls by superimposing the symbol of Túpac Inca Yupanqui's *panaca*, the rainbow (*cuychi*), over the symbol of Inca Pachacútec's panaca, the lightning bolt (*illapa*), the latter of which the walls were actually constructed to invoke (Mazzotti 1996b: 197–211). Mazzotti has additionally suggested that Inca Garcilaso's insertion of a historically nonexistent tenth Inca, named Inca Yupanqui, between the reigns of Pachacútec Inca and Túpac Inca Yupanqui follows the same partisan logic. Pachacútec Inca, the ninth ruler, was the father of Túpac Inca Yupanqui, the tenth ruler, and Inca Garcilaso's addition of a cipher named Inca Yupanqui between the two allows him to further distance his own panaca from that of Pachacútec Inca to the diminution of the latter (Mazzotti 1996b: 200n7).

19. Luis Millones likewise contends the knowledge that allows Inca Garcilaso to defend his own version of Inca history and religion over and above its disagreements with other sources "pertained to the Cuzcan nobility in which he takes pride of being a member, including his self-baptism as 'Inca'" (Millones 2010: 169 quote, 173–174; my translation).

20. For the myths of Huarochirí, see *Hijos de Pariya Qaqa* (1983: vol. 2, 173–185); Guaman Poma de Ayala (1980: vol. 1, 236, f. 265); Cieza de León (1985: Chapter 72); and Santillán (1968: Chapter 28).

21. Numerous modern scholars have demonstrated not only a partial identification between Pachacámac and Viracocha in Andean religions, but also that the two deities were seen as regional variants of the same manifold godhead with their

own specific and respective functions. Pachacámac was the principal deity of the Central and Southern coastal regions and Viracocha held sway in the sierras. See Demarest (1981: 52–54) and Rostworowski (1983: 30–31 and 42–49).

22. Inca Garcilaso, however, places the conquest of the Pachacámac valley and the Yunga Indians within the reign of Pachacútec Inca (Part 1, Book VI, Chapter XXX–XXXI).
23. It is quite possible that Inca Garcilaso did, in fact, have access to numerous, regional versions of indigenous history from which he complied his own. In the chapter entitled, "Author's Declaration about this History" (Part 1, Book I, Chapter XIX), he informs us that once he had decided to compose a history of the Incas, he wrote to his classmates from Cuzco requesting that they send him the accounts recorded in the *quipus* of each province. There is no reason to think this is a blatant falsehood, although the letters have never been recovered.
24. For example, while maintaining that Inca Garcilaso's account of the phantasm Viracocha incorporates a "combination of Andean and Spanish perspectives" that "presents a transatlantic vision of Hispanic cultures, where different languages, cultures, and beliefs coexist in their diversity," Raúl Marrero Fente intriguingly suggests that the account "belongs to the complex oral tradition of Cuzco," and that "the spectral condition of the narration is an integral part of the Andean historiographical tradition," which especially highlights "the names of protagonists excluded from Inca history," such as Inca Yupanqui (Fente 2010: 209–10).
25. See Appendix.
26. From the original: "mediante sus grandes trabajos e increíbles hazañas, les quitaron las infernales tinieblas en que morían y les dieron la luz envangélica en que hoy viven!"
27. In his last will and testament, Manco Cápac very curiously "encommended to the prince-heir and all his other sons the love and benefit of the vassals" (*encomendado al príncipe heredero y a los demás sus hijos el amor y beneficio de los vasallos*). Moreover, Manco Cápac "ordered that everything he had encommended to them they should encommend to their sons and descendants from generation to generation" (*Mandoles que todo lo que le dejaba encomendado lo encomendasen ellos a sus hijos y descendientes de generación en generación*) (Part 1, Book I, Chapter XXV, vol. 1, 60). As such, Inca Garcilaso implies that the transfer of Inca rule was based on an indigenous encomienda system granted in perpetuity in which the Incas were entitled to the labor-tribute, but not the land, of their "vassals." As Silvio Zavala has shown, the Spanish encomienda was, in fact, a grant of labor, in this case Indian, and not land, which was later changed to payment in goods in 1549 (Zavala 1943: 80–92). In discussing Inca Garcilaso's portrayal of Inca tribute, which

comes directly from Blas Valera and is found in Book V, Chapter XV of the First Part, Franklin Pease has demonstrated its congruence with Andean notions of reciprocity, which were based on the exchange of productive energies and not land rights (Pease 1984: 41–52). It can therefore be seen that Inca Garcilaso tried to create a correspondence between the traditional practices of Inca rule and tribute with the original form of the Spanish encomienda system. Due to the similarity between the practices of the Incas and the encomenderos, this resemblance once again suggests, according to Inca Garcilaso, that indigenous Andeans could have quite easily accepted the Spanish conquerors and settlers as potential successors to the Inca dynasty, because their rule was implicitly based on indigenous customs. See also Francisco Falcón's early criticism of the viceregal administration in Peru (1567), which apparently served as a source for Blas Valera's work and therefore Inca Garcilaso's, in which Falcón called for lower rates of tribute by indigenous Andeans to their encomenderos and more of an emphasis on agricultural labor to serve the common good (rather than work in the mines), as had been the case under the Incas (Mazzotti 2011: 193–95). For a more critical estimation of Inca Garcilaso's support of the encomienda system in Peru, see Stein (2005).

28. The indigenous association of Spaniards and Viracocha may be the result of panaca rivalries and political manipulation of Inca history. For as the Licentiate of Cuzco, Juan Polo de Ondegardo, reported in 1561, only Inca elites from Cuzco called Spaniards "Viracochas." In contrast, Atahualpa's supporters, who had ties in Cuzco linking them to Quito, called the Spaniards "Zungazapa, which means bearded" (my translation). It should be kept in mind, therefore, that the partial deification of Spaniards was by no means espoused by all, and perhaps no more than a select group, of indigenous Andeans (Polo de Ondegardo 1940: 129–96, quote on 154).

29. José de Acosta claims that in addition to worshipping Viracocha, the Sun, Moon, and stars, the Incas worshipped a thunder-god under the three names of *Chuquilla*, *Catuilla*, and *Inti Illapa* (Acosta 1921: 303–04). Acosta's intent, however, was to demonstrate the polytheistic nature of Inca idolatry in order to illustrate the misguided and deplorable state of Inca culture. It was precisely this view that Inca Garcilaso challenged in the First Part; hence he denied Acosta's claim that the Incas had worshipped thunder, illapa, and suggested instead that lightning, thunder, and the thunderbolt were respected as divine agents, but not as deities.

30. Pease also points out that the imposition of a justification of this nature, attempting to convince indigenous peoples that their conquerors had supernatural powers and were therefore invincible, represents another form of violence exercised in the conquest (Pease 1995: 151).

31. Inca Garcilaso rationalizes this "fable" by explaining that Manco Cápac had

invented it in order to convince the Indians of the divine authority of his civilizing mission and thereby persuade them to accept him (Part 1, Book I, Chapter XXV, vol. 1, 61). In this way, the "fable" of Inca solar descent bears a strong resemblance to the "noble lie" in Plato's *Republic*, whose function would have been readily understandable to his European readers. Keith David Howard provides an analysis of Manco Cápac's "lie" in the context of reason of state politics, albeit without linking it to Plato (Howard 2012).

It is also worth noting Juan M. Ossio's insight, that Inca Garcilaso "homologizes the role of the primordial pair [Manco Cápac and Mama Ocllo Huaco] a little with Viracocha," regarding how the latter's founding and civilizing mission is portrayed in other sources (Ossio 2010: 71; my translation). If true, the ensuing displacement and various transformations of Viracocha in the *Royal Commentaries* may be signaled or foregrounded for Andean readers very early in the text.

32. From the original: "Sobrino, yo soy hijo del sol y hermano del Inca Manco Cápac y de la Coya Mama Ocllo Huaco."
33. It should be noted that Hilton was the first to make this argument, which Duviols developed and extended.
34. From the original: "esperemos más en la rectitud de los que tenemos por dioses, que no en nuestras diligencias, que si son verdaderos hijos del Sol, como lo creemos, harán como Incas."
35. From the original: "hasta que la avaricia, luxuria, crueldad y aspereza con que muchos dellos les trataban, los desengañaron de su falsa creencia, por do les quitaron el nombre Inca."
36. According to Diego González Holguín's *Vocabulario de la lengua general del todo Perú* (Vocabulary of the General Language of All Peru, 1608), the suffix "cuna" conferred plurality (González Holguín 1952: 54).
37. From the original: "Mas el Demonio, enemigo del género humano, procuraba en contra, con todas sus fuerzas y mañas, estorbar la conversión de aquellos indios; y aunque no pudo estorbarlo del todo, a lo menos la estorbó muchos años, con el ayuda y buena diligencia de sus ministros, los siete pecados mortales, que, en tiempo de tanta libertad y ocasiones, podía cada cual de los vicios lo que quería."
38. Doña Angelina Yupanque was first betrothed to Atahualpa and then became Francisco Pizarro's concubine before finally marrying Betanzos. Additionally, she was a member of Inca Pachacútec's panaca, which included Atahualpa, and who were the fiercest rivals of Inca Garcilaso's own panaca, that of Túpac Inca Yupanqui. For this reason, among several others, it is often quite illuminating to compare Inca Garcilaso's views with those of Betanzos, for they are both firmly rooted in the oral traditions of the Inca elite in Cuzco, yet they represent the diametrically opposed

political views of ruling indigenous factions (Hamilton 1996: ix–xiv). Although Inca Garcilaso mentions Juan de Betanzos on a couple of occasions in the *Royal Commentaries* (Part 2, Book VIII, Chapters VIII–IX), there is no evidence that he had access to Betanzos's work, which was unpublished during his lifetime and only rediscovered and edited by Marco Jiménez de la Espada in the late nineteenth century (Buchanan 1996: xvi).

39. On the multiple identities, roles, and status of Viracocha in Andean religions, see Pease (1973); Demarest (1981); Urbano (1981); Rostworowski (1983); Szemiñski (1987, 1997); and Duviols (1993).

40. For those readers familiar with the primary indigenous sources that have shaped contemporary understanding of Andean religions, Joan de Santacruz Pachacuti Yamqui Salcamaygua's famous drawing of *Coricancha*, the Inca "House of the Sun" in Cuzco, immediately comes to mind. For English readers less familiar with Santacruz Pachacuti's work, chapter 3 of Regina Harrison's *Signs, Songs, and Memory in the Andes* (1989) offers an insightful analysis, included in which is not only Santacruz Pachacuti's diagram (67, figure 11; 69, figure 12), but also a succinct explanation of much of its symbolism (55–84). See also Harrison (1982: 65–99).

41. From the original: "en sus historias dan otro nombre a Dios, que es *Tici Huiracocha*, que yo no sé qué signifique. Ni ellos tampoco."

It may also be the case that Inca Garcilaso knew very well how variants of Tici Viracocha had been translated by other commentators but simply refused to repeat them. For instance, taking Blas Valera as the author of the *Relación de las costumbres antiguas de los naturales del Pirú* (1594), "Anonymous Account," Sabine Hyland has noted the claim in that work that early Peruvians honored Illa Tecce for creating "the world, heavens and earth, sun and moon," and that the compound name meant "'Light Eternal' (*Luz Eterna*)" and "referred to the same God as *El* in Hebrew, *Theos* in Greek and *Deus* in Latin." On its own Tecce meant "'the first thing without beginning' (*principium rerum sine principio*)," while the word Viracocha, "the immense god of Pirua," had been added in more recent times and meant the same as the Latin word *numen*, which is to say "the will and power of god," as quoted by Inca Garcilaso from Valera's manuscript (Part 1, Book V, Chapter XXI, vol. 1, 301; Hyland 2003: 157). Taken together, Hyland contends that Valera saw Illa Tecce Viracocha or Tecce Viracocha as "Christ himself" (Hyland 2003: 145 quote, 158), and this heretical view was the reason he was imprisoned by the Jesuits in their house in Lima (Hyland 2003: 183–94). It may be the case that the badly damaged manuscript of Valera's *Historia Occidentalis*, which Inca Garcilaso quotes so liberally in the *Royal Commentaries*, contained the same etymologies and theological claims as the "Anonymous Account," if Valera was indeed the author of both, and that Inca Garcilaso learned the meaning of Tecce Viracocha there. It is also possible that Inca Garcilaso did not simply receive Valera's manuscript from Jesuit Pedro Maldonado de Saavedra, but also learned from the latter the suppressed history of Valera's heretical views regarding indigenous religion as well as his fate, which Inca Garcilaso prudently avoided by feigning ignorance on the matter.

42. From the original: "Dícenlo no porque signifique esto el nombre Huiracocha sino por la deidad en que los indios tuvieron al fantasma, que después del sol le adoraron por dios y le dieron segundo lugar. Y en pos de él adoraron a sus Incas y reyes. Y no tuvieron más dioses."

43. According to Inca Garcilaso, the Quechua term *huauque* was the word for brother used only between males (Part 1, Book IV, Chapter XI, vol. 1, 222). It was also, however, the symbolic brother or double of each Inca, of which numerous examples can be found in Sarmiento de Gamboa's *History of the Incas* (Sarmiento de Gamboa 1999: 61).

44. The differences in time of occurrence and importance between *Cápac Raymi* and *Inti Raymi* are briefly described in Book 5, Chapter 28 of Acosta's *Natural and Moral History* (Acosta 1921: 372–76).

45. From the original: "vendrá aquella gente nueva cumplirá lo que nuestro padre el sol nos ha dicho y ganará nuestro imperio y serán señores de él . . . su ley será mejor que la nuestra y sus armas poderosas e invencibles, más que las vuestras."

46. From the original: "*Cápac* quiere decir 'rico,' no de bienes de fortuna sino de excelencia y grandeza de ánimo . . . Y así otras cosas semejantes que querían engrandecer con este apellido Cápac."

47. From the original: "Veis aquí la cara y figura y hábito de nuestro Dios Viracocha al propio, como nos dejó retratado, en la estatua y bulto de piedra, nuestro ancestro el Inca Viracocha, a quien se le apareció en esta figura."

48. For instance, Guaman Poma de Ayala describes five ages in Andean history: Uari Vira Cocha Runa, Uari Runa, Purun Runa, Auca Runa, and Yncap Runa (Guaman Poma de Ayala 1980: vol. 1, 41–61, fs. 49[49]–81[81]). For a more comprehensive study of this notion, see MacCormack (1988).

49. From the original: "En su tienpo deste dicho *Ynga* abía muy mucho mortansa de indios y hambre y sed y pestilencia y castigo de Dios, que no llouió ciete años; otros dizen que dies años. Y abía tenpestades, lo ms tienpo era todo llorar y enterrar defuntos. Y ací este dicho *Ynga* se llamó *Pachacuti Ynga*, grandícimos castigos de Dios en este rreyno y en el mundo." Rolena Adorno points out that, unlike Garcilaso, Guaman Poma does not classify the conquest itself as a *pachacuti*, but rather attributes the concept to the war between Huáscar and Atahualpa as well

as to the reign of Inca Pachacútec, indicating "that these events belonged to the old order, when periodic cataclysm had not yet been replaced by permanent chaos" (Adorno 1982b: 112).

50. From the original: "*pácham cútin:* quiere decir 'el mundo se trueca.' Y por la mayor parte lo dicen cuando las cosas grandes se truecan de bien en mal. Y raras veces lo dicen cuando se truecan de mal en bien, porque dicen que más cierto es trocarse de bien en mal que de mal en bien." It is worth noting that Chapter XXVIII of Book V of the First Part both encapsulates and models the term pachacuti that it defines and explains. After giving its significance and use in Quechua and the reasons why the name Pachacútec was given to Titu Manco Cápac rather than Inca Viracocha in the first half of the chapter, in the second half Inca Garcilaso pivots to explain Inca Viracocha's prediction regarding the end of the Inca dynasty and the arrival of the Spaniards that was kept as a royal secret until the time of Huayna Cápac, about which Inca Garcilaso declares, "We have put this before its place to account for the marvelous prediction that the Inca kings had many years before. It was fulfilled in the time of Huáscar and Atahualpa, who were great-great-great grandsons of Inca Viracocha" (*Hemos antepuesto de su lugar por dar cuenta de este maravilloso pronóstico, que tántos años antes lo tuvieron los reyes Incas. Cumpliose en los tiempos de Huáscar y Atahuallpa, que fueron chosnos del Inca Huiracocha*; 320). In very short order, Inca Garcilaso not only underscores the meaning and importance of pachacuti but also provides examples of crucial moments in his version of Inca history to which it will apply.

51. Guaman Poma de Ayala's reasons for holding such a view of Inca Pachacútec's reign reflect the same conflicts in Inca politics that Inca Garcilaso inherited, but at a lower level in the imperial hierarchy. Guaman Poma's father, Don Martín Guaman Mallqui de Ayala, was a *curaca* (local ethnic lord) in the region of Lucanas, and "second person," or double, to Túpac Inca Yupanqui. Further, Guaman Poma's mother, Doña Juana Curi Ocllo, was the "daughter" of Túpac Inca Yupanqui and "his sons" (Guaman Poma de Ayala 1980: 11, f. 15[15]). In other words, Martín Guaman Mallqui de Ayala's status as curaca stemmed from his relationship, either through marriage or coalition, with the panaca of Túpac Inca Yupanqui, and as such, the abhorrence of that panaca for Pachacútec Inca's panaca appears to have carried over. Add to this the point that Inca Pachacútec's reign initiated the major intensification of Inca expansion efforts, which in turn resulted in the loss of freedom for local lords, and it is easy to see why Guaman Poma held Inca Pachacútec's rule to be nothing short of disastrous.

52. Elena Romiti contends that the repetitive and formulaic aspects of the First Part of the *Royal Commentaries* may have to do with the numerical organization of

information in "historical quipus" (*quipus historiales*), which she argues Inca Garcilaso appears to be simulating in his work (Romiti 2009: 87).

53. From the original: "Y que los descendientes de aquel, *procediendo de bien en mejor*, cultivasen aquellas fieras y las convirtiesen en hombres" (my emphasis). Livermore's translation of the *Royal Commentaries of the Incas* has at this point, "The descendants of this leader should thus tame those savages and convert them into men," completely omitting the phrase "proceeding from good to better" (*procediendo de bien en mejor*), which marks the moment as a pachacuti (Garcilaso de la Vega 1966: vol. 1, 40).
54. From the original: "digo que tengo estos tiempos por felicíssimos, por habernos embiado en ellos el Dios Huiracocha tales huéspedes, y que los mismos tiempos nos prometen que el *estado de la república se trocará en mejor suerte, la cual mudanza y trueque certifican la tradición de nuestros mayores y las palabras del testamento de mi padre Huayna Cápac*" (my emphasis).
55. From the original: "aclamando a grandes voces, *llamándole Inca* y otros renombres que a sus Reyes naturales solían decir en sus triunfos" (my emphasis).
56. From the original: "El Inca alzó el brazo derecho con la mano abierta, y la puso en derecho del oído. Y de allí la bajó poco a poco, hasta ponerla sobre el muslo derecho. Con lo cual, sintiendo los indios que les mandaba callar, cessaron de su grita y vocería, y *quedaron con tanto silencio, que parecía no haber ánima nacida en toda aquella ciudad*" (my emphasis).
57. Also see Zamora (2010a: 125–26).
58. Antisuyu, Cuntisuyu, Chinchasuyu, and Collasuyu were the names of the four districts within Tahuantinsuyu, "the four corners of the world united," the Inca empire. The *suyus* represented not only a geographical relationship within Cuzco (Antisuyu was the Northeast district; Cuntisuyu, Southeast; Chinchasuyu, Southwest; and Collasuyu, Northwest), but also the symbolization of the outward expanse of Inca rule in each of these directions from the focal point in Cuzco. For Inca Garcilaso's account of the four *suyus*, see Part 1, Book II, Chapter XI, and for his explanation of how Cuzco "contained the description of the entire empire," see Part 1, Book VII, Chapter VIII–XI.
59. From the original: "En estos nuestros días el virrey Francisco de Toledo trocó, mudó y revocó muchas leyes y estatutos de los que este Inca estableció. Los indios, admirados de su poder absoluto, le llamaron 'segundo Pachacútec,' por decir que era reformador del primer reformador."
60. *Pachacuticuna* is based on Adorno's usage (1982b: 112), combining the nominative *pachacuti* with *cuna*, the particle or suffix for plurality (González Holguín 1952: 54).
61. There is no English equivalent for *behetrías*, so I have left it untranslated. In

Sebastián de Covarrubias's seventeenth-century dictionary, *behetrías* is given a specific first definition: towns in Old Castile, which from time immemorial had the custom of electing and removing leaders at whim. Covarrubias's entry, however, is quite extensive and in exploring the possible Arabic, Hebrew, and Spanish roots as well as the philological work of Inca Garcilaso's close friend, Ambrosio de Morales, the connotations of either leaderlessness or lords and kings with limited rights and privileges, a "popular" liberty to select and remove rulers, and the idea of a general mixing and confusion of peoples due to the lack of a duly constituted figurehead are all included. See Covarrubias (1943: 203–04). In general terms, therefore, *behetrías* refers to an ancient or primitive condition of the relationship between autochthonous and semi-autonomous villages or towns with varying degrees of popular sovereignty. The term, moreover, was frequently employed to describe the social organization of either provincial (meaning "rural" as opposed to "urban" in accordance with then-current European expectations) or primordial indigenous communities, as in Sarmiento de Gamboa's *History of the Incas*, Chapter VIII, "The Ancient *Behetrías* of These Kingdoms of Peru and Their Provinces" (Sarmiento de Gamboa 1999: 37–39). For additional historical examples and analysis of the term, see MacCormack (2007: 206–07) and Ossio (2010: 66–67).

62. From the original: "Ni tenían pueblos ni adoraban dioses ni tenían cosas de hombres. Vivían como bestias, derramados por los campos, sierras y valles, matándose unos a otros sin saber por qué. No reconocían señor y así no tuvieron nombre sus provincias."

63. Against this view, Ossio maintains: "I fear that in this intent Garcilaso forgets the connection of the term 'Pachachuti' with a cyclical notion of time, very much intrinsic to Andean culture but also very far from the markedly linear, European conception that he utilizes" (*Yo temo que en este intento Garcilaso olvida el vínculo del término 'Pachacuti' con una concepción cíclica del tiempo, muy intrinseca a al cultura andina pero muy ajena a la concepción europea marcadamente lineal gue esgrime*) (Ossio 2010: 72). I argue that both temporal conceptions are equally operative in the *Royal Commentaries*.

64. It could be added here, according to the report of Pedro Pizarro, the younger cousin of Francisco, that there appears to have been a falling out between Atahualpa, and perhaps the rest of Inca Pachacútec's panaca, and Pachacámac. After his capture by the Spaniards, Pizarro relates, Atahualpa renounced Pachacámac as a "liar" (*mentiroso*) for having given him a false prognostication about his future, and he later sent soldiers to destroy the Temple of Pachacámac on the central coast (Pizarro 1978: 57; Millones 2010: 176–77). Although nothing of this is mentioned by Inca Garcilaso, if Atahualpa had behaved in this or a similar way toward

Pachacámac, it would have certainly contributed to the preference for Pachacámac evinced by Atahualpa's staunchest enemies, the members of Túpac Inca Yupanqui's panaca. See also Mazzotti (1996a: 213–14n22 and 2008: 174n27).

65. It will be remembered that Andean conceptions of space were fundamentally dual and divided the world into complementary and symmetrical halves. *Hanan* was the upper or major half and symbolically represented the sierras, and *hurin* was the lower or minor half and represented either the lowland valleys or the coast.

66. From the original: "Decían, al eclipse solar, que el sol estaba enojado por algún delito que habían hecho contra *él pues mostraba su cara turbada, como hombre airado.* Y pronosticaban, a semejanza de los astrólogos, que les había de venir algún grave castigo" (my emphasis).

67. From the original: "Al eclipse de la luna, viéndola ir ennegreciendo decían que enfermaba la luna y que si acababa de oscurecerse había de morir y caerse del cielo y cogerlos a todos debajo y matarlos y que se había de acabar el mundo."

68. From the original: "Cuando veían que la luna iba poco a poco volviendo a cobrar su luz decían que convalecía de su enfermedad porque el Pachacámac (que era el sustentador del universo) la había dado salud y mandádole que no muriese, para que no pereciese el mundo" (my emphasis).

69. Perhaps tellingly, in an earlier chapter in the First Part that recounts Cusi Yupanqui's peaceful conquest of the Yuncas and which is discussed below, we are told that one of the conditions to which the Yunga chief Cuismancu agreed was that "they would adore Pachacámac in their hearts without putting up any statue to him because, not having allowed himself to be seen, *they did not know what form he took*" (*que al Pachacámac le adorasen en el corazón y no le pusiesen estatua alguna porque, no habiendo dejado verse,* no sabían qué figura tenía) (Part 1, Book VI, Chapter XXXI, vol. 1, 396; my emphasis). In this sense, Inca Garcilaso portrays indigenous Andeans as not only waiting for Pachacámac to arrive, but also to reveal his precise manifestation—sustainer of the world universe or destroyer of it—which in turn feeds into the uncertainty indigenous actors experience upon the Spanish arrival.

70. From the original: "Tenían este nombre en tan gran veneración que *no le osaban tomarlo en la boca.* Y *cuando les era forzoso tomarlo* era haciendo afectos y muestras de mucho acatamiento" (my emphasis).

71. From the original: "habiéndolos recebido y adorado con suma veneración, dijo a sus capitanes y soldados: 'Éstos son hijos de Nuestro Dios Viracocha.'"

72. From the original: "o que vuestro Príncipe y todos vosotros sois tiranos que andáis destruyendo el mundo, quitando reinos ajenos, matando y robando a los que no os han hecho injuria ni os deben nada, *o que sois ministros del Dios, a quien nosotros llamamos Pachacámac, que os ha elegido para castigo y destrucción nuestra*" (my emphasis).

73. From the original: "Quizá, pues dicen que son mensajeros del Dios Pachacámac, le temerán . . . si son verdaderos hijos del Sol, como lo creemos, harán como Incas."

74. From the original: "Parésceme que visiblemente lo ha contradicho el Pachacámac . . . Todo lo cual, bien mirado, nos dice a la clara que no son obras de hombres, sino del Pachacámac."

75. From the original: "pero más eran sus fiestas para llorarlas que para gozarlas, según *la miseria de lo presente a la grandeza de lo pasado*" (my emphasis).

76. In his "Cinco memoriales" (ca. 1650), the Peruvian mestizo Jesuit and doctrina priest Juan de Cuevas Herrera includes nearly all of the signal elements of Inca Garcilaso's unique rendition of Inca history: identification of Pachacámac with the Christian god and Divine Will (*Divina voluntad*); the prophecy of Inca Viracocha, which he received from a nonhuman figure (*figura*) while banished by his father Inca Yáhuar Huácac in Chita and which told of white, bearded men who would arrive with the true religion; repetition and publicizing of the prophecy by Huayna Cápac; and use of the prophecy to explain the tyrant Atahualpa's lack of resistance to the Spaniards as well as Manco Inca's (Fusano: sic) failed rebellion in Cuzco. Cueva Herrera writes:

> The Inca Viracocha, to whom and for whose prophecy we attached the name, banished by his Father the Inca Yavarvacac [Yáhuar Huácac] to the Chita place [pasaje] near Cuzco, saw a thing, no human vision or corporal representation, but the figure of a white and blond man with a beard similar to ours: This figure spoke to him clearly that in forthcoming times a people who looked like the figure would come, bringing the true religion, better than the one they then professed, it was the will of Pachacámac, the Maker of the World, that this people subject the Indians, and that the Indians receive and obey them. This prediction, repeated between them from generation to generation, was repeated again by the oldest amongst them, Inca Guayna Cápac, saying that the time had arrived in which the men foretold by Inca Viracocha would come, and that upon arriving they should receive, obey, and serve them as Viracocha had ordered and he was ordering again: In conformity with this, the Inca Atagualpa, son of the same Guayna Cápac, although an intruder in the kingdom and tyrant in everything else, he received our fellows with the royal treatment [agasajo] and love, as is known, otherwise, as is believed, a heart so bellicose, so spirited, and ruined, surrounded by thousands of warriors, that he would humble himself like a lamb to a few strangers [forasteros], and that even though all were carrying steel, steel would have done little to such a multitude. Finally

Fusano Ynca[,] legitimate son of Guayna Cápaca, paternal and maternal brother of the aforementioned Guascar and heir of Guayna Cápac, leaving the fierce mountains of Vilcabamba with more than 200 D soldiers near the city of Cuzco, where only 150 Spaniards remained, that with obvious miracles Our Lord God sustained and freed Cuzco from that infinite multitude like the Gospel's seed: having seen which, the Inca came to believe that the prognostication of his ancestors Viracocha and Guayna Cápac was true, and he withdrew, saying that it was without doubt the will of Pachacámac that these kingdoms passed to the Spaniards and making a gentle argument to his people, he charged them to accommodate those decreed by heaven: he returned to his retreat where he was paid with death by the ingratitude and discourtesy of a Spaniard, whose life he had graciously and courteously saved. (El Inca Viracocha, de quien, y de cuya profesia senos [se nos] pegó el nombre, desterrado por su Padre el Inca Yavarvacac al pasaje de Chita, cerca del Cuzco, vió una cosa, no human vision o representacion corporal, una figura como de hombres de aspecto blanco, y rubio, la barba al modo dela nuestra; Esta figura le dijo claramente, que en tiempos venideros vendria una gente a ella parecida, que traheria la verdadera religion, mejor, que la que entonces se profesava, que era voluntad del Pachacámac, esto es del Hacedor del Mundo, sele [se les] sujetasen los Indios la recivieren, y obediciesen. Este vaticinio repetido entre ellos de generación en generación bolvió a repetir el mayor de los Yncas Guayna Cápac diciendo, que ya llegava el tiempo, en que havian de venir aquellos hombres pronunciados por el Ynca Viracocha, que en viniendo los recivieren, obediecesen, y sirvieresen, como lo havía mandado, y el lo bolvía amandar [a mandar]: En conformidad desto el Ynca Atagualpa, hixo del mismo Guayna cápac aunque intruso en el reyno, y tirano en lo demás, recivió a los nuestros con el agasajo y amor, quesesave [que se sabe], que porlo demás como es creible, que un corazón, tan belicoso, tan animoso, y arruinado [?] cercado de tantos millones de gente de guerra, se humillase como un cordero a unos pocos forasteros, que aunque todos fueran de acero, hexa [hecha] acero mui poco para tanta muchedumbre. Finalmente Fuanso Ynca hijo legítimo de Guayna cápac hermano de padre, y madre del desdicha Guascar y heredero de Guayna capac, saliendo de las brabas montañas de Vilcapampa con mas de 200 D combatientes cerca la ciudad del Cusco, donde solo quedaron 150 Españoles, que con evidentes milagros sustentó Dios nuestro Señor, y libró de aquella infinita multitud, como semilla del Evangelio: visto lo cual acavo de creer el Ynca, que era verdadero el pronostico de sus ancianos

> Viracocha y Guayna cápac, retírose diciendo que sin duda era voluntad del Pachacámac que estos reynos pasavan a los Españoles y hacinedo un tierno razonamiento a los suyos les encargó se acomodasen a los decretado por el cielo: bolviase a su retiro donde le dió la muerta la ingratitude y descortesia de un Español, a quien el graciosa y cortesmente le havia dado la vida.) (Cuevas Herrera 219–19v)

If Inca Garcilaso fashioned his account of Inca religion and dynastic history partially to reformulate or revise specific notions and concepts within an Andean frame of reference, then it appears that he succeeded to a very high degree with a mestizo reader like Cuevas Herrera.

77. From the original: "Los unos y los otros pelearon tan obstinadamente, que, aunque el sol era ya puesto y la noche cerrada, no dejaban de pelear, sin conocerse los unos a otros de por el apellido, que los unos decían 'Chili!' y los otros 'Pachacámac!,' en lugar de Pizarros y Almagros, que también alcanzaron estos renombres aquellos vandos."
78. From the original: "los Incas reyes del Perú, con la lumbre natural que Dios les dio alcanzaron que había un Hacedor de todas las cosas, al cual llamaron Pachacámac. . . . Esta doctrina salió primero de los Incas y se derramó por todos sus reinos, antes y después de conquistados."
79. From the original: "El general Cápac Yupanqui le envió a decir que tuviese por bien que *no peleasen hasta que hubiesen hablado más largo acerca de sus dioses* porque le hacía saber que los Incas, además de adorar al sol, adoraban también al Pachacámac . . . pues los unos y los otros adoraban a un mismo dios, no era razón que riñesen ni tuviesen guerra sino que fuesen amigos y hermanos" (my emphasis).

CHAPTER 4: *AUCA*

1. For the *requerimiento*, see Hanke (1938: 25–34) and Seed (1995: 69–99).
2. The debate between Spanish jurists and theologians over the justifications of conquest and the rational capacities and moral nature of the inhabitants of the New World continued to grow in intensity throughout the 1540s, reaching a climax in the famous yet indecisive debate at Valladolid in 1550 between Las Casas and the Spanish humanist Juan Ginés de Sepúlveda. For these developments, see Hanke (1974) and Pagden (2012).
3. Although Sarmiento de Gamboa's text bears the date 1572, it remained unpublished and unknown until being rediscovered in the early twentieth century. See Markham (1999: ix–xi).

4. The phrase is from Bermúdez-Gallegos (1992: 607–28).
5. Citing González Holguín's Spanish–Quechua dictionary (1608), Sabine MacCormack points out that *auca* also meant "warrior" in Quechua and that "the negative dimension of 'tyrant' did not readily translate" into the language (MacCormack 2007: 268n81). Although this is certainly true, Inca Garcilaso is nevertheless at pains in the *Royal Commentaries* to clarify and underscore the latter sense of the term for potential Andean readers in his portrayal of Atahualpa.
6. See, for instance, Sarmiento de Gamboa's account of the blocked succession of Inca Urco in Chapter XXV (1999: 85). For a fuller account of the portrayals Atahualpa's tyranny in colonial Peruvian historiography, see Pease (1995: 15–39).
7. For Ribadeneira's comparison of the king and tyrant, see (1952: Book II, Chapter IX, 532–33). For Mariana's see (1961: vol. 1, Book I, Chapter V, 91–100), also Braun (2007: 80–90) for Mariana on tyrannicide.
8. For the Jesuits and tyrannicide, see Lewy (1960: 66–78 and 133–51) and Höpfl (2004: 314–38).
9. As Richard Tuck and J.A. Fernández-Santamaría have respectively argued, this is by no means a fair characterization of Mariana's views. Strongly influenced by Tacitus, Mariana's work illustrates a more complex relation to reason of state doctrines than many commentators have allowed. See Tuck (1993: 79–80) and Fernández-Santamaría (1983: 96–101). For a thorough reexamination of Mariana's political thought, see Braun (2007).
10. For instance, see Sarmiento de Gamboa (1999: Chapter LXX, 190–94). The chapter title alone, however, says it all, "It is noteworthy how these Incas were tyrants against themselves, besides being so against the natives of the land."
11. For an interesting analysis of this moment in early Peruvian history, see Seed (1991).
12. From the original: "Pues si este Carlos es Príncipe y señor de todo el mundo, ¿qué necesidad tenía de que el Papa le hiciera nueva concessión y donación para hacerme guerra y usurpar estos reinos? Y si la tenía, luego el Papa es mayor señor que no él, y más poderoso, Príncipe de todo el mundo?"
13. From the original: "Pero si dices que a éstos no debo nada, menos debo a Carlos, que nunca fué señor destas regiones ni las ha visto."
14. From the original: "mis vassallos y yo nos ofrecemos a la muerte y a todo lo que de nosotros quisiéredes hacer, no por temor que tengamos de vuestras armas y amenazas, sino por cumplir lo que mi padre Huayna Cápac dejó mandado a la hora de su muerta."
15. From the original: "Castigo es del cielo muy ordinario contra los que fían más de sus astucias y tiranías que en la razón y justicia. Y assí permite Dios que caigan en ellas mismas y en otras peores, como luego veremos."

16. It should be noted, however, that Pizarro did in fact forward the "reason of state" justification for his execution of Atahualpa in a writ to Charles V during November 1535. Indeed, Pizarro's writ is almost verbatim with the arguments Inca Garcilaso gives to Atahualpa's prosecutors: "And as pertains to the death of Atabáliba . . . we deem it a higher disservice if the Spaniards all died and His Majesty lost the land." See Varón Gabai (1997: 60).
17. From the original: "'Vos mandastis matarlo; yo lo averiguaré, y castigaré como meresce vuestro delito,' es cierto que no lo matara."
18. Carlos Araníbar has identified this figure as Francisco Ninancoro Atahualpa, who died in Cuzco circa 1558 (Araníbar 1991: 670).
19. From the original: "Inca, ¿cómo nos hemos de holgar de la muerte de don Francisco, siendo tan pariente nuestro?"
20. From the original: "¿Tú has de ser pariente de un *auca*, hijo de otro *auca* (que es 'tirano traidor')?"
21. From the original: "Que si él fuera Inca no sólo no hiciera las crueldades y abominaciones que hizo, mas no las imaginara."
22. From the original: "Por tanto, no digas que es nuestro pariente el que fue tan en contra de todos nuestros pasados. Mira que a ellos y nosotros y a ti mismo te haces mucha afrenta en llamarnos parientes de un tirano cruel, que de reyes hizo siervos a esos pocos que escapamos de su crueldad."
23. From the original: "el nombre *auca*, tan significativo de tiranías, crueldades y maldades, digno apellido y blasón de los que lo pretenden."
24. From the original: "el bravo Rey Atahuallpa, tan contento y ufano de pensar que con sus crueldades y tiranías iva asegurando su Imperio."
25. Tellingly, Inca Garcilaso never uses the word "Inca" to refer to Atahualpa when speaking from his own perspective or that of his panaca. Rather, he only uses the Spanish words for "king," *rey*, or "prince," *príncipe*.
26. From the original: "Por lo cual dieron en decir que matassen al Inca, para que huviessen su parte de lo que de allí adelante se ganasse. A esta demanda y a su buena razón añadieron otras tan flacas y más. Pero con ser tales, fueron bastantes para que matassen un tan gran Príncipe como era Atahuallpa, el cual estaba con gran temor de su muerte, viendo el descontento y desabrimiento que los españoles traían unos con otros, y las muchas porfías que a gritos y voces, por horas y momentos, entre ellos había."
27. From the original: "o que vuestro Príncipe y todos vosotros sois tiranos que andáis destruyendo el mundo, quitando reinos ajenos, matando and robando a los que no os han hecho injuria ni os deben nada, o que sois ministros del Dios, a quien nosotros llamamos Pachacámac, que os ha elegido para castigo y destrucción nuestra."

28. From the original: "Urdióse la muerta de Atahuallpa por donde menos pensaban, ca Felipillo, lengua, se enamoró y amigó de una de sus mujeres, para casar con ella, si él moría. Dixo a Pizarro, y a otros, que Atabáliba juntava de secreto gente para matar los cristianos y librarse. Como esto se comenzó a sonruir entre los españoles, comenzaron ellos a creerlo; y unos dezían que lo matassen, para la seguridad de sus vidas y aquellos reinos; y otros, que lo embiassen al Emperador y no matassen tan gran Príncipe, aunque culpa tuviesse."
29. A similar proposal was made by Jesuit missionary José de Acosta in his *De procuranda indorum salute* (On procuring the Salvation of the Indians, 1588) (Acosta 1987: vol. XXIV, Book IV, Chapter IV, 37).
30. From the original: "los indios de un vando y otro, muertos los Incas, quedaron como ovejas sin pastor, sin tener quién los governasse en paz ni en guerra, ni en beneficio propio ni en daño ajeno. Antes quedaron enmistados los de Huáscar con los de Atahuallpa; y por prevalecer los unos contra los otros, procuró cada uno de los vandos servir y agradar a los españoles, por hazerlos de su parte contra la contraria."
31. From the original: "La guerra de los Reyes hermanos, Huáscar y Atahuallpa, fué la total destruición de aquel Imperio, que facilitó la entrada de los españoles en la tierra, para que la ganassen con la facilidad que la ganaron."
32. It will be remembered that the structure of the formula of foundation, beginning with the myth of Inca origins (Part 1, Book I, Chapter XV) is Subject + Adverbial Phrase (beginning with a gerund) + Verb Phrase. See Chapter 2, n96; and Mazzotti (1996a: 125ff. and 2008: 99–106).
33. From the original: "Mas Dios Nuestro Señor, habiendo misericordia de aquella gentilidad, permitió la discordia de los dos hermanos, para que los predicadores de su Evangelio y Fe Católica entrassen con más facilidad y menos resistencia."
34. The depth and pervasiveness of indigenous factions among the diverse ethnic groups under Inca rule are captured in Inca Garcilaso's anecdote about Don Francisco Cañari's antagonistic behavior during a Corpus Christi celebration in Cuzco, in which he recalled his killing of an Inca warrior in the service of the Spaniards during the conquest (Part 2, Book VIII, Chapter I).
35. Sarmiento de Gamboa had it that Titu Atauchi was a son of Huayna Cápac and one of Huáscar's generals who had been killed by Atahualpa (Sarmiento de Gamboa 1999: 160 and 189). If true, this seems like the sort of information Inca Garcilaso would have known from his relatives, and it may be the case that he was altering the record. However that stands, more important is that Inca Garcilaso portrays Titu Atauchi as both an Inca and a partisan of Atahualpa in order to affect a possible reconciliation between the two panacas.

36. From the original: "'A este *auca* manda el Pachacámac que ahorquen, y a todos los que mataron nuestro Inca.'"

A point of clarification is necessary. In this chapter (Part 2, Book II, Chapter VI), the Indians who are in charge of the proceedings are supposed to be taken as supporters of Atahualpa. As such, when reference is made to him, the possessive pronouns "their" (*su*) or "our" (*nuestro*) are used, as in "their king" (*su rey*) or, in a direct quotation "our Inca" (*nuestro Inca*). This much is to be expected given that Titu Atauchi and Quizquiz are avenging the death of "their king." These possessive pronouns, however, are by no means intended to be generalizable either to Huáscar's partisans, including Inca Garcilaso, or the entire empire for all of the reasons given above. I call attention to this because in Livermore's English translation of the *General History of Peru* this specificity is lost. For example, in the first four sentences of the chapter, Inca Garcilaso has, in order, "su Rey Atahuallpa," "su Rey," "su Inca," "su Rey," and "su Inca," which should be translated as "their King Atahuallpa," "their King," and "their Inca." Livermore, on the other hand, has "King Atahualpa," "Atahualpa," "the Inca," "the king," and "the Inca." In using definite articles, if any, Livermore makes it appear to English readers that Atahualpa, quite literally, was *the* Inca, although that is not what Inca Garcilaso wanted to convey. See Garcilaso de la Vega (1966: vol. 2, 743–44).

37. Hemming, for instance, points out that Cuéllar, Chaves, and Haro had not even arrived in Peru when Atahualpa's "trial" was conducted (Hemming 1970: 83 and 559n). In this Hemming followed the work of Raúl Porras Barrenechea, who argued that "the slightest engagement with the documents of the conquest will demonstrate the novelesque and legendary character of these episodes" (Porras Barrenechea 1986: 709; my translation). This version of events, however, appears to have originated with Blas Valera, the Peruvian mestizo Jesuit and one of Inca Garcilaso's favorite sources. In addition to his Latin history of Peru, the only remaining evidence of which is to be found in the many passages translated by Inca Garcilaso in the *Royal Commentaries*, Valera is credited by many scholars of Peruvian history as being the "anonymous Jesuit" who authored *Relación de las costumbres antiguas de los naturales del Pirú* (An Account of the Ancient Customs of the Natives of Peru, 1590[?]), known more commonly as *Relación anónima* (Anonymous Account). Curiously enough, there is a footnote in the *Relación anónima* to a section entitled, "That there were no sacrifices of men and children amongst Peruvians," in which we find the following: "Francisco de Chaves, from Jerez, who was a great friend of Titu Atauchi, brother of Atahualpa." (*Relación de las costumbres antiguas* 1992: 53n20). If Valera was in fact the author of the *Relación anónima* as well as the history Inca Garcilaso so frequently consulted, then

there is reason to suspect that the capitulations in the *Royal Commentaries* are an elaboration of statements that may have appeared in both of Valera's texts. However that may be, Henrique Urbano has argued that the version alluded to in the *Relación anónima* bares "all the signs of an oral tradition," similar in many respects to the sixteenth-century Quechua tragedy, "The Death of Atahualpa." Urbano further states that it fits "perfectly within the early preoccupations, indigenous and Spanish, of reviving the memory and constructing from this base a proper consciousness of the Andean past" (Urbano 1992: 33, 35 respectively; my translation). We should not conclude from this that Inca Garcilaso had access to the *Relación anónima*, nor does this in any way prove Valera's authorship of that document (for the controversy on this last issue, see Urbano 1992: 7–38 and Hyland 2003: 82–87). Rather, there is some ground for believing that Inca Garcilaso was repeating and authorizing a conciliatory version of Atahualpa's execution that resonated with both Spanish and indigenous oral histories in Peru.

38. Inca Garcilaso completely omits reference to Túpac Huallpa, who was appointed Inca by Pizarro after Atahualpa's execution and who died shortly thereafter (Hemming 1970: 86–99). Furthermore, he downplays the claims to the throne of the other surviving son of Huayna Cápac, Paullu Inca. About Paullu's chances for the crown, Inca Garcilaso says he was given the scarlet fringe by Quizquiz, but he rejected it, for Paullu "thought little of it because he had no right to the kingdom, since Manco Inca was the legitimate heir" (*él hizo poco caso della, porque no tenía derecho al reino, que Manco Inca era el legítimo heredor*) (Part 2, Book I, Chapter XXXIX, vol. 1, 104). For more on the rivalry between Paullu and Manco Inca for the dynastic title, see Regalado de Hurtado (1993: 106–15).

39. Höpfl underscores the same point in his discussion of tyrannicide in Jesuit political thought (2004: 314–38), as does Braun in his study of Mariana (2007: 80–90).

40. Pizarro's coronation of Manco Inca took place in December 1533 (Hemming 1970: 126–27 and 501).

41. From the original: "acordaron, con buen consejo militar, restituir el Imperio a quien legítimamente le pertenecía, por que todos los indios fuessen a unas para resistir y echar del reino a los españoles, o para vivir juntamente con ellos, porque assí serían más estimados y más temidos que no estando divididos en vandos y parcialidades."

42. The same doctrines constrained Guaman Poma's representation of the conquest, which he depicts as a "nonconquest" (*no ubo conquista*) of Spanish arrival in Peru amidst peaceful, welcoming, and cooperative Andeans. See Guaman Poma (1980: vol. 2, 341–403) and Adorno (1982b: 123–30; 1986: 13–35).

43. From the original: "el Demonio, enemigo del género humano . . . con el ayuda y buena diligencia de sus ministros, los siete pecados mortales."

CHAPTER 5: "DIE A KING"

1. "R. Provision de Las Leyes Nuevas," in Konetzke (1953: vol.1, 216–20).
2. On Christopher and Diego Columbus see Haring (1975: 8–22), on Cortés see Liss (1975: 26–30), and on Pizarro see Varón Gabai (1997: 70–89).
3. The letter of Gonzalo Pizarro's appointment can be found in *Documents from Early Peru* (1936: 181–87).
4. From the original: "era hombre de bastante entendimiento, no caviloso ni engañador ni de promesas falsas ni de palabras dobladas, sino senzillo, hombre de verdad, de bondad y nobleza, confiado de sus amigos, que le destruyeron."
5. From the original: "Fué Gonzalo Pizarro gentilhombre de cuerpo, de muy buen rostro, de próspera salud, gran sufridor de trabajos, como por la historia se havrá visto. Lindo hombre de a caballo, de ambas sillas; diestro arcabuzero y ballestero, con un arco de bodoques pintava lo que quería en la pared. Fué la mejor lanza que ha pasado al Nuevo Mundo, según conclusión de todos los que hablaban de los hombres famosos que a él han ido."
6. Gonzalo's purported lack of cognitive prowess may be true or exaggerated, but it is a description that appears to have stuck, see Lockhart (1972: 175–89). Of the three colonial historians mentioned above, Zárate's work is often charitable toward Gonzalo, but it highlights his lack of intelligence and is quite far from the endorsement found in the *Royal Commentaries*. See Zárate (1991: Book 5, Chapter 1 to Book 7, Chapter 8, 185–375).
7. From the original: "Pero la obligación del que escribe los sucesos de sus tiempos, para dar cuenta dellos a todo el mundo, me obliga, y aun fuerza, si así puede decir, a que sin pasión ni afición diga la verdad de lo que pasó."
8. For an opposing view, see González Echevarría (1990: 43–92). As part of his broader argument concerning the importance of *artis notoriae*, or notarial rhetoric, in the historical development of the Latin American novel, González Echevarría suggests that the Second Part of the *Royal Commentaries* is best understood as a legal petition in the form of a *relación*, or relation (70). More precisely, he argues "the book is actually a relación, a letter of appeal to the Council of Indies to have Sebastián's name cleared and Garcilaso's petitions granted" (73), and he adduces the foregoing statement as the "compelling and concrete reason to view the entire book as in many ways determined by the *artis notariae*" (72). For insightful critiques of González Echevarría's views relative to legal writing and colonial historiography, see Durand (1988b: 209–27) and Adorno (1995).
9. As Silvio Zavala points out, the Spanish conquest of the New World was carried out by private individuals who contracted with the crown. As recompense for their services, the conquistadors expected to become lords of Indian vassals in the terri-

tories they subdued. There was, thus, an immediate and enduring conflict between the encomienda system used to achieve these purposes and monarchical interests. For, as a grant of Indian labor and tributary rights, encomiendas effectively removed a large portion of the indigenous populations from direct monarchical control and limited the amount of tribute the crown could exact from the territories. These logistical loggerheads, however, signaled a deeper ideological divide. The conquerors were operating from the medieval and semi-feudal perspective of achieving aristocratic or hidalgo status through military service, which had been dominant through the Spanish reconquest of the Iberian peninsula from the Muslims (711–1492). At least since Ferdinand and Isabella, however, the Spanish monarchs had consciously attempted to erode the power of the aristocracy in favor of a more powerful monarchy and centralized state. The viceregal system in the New World was therefore an extension of royal supremacy and state-centralization over the competing idea of the New World as a locus for the erection of new feudal estates (Zavala 1943: 69–92).

10. The early myths have it that Viracocha departs at Pachacámac, yet through Inca manipulation to express the expanse and greatness of their empire, many later versions place Viracocha's departure at the northwestern most point of Puerto Viejo, Ecuador. See Demarest (1981: 43–49). For at least one version of this myth collected in Cuzco, see Sarmiento de Gamboa (1999: 32–37). For a collection of additional versions as well as an excellent analysis, see Urbano (1981).

11. From the original: "illapas, que, como está dicho, en lengua de indios significa relámpagos, truenos y rayos, que tales fueron aquellos arcabuzes para el nobilísimo y hermoso ejército del general Diego Centeno . . . casi todos perecieron en aquella desdicha y cruel batalla."

12. From the original: "aclamando a voces grandes, llamándole Inca y otros renombres que a sus Reyes naturales solían decir en sus triunfos."

Regardless of his actual itinerary, Inca Garcilaso only traces Gonzalo's movements from the all-important battle of Huarina (Lake Titicaca, Bolivia) through Pucara and his triumphant entrance in Cuzco (Part 2, Book V, Chapters XIX–XX). All three of these sites have mythological importance. Lake Titicaca marks the beginning of the god Viracocha's journeys and, as Inca Garcilaso notices, it is also the first Incas' place of origin (Part 1, Book I, Chapter XV). Cuzco was not only the capital of the empire, but also the center or navel of the world-universe as far as the Incas were concerned (Part 1, Book II, Chapter XI). In Pucara, which is the geographical mid-point on the northwestern diagonal between Titicaca and Cuzco, there was a shrine to Viracocha commemorating his exemplary punishment of unruly tribes, which he turned into stone (Sarmiento de Gamboa 1999: 29–30).

13. From the original: "procuró Gonzalo Pizarro hazer leyes y ordenanzas para el buen gobierno de la tierra, para la quietud y beneficio de indios y españoles, y aumento de la religión cristiana."
14. It should be pointed out that while strictly speaking Inca Garcilaso does indeed mention Carvajal's "long letter" (*carta larga*) to Gonzalo Pizarro, he does not claim to report its contents. Rather, Inca Garcilaso prefaces Carvajal's advice with, "but when [Carvajal] met with Gonzalo Pizarro in Rímac (although we put this passage ahead of its place) *he said* to him," which is followed by a direct quotation of Carvajal's words (*Mas cuando se vió con Gonzalo Pizarro en Rímac* [*aunque adelantamos este paso de su lugar*] *le dijo*) (Part 2, Book IV, Chapter XL, vol. 2, 133). This may seem a trivial point, but it is just as well to note that Inca Garcilaso is reporting Carvajal's speech, clearly of his own creation, and not the letter mentioned by previous historians.
15. The peace treaty between Titu Atauchi, Francisco de Chaves, and Hernando de Haro (Part 2, Book II, Chapter VI) discussed in chapter 4 of this work is another important example.
16. From the original: "Señor, muerto un Virrey en batalla campal, y cortada su cabeza y puesta en la picota, y que la batalla fué contra el estandarte de Su Majestad . . . no hay para qué esperar perdón del Rey ni otro concierto alguno, aunque Vuesa Señoría dé sus disculpas bastantíssimas, y quede más inocente que un niño de teta, ni hay para qué fiar de promesas ni de palabras, por certificadas que vengan, sino que Vuessa Señoría se alce y se llame Rey, y la gobernación y el mando que espera de mano ajena se lo tome de la suya, y ponga corona sobre su cabeza, y reparta lo que hay vaco en la tierra por sus amigos y valedores; y lo que el Rey les da temporal por dos vidas, se lo dé Vuessa Señoría en mayorazgo perpetuo, con título de duques, marqueses y condes, como los hay en todos los reinos del mundo, que, por sustentar y defender ellos sus estados, defenderán el de Vuessa Señoría.

    "Levante órdenes militares con nombre y apellido de los de España o de otros santos, sus devotos, con las insignias que por bien tuviere; y para los caballeros de los tales hábitos señale rentas y pinsiones de que puedan comer y gozar por sus días, como lo hazen en todas partes los caballeros militares. Con este que he dicho en suma, atraerá Vuesa Señoría a su servicio toda la caballería y nobleza de los españoles que en este Imperio están, y pagará por entero a los que lo ganaron y sirvieron a Vuessa Señoría, que ahora no lo están. Y para atraer a los indios a su servicio y devoción, para que mueran por Vuessa Señoría con el amor que a sus Reyes Incas tenían, tome Vuessa Señoría por mujer y esposa la infanta que entre ellos se hallare más propincua al árbol real, y embie sus embajadores a las montañas donde está el Inca heredero deste Imperio, pidiéndole salga a restituirse en su majestad y grandeza, y que de su mano dé a Vuessa Señoría por mujer la hija o hermana que tuviere, que bien sabe Vuessa Señoría cuánto estimará aquel príncipe su parentesco y amistad, y, demás de ganar el amor universal de todos los indios con la restitución de su Inca, ganará Vuessa Señoría que harán muy de veras lo que su Rey les mandare en vuestro servicio . . . en fin, serán todos los indios de vuestro vando, que, no ayudando ellos a los contrarios de Vuessa Señoría con bastimentos ni con llevar las cargas, no pueden prevalecer ni ser parte en esta tierra; y el príncipe se contentará con el nombre de Rey, y que sus vassallos le obedezcan como antes, y gobiernen en la paz a sus indios como hicieron sus passados, Vuessa Señoría y sus ministros y capitanes gobernarán a los españoles, y administrarán lo que tocare de la guerra, pidiendo al Inca que mande a los indios hagan y cumplan lo que Vuessa Señoría ordenare y mandare. . . .

"Demás desto, terná Vuessa Señoría del Inca, no solamente todo el oro y plata que los indios sacaren en este Imperio, pues ellos no lo tenían por riqueza ni tesoro, sino también todo el tesoro que tienen escondido (como es notorio) de los Reyes, sus antecesores, que todo se lo dará y entregará a Vuessa Señoría, así por el parentesco como por verse restituído en su majestad y grandeza; y con tanto oro y plata como la fama dice, podrá Vuessa Señoría comprar a todo el mundo, si quisiere ser señor dél; y no repare Vuessa Señoría en que le digan que hace tiranía al Rey de España; que no se la hace, porque, como el refrán dice, no hay Rey traidor. Esta tierra era de los Incas, señores naturales della, y, no habiendo de restituírsela a ellos, más derecho tiene Vuessa Señoría a ella que el Rey de Castilla, porque la ganó por su persona, a su costa y riesgo, juntamente con sus hermanos; y ahora, en restituírsela al Inca, haze lo que debe en ley natural, y en quererla gobernar y mandar por sí, como ganador della, y no como súbdito y vassallo de otro, también hace lo que debe a su reputación, que, quien puede ser Rey por el valor de su brazo, no es razón que sea siervo por flaqueza de ánimo: todo está en dar el primer paso y la primera voz . . . y por conclusión digo que como quiera que el hecho salga, Vuessa Señoría se corone y se llame Rey, que, a quien lo ha ganado por sus brazos y valor, no le está bien otro nombre, y muera Vuessa Señoría Rey; y muchas veces vuelvo a dezir que muera Rey y no súbdito, que quien consiente estarse mal, meresce estar peor."

17. From the original: "fueron los que hicieron la guerra a Gonzalo Pizarro y dieron aquel Imperio a licenciado la Gasca."
18. From the original: "se haya entendido por Su Majestad y por los demás de España, no por género de rebelión ni infidelidad contra su Rey, sino por defensa de su justicia derecha, que debaxo de tal suplicación que para su Príncipe se havía interpuesto tenían."
19. From the original: "para persuadir a Gonzalo Pizarro que se rindiese y sometiese a su Príncipe, contra quien no podía tener fuerzas para resistirle."

20. From the original: "muy buenas bulas son éstas; paréceme que no es razón que Vuessa Señoría las dexe de tomar, y todos nosotros hagamos lo mismo, porque traen grandes indulgencias."
21. From the original: "Señor, que son muy buenas y muy baratas, pues nos ofrecen rebocación de las ordenanzas y perdón de todo lo passado, y que *en el porvenir se tome orden y parecer de los regimientos de las ciudades*, para ordenar lo que al servicio de Dios y al bien de la tierra y beneficio de los pobladores y vecinos della convenga, que es todo hemos desseado y podemos dessear, porque con la rebocación de las ordenanzas nos assiguran nuestros indios, que es lo que nos hizo tomar las armas y ponernos en contingencia de perder las vidas, y con el perdón de lo passado las asiguran, y *con el orden que se ha de tener de aquí adelante, en que gobierne lo que convenga, con el parecer y consejo de los regimientos de las ciudades, nos hacen señores de la tierra, pues la hemos de gobernar nosotros.* Por todo esto, soy de parecer que se tomen las bulas y que se elijan nuevos embaxadores que vayan al Presidente con la respuesta, y lo traigan en hombros a esta ciudad y le enladrillen los caminos por do viniere con barras de plata y tejos de oro, y se le haga todo el mayor regalo que fuere possible, en agradacimiento de que nos truxo tan buen despacho, y para obligarle a que adelante nos trate como a amigos y nos descubra si trae otra mayor facultad y poder para dar a Vuessa Señoría la gobernación deste Imperio, que yo no dudo que lo traiga, que, pues del primer lance nos embida lo que nos ha embidado, señal es que le queda más resto que rebidarnos. Tráigale como he dicho, que, si no nos estuviere bien su venida, después podremos hazer dél lo que quisiéremos" (my emphasis).
22. For a thorough examination of the role of the *cortes* in Spanish political life and the *comunero* revolt, see Espinosa (2008: 35–82).
23. From the original: "assí en México como en el Perú había costumbre entonces, y hasta el año de quinientos y sesenta que yo salí de allá, que aun no se havían perpetuado los oficios, y era que en cada pueblo de los españoles se elegían cuatro cavalleros de los más principales, de más crédito y confianza que se podían hallar, para oficiales de la hazienda real y para guardar el quinto del oro y plata que en toda la tierra se sacava. . . . Sin estos oficios, eligían cada año en cada pueblo de españoles dos alcaldes ordinarios, un corregidor y tiniente de corregidor, y seis o ocho o diez regidores, más o menos como era el pueblo, y con los demás oficios necessarios para el buen gobierno de la república."
24. From the original: "Pudieron hazer esto con buen título los de aquella ciudad, porque, a falta de gobernador nombrado por Su Majestad, podía el cabildo de Cuzco (como cabeza de aquel Imperio) nombrar ministros para la guerra y para la justicia, entre tanto que Su Majestad no los nombrava."

25. From the original: "Este escándolo y temor acrecentava el rigor de la condición del Visorrey, y no querer oír en particular suplicación de ciudad alguna sobre las ordenanzas, sino que se havía de llevar todo a hecho por todo rigor. Por lo cual les pareció a las cuatro ciudades, que son Huamanca, Arequipa, Chuquisaca y el Cuzco, en las cuales aún no estava recebido el Visorrey, que eligiendo ellas un procurador general que hablasse por todas cuatro y por todo el reino, porque eligiéndolo el Cuzco, que era cabeza de aquel Imperio, era visto elegirlo todo él, se remedaría el daño que temían."
26. For the argument that the comunero movement represents the first "modern revolution," see Maravall (1970: 87–92).
27. For the Scholastic concept of polity or *ciudad*, see Aristotle 1996: Book 1, Chapter 1, 1252a1–5, 11) and Aquinas (1988: I–II, Question 96, Article 1, 65–66). Throughout the sixteenth and early seventeenth centuries this was the central idea in the theories of natural rights and popular sovereignty developed by Dominican and Jesuit theologians in Spain, such as Francisco de Vitoria, Domingo de Soto, Melchior Cano, Luis de Molina, and Francisco Suárez, see Hamilton (1963); Noreña (1975); Fernández-Santamaría (1977); Skinner (1978: vol. 2, 135–73); and Tuck (1979; 1993: 137–46). For an analysis of how Jesuits in particular derived political authority from the notion of polity or commonwealth, see Höpfl (2004: 192–217).
28. For more on Charles V's political views, see Maravall (1999: 67–107).
29. José Antonio Maravall has argued that the defeat of the comuneros resulted in the end of resistance to the increasing power of the Caroline monarchy, which was rapidly moving in the direction of centralized, bureaucratic absolutism, and ultimately undercut or delayed the creation of a modern state apparatus in Spain (1970: 12–13, 244, 266–67). In his comprehensive revision of the comunero movement and its historiography, Aurelio Espinosa contends that "the steps the Castilian republics took to change the government Charles first installed in 1517 gradually transformed the Spanish empire of cities and towns into a constitutional monarchy accountable to the parliament . . . by rejecting the Burgundian regime (c. 1517–1522) and laying the foundations for the reconstruction of a meritocratic bureaucracy" (2008: 83). According to Espinosa, the comuneros paradoxically lost the civil war, but in fact won the battle for political reform that they had initiated.
30. Unless Inca Garcilaso had access to this text in manuscript form, perhaps through his Jesuit friends, it is unlikely that he knew it because it was not published until centuries later.
31. A more comprehensive account of Don Pedro Laso de la Vega's leading role in the comunero movement can be found in Seaver (1928).

32. Interestingly enough, despite his obvious bias in the king's favor, Mejía also praises Don Pedro throughout his account of the revolt and credits him with being one of his sources (Mejía 1945: 137).

33. Both authors note that Don Pedro was eventually pardoned in 1526. Don Pedro's exile in Portugal and, as Seaver points out, the active refusal of the Portuguese court to allow his extradition to Spain (1928: 354) shed a tantalizing new light on Inca Garcilaso's dedications to both *La Florida del Inca* and the First Part of the *Royal Commentaries* to members of the Braganza family in Portugal. Inca Garcilaso certainly knew of his distant cousin's participation in the comunero revolt from his Spanish relatives or possibly, though this is much less likely, through Pedro de Mejía's *Historia del Emperador*, cited above (n30). The dedication in *La Florida del Inca* is to the "Most excellent Lord Don Theodosio, Duke of Braganza," and that of the First Part of the *Royal Commentaries* is to the "Most Serene Princess Doña Catalina of Portugal, Duchess of Braganza." Both belong to the same family as King João I, the ruler of Portugal who protected Don Pedro during his four years of exile in the 1520s. If this is what Inca Garcilaso had in mind, his language almost gives it away. In *La Florida* the dedication begins "During my childhood, Most Serene Prince, I heard from *my father and his relatives* of the heroic virtues and great deeds of the kings and princes of glorious memory who were *the forebears of Your Excellency*," and closes "May Our Lord preserve Your Excellency for many happy years as a refuge and defense for the needy poor" (*Por haber en mis niñeces, Serenísimo Príncipe, oído a* mi padre y a sus deudos *las heroícas virtudes y las grandes hazañas de los reyes y príncipes de gloriosa memoria* progenitores de vuestra Excelencia . . . *Nuestro Señor guarde a Vuestra Excelencia muchas y felices años para refugio y amparo de pobres necesitados*; my emphasis) (*La Florida*, "Dedication"). Inca Garcilaso explicitly calls attention to a possible historical connection between "my father and his relatives," the Laso de la Vega lineage, and the Duke of Braganza's forebears of "glorious memory," and prays that the Braganza family will continue to act as a "refuge and defense for the needy poor," which is what King João I did for Don Pedro, some of whose property had been confiscated and given away by King Charles (Espinosa 2008: 93). Likewise, in the first sentence of the dedication to Doña Catalina in the First Part of the *Royal Commentaries*, Inca Garcilaso claims it is customary for authors to dedicate their works "to generous monarchs and powerful kings and princes so that with their defense and protection they [authors] may live more favored by the virtuous and freer from the calumnies of the malicious" (*a generosos monarcas y poderosos reyes y príncipes para que con el amparo y protección de ellos vivan más favorecidos y más libres de las calumnias de los maldicientes*). He continues by saying Doña Catalina's

generosity is known to all "since you are the daughter and descendant of the illustrious kings and princes of Portugal" and that he would say more of her virtues "if Your Highness did not abhor praises as much as you desire silence about them" (*pues es hija y descendiente de los esclarecidos reyes y príncipes de Portugal . . . si Vuestra Alteza no aborreciera tanto sus alabanzas como apetece el silencio de ellas*) (Part 1, "Dedication"). Again, the themes of defense, protection, and the generosity of the Braganza ancestors are explicit and, this time, the suggestion of desiring "silence" about the virtues of Doña Catalina and her family is added. In this light, I think the dedications can be read as both a memorial and an act of gratitude on Inca Garcilaso's part to the Braganza family for having saved the life of his comunero cousin as well as a clever snub to the Spanish monarchy. Moreover, it expresses the undercurrent of Inca Garcilaso's sympathy toward the Braganzas and his resentment for Philip II's annexation of Portugal in 1580, in which the Braganza family, somewhat like his own relatives in Peru, became subjects of an expanding Spanish crown.

34. Whether or not Inca Garcilaso cloaked and concealed his views in the Second Part of the *Royal Commentaries* due to fears of Inquisitorial censorship or the remote possibility of being prosecuted by the Holy Office remains an open question. The strongest argument against fear of the Inquisition playing a role is the fact that Inca Garcilaso's close friend, Jesuit Francisco de Castro, Professor of Rhetoric at Cordoba, personally approved the Second Part for publication. With such a reputable and sympathetic censor, it is quite arguable that Inca Garcilaso had nothing to fear at all on this count. Nevertheless, there is more than enough circumstantial evidence, some of which is provided above, as well as further textual and contextual evidence to suggest that Inca Garcilaso was indeed wary of associating the comuneros with Gonzalo Pizarro. Chief among these are the prior difficulties he experienced with the Inquisition in his translation of Hebreo's *Dialoghi d'Amore*, in which certain passages on the Cabbala had been expurgated (Part 2, "Prologue"), and in *La Florida del Inca*, in which passages on indigenous belief in the immortality of the soul had to be removed (Book II, Part I, Chapter VII). He did, then, have some personal history with and knowledge of the censorial practices of the Inquisition. Moreover, we should take into consideration that hardly any political thinkers in sixteenth- and early-seventeenth-century Spain were espousing republican theories of government akin to those forwarded by the comuneros, with a possible exception being the Portuguese Jesuit Jerónimo de Osorio (Maravall 1970: 197), whose works Inca Garcilaso appears to have known (Durand 1948: 244 and 247). To a man, the influential early humanists such as Erasmus, Vives, and Fox Morcillo, the School of Salamanca theorists, including the Dominicans

Vitoria, Soto, and Cano, and Jesuits Suárez and Molina, and the Jesuit humanists Inca Garcilaso is known to have read, such as Pedro de Ribadeneira and Juan de Mariana, were all monarchists. While it is true that the Dominican and Jesuit theologians were developing evermore refined theories of natural rights, popular sovereignty, and rights of resistance to despotic government (with Vitoria being the originator and Suárez the capstone of this tradition), it is also the case that the central concerns of such thinkers were the legitimate foundations of and possible limits to monarchical power (n27 above). Further, although Inca Garcilaso uses comunero arguments to defend Gonzalo's right to rebel, he too distances himself from the more republican and democratic elements of their platform. If we take into consideration all of these factors, it is not unreasonable to conclude that Inca Garcilaso agreed with the rights upon which comunero resistance was based without endorsing their political goals. Yet, given the negative connotations of the comuneros in his day, he could not explicitly state such a view without raising additional suspicions about his work, suspicions that could have easily led to a shaking of his family trees and personal associations in which known rebels would have fallen out on two continents. This is precisely the kind of official scrutiny that could have been very dangerous for a mestizo who, by virtue of his birth alone, already occupied a precarious and suspect status in the social world of his day.

35. In simplest terms, Gonzalo's rebellion was first and foremost about taking the government of Peru for himself, of which he thought he had been cheated, and defending the interests of certain Peruvian encomenderos against the Spanish crown. Compared to the comprehensive and well-considered ideas of the comuneros, the arguments offered by Gonzalo's supporters appear piece-meal, grasping, and opportunistic. Lohmann Villena makes a persuasive case that the ostensible justifications for the rebellion were dubious claims at best and he uses the apt phrase "*la justificación de lo injustificable*" (the justification of the unjustifiable) to describe these efforts (1977: 39). That Gonzalo's rebellion was not a comunero movement, in terms of the contents of its political thought, see also Pérez (1998: 680).

36. Rolena Adorno has argued that the citation of other authors was one of the ways to avoid Inquisitorial censorship in sixteenth century Spain and that this was the strategy used by Augustinian Friar Jerónimo Román y Zamora in his *Repúblicas del mundo* (Republics of the World, 1575), which includes copious passages from Las Casas's *Apologética historia sumaria* (1560). Las Casas's other works were banned in Mexico in 1553, Peru in 1572, and sequestered by royal order of Philip II in 1579, and for including it in his own work, Román suffered official censorship. See Adorno (1992: 812–27). Since Inca Garcilaso had read and refers to *Repúblicas*

de las Indias Occidentales (Republics of the West Indies), the shortened, censored edition of Román's earlier text published in 1595, in the *Royal Commentaries* (Part 1, Book I, Chapter XLI; Book V, Chapter II; Book V, Chapter XVIII), it is quite possible that he picked up this strategy from the Augustinian author.

37. From the original: "no faltaron letrados que fundavan y les hazían entender cómo en todo esto no había ningún desacato, y que lo podían hazer de derecho, y que una fuerza se puede y debe repeler con otra, y que el juez que procede de hecho puede ser resistido de hecho. Y desta manera se resolvieron en que Gonzalo Pizarro alzasse banderas y hiziesse gente, y muchos de los vezinos del Cuzco se le ofrecieron con sus personas y haziendas, y aun algunos hubo dezían que perderían la ánimas en esta demanda."

38. From the original: "otros, que podían defender por armas sus vassallos y previlegios, *como los hidalgos de Castilla sus libertades*, las cuales tenían por haber ayudado a los Reyes a ganar sus reinos de poder de moros, como ellos por haber ganado el Perú de manos de idólatras; dezían en fin todos que no caían en pena por suplicar de las ordenanzas, y muchos que ni aun las contradecir, *pues no les obligavan antes de consentirlas y recebirlas por leyes*" (my emphasis).

39. From the original: "los cuales embía aquella mi tierra a toda España y a todo el mundo viejo, mostrándose cruel madrastra de sus propios hijos y apasionada madre de los ajenos."

40. For Maravall's linguistic analysis of the meaning and importance of these terms in the comunero revolt, see (1970: 92–123 and 193–203).

41. It should be noted that when the *Junta General* (General Court) elected Juan Padilla its Captain General, the movement became more "radicalized." It turned from the idea of compromising with the crown, attacked the privileges of the high aristocracy, and became a movement increasingly dominated by lower members of the caste society. It was at this moment that Don Pedro Laso de la Vega abandoned it (Seaver 1928: 281–287).

42. From the original: "pues era notorio que lo que más se pretendía era que los indios fuesse cristianos, y que esto no podía haber efecto estando en poder de sus caciques. Especialmente que era muy claro que si algún indio se hazía cristiano y después bolvía a poder de su cacique, hazía que le sacrificassen al Demonio."

43. From the original: "mucha comunicación y amistad que tenía con soldados, y ninguna con los vecinos, que era bastante indicio para sospechar mal de su intención y ánimo."

44. For a discussion of these perspectives, see Choy (1985: 17–48, 49–74, 75–103) and Delgado Díaz del Olmo (1991: Chapter 6).

CHAPTER 6: JESUIT AMAUTAS

1. See chapter 2, n24.
2. For this approach to Inca Garcilaso, see the insightful work of Enrique Pupo-Walker (1982).
3. For a recent analysis of how both the Jesuits and Inca Garcilaso adopted some of the views of Las Casas and his supporters while distancing themselves from others, see Serna (2010). It should be noted, however, that had Inca Garcilaso known the specifics of Las Casas's position regarding Peru, he would not have agreed completely. In *Las doce dudas* (The Twelve Doubts, 1564), Las Casas argues that Phillip II should restore the Inca throne to its rightful heir, and he names "Tito," the leader of Inca resistance in Vilcabamba, Titu Cusi Yupanqui, as the principal beneficiary (Las Casas 1995: 333–52). In the *Royal Commentaries*, however, Titu Cusi Yupanqui is an insignificant figure who is never mentioned by Inca Garcilaso as having any claim whatsoever to the Inca throne. He writes of both the prior Inca, Sairi Túpac, and the succeeding Inca, Túpac Amaru, but not Titu Cusi Yupanqui, whose reign was situated between the two. Inca Garcilaso's omission appears to be explicable, as Luis Millones has pointed out, by the likelihood that among indigenous Andeans Titu Cusi was not seen as an "Inca," for he in fact lacked that title. It appears that Titu Cusi was a temporary regent for Túpac Amaru who was to serve until the latter reached the age of maturity and was able to assume the scarlet fringe himself (Millones 1985: 7–15). Whatever the case may have been, it is clear that Inca Garcilaso did not see Titu Cusi as a legitimate claimant to the Inca throne, thus marking his disagreement with Las Casas in this instance.
4. Curiously, Inca Garcilaso omits her name.
5. From the original: "A lo cual me dicen que no sirven poco nuestros *Comentarios* de la primera parte, por la relación sucesiva que ha dado de aquellos Reyes Incas."
6. Similarly, Guaman Poma exhorts indigenous Peruvians to *sepan hacer peticiones*—know how to make petitions (Alparrine-Bouyer 2002: 162).
7. On the curacas' petition of 1560, see Hemming (1970: 386–89), and for the Inca document, see Rowe (1985: 193–245).
8. The phrase is Pierre Duviols's (1977: 145–63).
9. Inca Garcilaso dates Chapter XXXVIII of Book IX in the First Part as 1602, and Chapter XL, in which the results of Don Melchor's petition are mentioned, bears the year 1603.
10. From the original: "Y habiéndolas oído el príncipe y entendídolas bien, tomó la sobremesa que tenía delante, que era de terciopelo y guarnecida con un flueco de seda, y, arrancando una hebra de flueco, con ella en la mano, dijo al Arzo-

bispo: 'Todo este paño y su guarnición era mío, y ahora me dan este pelito par mi sustento y de toda mi casa.'"

11. From the original: "no quiso presentar los papeles por no confesar que había tantos de aquella sangre real, por parecerle que, si lo hacía, le quitarían mucha parte de las mercedes que pretendía y esperaba recebir, y así no quiso hablar en favor de sus parientes."
12. For an opposing view, see Roberto González Echevarría in chapter 5, n8.
13. Thomas Abercrombie has argued that *Taki Onqoy* was an indigenous resistance movement that arose in part as a response to the efforts of Peruvian encomenderos to have their grants of land and labor extended in perpetuity (Abercrombie 2002).
14. For instance, see the *memorial* to Philip II written in 1588 by Spanish Jesuit priest Bartolomé Álvarez, *De las costumbres y conversión de los indios del Perú* ("On the Customs and Conversion of Peruvian Indians"). In it, Álvarez, who was stationed in the indigenous town of Pampa Aullagas in Bolivia, saw the problem of indigenous idolatry to be so thoroughly pernicious and intractable that he attempted to persuade the monarch to employ the Office of the Holy Inquisition in Peru, to better uncover and stamp it out (Álvarez 1998; Villarías Robles and del Carmen Martín Rubio 1998: XV–XVII; Alaperrine-Bouyer 2002: 154–56).
15. For Aristotle on natural slaves, see *The Politics*, Book I, Chapters 3–5, 1253b1–55a1 (Aristotle 1993: 4–7).
16. Las Casas's arguments on human sacrifice can be found in the tract he read before the Court at Valladolid during his confrontation with Sepúlveda, usually referred to simply as *Apología*. For an English edition, see Las Casas (1974: 221–43).
17. Las Casas's views on evangelization can be found in *Del único modo a atraer a todos los pueblos a la verdadera religión* (The Only Way of Attracting All Peoples to the True Religion) (Las Casas 1942). For an analysis of the differences between Las Casas's and Acosta's positions on the proper methods of preaching, see Abbott (1996: 60–78).
18. Although Kenneth Mills cautions that "coercive actions that were meant to advance the conversion of Andeans to Christianity had been present from the beginning of the evangelization of Peru," he also adds that the "process of finding out about Andean religion in order to eradicate it guided and inspired the labors of those in particular in the Peruvian Church who advocated that a measure of force was necessary to wrest the Indians from their error-filled ways" (1997: 20). Acosta often seems to side with this camp.
19. Renowned Acostan scholar Fermín del Pino-Díaz has argued that Acosta's views on Amerindian cultures, especially Inca and Mexica cultures, are more laudatory than they are often given credit for. According to del Pino-Díaz, a close reading

of Acosta, who had several passages about the abuses of conquistadors edited out of *De procuranda*, suggests that the Jesuit appears to have self-censored his work so that it would be able to pass the inquisitorial auditors, with whom he had worked in Peru, through the insertion of formulaic passages that emphasize the superstition, idolatry, or satanic inspiration of indigenous rituals and beliefs. With regard to the Devil's influence on native religions, del Pino-Díaz contends that the Jesuits viewed the Devil as a conquered or marginal figure and that his attempts to establish a counterfeit church in the New World had paradoxically paved the way for the spreading of the Christian faith in the vein of *praeparatio evangelica*. See del Pino-Díaz (2002a, 2008).

20. To this list Acosta adds the veneration of man-made images in *Natural and Moral History* (Acosta 1921: Book 5, Chapter 9, 317–23).
21. According to Mills, since the earliest days of proselytizing in Peru there were two rival methods of converting Indians, "a patient and gradualist tradition" and a more explicitly aggressive and coercive tack, and such a division could be seen within the Jesuits during the Third Council of Lima. He further suggests that Archbishop St. Toribio Alfonso de Mongrovejo and Acosta, his primary theologian and advisor, were proponents of the positive, gradualist approach, while Juan de Atienza, José de Arriaga, Juan Sebastián, and others preferred more severe and punitive measures (Mills 1997: 20–24). In this light, Acosta's "mixed" method of evangelization can be viewed as a compromise between opposing camps within the Jesuits, which may also help to account for the internal tensions within his published views.
22. From the original: "en aquella Primera Edad y antigua gentilidad unos indios había poco mejores de bestias mansas y otros mucho peores que fieras bravas . . . los tuvieron conforme a las demás simplicidades y torpezas que usaron." For an explanation of the term *gentilidad* and my translation as gentilism, see chapter 2, n47.
23. For example, Inca Garcilaso calls Acosta's account of the phantasm Viracocha "brief and confused" (*abreviada y confusamente*), although he attributes Acosta's error to the Indians from whom he heard it, due to their "difficulties of language" (*las dificultades del lenguaje*) and because "they have lost the memory of their historical traditions and say the substance of them confusedly, without maintaining order and time" (*Y porque tienen ya perdidos los memoriales de las tradiciones de sus historias dicen en confuso la sustancia de ellas, sin guardar orden ni tiempo*) (Part 1, Book V, Chapter XVIII, vol. 1, 293). Inca Garcilaso thereby deflects blame *away* from Acosta for his mistaken account of the phantasm of Viracocha while nevertheless criticizing it as mistaken due to the same nexus of problems for which Inca Garcilaso chastises other Spanish historians. For an opposing interpretation of this passage, see del Pino-Díaz (2010: 68–69).

24. It was precisely the providential role given to the Incas by Acosta in his work, according to del Pino Díaz, that inspired Inca Garcilaso and led to him laud the former as an "intellectual mentor" (*mentor intellectual*) in the *Royal Commentaries* (del Pino-Díaz 2010a: 67).
25. From the original: "Los españoles aplican otros muchos dioses a los Incas, por no saber dividir los tiempos y las idolatrías de aquella Primera Edad y las de la Segunda. Y también por no saber la propriedad del lenguaje para saber pedir y recibir la relación de los indios, de cuya ignorancia ha nacido dar a los Incas muchos dioses—o todos los que ellos quitaron a los indios que sujetaron a su imperio."
26. From the original: "De la cual pronunciación—y de todas demás que aquel lenguaje tiene—no hacen caso alguno los españoles por curiosos que sean (con importarles tánto el saberlas), porque no las tienen en la lenguaje español."
27. Acosta's discussion of Lactantius's view of the antipodes is but one of several examples.
28. From the original: "los cristianos españoles las abominan todas por cosas del demonio. Y los españoles tampoco advierten en pedir la noticia de ellas con llaneza, antes las confirman por cosas diabólicas como las imaginan."
29. In light of Inca Garcilaso's longstanding and numerous connections to the Jesuits in both Peru and Spain, Mercedes Serna claims that "the result was a political and educational text [the *Royal Commentaries*] that reflected and expounded the ideas of both parties" (Serna 2010: 351). As we have seen with Inca Garcilaso's treatment of Acosta above and will see again in his use of Valera below, not only are the views of both parties "reflected and expounded" in the *Royal Commentaries* but they are interwoven in such a way as to make it often very difficult to identify which party is saying what.
30. From the original: "En la cual idolatría—y en que antes de ellos hubo—son mucho de estimar aquellos indios, así los de la Segunda Edad como los de la Primera. Que en tanta diversidad y tanta burlería de dioses como tuvieron no adoraron deleites ni los vicios como los de la antigua gentilidad del mundo viejo—que adoraban a los que ellos confesaban por adúlteros, homicidas, borrachos (y sobre todo el Priapo), con ser gente que presumía tanto de sus letras y saber y esta otra tan ajena de toda buena enseñanza."
31. From the original: "en la filosofía moral se extremaron, así en la enseñanza de ella como en usar las leyes y costumbres que guardaron . . . en el ejercicio de esta ciencia se desvelaron tanto que ningún encarecimiento llega a ponerla en su punto."
32. From the original: "estos Incas del Perú deben ser preferidos no sólo a los chinos y japones y a los indios orientales, mas también a los gentiles naturales de Asia y de Grecia."
33. Cápac Cocha, the Inca practice of human sacrifice, occurred during the festival

of Cápac Raymi and included the interment of sacrificial victims, which appear to have been children. The practice is described at length in the work of Cristóbal de Molina the Cuzqueño, *Relación de las fábulas i ritos de los ingas* (Account of the Fables and Rights of the Incas, 1573) (Molina 1989: 120–28), and it is also mentioned by Guaman Poma de Ayala in his description of Cápac Raymi (Guaman Poma 1980: vol. 1, f. 259[261], 233). The Inca practice of burying their sacrificial victims alive was different from the Mexica practice, which included the removal of vital organs, and in this sense, there is some truth to Inca Garcilaso's denial of the claim that in Cuzco "they sacrificed human blood" (*sacrificaban sangre humana*). Nevertheless, against the claim that "Incas sacrificed men and children," he unequivocally states, "it is certain they did not do so" (*Hace dicho todo esto por ir contra la opinión de los que dicen que los Incas sacrificaban hombres y niños. Que, cierto, no hicieron tal*) (Part 1, Book II, Chapter X, vol. 1, 94).

34. From the original: "Mas un caso tan inhumano no se debía decir si no es sabiéndolo muy sabido."
35. From the original: "dijo que le dejase decir todo lo que sabía en aquel caso, porque diciendo una parte y callando otra entendía que mentía y que no había dicho entera verdad como la había prometido."
36. For an illuminating analysis of this chapter in the *Royal Commentaries* against the context of racial theories of the sixteenth century, see Zamora (2010b; 2016).
37. For Acosta's involvement in this dispute, see Hyland (1994: 266–93).
38. Hyland notes the "degree of ambivalence" within Acosta's activities surrounding mestizo ordination, but claims that he was a "relatively moderate figure, balancing such radicals as Valera against individuals—such as [Juan de] Atienza and [Juan] Sebastián—who were hostile to mestizos and in favor of aggressive actions to eradicate idolatry" (2003: 181–82). Read in tandem with del Pino-Díaz's numerous reevaluations of Acosta's tolerance for non-Christians (Acosta himself being of *converso* [Jewish convert to Catholicism or a descendant of one] stock), his proindigenous stance vis-à-vis the Incas, and his closeness in perspective to Inca Garcilaso, the two make a compelling case for Acosta as one who not only actively supported but also consistently worked in his administrative capacities for the betterment of Peruvian Indians, mestizos, and criollos alike. See del Pino-Díaz (2002b, 2008, 2010b, 2011). Nevertheless, there remains a pronounced ambivalence regarding indigenous culture within Acosta's *published* texts that cannot lightly be set aside, and it is these moments of apparent tension or inconsistency that Inca Garcilaso exploits for his own ends.
39. Both Mills (1997: 20–24) and Hyland (2003: 178–82) argue that Mogrovejo's policy decision was based on Acosta's council and intervention.

40. From the original: "Diego de Alcobaza, el cual en muchas provincias de aquel reino ha sido vicario y predicador de los indios. Que sus prelados lo han mudado de unas partes a otras porque, como mestizo natural del Cuzco, sabe mejor la lengua de los indios que otros no naturales de la tierra. Y hace más fruto."
41. Acosta continued to praise and support Valera before, during, and after the latter was imprisoned by the Jesuits in Lima and even wrote on his behalf to have him removed to Spain. For Valera's imprisonment, see Hyland (2003: 183–192) and for his complicated relationship with Acosta see (169–83).
42. Christian Fernández argues that Inca Garcilaso in some sense needed to "create" the unpublished Blas Valera as an "author" in order to establish the authority of his own work (Fernández 2011).
43. From the original: "han trabajado mucho los padres de la santa Compañía de Jesús . . . para saberla bien hablar. Y con su buen ejemplo (que es lo que más importa) han aprovechado mucho en la doctrina de los indios."
44. From the original: "Los que ahora son deben dar muchas gracias a Dios porque les envió la Compañía de Jesús, con la cual hay tanta abundancia de todas ciencias y de toda buena enseñanza."
45. From the original: "Porque es así que aquella gente a ninguna cosa atiende tanto como a mirar si lo que hacen los maestros conforma con lo que dicen y hallando conformidad en la vida y en la doctrina no han menester argumentos para convencerlos a lo que quisieren hacer de ellos."
46. The mentions are in the First Part, Book V, Chapter X; Book VI, Chapter IV; and Book VII, Chapter X. In the Second Part see Book I, Chapter XXXII; Book II, Chapters VII and XXIV; and Book V, Chapter IX.
47. Sarmiento de Gamboa, who was an expert on the *huauquis*, brothers or doubles, likewise states that the *huauqui* or symbolic brother adopted by Viracocha Inca was *amaru* (Sarmiento de Gamboa 1999: 86).
48. It appears that Inca Garcilaso may have been directing indigenous and mestizo descendants of the Incas in Cuzco to the Jesuit *Colegio de la Transfiguración* (College of the Transfiguration) housed in Amarucancha. Inaugurated and designed by Jesuit Provincial Jerónimo Ruiz de Portillo in 1578, the college was constructed on land that formerly belonged to Hernando Pizarro, at one time housed Alonso de Barzana and Blas Valera, was run by Father Antonio de Vega at the turn of the seventeenth century, and offered classes to students in "Latin and humane letters," including mestizo and Indian students, in a space formerly occupied by Inca *amautas* (Carrión 2010: 163–64). In his history of the college in 1600, Vega dedicates an entire chapter to describing the piety and good works of the indigenous confraternity *Nombre de Jesús* (Name of Jesus) that operated out of the Jesuit

church and college, and he singles out Barzana and Valera as two of the Jesuits who were instrumental in helping the confraternity to thrive and grow (Vargas-Ugarte 1948: 42–46). Vega goes on explicitly to thank the "Indians of Cuzco" (*los indios de Cuzco*) for the college's success, putting them in the second rank of benefactors right after the Jesuit hierarchy and Philip II, stating, "because nothing of importance has been done in this College, in which they do not take the principal part" (*pues ninguna cosa se ha hecho de importancia en este Colegio, en que no tengan en ellas la principal parte*; my translation) (Vargas-Ugarte 1948: 71). As such, there is reason to think that Inca Garcilaso is in fact underscoring a practice at the turn of the seventeenth century that was already fairly well established among the Inca elite in Cuzco.

49. One also wonders whether Inca Garcilaso's frequent and extended quotations of Valera might not possibly feed into this association, or perhaps be in reference to a more recent oral tradition of the Inca elite in Cuzco, which the historian learned from his relatives. For instance, Valera was at the Jesuit college in Cuzco in 1576, residing in Amarucancha, where he taught Latin and both confessed and preached to Indians. According to Sabine Hyland, he also "was the spiritual advisor of the Nombre de Jesús confraternity, whose membership included many important Inca nobles. Every Wednesday and Friday, the confraternity met for 'spiritual discussions' and communal prayer, led by the young mestizo Jesuit . . . it appears that Valera's 'spiritual discussions' with certain of the native elites were wide-ranging yet focused on the similarities between the ancient Andean faith and the Christian religion" (Hyland 2003: 54). Hyland has surmised that at least three of the members of the Nombre de Jesús confraternity were Don Luis Inca, "a Cuzco nobleman who wrote two works in Quechua about native religion," Francisco Yutu Inca, and Juan Huallpa Inca, who had been the wardrobe supervisor for Huayna Cápac, "a position of considerable importance" (54–55). Interestingly, the historical record shows Valera possessing all of the attributes Inca Garcilaso ascribes to Jesuit *amautas* and Incas by privilege, opening the door for speculation as to whether Inca Garcilaso was revising/reimagining Inca history on this score or elaborating on a newer development within it. As a final note on how profound an impression Valera made on the Inca elite in Cuzco, when the Jesuits decided to move Valera and Alonzo de Barzana, the Spanish Jesuit who begged Viceroy Toledo to spare Túpac Amaru's life, to Potosí, "the 'Indians of Cuzco' passed one day and one night crying outside the Jesuit college and then marched through the streets, shouting and crying to voice their distress at Valera's impending transfer." This was reported to General Mercurian in a letter written on February 15, 1577 by none other than José de Acosta, who in turn had

already delayed Valera's transfer, to the "great consolation and gratitude" of the Indians (55).

50. A famous portrait of their marriage was prominently displayed at the entrance to the Jesuit church in Cuzco toward the end of the seventeenth century (Dean 1999: 112; 2002: 176–79).

51. Inca Garcilaso was not alone in this. Guaman Poma holds the Jesuits out for special approbation as well, praising them for their humility and Christian charity, the extent to which they call everyone "brothers" and "sisters" (hermanos, hermanas) regardless of whether they are Spanish or Indian, but also for their role as "holy reverend prelates and preachers and lettered college men, teachers of arts and Latins, and preachers, linguists of the Inca language, Quechua, Aymara, Chinchaysuyo of this kingdom" (*santos rrebrendos perlados y predicadores y letrados coligiales, maystros de artes y latines y predicadores, lenguarases de la lengu ynga, quichiua, aymara, chinchaysuyo deste reyno*) (Guaman Poma de Ayala 1980: vol. 2, 490, f. 479[483]). Moreover, that the entrance of the indigenous and mestizo elite in Jesuit colleges became a trend in early seventeenth-century Peru that extended well beyond Inca Garcilaso's or Guaman Poma's exhortations is underscored by John Charles's study of indigenous *letrados*, aptly titled "Trained by Jesuits" (Charles 2010b).

52. From the original: "parte de aquella población usó la religión para mejorar su condición y situarse en la nueva sociedad colonial. Esta clase mejor posicionada para aprovecharse de las nuevas condiciones sociales era la elite política y social indígena, principalmente los incas, porque ya tenían más movilidad dentro de su propia sociedad y también porque recibieron de parte de los mismos conquistadores un tratamiento privilegiado."

53. From the original: "un privilegio que equivalía al reconocimiento de su nobleza. Era la única vía de una hipotética integración en la sociedad peruana que les era hostil pero les necesitaba."

54. In addition to the Incas and mestizos who enrolled at the College of the Transfiguration mentioned above (n49), "the alliance of the royal Inkas and the Jesuits was a union from which both profited and one," according to Carolyn Dean, "that was inculcated at the Colegio de San Borja [in Cuzco]," where "noble Inka youth—future *caciques*—not only learned Christian doctrine, Castilian, math, music, and other 'essential' categories of Western knowledge, they also learned the importance of their own nobility. While certainly aiming to acculturate native elite males who would be future leaders of their communities, the Jesuits also, simultaneously, encouraged the expression of a noble alterity" (Dean 1999: 112–13; Rowe 1976: 13–17).

55. Christian Fernández rightly notes that Inca Garcilaso's citations of Valera often make it difficult to distinguish who is actually speaking and verge in many instances on a species of ventriloquism (Fernández 2011: 102). This chapter (Part 1, Book V, Chapter XXIX) is also the one in which Inca Garcilaso recalls seeing the mallquis (mummy bundles) of Inca Viracocha, Túpac Inca Yupanqui, Huayna Cápac, Coya Mama Runtu, and Coya Mama Ocllo in Polo de Ondegardo's chamber before leaving for Spain in 1560 and touching Huayna Cápac with his finger. In his perceptive analysis, Paul Firbas highlights Inca Garcilaso's description of the expert preservation of the embalmed corpses, so well maintained and lifelike that "they the lacked nothing, except speech" (*no les faltaba nada, sino hablar*) (Part 1, Book V, Chapter XXIX, vol. 1, 322; Firbas 2009: 52). By ending this moving personal remembrance with a passage from Blas Valera, which in turn ends with a quote from Inca Viracocha, perhaps Inca Garcilaso is recalling his earlier simulation of Inca oral traditions—as seen in his quotation of his uncle Cusi Huallpa on Inca origins—and extending it to Inca Viracocha, Valera, and himself, thereby imbuing the figures of the Inca past, once again, with the ability to speak.
56. From the original: "Los padres muchas veces son causa de que los hijos se pierdan o corrompan con las malas costumbres que les dejan tomar en la niñez. Porque algunos los crían con sobra de regalos y demasiada blandura. Y como encantados con la hermosura y ternura de los niños los dejan ir a toda su voluntad sin cuidar de lo que adelante, cuando sean hombres, les ha de suceder. Otros hay que los crían con demasiada aspereza y castigo, que también los destruyen. Porque con el demasiado regalo se debilitan y apocan las fuerzas del cuerpo y del ánimo y con el mucho castigo desmayan y desfallecen los ingenios, de tal manera que pierden la esperanza de aprender y aborrecen la doctrina. Y los que lo teme todo no pueden esforzarse a hacer cose digna de hombres. El orden que se debe guardar es que los críen en un medio, de manera que salgan fuertes y animosos para la guerra y sabios y discretos para la paz. Con este dicho acaba el padre Blas Valera la vida de este Inca Huiracocha."
57. See the appendix.

APPENDIX

1. The text has "Setentrión," which means North.
2. "Ask of me and I will give you the nations for your inheritance, and the ends of the earth for your possession," Psalms 2:8.

3. "Carried a full day's burden in the scorching heat," Matthew 20:12.
4. The Capitolio was the smallest of the seven hills in Rome, upon which Jupiter's temple was located.
5. For the flowering of Aaron's staff, see Numbers 17:16–26. Jesse's staff, that of a shepherd, passed to his son David, 1 Samuel 17. In these respective instances the staff symbolizes God's law and the coming of Christ's Empire, as was prophesied by Nathan to David in 2 Samuel 17:16, "Your house and your kingdom shall endure forever before me; your throne shall stand firm forever."

BIBLIOGRAPHY

Abbott, Don Paul. *Rhetoric in the New World.* Columbia: University of South Carolina Press, 1996.

Abercrombie, Thomas A. "La perpetuida traducida: del 'debate' al Taqui Onkoy y una rebellion comunero peruana." In *Incas e indios cristianos: Elites indígenas e identidades cristianas en los Andes coloniales.* Edited by Jean-Jacques Decoster, 79–120. Cusco/Lima: CBC, Asociación Kuraka/IFEA, 2002.

Ackrill, J.L. *A New Aristotle Reader.* Princeton: Princeton University Press, 1987.

Acosta, José de. *De procuranda indorum salute* [1588]. In *Corpus Hispanorum de Pace.* Vols. XXIII–XXIV. Madrid: Consejo Superior de Investigaciones Científicas, 1987.

Acosta, José de. *Historia natural y moral de las Indias* [1590]. Edited by Fermín del Pino-Díaz. Madrid: Consejo Superior de Investigaciones Científicas, 2008.

Acosta, José de. *Natural and Moral History of the Indies* [1590]. Translated by Edward Grimston [1604]. Edited by Clements R. Markham. 2 Vols. New York: Burt Franklin, 1921.

Adams, Robert M. *Desiderius Erasmus: The Praise of Folly and Other Writings.* New York: Norton, 1989.

Adorno, Rolena. "Censorship and Its Evasion: Jerónimo Román and Bartolomé de Las Casas." *Hispania* 75: no. 4 (1992): 812–27.

Adorno, Rolena. "Discurso jurídico, discurso literario: el reto de leer en el siglo XX los escritos del XVI." In *Memorias. Jornadas Andinas de la Literatura Latino Americana*, 15–25. La Paz: Plural Editores, 1995.

Adorno, Rolena, ed. *From Oral to Written Expression*. Syracuse: Maxwell School of Citizenship and Public Affairs, 1982a.

Adorno, Rolena. *Guaman Poma: Writing and Resistance in Colonial Peru*. Austin: University of Texas Press, 1986.

Adorno, Rolena. "Images of Indios Ladinos in Early Colonial Peru." In *Transatlantic Encounters: Europeans and Andeans in the Sixteenth Century*. Edited by Kenneth Andrien and Rolena Adorno, 232–70. Berkeley: University of California Press, 1991.

Adorno, Rolena. "El Inca Garcilaso: Writer of Hernando de Soto, Reader of Cabeza de Vaca." In *Beyond Books and Borders: Garcilaso de la Vega and* La Florida del Inca. Edited by Raquel Chang-Rodríguez, 119–33. Lewisburg: Bucknell University Press, 2006.

Adorno, Rolena. "The Language of History in Guaman Poma's *Nueva Corónica y Buen Gobierno*." In *From Oral to Written Expression*. Edited by Rolena Adorno, 109–73. Syracuse: Maxwell School of Citizenship and Public Affairs, 1982b.

Aguilar Priego, Rafael. "El Hijo del Inca Garcilaso." *Boletín de la Real Academia de Ciencias, Bellas Letras y Nobles Artes de Córdoba* XVI: no. 54, July–December (1945): 281–300.

Alaperrine-Bouyer, Monique. *La educación de las elites indígenas en el Perú colonial*. Lima: Instituto Francés de Estudios Andinos, 2007.

Alaperrine-Bouyer, Monique. "Saber y poder: la cuestión de la educación de las elites indígenas." In *Incas e indios cristianos: Elites indígenas e identidades cristianas en los Andes coloniales*. Edited by Jean-Jacques Decoster, 145–68. Cusco/Lima: CBC, Asociación Kuraka/IFEA, 2002.

Álvarez, Bartolomé. *De las costumbres y conversión de los indios del Perú* [1588]. Edited by María del Carmen Martín Rubio, Juan J. R. Villarías Robles, and Fermín del Pino Díaz. Madrid: Ediciones Polisemo, 1998.

Amat Olazábal, Hernán. *El Inca Garcilaso de la Vega: IV Centenario de los* Comentarios reales de los Incas. Lima: Universidad Alas Peruanas, 2012.

Anadón, José, ed. *Garcilaso Inca de la Vega: An American Humanist. A Tribute to José Durand*. Notre Dame: University of Notre Dame Press, 1998.

Andrien, Kenneth J. and Rolena Adorno, eds. *Transatlantic Encounters: Europeans and Andeans in the Sixteenth Century*. Berkeley: University of California Press, 1991.

Aquinas, Thomas. *On Law, Morality, and Politics.* Edited by William P. Baumgarth and Richard J. Regan, S.J. Cambridge: Hackett Publishing, 1988.

Aranda, Antonio Garrido, ed. *El Inca Garcilaso entre Europa y América.* Córdoba: Caja Provincial de Ahorros de Córdoba, 1994.

Araníbar, Carlos. "Índice Analítico y Glosario." In Inca Garcilaso de la Vega, *Comentarios reales de los Incas* (Primera Parte). Vol. 2. Edited by Carlos Araníbar, 653–880. Lima: FCE, 1991.

Aristotle. *The Nichomachean Ethics.* Translated by David Ross. Oxford: Oxford University Press, 1980.

Aristotle. *On Rhetoric.* Translated by George A. Kennedy. Oxford: Oxford University Press, 1991.

Aristotle. *The Politics and the Constitution of Athens.* Edited by Stephen Everson. Cambridge: Cambridge University Press, 1993.

Arocena, Luis. *El Inca Garcilaso y el humanismo renacentista.* Buenos Aires, 1949.

Ascher, María, and Robert Ascher. *The Code of the Quipu. A Study in Media, Mathematics, and Culture.* Ann Arbor: University of Michigan Press, 1981.

Asensio, Manuel. "Dos cartas desconocidas del Inca Garcilaso." *Nueva Revista de Filología Hispánica* (Mexico) VII (1953): 582–93.

Augustine of Hippo. *City of God.* Translated by Henry Bettenson. New York: Penguin, 1984.

Avalle-Arce, Juan Bautista. *El Inca en sus "Comentarios"* (antología vivida). Biblioteca Románica Hispánica, VI, 21. Madrid: Gredos, 1970.

Bacon, Francis. *An Advertisement Touching a Holy War* [1629]. Edited by Laurence Lampert. Prospect Heights: Waveland Press, 2005.

Bataillon, Marcel. *Erasmo y España: estudios sobre la historia espiritual del siglo XVI.* Translated by Antonio Alatorre. Mexico: Fondo Cultural Económico, 1991.

Benand, Carmen. "Soles. Platón, Heliodoro, León Hebreo y el Inca Garcilaso." In *Humanismo, mestizaje y escritura en los* Comentarios reales. Edited by Carmen de Mora, Guillermo Serés, and Mercedes Serna Arnaiz, 31–50. Madrid/Frankfurt am Main: Iberoamericana/Vervuert, 2010.

Bermúdez-Gallegos, Marta. "Atahuallpa Inca: Axial Figure in the Encounter of Two Worlds." In *Amerindian Images and the Legacy of Columbus.* Edited by René Jara and Nicholas Spadaccini, 607–28. Minneapolis: University of Minnesota Press, 1992.

Betanzos, Juan de. *Narrative of the Incas* [1557]. Translated by Ronald Hamilton and Dana Buchanan. Austin: University of Texas Press, 1996.

Bethel, Leslie, ed. *Colonial Spanish America.* Cambridge: Cambridge University Press, 1987.

Beysterveldt, Antony A. Van. "Nueva interpretación de los *Comentarios Reales* de Garcilaso el Inca." *Cuadernos hispanoamericanos* 230 (1969): 353–90.

Brading, D. A. *The First America. The Spanish Monarchy, Creole Patriots and the Liberal State, 1492–1867*. New York: Cambridge University Press, 1991.

Brading, D. A. "The Incas and the Renaissance. The *Royal Commentaries* of Inca Garcilaso de la Vega." *Journal of Latin American Studies* (Cambridge, 1986): 1–23.

Braun, Harald E. *Juan de Mariana and Early Modern Spanish Political Thought*. Burlington: Ashgate, 2007.

Brown, John L. *The Methodus ad Facilem Historiarum Cognitionem of Jean Bodin*. Washington, DC: Catholic University of America Press, 1939.

Buchanan, Dana. "Note on the Translation." In Juan de Betanzos, *Narrative of the Incas*. Translated by Ronald Hamilton and Dana Buchanan, xv–xviii. Austin: University of Texas Press, 1996.

Buntix, Gustavo, and Luis Wuffarden. "Incas y reyes españoles en la pintura colonial peruana: La estela de Garcilaso." *Márgenes* 8 (1991): 151–210.

Burgaleta, Claudio M., S.J. *José de Acosta, S.J. (1540–1600) His Life and Thought*. Chicago: Loyola Press, 1999.

Burns, J. H., and Mark Goldie, eds. *The Cambridge History of Political Thought, 1450–1700*. Cambridge: Cambridge University Press, 1991.

Burns, Kathryn J. "Beatas, 'decencia' y poder: la formación de una elite indígena en el Cuzco colonial." In *Incas e indios cristianos: Elites indígenas e identidades cristianas en los Andes coloniales*. Edited by Jean-Jacques Decoster, 121–34. Cusco/Lima: CBC, Asociación Kuraka/IFEA, 2002.

Burns, Kathryn J., ed. *Into the Archive: Writing and Power in Colonial Peru*. Durham: Duke University Press, 2010.

Burns, Kathryn, J. "Making Indigenous Archives: The Quilcacamayoc of Colonial Cuzco." In *Indigenous Intellectuals: Knowledge, Power, and Colonial Culture in Mexico and the Andes*. Edited by Gabriela Ramos and Yanna Yannakakis, 237–60. Durham: Duke University Press, 2014.

Burns, Kathryn J. "Notaries, Truth and Consequences." *American Historical Review* 110, no. 2 (April 2005): 350–79.

Cabrera de Córdoba, Luis. *De historia, para entenderla y escribirla* [1611]. Edited by Santiago Montero Díaz. Madrid: Instituto de Estudios Politicos, 1948.

Campbell, S.J., Thomas J. *The Jesuits, 1534–1921*. Boston: Milford House, 1921.

Campos-Muñoz, Germán. "Cuzco, Urbs et Orbis: Rome and Garcilaso de la Vega's Self-Classicalization." *Hispanic Review* 81, no. 2 (Spring 2013): 123–44.

Canny, Nicholas, and Anthony Pagden, eds. *Colonial Identity in the Atlantic World, 1500–1800*. Princeton: Princeton University Press, 1987.

Carrión, Martín Oliver. *Cuzco's Intellectual and Artistic Renaissance: Juan Espinosa Medrano "El Lunarejo," Diego Tito Quispe and the Jesuits*. Ph.D. diss., Johns Hopkins University, 2010.

Cassirer, Ernst, Paul Oskar Kristeller, and John Herman Randall, Jr., eds. *The Renaissance Philosophy of Man*. Chicago: University of Chicago Press, 1948.

Castanien, Donald G. *El Inca Garcilaso de la Vega*. New York: Twayne Publishers, 1969.

Castro-Klarén, Sara. "For It Is a Single World: Marsilio Ficino and Inca Garcilaso de la Vega in Dialogue with Pagan Philosophies." In *Inca Garcilaso and Contemporary World-Making*. Edited by Sara Castro-Klarén and Christian Fernández, 195–228. Pittsburgh: University of Pittsburgh Press, 2016a.

Castro-Klarén, Sara. "Introduction." In *Inca Garcilaso and Contemporary World-Making*. Edited by Sara Castro-Klarén and Christian Fernández, 3–19. Pittsburgh: University of Pittsburgh Press, 2016b.

Castro-Klarén, Sara. "Writing Subalterity: Guaman Poma and Garcilaso, Inca." *Dispositio* 19, no. 46 (1994): 229–44.

Castro-Klarén, Sara, and Christian Fernández, eds. *Inca Garcilaso and Contemporary World-Making*. Pittsburgh: University of Pittsburgh Press, 2016.

Centro de Estudios Histórico-Militares del Perú. *Nuevos estudios sobre el Inca, Garcilaso de la Vega*. Lima, 1955.

Chang-Rodríguez, Raquel, ed. *Beyond Books and Borders: Garcilaso de la Vega and* La Florida del Inca. Lewisburg: Bucknell University Press, 2006a.

Chang-Rodríguez, Raquel. *Entre la espada y la pluma: el Inca Garcilaso de la Vega y sus* Comentarios reales. Lima: Fondo Editorial de la Pontificia Universidad Católica del Perú, 2010.

Chang-Rodríguez, Raquel. "Introduction." In *Beyond Books and Borders: Garcilaso de la Vega and* La Florida del Inca. Edited by Raquel Chang-Rodríguez, 15–32. Lewisburg: Bucknell University Press, 2006b.

Chang-Rodríguez, Raquel. "Traversing Cultures and Crisscrossing Territories in *La Florida del Inca*." In *Beyond Books and Borders: Garcilaso de la Vega and* La Florida del Inca. Edited by Raquel Chang-Rodríguez, 134–44. Lewisburg: Bucknell University Press, 2006c.

Chapple, Christopher, ed. *The Jesuit Tradition in Education and Missions*. Scranton: University of Scranton Press, 1993.

Charles, John. *Allies at Odds: The Andean Church and Its Indigenous Agents, 1583–1671*. Albuquerque: University of New Mexico Press, 2010a.

Charles, John. "Trained by Jesuits: Indigenous *Letrados* in Seventeenth-Century Peru." In *Into the Archive: Writing and Power in Colonial Peru*. Edited by Kathryn J. Burns, 60–78. Durham: Duke University Press, 2010b.

Chiapelli, Fred, ed. *First Images of America: The Impact of the New World on the Old.* Berkeley: University of California Press, 1976.

Choy, Emilio. *Antropología e historia.* Lima: Universidad Nacional Mayor de San Marcos, 1985.

Cicero, Marcus Tullius. *Brutus.* Loeb Edition. Translated by G. L. Hendrickson. Cambridge: Harvard University Press, 1939.

Cicero, Marcus Tullius. *De Inventione.* Loeb Edition. Translated by H. M. Hubbell. Cambridge: Harvard University Press, 1976.

Cicero, Marcus Tullius. *De Officiis.* Loeb Edition. Translated by Walter Miller. Cambridge: Harvard University Press, 1997a.

Cicero, Marcus Tullius. *De Oratore.* Loeb Edition. Translated by E. W. Sutton and H. Rackham. Cambridge: Harvard University Press, 1997b.

Cicero, Marcus Tullius. *De Re Publica* and *De Legibus.* Loeb Edition. Translated by Clinton Walker Keyes. Cambridge: Harvard University Press, 1994.

Cicero, Marcus Tullius. *Rhetorica ad Herennium.* Loeb Edition. Translated by Harry Caplan. Cambridge: Harvard University Press, 1989.

Cieza de León, Pedro. *La crónica del Perú* [1553]. Edited by Manuel Ballesteros Gaibrois. Lima: Historia 16, 1984.

Cieza de León, Pedro. *El señorío de los Incas* [1550]. Edited by Manuel Ballesteros Gaibrois. Lima: Historia 16, 1985.

Classen, Constance. *Inca Cosmology and the Human Body.* Salt Lake City: University of Utah Press, 1993.

Cobo, Bernabé. *History of the Inca Empire* [1653]. Translated by Roland Hamilton. Austin: University of Texas Press, 1979.

Cochrane, Eric. *Historians and Historiography in the Italian Renaissance.* Chicago: University of Chicago Press, 1981.

Cochrane, Eric. "The Transition from Renaissance to Baroque: The Case of Italian Historiography." *History and Theory* XIX (1980): 21–38.

Cornejo Polar, Antonio. "El discurso de la armonía imposible (El Inca Garcilaso de la Vega: discurso y recepción social)." *Revista de Crítica Literaria Latinoamericana* 38 (1993): 73–80.

Costas Rodríguez, Jenaro. "El Tópico de la Verdad en la Historiografía Latina Renacentista." In *La recepción de las artes clásicas en el siglo XVI.* Edited by Eustaquio Sánchez Salon, Luis Merino Jerez, and Santiago López Moreda Cáceres, 543–54. Universidad de Extremadura: Servicio de Publicaciones, 1996.

Covarrubias, Sebastián de. *Tesoro de la lengua castellano o española* [1611]. Edited by Martín de Riquer. Barcelona: S.A. Horta I.E., 1943.

Cox, Carlos Manuel. *Utopía y realidad en el Inca Garcilaso.* Lima: UNMSM, 1965.

Crowley, Frances G. *Garcilaso de la Vega: El Inca and His Sources in the* Comentarios Reales. Paris: Mouton, 1971.

Cuevas Herrera, Juan de. "Cinco memoriales en que breve y sucintamente se da noticia de los mayores impedimentos que hay para que estos indios del Perú no acaben de entrar en la ley y costumbres evangélicas. Dirigidos al nuestro señor por el Lizenziado Juan de Cuevas Herrera Cura beneficiado de los Pueblos de Andamarca y Hurinoca en la Provincia de los Carangas, natural de la Ciudad de la Plata en los Carchas." Biblioteca Real del Palacio de Madrid, Spain. Sign. II/2819, 218–69, ca. 1650.

Cusi Yupanqui, Titu. *Ynstrucción del Ynga Don Diego de Castro Titu Cusi Yupangui* [1570]. Edited by Luis Millones. Lima: El Virrey, 1985.

Davies, Nigel. *The Incas.* Niwot: University Press of Colorado, 1995.

Dean, Carolyn S. "Familiarizando el catolicismo en el Cuzco colonial." In *Incas e indios cristianos: Elites indígenas e identidades cristianas en los Andes coloniales.* Edited by Jean-Jacques Decoster, 195–208. Cusco/Lima: CBC, Asociación Kuraka/IFEA, 2002.

Dean, Carolyn S. *Inka Bodies and the Body of Christ: Corpus Christi in Colonial Peru.* Durham: Duke University Press, 1999.

Debicki, Andrew P., and Enrique Pupo-Walker, eds. *Estudios de literatura hispanoamericana en honor de José J. Arrom.* Chapel Hill: North Carolina Studies in the Romance Languages and Literatures, 1974.

Decoster, Jean-Jacques, ed. *Incas e indios cristianos: Elites indígenas e identidades cristianas en los Andes coloniales.* Cusco/Lima: CBC, Asociación Kuraka/IFEA, 2002.

Decoster, Jean-Jacques. "La sangre que mancha: la iglesia colonial temprano frente a indios, mestizo e ilegítimos." In *Incas e indios cristianos: Elites indígenas e identidades cristianas en los Andes coloniales.* Edited by Jean-Jacques Decoster, 251–94. Cusco/Lima: CBC, Asociación Kuraka/IFEA, 2002.

De la Fuente, Vicente, ed. *Obras escogidas del padre Pedro de Rivadeneira.* Madrid: Ediciones Atlas, 1952.

De la Torre y del Cerro, José. *El Inca Garcilaso de la Vega. Nueva documentación.* Madrid: Imprenta de José Murillo, 1935.

Delgado Díaz del Olmo, César. *El diálogo de los mundos: Ensayos sobre el Inca Garcilaso.* Arequipa: Universidad Nacional San Antonio Abad, 1991.

Demarest, Arthur A. *Viracocha: The Nature and Antiquity of the Andean High God.* Peabody Museum Monographs, Number 6. Cambridge: Harvard University, 1981.

Díaz, Junot. *The Brief Wonderous Life of Oscar Wao.* New York: Riverhead, 2007.

Di Biase, Carmine, ed. *Travel and Translation in the Early Modern Period.* New York: Rodopi, 2006.

Documents from Early Peru: The Pizarros and the Almagros, 1531–1578. The Harkness Collection in the Library of Congress. Washington, DC: United States Printing Office, 1936.

Dolan, John P. *The Essential Erasmus*. New York: Meridian, 1983.

Dueñas, Alcira. *Indians and Mestizos in the "Lettered City": Reshaping Justice, Social Hierarchy, and Political Culture in Colonial Peru*. Boulder: University Press of Colorado, 2010.

Durán Luzio, Juan. "Sobre Tomás Moro en el Inca Garcilaso." *Revista Iberoamericana* 96–97 (1976): 349–61.

Durand, José. "La Biblioteca del Inca." *Nueva Revista Filología Hispánica* II (1948): 239–64.

Durand, José. "Dos notas sobre el Inca Garcilaso. I. Aldrete y el Inca. II. Perú y Pirú." *Nueva Revista de Filología Hispánica* III (1949): 278–90.

Durand, José. *El Inca Garcilaso, clásico de América*. Mexico: Sepsetentas, 1976.

Durand, José. *El Inca Garcilaso de America*. Serie Perulibros. Lima: Paramonga, 1988a.

Durand, José. "El Inca jura decir la verdad." *Histórica* XIV, no. 1 (1990): 1–25.

Durand, José. "En torno a la prosa de Inca Garcilaso. A propósito de un artículo de Roberto González Echevarría." *Nuevo Texto Crítico* 2 (1988b): 209–27.

Durand, José. "Garcilaso between the World of the Incas and That of Renaissance Concepts." *Diogenes* (1964): 21–45.

Durand, José. "Garcilaso y su formación literaria e histórica." In Centro de Estudios Histórico-Militares del Perú, *Nuevos estudios sobre el Inca, Garcilaso de la Vega*, 63–85. Lima, 1955.

Durand, José. "Perú y Ophir en Garcilaso Inca, el jesuita Pineda y Gregorio García." *Histórica* III, no. 1 (1979): 33–54.

Durand, José. "Presencia de Garcilaso en Túpac Amaru." *Cuadernos Americanos* 6, no. 18 (1989): 172–77.

Duviols, Pierre. *La destrucción de las religiones andinas (conquista y colonia)*. Mexico: Universidad Nacional Autónoma de México, 1977.

Duviols, Pierre. "The Inca Garcilaso de la Vega, Humanist Interpreter of the Inca Religion." *Diogenes* 44 (1964): 36–52.

Duviols, Pierre. "Introducción." In Joan de Santacruz Pachacuti Yamqui Salcamaygua, *Relación de las antigüedades deste* reyno *del Pirú* [1613]. Edited by Pierre Duviols, 11–126. Lima: Instituto Francés de Estudios Andinos y Centro de Estudios Regionales Bartolomé de Las Casas, 1993.

Duviols, Pierre. "The Problematic Representation of Viracocha in the *Royal Commentaries*, and Why Garcilaso Bears and Deserves the Title of Inca." In *Garcilaso Inca de la Vega: An American Humanist. A Tribute to José Durand*. Edited by José Anadón, 46–58. Notre Dame: University of Notre Dame Press, 1998.

Elliot, J. H. *Empires of the Atlantic World: Britain and Spain in America, 1492–1830*. New Haven: Yale University Press, 2006.

Elliott, J. H. *History in the Making*. New Haven: Yale University Press, 2012.

Elliott, J. H. *Imperial Spain, 1469–1716*. New York: Penguin Books, 1963.

Elliott, J. H. *The Old World and the New, 1492–1650*. Cambridge: Cambridge University Press, 1970.

Elliott, J. H. *Spain and Its World, 1500–1700*. New Haven: Yale University Press, 1989.

Elliott, J. H. "The Spanish Conquest." In *Colonial Spanish America*. Edited by Leslie Bethel, 1–58. Cambridge: Cambridge University Press, 1987.

Emerton, Ephraim. *Humanism and Tyranny*. Cambridge: Harvard University Press, 1925.

Erasmus, Desiderius. *Ciceronianus*. Translated by Izora Scott. New York: Columbia University Teachers College, 1908.

Escobar, Alberto. *Patio de letras*, 11–40. Lima: Caballo de Troya: 1965.

Espinosa, Aurelio. *The Empire of the Cities: Emperor Charles V, the Comunero Revolt, and the Transformation of the Spanish System*. Boston: Brill, 2008.

Espinoza Soriano, Waldemar. *La destrucción del imperio de los Incas*. Lima: Amaru Editores, 1973.

Farrell, S.J., Allan P. *The Jesuit Code of Liberal Education*. Milwaukee: Bruce Publishing, 1938.

Fernández de Palencia, Diego. *Historia del Perú* [1565]. Edited by Lucas de Torre. Madrid: Biblioteca Hispania, 1913–1914.

Fernández Palacios, Christian. "Inca Garcilaso's Biography." In *Inca Garcilaso and Contemporary World-Making*. Edited by Sara Castro-Klarén and Christian Fernández, 20–32. Pittsburgh: University of Pittsburgh Press, 2016a.

Fernández Palacios, Christian. *Inca Garcilaso de la Vega: Imaginación, memoria e identidad*. Lima: Fondo Editorial de la Universidad Nacional Mayor de San Marcos, 2004.

Fernández Palacios, Christian. "Transatlantic Images and Paratexts in the *Royal Commentaries*." In *Inca Garcilaso and Contemporary World-Making*. Edited by Sara Castro-Klarén and Christian Fernández, 33–61. Pittsburgh: University of Pittsburgh Press, 2016b.

Fernández Palacios, Christian. "Traducción y apropriación: Los 'papeles rotos' y la creación de Blas Valera como un 'autor' en los *Comentarios reales* del Inca Garcilaso." In *El Inca Garcilaso de la Vega: entre varios mundos*. Edited by José Morales Saravia, and Gerhard Penzkopfer, 93–104. Lima: Universidad Nacional Mayor de San Marcos, 2011.

Fernández-Santamaría, J. A. *Reason of State and Statecraft in Spanish Political Thought, 1595–1640*. Lanham: University Press of America, 1983.

Fernández-Santamaría, J. A. *The State, War and Peace: Spanish Political Thought in the Renaissance, 1516–1559*. New York: Cambridge University Press, 1977.

Firbas, Paul. "La momia del Inca: cuerpo y palabra en los *Comentarios reales*." *Revista de Crítica Literaria Latinoamericana* 35, no. 70 (2009): 39–61.

Fitzmaurice-Kelly, Julia. *El Inca Garcilaso de la Vega*. Oxford: Oxford University Press, 1921.

Flores Quelopano, Gustavo. *El Inca Garcilaso como filósofo*. Lima: IIPCIAL, Fondo Editorial, 2008.

Foucault, Michel. *The Order of Things: An Archaeology of the Human Sciences*. New York: Vintage Books, 1994.

Franklin, Julian H. *Jean Bodin and the Sixteenth-Century Revolution in the Methodology of Law and History*. New York: Columbia University Press, 1963.

Frenk, Margarit. "Lectores y oidores. La difusión oral de la literatura en el Siglo de Oro." In *Actas del Septímo Congreso de la Asociación de Hispanistas*. Vol. 1, 101–23. Rome: Bulzoni, 1982.

Fuerst, James W. "Locke and Inca Garcilaso." In *Inca Garcilaso and Contemporary World-Making*. Edited by Sara Castro-Klarén and Christian Fernández, 269–96. Pittsburgh: University of Pittsburgh Press, 2016.

Fuerst, James W. *Mestizo Rhetoric: The Political Thought of El Inca Garcilaso de la Vega*. Ph.D. diss., Harvard University, 2000.

Fuerst, James W. "'El dios no conocido' y la vuelta del mundo en los *Comentarios reales*." In *Renacimiento mestizo: Los 400 años de los Comentarios reales*. Edited by José Antonio Mazzotti, 181–93. Madrid/Frankfurt am Main: Iberoamericana/Vervuert, 2010.

Garcés, María Antonia. "Lecciones del Nuevo Mundo: la estética de la palabra en el Inca Garcilaso de la Vega." *Texto y Contexto* 17 (1991): 125–51.

Garcés, María Antonia. "The Translator Translated: Inca Garcilaso and English Imperial Expansion." In *Travel and Translation in the Early Modern Period*. Edited by Carmine Di Biase, 203–28. New York: Rodopi, 2006.

Garcilaso de la Vega, el Inca. *Comentarios reales*. Edited by Mercedes Serna Arnaiz. Madrid: Editorial Castalia, 2000.

Garcilaso de la Vega, el Inca. *Comentarios reales de los Incas*. Edited by Horacio H. Urteaga. 6 Vols. Lima: Librería e Imprenta Sanmarti y Cía, 1918–1920.

Garcilaso de la Vega, el Inca. *Comentarios reales de los Incas* [1609]. Edited by Carlos Araníbar, 2 Vols. Lima: FondoCultural Económica, 1991.

Garcilaso de la Vega, el Inca. *The Florida of the Inca*. Translated by John Grier Varner. Austin: University of Texas Press, 1951a.

Garcilaso de la Vega, el Inca. *La Florida del Ynca. Historia del Adelantado Hernando de Soto, Gouernador y capitán general del Reyno de la Florida, y otros heroicos caualleros Españoles e Yndios, escrita por el Ynca Garcilasso de la Vega, capitan de su Magestad, natural de la gran ciudad del Cozco, cabeça de los Reynos y prouinçias del Peru* [1605]. Edited by Sylvia-Lyn Hilton. Madrid: Fundación Universitaria Espanola, 1982.

Garcilaso de la Vega, el Inca. *Historia general del Perú. Segunda parte de los Comentarios reales* [1617]. Edited by Ángel Rosenblat. 3 Vols. Buenos Aires: Emece Editores, S.A., 1944.

Garcilaso de la Vega, el Inca. *Obras completas*. Edited by Carmelo Saenz de Santa María, S.J. 4 Vols. Madrid: Ediciones Atlas, 1960–1965.

Garcilaso de la Vega, el Inca. *Relación de la descendencia de Garci Pérez de Vargas* [1596]. Facsimile reproduction of original manuscript with a prologue by Raúl Porras Barrenechea. Lima: Ediciones del Instituto Historia, 1951b.

Garcilaso de la Vega, el Inca. *The Royal Commentaries of the Incas and the General History of Peru*. Translated by Harold V. Livermore. 2 Vols. Austin: University of Texas Press, 1966.

Garcilaso de la Vega, el Inca. *The Royal Commentaries of the Incas and General History of Peru*. Translated by Harold V. Livermore. Edited by Karen Spalding. Indianapolis: Hackett Publishing, 2006.

Garcilaso de la Vega, el Inca. *Traducción de los Diálogos de Amor de León Hebreo* [1590]. Edited by Andrés Soriano Olmedo. Madrid: Biblioteca Castro, 1995.

Garrido Aranda, Antonio, ed. *El Inca Garcilaso entre Europa y América*. Córdoba: Caja Provincial de Ahorros de Cordoba, 1994.

Gates, Henry Louis. *Signifying Monkey: A Theory of Afro-American Literary Criticism*. New York: Oxford University Press, 1988.

Gerbi, Antonello. *The Dispute of the New World: The History of a Polemic, 1750–1900*. Translated by Jeremy Moyle. Pittsburgh: University of Pittsburgh Press, 1973.

Gilbert, Felix. *Machiavelli and Guicciardini: Politics and History in Sixteenth-Century Florence*. Princeton: Princeton University Press, 1965.

González, Jaime. *La Idea de Roma en la Historiografía Indiana, 1492–1550*. Madrid: Consejo Superior de Investigaciones Científicas, 1981.

González Echevarría, Roberto. "The Law of the Letter." In Roberto González Echevarría, *Myth and Archive: A Theory of Latin American Narrative*, 43–92. Cambridge: Cambridge University Press, 1990.

González Holguín, Diego. *Vocabulario de la lengua general del todo Perú llamada lengua qquichua o del Inca* [1608]. Edited by Raúl Porras Barrenechea. Lima: Universidad Nacional Mayor de San Marcos, 1952.

González Sánchez, Carlos Alberto. "Los *Comentarios reales* en la vida y menester indiano del licenciado Cristóbal Cacho de Santillan (1599–1641)." In *Entre la espada y la pluma: el Inca Garcilaso de la Vega y sus* Comentarios reales. Edited by Raquel Chang-Rodríguez, 31–54. Lima: Fondo Editorial de la Pontificia Universidad Católica del Perú, 2010.

Grafton, Anthony. *Defenders of the Text: The Traditions of Scholarship in an Age of Science, 1450–1800*. Cambridge: Harvard University Press, 1991.

Grafton, Anthony, April Shelford, and Nancy Siraisi, eds. *New Worlds, Ancient Texts: The Power of Tradition and the Shock of Discovery*. Cambridge: Harvard University Press, 1992.

Graubart, Karen B. "The Creolization of the New World: Local Forms of Identification in Urban Colonial Peru, 1560–1640." *Hispanic American Historical Review* 89, no. 3 (2009): 471–99.

Greenblatt, Stephen. *Marvelous Possessions: The Wonder of the New World*. Chicago: Chicago University Press, 1991.

Guaman Poma de Ayala, Don Felipe. *El primer nueva corónica y buen gobierno* [1615]. Edited by John V. Murra and Rolena Adorno. 3 Vols. Mexico City: Siglo XXI Editores, 1980.

Guibovich Pérez, Pedro M. "The Dissemination and Reading of the *Royal Commentaries* in the Peruvian Viceroyalty." In *Inca Garcilaso and Contemporary World-Making*. Edited by Sara Castro-Klarén and Christian Fernández, 129–53. Pittsburgh: University of Pittsburgh Press, 2016.

Guibovich Pérez, Pedro M. "Lectura y difusión de la obra del Inca Garcilaso en el virreinato peruano (siglos XVII–XVIII). El caso de los *Comentarios reales*." *Revista Histórica* 37 (1990–1992): 103–20.

Hamilton, Bernice. *Political Thought in Sixteenth-Century Spain*. Oxford: Oxford University Press, 1963.

Hamilton, Edith, and Huntington Cairns, eds. *The Collected Dialogues of Plato*. Princeton: Princeton University Press, 1961.

Hamilton, Roland. "Introduction." In Juan de Betanzos, *Narrative of the Incas*. Translated by Ronald Hamilton and Dana Buchanan, ix–xiv. Austin: University of Texas Press, 1996.

Hampe-Martínez, Teodoro. "The Diffusion of Books and Ideas in Colonial Peru: A Study of Private Libraries in the Sixteenth and Seventeenth Centuries." *Hispanic American Historical Review* 73, no. 2 (May 1993): 211–33.

Hampe-Martínez, Teodoro. "El renacentismo del Inca Garcilaso revisitado: los clásicos greco-latinos en su biblioteca y su obra." *Bibliotèque d'Humanisme et Renaissance* LVI, 3 (1994): 641–63.

Hanke, Lewis. *All Mankind Is One*. DeKalb: Northern Illinois University Press, 1974.

Hanke, Lewis. "The *Requerimiento* and Its Interpreters." *Revista de Historia de America* I (1938): 25–34.

Hanke, Lewis. *The Spanish Struggle for Justice in the Conquest of America*. Boston: Little, Brown, 1965.

Haring, C. H. *The Spanish Empire in America* [1947]. New York: Harcourt, Brace, Jovanovich, 1975.

Harrison, Regina. "Modes of Discourse: The *Relación de antigüedades deste reyno del Pirú* by Joan de Santacruz Pachacuti Yamqui Salcamaygua." In *From Oral to Written Expression*. Edited by Rolena Adorno, 65–99. Syracuse: Maxwell School of Citizenship and Public Affairs, 1982.

Harrison, Regina. *Signs, Songs, and Memory in the Andes*. Austin: University of Texas Press, 1989.

Hebreo, León. *The Philosophy of Love: Dialoghi d'Amore*. Edited by Frank Friedberg-Seely. Translated by Jean H. Barnes. London: Soncino Press, 1937.

Hemming, John. *The Conquest of the Incas*. New York: Harcourt Brace Jovanovich, 1970.

Hijos de Pariya Qaqa: La tradición oral de Waru Chiri. Edited by George L. Urioste. 2 Vols. Syracuse: Maxwell School of Citizenship and Public Affairs, 1983.

Hilton, Sylvia-Lyn. "Introducción." In Inca Garcilaso de la Vega, *La Florida del Ynca. Historia del Adelantado Hernando de Soto, Gouernador y capitán general del Reyno de la Florida, y otros heroicos caualleros Españoles e Yndios, escrita por el Ynca Garcilasso de la Vega, capitan de su Magestad, natural de la gran ciudad del Cozco, cabeça de los Reynos y prouinçias del Peru* [1605]. Edited by Sylvia-Lyn Hilton. Madrid: Fundación Universitaria Espanola, 1982.

Hobbes, Thomas. *Leviathan*. New York: Penguin Books, 1968.

Höpfl, Harro. *Jesuit Political Thought: The Society of Jesus and the State, c. 1540–1630*. Cambridge: Cambridge University Press, 2004.

Hosne, Ana Carolina. *The Jesuit Missions to China and Peru, 1570–1610*. New York: Routledge, 2013.

Howard, Keith David. "Inca Garcilaso de la Vega's 'Ways of Lying': Reason of State, Religion and Exemplary Prudence in Part I of the *Comentarios Reales*." *Neophilologus* 96 (2012): 541–52.

Hume, David. *Essays Moral, Political and Literary*. Edited by Eugene F. Miller. Indianapolis: Liberty Fund, 1985.

Huys, Johan. *José de Acosta y el origen de la idea de misión Perú, siglo XVI*. Cuzco: CBC, 1997.

Hyland, Sabine. *Conversion, Custom and "Culture": Jesuit Racial Policy in 16th Century Peru*. Ph.D. diss., Yale University, 1994.

Hyland, Sabine. "Illegitimacy and Racial Hierarchy in the Peruvian Priesthood: A Seventeenth-Century Dispute." *Catholic Historical Review*, 84, no. 3 (1998): 431–54.

Hyland, Sabine. *The Jesuit and the Incas: The Extraordinary Life of Padre Blas Valera, S.J.* Ann Arbor: University of Michigan Press, 2003.

Iberico, Manuel. "Discurso sobre el Inca Garcilaso de la Vega." *Revista Histórica* 73 (1939): 18–34.

Ilgen, William D. "La configuración mítica de la historia en los *Comentarios reales* del Inca Garcilaso de la Vega." In *Estudios de literatura hispanoamericana en honor de José J. Arrom*. Edited by Andrew Peter Debicki and Ernesto Pupo-Walker, 37–46. Chapel Hill: North Carolina Studies in the Romance Languages and Literatures, 1974.

Jákfalvi-Leiva, Susana. *Traducción, escritura y violencia colonizadora: un estudio de la obra del Inca Garcilaso de la Vega*. Syracuse: Maxwell School of Citizenship and Public Affairs, 1984.

Jara, René and Nicholas Spadaccini, eds. *Amerindian Images and the Legacy of Columbus*. Minneapolis: University of Minnesota Press, 1992.

Jerez, Francisco de. *A True Account of the Province of Cuzco* [1534]. Translated by Clements R. Markham. London: Hakluyt Society, 1921.

Kamen, Henry. *Philip of Spain*. New Haven: Yale University Press, 1997.

Kamen, Henry. *The Spanish Inquisition: A Historical Revision*. New Haven: Yale University Press, 1998.

Kelley, Donald R. *Foundations of Modern Historical Scholarship*. New York: Columbia University Press, 1970.

Kennedy, William J. *Rhetorical Norms in Renaissance Literature*. New Haven: Yale University Press, 1978.

Konetzke, Richard, ed. *Colección de documentos para la historia de la formación social de hispanoamerica, 1493–1810*. Vol. 1 (1493–1592). Madrid: Consejo Superior de Investigaciones Cientificas, 1953.

Konetzke, Richard. "El mestizaje y su importancia en el desarrollo de la poblacion hispanoamericana durante la epoca colonial." *Revista de Indias* VII, 23 (1946a): 7–44.

Konetzke, Richard. "El mestizaje y su importancia en el desarrollo de la poblacion hispanoamericana durante la epoca colonial (conclusion)." *Revista de Indias* VII, 24 (1946b): 215–37.

Kubler, George. "The Neo-Inca State, 1537–1572." *Hispanic American Historical Review* XXVII, no. 2 (1947): 189–203.

Kupperman, Karen Ordahl, ed. *America in European Consciousness, 1493–1750*. Chapel Hill: University of North Carolina Press, 1995.

Lamana, Gonzalo. "Signifyin(g), Double Consciousness, and Coloniality: The *Royal*

Commentaries as Theory of Practice and Political Project." In *Inca Garcilaso and Contemporary World-Making*. Edited by Sara Castro-Klarén and Christian Fernández, 297–315. Pittsburgh: University of Pittsburgh Press, 2016.

Las Casas, Bartolomé de. *A Brief Account of the Destruction of the Indies*. Translated by Nigel Griffin. New York: Penguin, 1992.

Las Casas, Bartolomé de. *In Defense of the Indians* [1552]. Translated by Stafford Poole, C.M. DeKalb: Northern Illinois University Press, 1974.

Las Casas, Bartolomé de. *History of the Indies*. Translated by Andrée Collard. New York: Harper and Row, 1971.

Las Casas, Bartolomé de. "Twelve Problems of Conscience." In *Indian Freedom: The Cause of Bartolomé de las Casas, 1484–1566*. Edited by Francis Patrick Sullivan, S.J., 333–52. Kansas City: Sheed and Ward, 1995.

Las Casas, Bartolomé de. *Del único modo a atraer a todos los pueblos a la verdadera religión*. Translated by Agustín Millares Carlo. Mexico City: Fondo de Cultural Económica, 1942.

Las siete partidas. Translated by Samuel Parsons Scott. New York: Commerce Clearing House, 1931.

Lavallé, Bernard. "La admisión de los Americanos en la compañía de Jesús: El caso de la provincia peruana en el siglo XVI." *Histórica* IX: no. 2 (1985): 137–53.

Lebsanft, Franz. "Etnografía e imaginación en los *Comentarios reales de los Incas*." In *El Inca Garcilaso: entre varios mundos*. Edited José Morales Saravia and Gerhard Penzkopfer, 163–83. Lima: Universidad Nacional Mayor de San Marcos, 2011.

Leckie, John D. "A Spanish Robinson Crusoe." *Chamber's Journal* XI (1908): 510–12.

Leonard, Irving. "The Inca Garcilaso de la Vega, First Classic Writer of America." In *Filología y crítica hispánica: homenaje al Prof. Federico Sánchez Escribano*. Edited by Alberto Porqueras Mayo and Carlos Rojas, 51–62. Madrid: Ediciones Alcalá, 1969.

Lewy, Guenther. *Constitutionalism and Statecraft During the Golden Age of Spain: A Study of the Political Philosophy of Juan de Mariana, S.J.* Geneva: Librairie E. Droz, 1960.

Liss, Peggy K. *Mexico Under Spain, 1521–1556*. Chicago: University of Chicago Press, 1975.

Livermore, Harold V. "Introduction." In Inca Garcilaso de la Vega, *Royal Commentaries of the Incas and General History of Peru*. Vol. 2. Translated by Harold V. Livermore, vii–xxvi. Austin: University of Texas Press, 1966.

Livy, Titus. *The Rise of Rome*. Translated by T. J. Luce. Oxford: Oxford University Press, 1998.

Lockhart, James. *The Men of Cajamarca*. Austin: University of Texas Press, 1972.

Lockhart, James. *Spanish Peru: 1532–1560*. Madison: University of Wisconsin Press, 1968.

Lohmann Villena, Guillermo. *Las ideas juridico-políticas en la rebelión de Gonzalo Pizarro*. Valladolid: Casa-Museo de Colón y Seminario Americanista, Secretario de Publicaciones de la Universidad de Valladolid, 1977.

Lohmann Villena, Guillermo. "La parentela española del Inca Garcilaso de la Vega." In *El Inca Garcilaso entre Europa y América*. Edited by Antonio Garrido Aranda, 257–83. Cordoba: Caja Provincial de Ahorros de Córdoba, 1994.

López-Baralt, Mercedes. *El Inca Garcilaso, traductor de culturas*. Madrid/Frankfurt am Main: Iberoamericana/Vervuert, 2011.

López de Gómara, Francisco. *Annales de Carlos Quinto* [1556?]. Edited by Roger Bigelow Merriman. Oxford: Clarendon Press, 1912.

López de Gómara, Francisco. *Historia general de las Indias y conquista de México* [1552]. Madrid: Espasa-Calpe, 1941.

López Martínez, Héctor. *Rebeliones mestizos y otros temas quinientistas*. Lima: Impresa Gráfica Villanueva, 1971.

Lorandi, Ana María. *The Spanish King of the Incas: The Epic life of Pedro Bohorques*. Translated by Ann de León. Pittsburgh: University of Pittsburgh Press, 2005.

Lovett, A. W. *Early Habsburg Spain, 1517–1598*. Oxford: Oxford University Press, 1986.

Lynch, John. *Spain, 1516–1598*. Oxford: Blackwell Press, 1991.

MacCormack, Sabine. "History, Historical Record, and Ceremonial Action: Incas and Spaniards in Cuzco." *Comparative Studies in Society and History* 43, no. 2 (April 2001): 329–63.

MacCormack, Sabine. "The Incas and Rome." In *Garcilaso Inca de la Vega: An American Humanist. A Tribute to José Durand*. Edited by José Anadón, 8–31. Notre Dame: University of Notre Dame Press, 1998.

MacCormack, Sabine. *On the Wings of Time*. Princeton: Princeton University Press, 2007.

MacCormack, Sabine. "Pachacuti: Miracles, Punishment, and Last Judgment: Visionary Past and Prophetic Future in Early Colonial Peru." *American Historical Review* 93, no. 4 (October 1988): 960–1006.

MacCormack, Sabine. *Religion in the Andes*. Princeton: Princeton University Press, 1991.

Madrigal, L. Iñigo, ed. *Historia de la literatura hispanoamericana*. Madrid: Ediciones Catédra, Vol. 1 (Epoca Colonial), 1992.

Maravall, Jose Antonio. *Las comunidades de Castilla: una primera revolución moderna*. Madrid: Revista de Occidente. 2nd edition, 1970.

Maravall, Jose Antonio. *Carlos V y el pensamiento político del renacimiento*. Madrid: Boletín Oficial del Estado, 1999.

Maravall, Jose Antonio. *Estudios de historia del pensamiento español*. 2 Vols. Madrid: Ediciones Cultura Hispánica, 1984.

Mariana, Juan de. *Del rey y la institución real* [1599]. Translated by Humberto Armella Maza. 2 Vols. Madrid: Publicaciones Españoles, 1961.

Marincola, John. *Authority and Tradition in Ancient Historiography*. Cambridge: Cambridge University Press, 1997.

Markham, Clement. "Introduction." In Pedro Sarmiento de Gamboa, *History of the Incas*. Edited by Clement Markham. Mineola: Dover Edition, 1999.

Marrero-Fente, Raúl. "La vision trasatlántica de las culturas en los *Comentarios reales*." In *Humanismo, mestizaje y escritura en los* Comentarios reales. Edited by Carmen de Mora, Guillermo Serés, and Mercedes Serna Arnaiz, 191–210. Madrid/Frankfurt am Main: Vervuert/Iberoamericana, 2010.

Martí-Abelló, Rafael. "Garcilaso Inca de la Vega." *Revista Hispánica Moderna* VII (1950), 99–111.

Martín, Luis. S.J. *The Intellectual Conquest of Peru: The Jesuit College of San Pablo, 1567–1768*. New York: Fordham University Press, 1968.

Martín, Luis. S.J. "The Peruvian Indian through Jesuit Eyes: The Case of José de Acosta and Pablo José de Arriaga." In *The Jesuit Tradition in Education and Missions*. Edited by Christopher Chapple, 205–14. Scranton: University of Scranton Press, 1993.

Mazzotti, José Antonio. *Coros mestizos del Inca Garcilaso, resonancias andinas*. Lima: Fondo de Cultura Económica, 1996a.

Mazzotti, José Antonio. "Garcilaso and the Origins of Garcilacism: The Role of the *Royal Commentaries* in the Development of a Peruvian National *Imaginaire*." In *Garcilaso Inca de la Vega: An American Humanist, A Tribute to José Durand*. Edited by José Anadón, 90–109. Notre Dame: University of Notre Dame Press, 1998.

Mazzotti, José Antonio. "Garcilaso y el 'bien común': mestizaje y posición política." In *El Inca Garcilaso: entre varios mundos*. Edited by José Morales Saravia and Gerhard Penzkopfer, 185–206. Lima: Universidad Nacional Mayor de San Marcos, 2011.

Mazzotti, José Antonio. "El Inca Garcilaso Translates León Hebreo: The *Dialogues of Love*, the Cabala, and Andean Mythology." In *Beyond Books and Borders: Garcilaso de la Vega and* La Florida del Inca. Edited by Raquel Chang-Rodríguez, 99–118. Lewisburg: Bucknell University Press, 2006.

Mazzotti, José Antonio. *Incan Insights: Inca Garcilaso's Hints to Andean Readers*. Madrid/Frankfurt am Main: Iberoamericana/Vervuert, 2008.

Mazzotti, José Antonio. "The Lightning Bolt Yields to the Rainbow: Indigenous History and Colonial Semiosis in the Royal Commentaries of El Inca Garcilaso de la Vega." *Modern Language Quarterly* 57, 2 (1996b): 197–211.

Mazzotti, José Antonio, ed. *Renacimiento mestizo: Los 400 años de los* Comentarios reales. Madrid/Frankfurt am Main: Iberoamericana/Vervuert, 2010.

Mazzotti, José Antonio, and U. Juan Zevallos Aguilar, eds. *Asedios a la heterogeneidad cultural: libro de homenaje a Antonio Cornelo Polar*. Philadelphia: Asociación Internacional de Peruanistas, 1996.

Mejía, Pedro de. *Historia del Emperador Carlos Quinto.* Edited by Juan de Mata Carriazo. Madrid: Espasa-Calpe, 1945.

Menéndez y Pelayo, Marcelino. *Historia de la poesía hispanoamericana*. Madrid: Consejo Superior de Investigaciones Científicas. 1948.

Mesa Gisbert, Isabel. "Pedro Serrano: la crónica de un naufragio en un cuento para niños." *Revista Cultural del Banco Central de Bolivia* XII, no. 54 (September–October, 2008).

Mignolo, Walter. "Cartas, crónicas y relaciones de la conquista y del descubrimiento." In *Historia de la literatura hispanoamericana*. Vol. 1 (Epoca Colonial). Edited by L. Iñigo Madrigal, 57–116. Madrid: Ediciones Catédra, 1992.

Mignolo, Walter. *The Darker Side of the Renaissance.* Ann Arbor: University of Michigan Press, 1995.

Mignolo, Walter. "El metatexto historiográfico y la historiografía indiana." *Modern Language Notes* 96 (1981): 358–402.

Milliones, Luis. "Las herejías del Garcilaso." In *Renacimiento mestizo: Los 400 años de los* Comentarios reales. Edited by José Antonio Mazzotti. Madrid/Frankfurt am Main: Iberoamericana/Vervuert, 2010.

Millones, Luis. "Introducción." In *Ynstrucción del Ynga Don Diego de Castro Titu Cusi Yupangui* (1570). Edited by Luis Millones, 7–15. Lima: El Virrey, 1985.

Mills, Kenneth. *Idolatry and Its Enemies: Colonial Andean Religion and Extirpation, 1640–1750*. Princeton: Princeton University Press, 1997.

Miró Quesada Sosa, Aurelio. *El Inca Garcilaso*. Madrid: Instituto de Cultura Hispánica, 1948.

Miró Quesada Sosa, Aurelio. *El Inca Garcilaso y otros estudios garcilacistas*. Madrid: Ediciones de Cultura Hispánica, 1971.

Molina, Cristóbal de. *Relación de las fábulas i ritos de los ingas* [1573]. In *Fábulas y mitos de los Incas*. Edited by Henrique Urbano and Pierre Duviols, 120–28. Lima: Historia 16, 1989.

Montero Díaz, Santiago. "La doctrina de la historia en los tratadistas del siglo de oro." In Luis Cabrera de Córdoba, *De historia, para entenderla y escribirla* [1611]. Edited by Santiago Montero Díaz, xi–lvi. Madrid: Instituto de Estudios Politicos, 1948.

Montiel, Edgar. "El Inca Garcilaso y la independencia de las Americas." *Cuadernos Americanos* (México) 1, no. 131 (2010): 113–32.

Mora, Carmen de. "La amistad del Inca Garcilaso con los humanistas de Córdoba." In *Renacimiento mestizo: Los 400 años de los* Comentarios reales. Edited by José

Antonio Mazzotti, 103–17. Madrid/Frankfurt am Main: Iberoamericana/Vervuert, 2010.

Mora, Carmen de. "*La Florida del Inca*: A Publication History." In *Beyond Books and Borders: Garcilaso de la Vega and* La Florida del Inca. Edited by Raquel Chang-Rodríguez, 154–70. Lewisburg: Bucknell University Press, 2006.

Mora, Carmen de. "Historia y ficción en *La Florida* del Inca Garcilaso." In *El Inca Garcilaso entre Europa y América*. Edited by Antonio Garrido Aranda, 229–36. Cordoba: Caja Provincial de Ahorros de Córdoba, 1994.

Mora, Carmen de, Guillermo Serés, and Mercedes Serna, eds. *Humanismo, mestizaje y escritura en los* Comentarios reales. Frankfurt am Main/Madrid: Vervuert/Iberoamericana, 2010.

Moraña, Mabel. "Alternatividad intelectual en el Inca Garcilaso." In *Renacimiento mestizo: Los 400 años de los* Comentarios reales. Edited by José Antonio Mazzotti, 381–93. Madrid/Frankfurt am Main: Iberoamericana/Vervuert, 2010.

Murra, John V. "The Expansion of the Inca State: Armies, War, and Rebellions." In *Anthropological History of Andean Polities*. Edited by John V. Murra, Nathan Wachtel, and Jacques Revel, 49–58. Cambridge: Cambridge University Press, 1986.

Murra, John V., Nathan Wachtel, and Jacques Revel, eds. *Anthropological History of Andean Polities*. Cambridge: Cambridge University Press, 1986.

Muthu, Sankar, ed. *Empire and Modern Political Thought*. New York: Cambridge University Press, 2012a.

Muthu, Sankar. *Enlightenment against Empire*. Princeton: Princeton University Press, 2003.

Muthu, Sankar. "Introduction." In *Empire and Modern Political Thought*. Edited by Sankar Muthu. New York: Cambridge University Press, 2012b.

Nadel, George H. "Philosophy of History before Historicism." *History and Theory* 3, no. 3 (1964): 291–315.

Navarro Ledesma, Francisco. *Cervantes: The Man and the Genius*. Translated by Don Bliss and Gabriela Bliss. New York: Charterhouse, 1973.

Nebrija, Antonio de. *Gramática de la lengua castellana* [1492]. Edited by Ignacio González Llubera. London: Oxford University Press, 1926.

Niles, Susan A. *The Shape of Inca History*. Iowa City: University of Iowa Press, 1999.

No, Song. "Los *Comentarios reales* en la tradición de la historiografía española." *Humanismo, mestizaje y escritura en los* Comentarios reales. Edited by Carmen de Mora, Guillermo Serés, and Mercedes Serna Arnaiz, 241–60. Madrid/Frankfurt am Main: Iberoamericana/Vervuert, 2010.

No, Song. "La desmarginalización del discurso en la *Historia general del Perú*." In *Entre la espada y la pluma: el Inca Garcilaso de la Vega en sus* Comentarios reales. Edited by Raquel Chang-Rodríguez, 97–108. Lima: Fondo Editorial PUCP, 2010b.

No, Song. "La oralidad y la violencia de la escritura en los *Comentarios reales* del Inca Garcilaso." *Revista de Crítica Literaria Latinoamericana* 25, no. 49 (1999): 27–39.

Noreña, Carlos G. *Studies in Spanish Renaissance Thought*. The Hague: Martinus Nijhoff, 1975.

North, Helen F. "Rhetoric and Historiography." *Quarterly Journal of Speech* XLII, no. 4 (1956): 234–42.

Novoa, James Nelson. "From Inca Realm to Italian Renaissance: Garcilaso el Inca and His Translation of Leone Ebreo's *Dialoghi d'Amore*." In *Travel and Translation in the Early Modern Period*. Edited by Carmine G. di Biase, 187–201. New York: Rodopi, 2006.

O'Gorman, Edmundo. *Cuatro historiadores de Indias, Siglo XVI*. Mexico: Secretaría de Educación Pública, 1972a.

O'Gorman, Edmundo. *The Invention of America*. Westport: Greenwood Press, 1972b.

O'Malley, S. J., John W. *The First Jesuits*. Cambridge: Harvard University Press, 1993.

O'Malley, S. J., John W. "Renaissance Humanism and the Religious Culture of the First Jesuits." *Heythrop Journal* XXXI, no. 4 (1990): 471–87.

Ong, Walter J. *Orality and Literacy*. New York: Routledge, 1982.

Ortega Martínez, Francisco A. "Writing the History of an Andean Ghost." In *Inca Garcilaso and Contemporary World-Making*. Edited by Sara Castro-Klarén and Christian Fernández, 229–59. Pittsburgh: University of Pittsburgh Press, 2016.

Ossio, Juan. "Los Mitos de Origen de los Incas en la Construcción de los *Comentarios reales*." In *Entre la espada y la pluma: el Inca Garcilaso de la Vega y sus* Comentarios reales. Edited by Raquel Chang-Rodríguez, 57–72. Lima: Fondo Editorial de la Pontificia Universidad Católica del Perú, 2010.

Pagden, Anthony. "Conquest and the Just War: The 'School of Salamanca' and the 'Affair of the Indies.'" In *Empire and Modern Political Thought*. Edited by Sankar Muthu, 30–60. New York: Cambridge University Press, 2012.

Pagden, Anthony. *European Encounters with the New World*. New Haven: Yale University Press, 1993.

Pagden, Anthony. *The Fall of Natural Man: The American Indian and the Origins of Comparative Ethnology*. Cambridge: Cambridge University Press, 1982.

Pagden, Anthony. *Lords of All the World: Ideologies of Empire in Spain, Britain, and France, c. 1500–c.1800*. New Haven: Yale University Press, 1995.

Pease G. Y., Franklin. *Las crónicas y los Andes*. Lima: Pontificia Universidad Católica del Perú, 1995.

Pease G. Y., Franklin. *El dios creador andino*. Lima: Mosca Azul Editores, 1973.

Pease G. Y., Franklin. "Garcilaso Andino." *Revista Histórica* XXXIV (1984): 41–52.

Pease G. Y., Franklin. *Los útimos Incas del Cuzco* [1972]. Lima: P. L. Villanueva, 1981.

Pérez, Joseph. *La revolución de las comunidades de Castilla, 1520–1521*. Translated by Juan José Faci Lacasta. Madrid: Siglo XXI de España Editores, 1998.

Petrarch, Francesco. *On His Own Ignorance and that of Many Others*. In *The Renaissance Philosophy of Man*. Edited by Ernst Cassirer, Paul Oskar Kristeller, and John Herman Randall, Jr. Chicago: University of Chicago Press, 1948.

Pérez de Tudela, Rocío Oviedo. "Desde la orilla española: modelos y huellas de los *Comentarios reales*." In *Entre la espada y la pluma: El Inca Garcilaso de la Vega y sus* Comentarios reales. Edited by Raquel Chang-Rodríguez, 149–70. Lima: Fondo Editorial de la Pontificia Universidad Católica del Perú, 2010.

Pino-Díaz, Fermín del. "Contribución del Padre Acosta a la constitución de la etnología: su evolucionismo." *Revista de Indias* 38 (1978): 507–46.

Pino-Díaz, Fermín del. "Cuzco y Roma, peruanos y andaluces en la obra del Inca Garcilaso." *Anthropológica* XXIX, no. 29 (December 2011): 7–30.

Pino-Díaz, Fermín del, ed. *Demonio, religión y sociedad entre España y América*. Madrid: Consejo Superior de Investigaciones Científicas, Departamento de Antropología de España y América, 2002a.

Pino-Díaz, Fermín del. "¿Dignidad cultural or proto-identidad cristiana de lo Inca? Acerca del sentido preferente de los 'Comentarios' garcilasianos al Padre Acosta." In *Renacimiento mestizo: Los 400 años de los* Comentarios reales. Edited by José Antonio Mazzotti, 51–77. Madrid/Frankfurt am Main: Iberoamericana/Vervuert, 2010.

Pino-Díaz, Fermín del. "Estudio Introductorio." In José de Acosta, *Historia natural y moral de las Indias* [1590]. Edited by Fermín del Pino Díaz, XVII–LVI. Madrid: Consejo Superior de Investigaciones Científicas, 2008.

Pino-Díaz, Fermín del. "Inquisidores, misioneros y demonios americanos." In *Demonio, religión y sociedad entre España y América*. Edited by Fermín del Pino-Díaz, 139–60. Madrid: Consejo Superior de Investigaciones Científicas, Departamento de Antropología de España y América, 2002b.

Pino-Díaz, Fermín del. "Mestizos americanos y conversos hispanos ¿Posibiles aliados?" In *Humanismo, mestizaje y escritura en los* Comentarios reales. Edited by Carmen de Mora, Guillermo Serés, and Mercedes Serna, 275–93. Madrid/Frankfurt am Main: Iberoamericana/Vervuert, 2010b.

Pitts, Jennifer. "Political Theory of Empire and Imperialism." In *Empire and Modern Political Thought*. Edited by Sankar Muthu, 351–87. New York: Cambridge University Press, 2012a.

Pitts, Jennifer. "Republicanism, Liberalism, and Empire in Postrevolutionary France."

In *Empire and Modern Political Thought*. Edited by Sankar Muthu, 261–91. New York: Cambridge University Press, 2012b.

Pitts, Jennifer. *A Turn to Empire: The Rise of Imperial Liberalism in Britain and France*. Princeton: Princeton University Press, 2005.

Pizarro, Pedro. *Discovery and Conquest of the Kingdoms of Peru* [1571]. Translated by Philip Ainsworth Means. New York: Cortes Society, 1921.

Pizarro, Pedro. *Relación del descubrimiento y conquista de lo reinos del Perú* [1571]. Edited by Guillermo Lohmann Villena. Lima: Fondo Editorial de la Pontificia Universidad Católica del Perú, 1978.

Plato. *Laws*. Loeb Edition. Translated by R. G. Bury. Cambridge: Harvard University Press, 1994.

Plato. *The Republic of Plato*. Translated by Allan Bloom. New York: Basic Books, 1991.

Polo de Ondegardo, Juan. "Informe del Licenciado Juan Polo de Ondegardo al Licenciado Briviesca de Muñatones sobre la perpetuidad de las encomiendas en el Perú" [1561]. *Revista Histórica* 13 (1940): 129–96.

Porqueras Mayo, Alberto. *El prólogo en el renacimiento español*. Madrid: Consejo de Investigaciones Científicas, 1965.

Porqueras Mayo, Alberto, and Carlos Rojas, eds. *Filología y crítica hispánica: homenaje al Prof. Federico Sánchez Escribano*. Madrid: Ediciones Alcalá, 1969.

Porras Barrenechea, Raúl. *Los cronistas del Perú, 1528–1630 y otros ensayos*. Lima: Banco de Crédito del Perú, 1986.

Porras Barrenechea, Raúl. *El Inca Garcilaso en Montilla*. Lima: Editorial San Marcos, 1955.

Potter, Tiffany. "A Colonial Source for Cannibalistic Breeding in Swift's *A Modest Proposal*." *Notes and Queries* 46, no. 3 (1999): 347–48.

Pupo-Walker, Enrique. *Historia, creación y profecía en los textos del Inca Garcilaso de la Vega*. Madrid: Porrúa Turranzas, 1982.

Queija, Berta Ares. "El Inca Garcilaso y sus 'parientes' mestizos." In *Humanismo, mestizaje y escritura en los* Comentarios reales. Edited by Carmen de Mora, Guillermo Serés, and Mercedes Serna Arnaiz, 15–30. Madrid/Frankfurt am Main: Vervuert/Iberoamericana, 2010.

Quintillian, Marcus Fabius. *Institutio Oratoria*. Loeb Edition. Translated by H. E. Butler. Cambridge: Harvard University Press, 1989.

Ramos, Gabriela. *Conversion and Death in the Andes*. Notre Dame: University of Notre Dame, 2010.

Ramos, Gabriela. "Indigenous Intellectuals in Andean Colonial Cities." In *Indigenous Intellectuals: Knowledge, Power, and Colonial Culture in Mexico and the Andes*. Edited by Gabriela Ramos and Yanna Yannakakis, 22–38. Durham: Duke University Press, 2014.

Ramos, Gabriela, and Yanna Yannakakis, eds. *Indigenous Intellectuals: Knowledge, Power, and Colonial Culture in Mexico and the Andes*. Durham: Duke University Press, 2014.

Rappaport, Joanne, and Tom Cummins. *Beyond the Lettered City: Indigenous Literacy in the Andes*. Durham: Duke University Press, 2012.

Regalado de Hurtado, Liliana. *Sucesión Incaíca*. Peru: Fondo Editorial, 1993.

Relación de las costumbres antiguas de los naturales del Pirú [1590?]. In *Antigüedades del Perú*. Edited by Henrique Urbano and Ana Sánchez. Lima: Historia 16, 1992.

Ribadeneira, Pedro de. *Tratado de la religion y virtudes que debe tener el príncipe cristiano* [1595]. In *Obras escogidas del padre Pedro de Ribadeneira*. Edited by Vicente de la Fuente. Madrid: Ediciones Atlas, 1952.

Rico Verdu, José. *La retorica española de los siglos XVI y XVII*. Madrid: Consejo Superior, 1973.

Riva-Agüero, José de la. "Elogio del Inca Garcilaso." In Inca Garcilaso de la Vega, *Comentarios reales de los Incas*. 6 Vols. Edited by Horocio H. Urteaga. Lima: Librería e Imprenta Sanmarti y Cía, 1918–1920.

Riva-Agüero, José de la. "Examen de la Segunda Parte de los *Comentarios reales*." In Inca Garcilaso de la Vega, *Historia general del Perú*. Edited by Ángel Rosenblat. 3 Vols., xliv–xlix. Buenos Aires: Emecé Editores, 1944.

Riva-Agüero, José de la. *La historia en el Perú*. Lima: Imprenta Nacional de F. Barrionuevo, 1910.

Rivarola, José Luis. "La génesis de los *Comentarios reales*. Examen de algunas apostillas del Inca a la *Historia* de Gómara." In *El Inca Garcilaso: entre varios mundos*. Edited by José Morales Saravia and Gerhard Penzkopfer, 75–91. Lima: Universidad Nacional Mayor de San Marcos, 2011.

Rodríguez, Eduardo Hopkins. "Fortuna y escritura en *La Florida del Inca* de Garcilaso de la Vega." In *El Inca Garcilaso de la Vega: entre varios mundos*. Edited by José Morales Saravia and Gerhard Penzkofer, 55–74. Lima: Universidad Nacional Mayor de San Marcos, 2011.

Rodríguez Garrido, José Antonio. "El título de los *Comentarios reales*: una nueva aproximación." In *Humanismo, mestizaje y escritura en los* Comentarios reales. Edited by Carmen de Mora, Guillermo Serés, and Mercedes Serna Arnaiz, 295–318. Madrid/Frankfurt am Main: Vervuert/Iberoamericana, 2010.

Rodríguez-Vecchini, Hugo. "*Don Quijote* y *La Florida del Inca*." *Revista Iberoamericana* 48 (1982): 587–620.

Romiti, Elena. *Los hilos de la tierra. Relaciones interculturales y escritura: el Inca Garcilaso de la Vega*. Montevideo: Biblioteca Nacional/Facultad de Humanidades y Ciencias de la Educación, 2009.

Rose, Sonia V. "Los incas en la corte de Luis XIII: Jean Baudoin y su traducción al francés de la primera parte de *Comentarios reales* (1633)." In *Entre la espada y la pluma: El Inca Garcilaso de la Vega y sus* Comentarios reales. Edited by Raquel Chang-Rodríguez, 131–48. Lima: Fondo Editorial de la Pontificia Universidad Católica del Perú, 2010.

Rostworowski de Diez Canseco, María. *Estructuras andinas del poder*. Lima: Instituto de Estudios Peruanos, 1983.

Rostworowski de Diez Canseco, María. *History of the Inca Realm*. Translated by Harry B. Iceland. Cambridge: Cambridge University Press, 1999.

Rostworowski de Diez Canseco, María. *Pachacutec Ynca Yupanqui*. Lima: Editorial Torres Aguirre, 1953.

Roth, Cecil. "Introduction." In León Hebreo, *Philosophy of Love*: *Dialoghi d'Amore*. Edited by Frank Friedberg-Seely. Translated by Jean H. Barnes, ix–xv. London: Soncino Press, 1937.

Rowe, John Howland. "Inca Culture at the Time of the Spanish Conquest." In *Handbook of South American Indians*. Edited by Julian H. Steward. 2 Vols. Washington, DC: United States Government Printing Office. 1946.

Rowe, John Howland. "El movimiento nacional inca del siglo XVIII." In *Túpac Amaru II—1780*. Edited by Alberto Galindo Flores, 13–46. Lima: Retablo de Papel Ediciones, 1976.

Rowe, John Howland. "Probanza de los Incas nietos de conquistadores." *Histórica* 9, no. 2 (1985): 193–245.

Saenz de Santa María, Carmelo. "Estudio preliminar." In Inca Garcilaso de la Vega, *Obras completas*. 4 Vols. Edited by Carmelo Saenz de Santa María, S.J., vol. 1., vii–lxxvii. Madrid: Ediciones Atlas, 1960–1965.

Sánchez Alonso, Benito. *Historia de la historiografía española*. Madrid: Consejo Superior, 1944.

Sánchez Salon, Eustaquio, Luis Merino Jerez, and Santiago López Moreda Cáceres, eds. *La recepción de las artes clásicas en el siglo XVI*. Universidad de Extremadura: Servicio de Publicaciones, 1996.

Sancho de la Hoz, Pedro [1550]. Translated by Philip Ainsworth Means. New York: Cortes Society, 1917.

Santacruz Pachacuti Yamqui Salcamaygua, Joan de. *Relación de las antigüedades deste reyno del Pirú* [1613?]. Edited by Pierre Duviols. Lima: Instituto Francés de Estudios Andinos y Centro de Estudios Regionales Bartolomé de Las Casas, 1993.

Santisteban Ochoa, Julián. "Dos documentos importantes sobre el Inca Garcilaso." *Revista Universitaria 94* (1st semester, 1948): 234–52.

Santo Tomás, Domingo de. *Lexicon o vocabulario de la lengua general del Perú* [1560]. Edited by Raúl Porras Barranechea. Lima: Edición del Instituto de Historia, 1951.

Santos Hernández, Ángel, S.J. *Los Jesuitas en América*. Madrid: Editorial MAPFRE, 1992.

Saravia, José Morales. "Garcilaso de la Vega, el Inca, en un nuevo siglo. El estado de la discussion." In *El Inca Garcilaso: entre varios mundos*. Edited by José Morales Saravia and Gerhard Penzkopfer, 15–52. Lima: Universidad Nacional Mayor de San Marcos, 2011a.

Saravia, José Morales, and Gerhard Penzkopfer, eds. *El Inca Garcilaso: entre varios mundos*. Lima: Universidad Nacional Mayor de San Marcos, 2011b.

Sarmiento de Gamboa, Pedro de. *Historia de los Incas* [1572]. Madrid: Miraguando Ediciones, 1988.

Sarmiento de Gamboa, Pedro de. *History of the Incas* [1572]. Edited by Clements R. Markham. Mineola: Dover, 1999.

Scott, James Brown. *The Spanish Origin of International Law*. Oxford: Clarendon, 1934.

Seaver, Henry Latimer. *The Great Revolt in Castile: A Study of the Comunero Movement in Castile, 1520–1521*. Boston: Houghton Mifflin, 1928.

Seed, Patricia. *Ceremonies of Possession in Europe's Conquest of the New World, 1492–1640*. Cambridge: Cambridge University Press, 1995.

Seed, Patricia. "Failing to Marvel: Atahualpa's Encounter with the Word." *Latin American Research Review* 26, no. 1 (1991): 7–32.

Sepúlveda, Juan Ginés de. *Democrates secundus o de las justas causas de la guerra contra los Indios* [1547]. Edited by Ángel Losada. Madrid: Consejo Superior de Investigaciones Científicas, 1984.

Serna Arnaiz, Mercedes. "Introducción." In el Inca Garcilaso de la Vega, *Comentarios reales*. Edited by Mercedes Serna Arnaiz, 9–81. Madrid: Editorial Castalia, 2000.

Serna Arnaiz, Mercedes. "Lascasismo y método jesuita en el pensamiento del Inca Garcilaso de la Vega." In *Humanismo, mestizaje y escritura en los* Comentarios reales. Edited by Carmen de Mora, Guillermo Serés, and Mercedes Serna, 349–60. Madrid/Frankfurt am Main: Iberoamericana/Vervuert, 2010.

Serna Arnaiz, Mercedes. "Pensamiento medieval y renacentista en el Inca Garcilaso de la Vega." In *El Inca Garcilaso de la Vega: entre varios mundos*. Edited by José Morales Saravia and Gerhard Penzkopfer, 147–62. Lima: Universidad Nacional Mayor de San Marcos, 2011.

Shakespeare, William. *The Norton Shakespeare*. Edited by Stephen Greenblatt, Walter Cohen, Jean E. Howard, Katharine Eisaman Maus, and Andrew Gurr. New York: W. W. Norton, 1997.

Siegel, Jerold F. *Rhetoric and Philosophy in Renaissance Humanism.* Princeton: Princeton University Press, 1968.

Silverblatt, Irene. *Sun, Moon and Witches.* Princeton: Princeton University Press, 1987.

Skinner, Quentin. *The Foundations of Modern Political Thought.* 2 Vols. Cambridge: Cambridge University Press, 1978.

Skinner, Quentin. *Reason and Rhetoric in the Philosophy of Hobbes.* Cambridge: Cambridge University Press, 1996.

Sommer, Doris. "At Home Abroad: El Inca Shuttles with Hebreo." *Poetics Today* 17, no. 3 (1996a): 385–415.

Sommer, Doris. "Mosaico y mestizo: el amor bilingüe de León Hebreo al Inca Garcilaso." In *Asedios a la heterogeneidad cultural: libro de homenaje a Antonio Cornelo Polar.* Edited by José Antonio Mazzotti and U. Juan Zevallos Aguilar. Philadelphia: Asociación Internacional de Peruanistas, 1996b.

Spalding, Karen. "Introduction." In Inca Garcilaso de la Vega, *The Royal Commentaries of the Incas and General History of Peru.* Translated by Harold V. Livermore. Edited by Karen Spalding, xi–xxviii. Indianapolis: Hackett Publishing, 2006.

Soons, Alan. *Juan de Mariana.* Boston: Twayne, 1982.

Steigman, Jonathan D. *La Florida del Inca and the Struggle for Social Equality in Colonial Spanish America.* Tuscaloosa: University of Alabama Press, 2005.

Stein, Susan Isabel. "Los trataban como a hijos": The Indians in Inca Garcilaso's *Historia general del Perú." A contracorriente* 2, no. 3 (Spring 2005): 75–101. acontracorriente.chass.ncsu.edu/index.php/acontracorriente/article/view/85/242

Stern, Stephen J. *Peru's Indian Peoples and the Challenge of Spanish Conquest: Huamanga to 1640.* 2nd edition. Madison: University of Wisconsin Press, 1993.

Steward, Julian H, ed. *Handbook of South American Indians.* 2 Vols. Washington, DC: United States Government Printing Office. 1946.

Struever, Nancy S. *The Language of History in the Renaissance.* Princeton: Princeton University Press, 1970.

Sullivan, Francis Patrick, ed. *Indian Freedom: The Cause of Bartolomé de las Casas, 1484–1566.* Kansas City: Sheed and Ward, 1995.

Szemiński, Juan. *Un kuraka, un dios, y una historia.* Jujuy: Proyecto ECIRA, 1987.

Szemiński, Juan. *Wira Quchan y sus obras: Teología andina y lenguaje, 1550–1662.* Lima: IEP, 1997.

Tacitus, Cornelius. *The Agricola* and *The Germania.* Translated by Harold Mattingly. New York: Penguin, 1970.

Tacitus, Cornelius. *The Annals of Imperial Rome.* Translated by Michael Grant. New York: Penguin, 1996.

Tacitus, Cornelius. *The Histories*. Translated by Kenneth Wellesley. New York: Penguin, 1995.

Taylor, William B., and Franklin Pease G. Y., eds. *Violence, Resistance, and Survival in the Americas*. Washington, DC: Smithsonian Institution Press, 1994.

Tocqueville, Alexis de, and Jennifer Pitts. *Writings on Empire and Slavery*. Baltimore: Johns Hopkins University Press, 2001.

Tuck, Richard. *Natural Rights Theories*. Cambridge: Cambridge University Press, 1979.

Tuck, Richard. *Philosophy and Government, 1572–1651*. Cambridge: Cambridge University Press, 1993.

Urbano, Henrique, and Pierre Duviols, eds. *Fábulas y mitos de los Incas*. Lima: Historia 16, 1989.

Urbano, Henrique. "Introducción." In *Antigüedades del Perú*. Edited by Henrique Urbano and Ana Sánchez, 7–38. Lima: Historia 16, 1992.

Urbano, Henrique. *Wiracocha y Ayar: héroes y funciones en las sociedades andinas*. Cuzco: Centro de Estudios Rurales Andinos "Bartolomé de Las Casas," 1981.

Urteaga, Horacio H. *El imperio incaico*. Lima: Museo Nacional, 1931.

Urton, Gary H. *The History of a Myth: Pacariqtambo and the Origin of the Incas*. Austin: University of Texas Press, 1990.

Valcárcel, Luis Eduardo. *Garcilaso el Inca. Visto de ángulo indio*. Lima: Imprenta del Museo Nacional, 1939.

Vargas Llosa, Mario. "El Inca Garcilaso y la lengua de todos." In *Entre la espada y la pluma: el Inca Garcilaso de la Vega en sus* Comentarios reales. Edited by Raquel Chang-Rodríguez, 19–28. Lima: Fondo Editorial PUCP, 2010.

Vargas-Ugarte S.J., Rubén. *Historia del colegio y universidad de San Ignacio de Loyola de la ciudad de Cuzco*. Lima: Biblioteca Histórica Peruana, 1948.

Vargas-Ugarte S.J., Rubén. *Historia general del Perú*. Vol. 1. Lima: Carlos Milla Batres, 1966.

Vargas-Ugarte S.J., Rubén. "Nota sobre Garcilaso." *Mercurio peruano* XX, January–February (1930): 47–50.

Varón Gabai, Rafael. *Francisco Pizarro and His Brothers: The Illusion of Power in Sixteenth-Century Peru*. Translated by Javier Flores Espinoza. Norman: University of Oklahoma Press, 1997.

Varner, John Grier. *El Inca: The Life and Times of Garcilaso de la Vega*. Austin: University of Texas Press, 1968.

Villarías Robles, Juan J. R., and María del Carmen Martín Rubio. "Sobre el autor." In Bartolomé Álvarez, *De las costumbres y conversión de los indios del Perú* [1588]. Edited by María del Carmen Martín Rubio, Juan J. R. Villarías Robles, and Fermín del Pino Díaz, XV–XXII. Madrid: Ediciones Polisemo, 1998.

Vitoria, Francisco de. *Political Writings*. Edited by Anthony Pagden and Jeremy Lawrence. Cambridge: Cambridge University Press, 1991.

Vives, Juan Luis. *Obras completas*. Edited by Lorenzo Riber. 2 Vols. Madrid: M. Aguilar, 1948.

Voigt, Lisa. *Writing Captivity in the Early Modern Atlantic: Circulations of Knowledge and Authority in the Iberian and English Imperial Worlds*. Chapel Hill: Published for the Omohundro Institute of Early American History and Culture, Williamsburg, University of North Carolina Press, 2009.

Wachtel, Nathan. *The Vision of the Vanquished: The Spanish Conquest of Peru through Indian Eyes, 1530–1570*. Sussex: Harvester Press, 1977.

Wachtel, Nathan. *Sociedad e ideología*. Lima: Instituto de Estudios Peruanos, 1973.

Ward, Thomas. "Modern Nativist Readings of Garcilaso in Peru." In *Entre la espada y la pluma: el Inca Garcilaso de la Vega en sus* Comentarios reales. Edited by Raquel Chang-Rodríguez, 171–89. Lima: Fondo Editorial PUCP, 2010.

White, Hayden V. *The Content of the Form*. Baltimore: Johns Hopkins University Press, 1987.

White, Hayden V. *Tropics of Discourse*. Baltimore: Johns Hopkins University Press, 1978.

Woodman, A. J. *Rhetoric in Classical Historiography*. Portland: Aeropagitica Press, 1988.

Zamora, Margarita. *Language, Authority and Indigenous History in the* Comentarios reales. Cambridge: Cambridge University Press, 1988.

Zamora, Margarita. "Regarding Colonialism in Garcilaso's *Historia general del Perú*." In *Entre la espada y la pluma: el Inca Garcilaso de la Vega en sus* Comentarios reales. Edited by Raquel Chang-Rodríguez, 121–28. Lima: Fondo Editorial PUCP, 2010a.

Zamora, Margarita. "Sobre la cuestión de la raza en los *Comentarios reales*." In *Renacimiento mestizo: Los 400 años de los* Comentarios reales. Edited by José Antonio Mazzotti, 361–79. Madrid/Frankfurt am Main: Iberoamericana/Vervuert, 2010.

Zamora, Margarita. "'Mestizo . . . me llamo a boca llena y me honro con él': Race in Inca Garcilaso's *Royal Commentaries of the Incas* and *General History of Peru*." In *Inca Garcilaso and Contemporary World-Making*. Edited by Sara Castro-Klarén and Christian Fernández, 174–94. Pittsburgh: University of Pittsburgh Press, 2016.

Zárate, Agustín de. *Historia del descubrimiento y conquista del Perú* [1555]. Edited by Franklin Pease G. Y. and Teodoro Hampe Martínez. Lima: Fondo Editorial de la Pontificia Universidad Católica del Perú, 1991.

Zavala, Silvio. *New Viewpoints on the Spanish Colonization of America*. Philadelphia: University of Pennsylvania Press, 1943.

Zavala, Silvio. *The Political Philosophy of the Conquest of America*. Translated by Teener Hall. Mexico: Editorial Cultura, 1953.

Zuidema, R. Tom. *Inca Civilization in Cuzco.* Translated by Jean-Jacques Decoster. Austin: University of Texas Press, 1990.

Zuidema, R. Tom. "The Relationship between Mountains and Coast in Ancient Peru." In *The Wonder of Man's Ingenuity.* Members of the Academic Staff of the National Museum of Ethnology. Leiden: Mededelingen Van Het Rijksmuseum voor Volkenkunde, 1962.

INDEX